T0202676

Lecture Notes in Computer Science 12226

More information about this series at http://www.springer.com/series/7408

Javier Camara · Martin Steffen (Eds.)

Software Engineering and Formal Methods

SEFM 2019 Collocated Workshops:
CoSim-CPS, ASYDE, CIFMA, and FOCLASA
Oslo, Norway, September 16–20, 2019
Revised Selected Papers

 Springer

Editors
Javier Camara
Department of Computer Science
University of York
York, UK

Martin Steffen
Department of Informatics
University of Oslo
Oslo, Norway

ISSN 0302-9743 ISSN 1611-3349 (electronic)
Lecture Notes in Computer Science
ISBN 978-3-030-57505-2 ISBN 978-3-030-57506-9 (eBook)
https://doi.org/10.1007/978-3-030-57506-9

LNCS Sublibrary: SL2 – Programming and Software Engineering

This Springer imprint is published by the registered company Springer Nature Switzerland AG
The registered company address is: Gewerbestrasse 11, 6330 Cham, Switzerland

Preface

This volume contains the technical papers presented at the four workshops co-located with the 17th International Conference on Software Engineering and Formal Methods (SEFM 2019). The workshops were hosted by the Department of Computer Science, University of Oslo, and took place at the Oslo Science Park, during September 16–17, 2019, preceding the main conference held at the same place.

The SEFM 2019 conference brought together researchers and practitioners from academia, industry, and government, to advance the state of the art in formal methods, to facilitate their uptake in the software industry, and to encourage their integration within practical software engineering methods and tools. The satellite workshops provided an interactive and collaborative environment to discuss emerging areas of software engineering, software technologies, model-driven engineering, and formal methods. The four workshops whose contributions are included in this volume are:

- **CoSim-CPS 2019** – Third International Workshop on Formal Co-Simulation of Cyber-Physical Systems. Organized by: Cláudio Gomes, University of Antwerp, Belgium; Cinzia Bernardeschi, University of Pisa, Italy; Paolo Masci, National Institute of Aerospace (NIA), USA; and Peter Gorm Larsen, Aarhus University, Denmark.
- **ASYDE 2019** – International Workshop on Automated and verifiable Software sYstem DEvelopment. Organized by: Farhad Arbab, Centre for Mathematics and Computer Science (CWI), The Netherlands; Marco Autili, University of L'Aquila, Italy; Federico Ciccozzi, Malardalen University, Sweden; Pascal Poizat, Sorbonne Université, France; and Massimo Tivoli, University of L'Aquila, Italy.
- **CIFMA 2019** – International Workshop on Cognition: Interdisciplinary Foundations, Models and Applications. Organized by: Antonio Cerone, Nazarbayev University, Kazakhstan; and Alan Dix, Computational Foundry, Swansea University, UK.
- **FOCLASA 2019** – 17th International Workshop on Coordination and Self-Adaptiveness of Software Applications. Organized by: Ernesto Pimentel, University of Málaga, Spain; and Jacopo Soldani, University of Pisa, Italy.

We would like to thank all organizers of the workshops at SEFM 2019 for the interesting topics and resulting talks, as well as the respective Program Committee members and reviewers for their thorough and careful reviews, for selecting the program for each workshop, and for making the compilation of this volume possible. We also thank the paper contributors and attendees of all workshops, including the keynote speakers for their excellent presentations. Finally, we would like to thank the organizers of general chairs of SEFM 2019, Peter Csaba Ölveczky and Gwen Salaün, and University of Oslo as hosting institution, for making the event possible.

June 2020   Javier Camara
                                                                              Martin Steffen

Organization

General SEFM Chairs

Gwen Salaün   Inria Grenoble Rhône-Alpes, France
Peter Csaba Ölveczky   University of Oslo, Norway

General Workshop Chairs

Javier Camara   University of York, UK
Martin Steffen   University of Oslo, Norway

Contents

CIFMA 2019

FOCLASA 2019

CoSim-CPS 2019

Organization

CoSim-CPS 2019 – Workshop Chairs

Cláudio Gomes	University of Antwerp
Cinzia Bernardeschi	University of Pisa
Paolo Masci	National Institute of Aerospace (NIA)
Peter Gorm Larsen	Aarhus University

CoSim-CPS 2019 – Program Committee

Adriano Fagiolini	University of Palermo, Italy
Akshay Rajhans	MathWorks, USA
Andrea Domenici	University of Pisa, Italy
Fabio Cremona	University of California, Berkeley, CA, USA
Frank Zeyda	University of York, UK
Giovanna Broccia	University of Pisa, Italy
Hans Vangheluwe	University of Antwerp, Belgium
Jean-Philippe Tavella	Électricité de France, France
Joachim Denil	University of Antwerp, Belgium
Jörg Brauer	Verified Systems International GmbH, Bremen
Julien De Antoni	Inria, France
Leo Freitas	Newcastle University, UK
Marco Di Natale	Scuola Superiore Sant'Anna, Italy
Mario Porrmann	Osnabrueck University, Germany
Marjan Sirjani	Malardalen University & Reykjavik University, Iceland
Maurizio Palmieri	University of Florence and University of Pisa, Italy
Neeraj Singh	INPT-ENSEEIHT/IRIT and University of Toulouse, France
Paul De Meulenaere	University of Antwerp, Belgium
Paul Curzon	Queen Mary University of London, UK
Stylianos Basagiannis	United Technologies Research Centre, Ireland
Yi Zhang	Center for Devices and Radiological Health, US Food and Drug Administration (CDRH/FDA), USA

Co-simulation and Verification of a Non-linear Control System for Cogging Torque Reduction in Brushless Motors

Cinzia Bernardeschi[(✉)], Pierpaolo Dini, Andrea Domenici, and Sergio Saponara

Department of Information Engineering, University of Pisa, Pisa, Italy
cinzia.bernardeschi@ing.unipi.it

Abstract. This work aims at demonstrating the benefits of integrating co-simulation and formal verification in the standard design flow of a brushless power drive system for precision robotic applications. A sufficient condition on controller gain for system stability is derived from the system's mathematical model, including a control algorithm for the reduction of cogging torque. Then, using co-simulation and design space exploration, fine tuning of the controller gain parameters has been executed, exploiting the results from the formal verification.

1 Introduction

Electronic power drive systems in hybrid vehicles in which mechanical and electrical parts coexist with electronic controllers have very complex dynamics [28].

Standard methods in the development of such systems are based on a hierarchical simulation workflow [22]: An abstract model of the system is first described and simulated in some modeling language such as Simulink or Open Modelica (model-in-the-loop, MIL); then the control algorithms, implemented in the C/C++ programming language, are simulated with the rest of the system in Matlab/Simulink (software-in-the-loop, SIL). Successively, the implemented algorithms are run on the target processor mounted on a development board (processor-in-the-loop, PIL) and on the target processor mounted in the deployed Electronic Control Unit (ECU) that interacts with an emulated physical plant (hardware-in-the-loop, HIL).

Special HW and SW tools have been developed to support the hardware-in-the-loop phase (e.g., dSPACE or Speedgoat). However, HIL simulation is very time-consuming and expensive. Most of the time, new control algorithms are simulated at the PIL level. Moreover, most simulators available capture the

Work partially supported by the Italian Ministry of Education and Research (MIUR) in the framework of the CrossLab project (Departments of Excellence), and by the PRA 2018_81 project entitled "Wearable sensor systems: personalized analysis and data security in healthcare" funded by the University of Pisa.

J. Camara and M. Steffen (Eds.): SEFM 2019 Workshops, LNCS 12226, pp. 3–19, 2020.
https://doi.org/10.1007/978-3-030-57506-9_1

performance of controllers when the code is executed on the specific instruction set of the processor, while they offer limited support for verification.

Finally, state space exploration of the controller during the design phase often considers only the variation of one of a set of parameters at a time, assuming the others constant. Therefore, the coverage of the design space is often time consuming and not exhaustive.

This work reports our experience in the application of co-simulation and formal verification supported by the INTO-CPS framework [16] to a real case study for the reduction of the cogging torque in brushless motors by a non-linear control system [7]. The effect of the cogging torque is due to the interaction between permanent magnets and the teeth of the stator slots. This is a main issue in precision electric drive applications, which is often solved with physical modification of the electrical machine.

The added value of the proposed approach is to include co-simulation and formal verification, in parallel with the standard approach, for the calibration of design parameters. Co-simulation improves flexibility because it does not require a single modeling language for all system parts (e.g., discrete and continuous parts), and formal verification enables proofs of correctness for fundamental properties of the system. In this work, OpenModelica has been used to model the physical part, while PVSio-web has been used to model the feedback linearization control part. Moreover, The Prototype Verification System (PVS) [23] has been used to describe the theory of the closed loop system in a formal language and prove sufficient conditions for stability. In particular, after finding the parameter ranges ensuring stability, co-simulation and design space exploration have been used to find a combination of control gains optimizing power consumption and precision according to the Pareto criterion.

The paper is structured as follows: Sect. 2 reports on related work; Sect. 3 describes the non-linear control technique for cogging torque reduction and the tools used for co-simulation and formal verification. The mathematical model of the motor and control is shown in Sect. 4. Section 5 shows results of co-simulation. Section 6 shows how the PVS theorem prover can perform proofs of properties for the non-linear control algorithm. Design space exploration is reported in Sect. 7. Finally, Sect. 8 concludes the paper.

2   Related Work

Proposals to apply formal methods to cyber-physical systems follow many different approaches and languages.

An important family of languages is that of hybrid automata [14], a conceptual model that lends itself to the integration of discrete- and continuous-time behaviors. In particular, timed automata [1] are supported by such tools as the UPPAAL environment [2].

Another approach is based on logic-based methods, which use various forms of logic languages to model and analyze systems. These logic languages include temporal logics [20,27], normally used in conjunction with state-machine representations, and higher-order logics [18].

KeYmaera [11] is a theorem prover, recently developed and applied successfully for the verification of cyber-physical systems. Its language includes conditions, non-determinism, loops, composition, and continuous dynamics, i.e., behaviors defined by differential equations.

In [3], the Prototype Verification System theorem prover is used to prove basic safety properties of a nonlinear (hybrid) control system (a storage tank).

In [8], co-simulation and formal verification have been applied to a simple autonomous vehicle. The vehicle kinematics have been simulated in Simulink, whereas the controller has been modeled in PVS. Co-simulation and formal verification were also applied to a bio-medical system, namely, a pacemaker and a human heart, modeled in PVS and Simulink, respectively [4].

The Vienna Definition Method (VDM) [10] family of languages and tools, in particular the *Crescendo* tool [17] have also been used extensively.

Palensky et al. [24, 25] advocate the integration of HIL simulation with co-simulation in the analysis of intelligent power grid systems. In [5], mixing formal verification with simulation-based techniques is proposed to create a new formal-verification-in-the-loop methodology.

3   Background

In this work, we refer to a three-phase permanent-magnet brushless motor, basically composed of a *stator* bearing three electric windings, and a *rotor* bearing permanent magnets on its surface. The currents in the windings create a rotating magnetic field that interacts with the magnets creating a torque T_{em} causing the rotor to spin and transmit mechanical power to its load. The three currents are a *three-phase system* characterized by the respective *phasors*, each defined by the amplitude and phase shift of the corresponding current. The basic three-phase representation can be transformed into other representations by a change of coordinate frame. In the following, two coordinate frames called $d - q$ and $\alpha - \beta$ will be used [28].

3.1   Cogging Torque in Brushless Motors

In this section we describe briefly the cogging torque phenomenon, which is an intrinsic feature of synchronous motors. Basically the cogging torque is due to the magnetic interaction between permanent magnets on the rotor surface and the stator teeth. In particular, it produces a tangential force on the magnets.

The tangential force (hence, the torque) on each magnet depends on its position with respect to nearby stator teeth, i.e., on the rotor's angular position θ. This force varies between opposite orientations as the magnet approaches or recedes from each tooth, therefore it has a null mean value, as shown in Fig. 1. The top part shows that during the movement of the rotor different configurations occur. The lower part shows schematically that the movement of a magnet with respect to a stator tooth generates a null mean contribution of cogging torque.

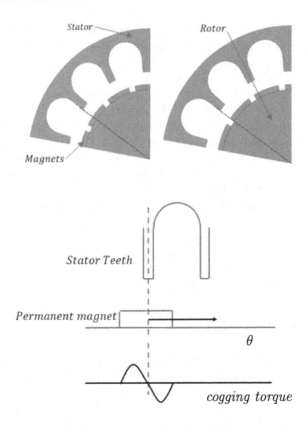

Fig. 1. Schematic representation of torque ripple due to the interaction between permanent magnets and stator teeth.

Therefore the cogging torque can be described as an additive disturbance to the electromagnetic torque, periodic and with zero mean. In this work we use a result from [29] describing the cogging torque through the following Fourier development:

$$T_{\text{cog}} = \sum_{k=1}^{m} T_k \sin(kZ\theta + \alpha_k) \tag{1}$$

In the above formula, T_k and α_k are the amplitude and the phase shift relative to the kth harmonic of the development, Z is the number of stator teeth, θ is the absolute (mechanical) angular position of the rotor and m is the number of harmonics necessary to approximate the actual cogging torque. The formula has been obtained through a finite element analysis (FEM) [29], in which it has also been verified that a limited number of harmonics, in particular four, is adequate for the mathematical description of the phenomenon.

3.2 The INTO-CPS Framework

Simulation in cyber-physical systems often takes the form of co-simulation [13], i.e., integrated simulation of different subsystems, each modeled with a specific formalism and simulated by a specific simulation engine. The Functional Mockup Interface (FMI) [6] is a standard for co-simulation: sub-models implemented as Functional Mockup Units (FMUs) are orchestrated by a master that communicates with them through proxy modules (FMI wrappers) whose interfaces are FMI-compliant. Recently, the INTO-CPS project [16] created an integrated co-simulation framework based on FMI.

INTO-CPS also supports the possibility of looking for optimal design parameter values by using the Design Space Exploration (DSE) functionality. This functionality allows developers to choose a set of values for each parameter and define objective functions on simulation results. The design exploration engine then executes one simulation for each combination of parameter values, retrieves results, computes objective functions, and ranks the resulting values.

3.3 The Prototype Verification System

The *Prototype Verification System* (PVS) [23] is an interactive theorem-proving environment whose users can define theories in a higher-order logic language and prove theorems with respect to them. Moreover, the PVSio extension [21] allows a PVS theory to be used as an executable model for simulation, and the PVSio-web [26] framework extends prototypes with interactive user interfaces, and converts stand-alone device prototypes into FMUs capable of exchanging commands and data with any FMI-compliant co-simulation engine. The PVS environment includes the NASALIB theory libraries [9] providing axioms and theorems addressing many topics in mathematics, including real number analysis, and it can be applied to model both the discrete and the continuous part of the system [3].

4 Mathematical Model of Motor and Control

The behavior of the brushless motor considered in this paper is modeled by parameters representing its physical characteristics and by a set of equations combining the electromagnetic, mechanical, and control laws [28]. The latter have been adapted from [7]. The electromagnetic laws are expressed in terms of $d - q$ phasors [28]. For simplicity, the law describing the cogging torque considers only its first harmonic. Tables 1 and 2 show the parameters and variable magnitudes, respectively, used in the model.

4.1 Motor Model

In the following, u_d and u_q are the $d - q$ components of the supplied voltage and i_d and i_q are the current components, while L and R are the inductance and equivalent resistance, respectively. The supplied voltage is then:

Table 1. Parameters

Parameter	Value	Meaning
Z	10	Number of stator teeth
p	3	Number of pole pairs
T_1	4.0 N $\cdot$ m	Amplitude of cogging torque's first harmonic
α_1	0.009 rad	Phase of cogging torque's first harmonic
R	3.3 Ω	Resistance
L	0.05 H	Inductance
k	0.5 Wb	Magnetic flux
J	0.01 kg $\cdot$ m^2	Rotational inertia
β	0.01 N $\cdot$ s/m	Friction coefficient

Table 2. Variables

Variable	Meaning
i_d, i_q	Direct and quadrature components of current
u_d, u_q	Direct and quadrature components of voltage
θ, ω	Angular position and speed
$\bar{i}_d, \bar{\theta}$	Desired values of i_d and θ
T_{em}, T_{cog}	Electromagnetic and cogging torques

$$\begin{pmatrix} u_d \\ u_q \end{pmatrix} = R \begin{pmatrix} i_d \\ i_q \end{pmatrix} + L \frac{d}{dt} \begin{pmatrix} i_d \\ i_q \end{pmatrix} + \begin{pmatrix} e_d \\ e_q \end{pmatrix} \tag{2}$$

where

$$\begin{pmatrix} e_d = -p\omega L i_q \\ e_q = p\omega(k + L i_d) \end{pmatrix}$$

is the counter-electromotive force vector.

Equations (3) represent the useful electromagnetic torque T_{em} and the cogging torque T_{cog}, and Eqs. 4 represent the resulting mechanical behavior.

$$T_{em} = \frac{3}{2} p k i_q$$
$$T_{cog} = T_1 \sin(Z\theta + \alpha_1) \tag{3}$$

$$J\dot{\omega} + \beta\omega = T_{em} + T_{cog}$$
$$\omega = \dot{\theta} \tag{4}$$

4.2   Controller Model

The controller shown here is based on the one presented in [7] and uses a feedback linearization technique.

Table 3. Numerical coefficients

Coefficient	Value	Coefficient	Value
C_1	4040	C_2	1237529
C_3	9/1000	C_4	153666659/90000
C_5	1597813728139/27000000	C_6	6371/300

Its inputs are the desired values of current $\bar{i}_d$ and angular position $\bar{\theta}$, and the feedback values of current (i_d and i_q), angular position θ, and angular speed ω. Its characteristic parameters are the gains K_{11} and K_{22}, used to compute a signal proportional to the error on the motor outputs (see [7] for details):

$$\begin{pmatrix} v_1 \\ v_2 \end{pmatrix} = \begin{pmatrix} K_{11} & 0 \\ 0 & K_{22} \end{pmatrix} \begin{pmatrix} i_d - \bar{i}_d \\ \theta - \bar{\theta} \end{pmatrix} \tag{5}$$

The control voltages u_d and u_q are computed according to (6).

$$\begin{cases} u_d = Lv_1 + Ri_d - Lpi_q\omega \\ u_q = \dfrac{2JL}{3pk}[v_2 - \dfrac{3pk}{2J}(-Ri_q - p\omega(Li_d + k))] \\ \quad + Z\omega(T_1\cos(Z\theta + \alpha_1)) - \dfrac{\beta}{J}[\dfrac{3}{2}pki_q + (T_1\sin(Z\theta + \alpha_1))]) \end{cases} \tag{6}$$

4.3 Choice of Gain Coefficients

The values of the controller's gain coefficients are a design choice. A standard method to choose their values is based on linearizing the system's dynamics around a given operating condition. The behavior of the system under analysis is given in matrix form by (7), where the first derivative of each controlled variable is equated to the respective *generating function* and $E_{dq} = (e_d, e_q)^T$ is the counter-electromotive force vector. The system's Jacobian is the matrix of the partial derivatives of the generating functions with respect to their variables. The gain coefficients must then be chosen so that the real part of the Jacobian's eigenvectors is less than or equal to zero, as is well known from control theory [15].

The four eigenvalues of the Jacobian have been computed with the Matlab symbolic toolbox in terms of the numerical coefficients reported in Table 3 and of the auxiliary functions Φ_1 and Φ_2 defined in (8). Note that the coefficients are expressed as exact rational numbers.

$$\begin{cases} \dot{\boldsymbol{I}}_{dq} = L_{dq}^{-1}(\boldsymbol{U}_{dq} - R_{dq}\boldsymbol{I}_{dq} - \boldsymbol{E}_{dq}) \\ \dot{\theta} = \omega \\ \dot{\omega} = \dfrac{T_{em} + T_{cog} - \beta\omega}{J} \end{cases} \tag{7}$$

$$\Phi_1(\theta) = C_1 \cos(10\theta + C_3)/3 - C_4$$
$$\Phi_2(\theta) = C_2 \cos(10\theta + C_3)/15 + C_5$$
(8)

The real parts of the eigenvalues λ_1, λ_2, λ_3, and λ_4 are shown in (9) below:

$$\mathrm{Re}(\lambda_4) = K_{11}$$

$$\mathrm{Re}(\lambda_3) = \frac{\Phi_1(\theta)}{\sqrt[3]{\frac{K_{22}}{2} + \Phi_2(\theta) + \sqrt{\left(\frac{K_{22}}{2} + \Phi_2(\theta)\right)^2 - \Phi_1(\theta)^3}}}$$

$$+ \sqrt[3]{\frac{K_{22}}{2} + \Phi_2(\theta) + \sqrt{\left(\frac{K_{22}}{2} + \Phi_2(\theta)\right)^2 - \Phi_1(\theta)^3}}$$

$$- C_6$$
(9)

$$\mathrm{Re}(\lambda_2) = -\frac{\Phi_1(\theta)}{2\sqrt[3]{\frac{K_{22}}{2} + \Phi_2(\theta) + \sqrt{\left(\frac{K_{22}}{2} + \Phi_2(\theta)\right)^2 - \Phi_1(\theta)^3}}}$$

$$- \frac{1}{2}\sqrt[3]{\frac{K_{22}}{2} + \Phi_2(\theta) + \sqrt{\left(\frac{K_{22}}{2} + \Phi_2(\theta)\right)^2 - \Phi_1(\theta)^3}}$$

$$- C_6$$
$$\mathrm{Re}(\lambda_1) = \mathrm{Re}(\lambda_2)$$

5   Co-simulation

Figure 2 shows the architecture of the power drive system. The full system consists of six blocks: FLC represents the controller function derived from (6) for the reduction of the cogging torque, dq2alfa transforms the electrical values from the $d - q$ representation to an intermediate $\alpha - \beta$ frame, alfa2abc transforms them to the three-phase form, Motor implements the dynamic model of the motor, abc2alfa is the transformation block from three-phase to the $\alpha - \beta$ frame and alfa2dq is the last coordinate transformation into the $d - q$ frame.

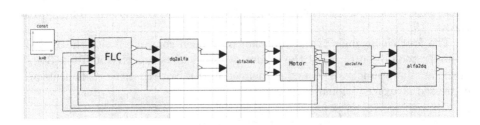

Fig. 2. System model in OpenModelica.

In the co-simulation, blocks relative to the modeling of the electrical machine and coordinate transformation are implemented in OpenModelica, while the FLC block is implemented in Misra C. Every block is exported as an FMU. The FMUs are linked together in a multimodel created by the INTO-CPS application.

Figures 3 and 4 show two runs with a duration of 1 s and a step size of 5 μs. The initial values of current and rotor position are 0 A and 10 rad, with a zero set-point for rotor position. The values of the controller gains are ($K_{11} = -2500, K_{22} = 250000$) for the first run (Fig. 3), and ($K_{11} = -3000, K_{22} = 300000$) for the second one.

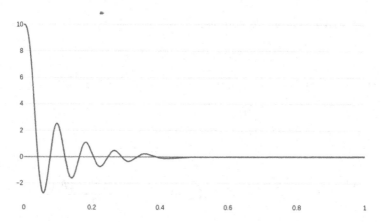

Fig. 3. Co-simulation for $K_{11} = -2500$, $K_{22} = -250000$ (y axis: $\theta - \bar{\theta}$; x axis: time).

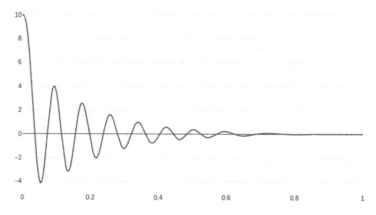

Fig. 4. Co-simulation for $K_{11} = -3000$, $K_{22} = -300000$ (y axis: $\theta - \bar{\theta}$; x axis: time).

6   Proofs

From the conditions for stability on the eigenvalues, we can find allowable ranges of values for the elements of the control gain matrix. The range for K_{11} is found immediately to be $K_{11} \leq 0$, while K_{22} requires more work.

First, let us define

$$X(K_{22}, \theta) = \sqrt[3]{\frac{K_{22}}{2} + \Phi_2(\theta) + \sqrt{\left(\frac{K_{22}}{2} + \Phi_2(\theta)\right)^2 - \Phi_1(\theta)^3}} \ .$$

It can be shown that $\Phi_1(\theta) \leq 0$, hence

$$X(K_{22}, \theta) \geq 0.$$

The condition on λ_3, $\mathrm{Re}(\lambda_3) \leq 0$, can be rewritten as

$$\frac{\Phi_1(\theta)}{X(K_{22}, \theta)} + X(K_{22}, \theta) - C_6 \leq 0 \tag{10}$$

yielding

$$\frac{C_6 - \sqrt{C_6^2 - 4\Phi_1(\theta)}}{2} \leq X(K_{22}, \theta) \leq \frac{C_6 + \sqrt{C_6^2 - 4\Phi_1(\theta)}}{2} \tag{11}$$

Similarly, the condition on λ_2 and λ_1 can be written as

$$\frac{-\Phi_1(\theta)}{2X(K_{22}, \theta)} - \frac{X(K_{22}, \theta)}{2} - C_6 \leq 0$$

yielding

$$X(K_{22}, \theta) \leq -C_6 - \sqrt{C_6^2 - \Phi_1(\theta)} \quad \lor \quad X(K_{22}, \theta) \geq -C_6 + \sqrt{C_6^2 - \Phi_1(\theta)} \tag{12}$$

Finally, it can be proved that:

$$-C_6 + \sqrt{C_6^2 - \Phi_1(\theta)} \leq X(K_{22}, \theta) \leq \frac{C_6 + \sqrt{C_6^2 - 4\Phi_1(\theta)}}{2} \tag{13}$$

Let us first determine the possible ranges for the bounds of $X(K_{22}, \theta)$, depending on $\Phi_1(\theta)$:

$$\begin{cases} -C_6 + \sqrt{C_6^2 - \Phi_1(\theta)} \in (7.37, 38) \\ \dfrac{C_6 + \sqrt{C_6^2 - 4\Phi_1(\theta)}}{2} \in (32.6, 67) \end{cases} \tag{14}$$

Let us now consider the lower bound

$$X(K_{22}, \theta) \geq -C_6 + \sqrt{C_6^2 - \Phi_1(\theta)} = c \ , \tag{15}$$

which leads to

$$\sqrt{\left(\frac{K_{22}}{2} + \Phi_2(\theta)\right)^2 - \Phi_1(\theta)^3} \geq c^3 - \left(\frac{K_{22}}{2} + \Phi_2(\theta)\right).$$

Assuming

$$c^3 - \left(\frac{K_{22}}{2} + \Phi_2(\theta)\right) \geq 0 \qquad (16)$$

we get

$$K_{22} \geq c^3 + \frac{\Phi_1(\theta)^3}{c^3} - 2\Phi_2(\theta). \qquad (17)$$

Considering the allowable ranges in (14), we find

$$K_{22}^{\min} \geq (7.37)^3 + \frac{(1346 - 1707)^3}{(7.37)^3} - 2 \cdot (82501 + 59178) \geq -400000$$

$$K_{22}^{\max} \geq (38)^3 + \frac{(-1346 - 1707)^3}{(38)^3} - 2 \cdot (82501 + 59178) \geq -417000 \qquad (18)$$

Discharging Assumption (16), we get two more bounds on K_{22}, i.e.,

$$K_{22} \leq 47446$$

$$K_{22} \leq -173614 \qquad (19)$$

With a similar procedure, for the upper bound we obtain

$$K_{22}^{\min} \leq (32.6)^3 + \frac{(1346 - 1707)^3}{(32.6)^3} - 2 \cdot (82501 + 59178) \leq -250000$$

$$K_{22}^{\max} \leq (67)^3 + \frac{(-1346 - 1707)^3}{(67)^3} - 2 \cdot (-82501 + 59178) \leq -254000 \qquad (20)$$

$$K_{22} \leq 115998$$

$$K_{22} \leq 318168 \qquad (21)$$

We can finally gather the required bounds on K_{22} and take their intersection to obtain a sufficient condition for stability:

$$-400000 \leq K_{22} \leq -250000$$

6.1 A PVS Theory

The preceding proofs have been carried out with the PVS theorem prover. The system under study has been specified in the **cogging** theory:

```
cogging: THEORY BEGIN
IMPORTING trig_fnd@sincos_def, power@root, reals@quadratic

C_1: posrat = 4040
%...

Phi_1(theta: real): real = C_1*cos(10*theta + C_3)/3 - C_4
Phi_2(theta: real): real = C_2*cos(10*theta + C_3)/15 + C_5
cubicrt(x: real): real = root(x, 3)
%...
```

The theory imports library theories on trigonometry and properties of roots and quadratic equations, then it defines the numeric coefficients as positive rational (*posrat*) constants, and introduces functions Φ_1 and Φ_2. Function *cubicrt* is an abbreviation for the predefined nth-root function.

Then the real parts of the eigenvalues are defined. For example, the real part of λ_3 is:

```
re_lambda_3(k_22, theta: real): real =
  Phi_1(theta)/cubicrt(k_22/2 + Phi_2(theta)
    + sqrt((k_22/2 + Phi_2(theta))^2 - Phi_1(theta)^3))
    + cubicrt(k_22/2 + Phi_2(theta)
    + sqrt((k_22/2 + Phi_2(theta))^2 - Phi_1(theta)^3)) - C_6
```

After the real parts of the eigenvalues, the definition of function X, using an auxiliary function a:

```
a(k_22, theta: real): real = k_22/2 + Phi_2(theta)
X(k_22, theta: real): real =
  cubicrt(a(k_22, theta) + sqrt(sq(a(k_22, theta)) - Phi_1(theta)^3))
```

The definitions of the eigenvalues' real parts have been obtained with Matlab, and can be rewritten more compactly in terms of X. The correctness of the rewriting is verified by proving a simple lemma:

```
real_lam3(k_22, theta: real): real =
    Phi_1(theta)/X(k_22, theta) + X(k_22, theta) - C_6

lem_1: LEMMA
      FORALL (k_22, theta: real):
         real_lam3(k_22, theta) = re_lambda_3(k_22, theta)
```

The theory includes several lemmas corresponding to proofs of the steps shown above. For example, it has been proved that $\mathrm{Re}(\lambda_3) \leq 0$ implies that $X_{\lambda_3,1}(\theta) \leq X(K_{22}, \theta) \leq X_{\lambda_3,2}(\theta)$, where $X_{\lambda_3,1}(\theta)$ and $X_{\lambda_3,2}(\theta)$ are the roots of the quadratic equation associated with inequality 10:

```
X_lam3_1(theta: real): real = root(1, -C_6, Phi_1(theta), -1)
X_lam3_2(theta: real): real = root(1, -C_6, Phi_1(theta), 1)

lem_3: LEMMA
      FORALL (k_22, theta: real):
```

```
real_lam3(k_22, theta) <= 0 IMPLIES
X(k_22, theta) >= X_lam3_1(theta)
AND X(k_22, theta) <= X_lam3_2(theta)
```

Table 4. DSE experiment 1.

Rank	K_{22}	K_{11}	Power_consumption	Object_error	Row
1	−250000	−2500	1461.0512489	2.61001161113	1
2	−262000	−2620	1778.52854857	2.69090121223	2
3	−275000	−2750	2213.32403129	2.81849055117	3
4	−288000	−2880	2799.8888976	3.01450451582	4
5	−300000	−3000	3539.7916041	3.27898211731	5
6	−312000	−3120	4599.74043917	3.67639575642	6
7	−325000	−3250	6450.85181919	4.39867095785	7

Some proofs consist in the invocation of a single PVS command, while others may require longish manipulations and the introduction of lemmas from predefined theories. The effort results in a rigorous and reliable characterization of the allowable ranges for design parameters.

7   Design Space Exploration

The DSE feature of INTO-CPS has been applied to analyze the behavior of the feedback controlled system in the range of controller gains obtained in Sect. 6. The analysis uses the *Pareto method* [12,19] to rank the (K_{11}, K_{22}) pairs for the following objective functions, where N is the number of time samples collected in each simulation: (i) the absorbed power, $power\_consumption = \sum_{k\in[1..N]}(U_k I_k)$; and (ii) the sum of the mean square errors on θ and i_d, $object\_error = \frac{1}{N}\sum_{k\in[1..N]}((\theta_k - \bar{\theta})^2 + (i_{dk} - \bar{i}_d)^2)$. All co-simulation runs have a duration of 1 s with a step-size of 5 μs.

Each DSE experiment can be configured with a specific search strategy in the design space. As an example, the following paragraphs present two experiments with different aims.

First Experiment. This experiment aims at locating optimal values for K_{22}, under the arbitrary constraint $K_{11} = \frac{1}{100}K_{22}$. Gain K_{22} takes values in the range $(-325000, -250000)$. Table 4 shows that, when the modulus of K_{22} increases, the power consumption increases, since higher absolute values of K_{22} correspond to higher voltages. Also the error increases with K_{22}. Figure 5 shows the corresponding Pareto plot, where the circled numbers refer to the table rows.

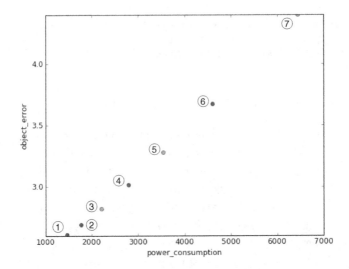

Fig. 5. Pareto front experiment 1.

Table 5. Experiment 2.

Rank	K_{22}	K_{11}	Power_consumption	Object_error	Row
1	−250000	−2750	1460.4785694	2.6092047542	1
2	−250000	−2500	1461.0512489	2.61001161113	2
3	−250000	−2250	1461.71978471	2.61099274616	3
4	−250000	−2000	1462.50680786	2.61221096464	4
5	−250000	−1000	1467.16692601	2.62267780615	5
6	−262000	−2750	1778.08149989	2.69034252751	6
			...		
11	−275000	−2750	2213.32403129	2.81849055117	11
			...		
16	−288000	−2750	2801.06586543	3.01561930304	16
			...		
21	−300000	−2750	3543.85886091	3.2822939417	21
22	−300000	−2500	3548.61453009	3.28623379906	22
23	−300000	−2250	3554.23990985	3.29099668275	23
24	−300000	−2000	3560.97904403	3.29686612091	24
25	−300000	−1000	3606.61555253	3.34495731412	25

Second Experiment. This experiment compares the influence of the two gains on the evaluation criteria, by considering different combinations of values for K_{11} and K_{22}, taken from discrete sets: $K_{22} \in \{-300000, -288000, -275000, -262000, -250000\}$ and $K_{11} \in \{-2750, -2500, -2250, -2000, -1000\}$, performing 25 different simulations. From Table 5 and the corresponding plot in Fig. 6, it turns out that K_{22} is the dominant factor. In fact, for each distinct value of K_{22} there is a cluster of five closely spaced points corresponding to values of K_{11}.

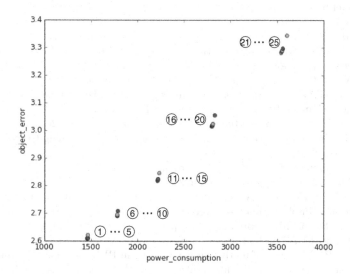

Fig. 6. Pareto front experiment 2.

8   Conclusions

A main theme of this work is the integration and complementarity of different tools. In particular, finding the allowable ranges for the controller gain has relied on Matlab and PVS. The symbolic and numerical computational capabilities of Matlab made it possible to obtain quickly the expressions for the system's eigenvalues. Then, interactive theorem proving made it possible to determine the conditions for stability on the eigenvalues, starting from the Matlab results and performing the necessary logical steps under the continuous check for correctness enforced by the PVS prover. Finally, co-simulation and design-space exploration with INTO-CPS led to the final design choices.

Acknowledgments. The authors wish to thank the anonymous referees for their valuable suggestions. The authors also thank the INTO-CPS project for providing the co-simulation environment.

References

1. Alur, R., Dill, D.L.: A theory of timed automata. Theoret. Comput. Sci. **126**(2), 183–235 (1994)
2. Behrmann, G., et al.: UPPAAL 4.0. In: Third International Conference on Quantitative Evaluation of Systems (QEST 2006), pp. 125–126, September 2006

3. Bernardeschi, C., Domenici, A.: Verifying safety properties of a nonlinear control by interactive theorem proving with the Prototype Verification System. Inf. Process. Lett. **116**(6), 409–415 (2016)
4. Bernardeschi, C., Domenici, A., Masci, P.: A PVS-simulink integrated environment for model-based analysis of cyber-physical systems. IEEE Trans. Software Eng. **44**(6), 512–533 (2018)
5. Bernardeschi, C., Domenici, A., Saponara, S.: Formal verification in the loop to enhance verification of safety-critical cyber-physical systems. In: Proceedings of Interactive Workshop on the Industrial Application of Verification and Testing, InterAVT 2019 (ETAPS 2019), Electronic Communications of the EASST (2019)
6. Blochwitz, T., et al.: Functional mockup interface 2.0: the standard for tool independent exchange of simulation models. In: Proceedings of the 9th International MODELICA Conference, Munich, Germany, 3–5 September 2012, pp. 173–184. No. 76 in Linköping Electronic Conference Proceedings, Linköping University Electronic Press (2012)
7. Dini, P., Saponara, S.: Cogging torque reduction in brushless motors by a nonlinear control technique. Energies **12**(11), 2224 (2019)
8. Domenici, A., Fagiolini, A., Palmieri, M.: Integrated simulation and formal verification of a simple autonomous vehicle. In: Cerone, A., Roveri, M. (eds.) SEFM 2017. LNCS, vol. 10729, pp. 300–314. Springer, Cham (2018). https://doi.org/10.1007/978-3-319-74781-1_21
9. Dutertre, B.: Elements of mathematical analysis in PVS. In: Goos, G., Hartmanis, J., van Leeuwen, J., von Wright, J., Grundy, J., Harrison, J. (eds.) TPHOLs 1996. LNCS, vol. 1125, pp. 141–156. Springer, Heidelberg (1996). https://doi.org/10.1007/BFb0105402
10. Fitzgerald, J.S., Larsen, P.G., Verhoef, M.: Vienna development method. In: Wah, B. (ed.) Wiley Encyclopedia of Computer Science and Engineering. Wiley (2007)
11. Fulton, N., Mitsch, S., Quesel, J.-D., Völp, M., Platzer, A.: KeYmaera X: an axiomatic tactical theorem prover for hybrid systems. In: Felty, A.P., Middeldorp, A. (eds.) CADE 2015. LNCS (LNAI), vol. 9195, pp. 527–538. Springer, Cham (2015). https://doi.org/10.1007/978-3-319-21401-6_36
12. Gamble, C.: DSE in the INTO-CPS platform. Technical report, D5.3e, INTO-CPS Deliverable (2017)
13. Gomes, C., Thule, C., Broman, D., Larsen, P.G., Vangheluwe, H.: Co-simulation: State of the art. CoRR abs/1702.00686 (2017)
14. Henzinger, T.A.: The theory of hybrid automata. In: Proceedings of the 11th Annual IEEE Symposium on Logic in Computer Science, LICS 1996, pp. 278–292. IEEE Computer Society, Washington (1996)
15. Isidori, A.: Nonlinear Control System. Communications and Control Engineering. Springer, London (1995). https://doi.org/10.1007/978-1-84628-615-5
16. Larsen, P.G., et al.: Integrated tool chain for model-based design of Cyber-Physical Systems: the INTO-CPS project. In: 2016 2nd International Workshop on Modelling, Analysis, and Control of Complex CPS (CPS Data), pp. 1–6, April 2016
17. Larsen, P.G., Gamble, C., Pierce, K., Ribeiro, A., Lausdahl, K.: Support for co-modelling and co-simulation: the Crescendo tool. In: Fitzgerald, J., Larsen, P.G., Verhoef, M. (eds.) Collaborative Design for Embedded Systems. LNCS, pp. 97–114. Springer, Heidelberg (2014). https://doi.org/10.1007/978-3-642-54118-6_5
18. Leivant, D.: Higher order logic. In: Gabbay, D.M., Hogger, C.J., Robinson, J.A. (eds.) Handbook of Logic in Artificial Intelligence and Logic Programming, pp. 229–321. Oxford University Press Inc., New York (1994)

19. Lotov, A.V., Miettinen, K.: Visualizing the Pareto frontier. In: Branke, J., Deb, K., Miettinen, K., Słowiński, R. (eds.) Multiobjective Optimization. LNCS, vol. 5252, pp. 213–243. Springer, Heidelberg (2008). https://doi.org/10.1007/978-3-540-88908-3_9
20. Manna, Z., Pnueli, A.: The Temporal Logic of Reactive Systems: Safety. Springer, New York (1995). https://doi.org/10.1007/978-1-4612-4222-2
21. Muñoz, C.: Rapid prototyping in PVS. Technical report, NIA 2003–03, NASA/CR-2003-212418, National Institute of Aerospace, Hampton, VA, USA (2003)
22. Nibert, J., Herniter, M.E., Chambers, Z.: Model-based system design for MIL, SIL, and HIL. World Electr. Veh. J. **5**(4), 1121–1130 (2012)
23. Owre, S., Rushby, J.M., Shankar, N.: PVS: a prototype verification system. In: Kapur, D. (ed.) CADE 1992. LNCS, vol. 607, pp. 748–752. Springer, Heidelberg (1992). https://doi.org/10.1007/3-540-55602-8_217
24. Palensky, P., van der Meer, A., Lopez, C., Joseph, A., Pan, K.: Applied cosimulation of intelligent power systems: implementing hybrid simulators for complex power systems. IEEE Ind. Electron. Mag. **11**(2), 6–21 (2017)
25. Palensky, P., Meer, A.A.V.D., Lopez, C.D., Joseph, A., Pan, K.: Cosimulation of intelligent power systems: fundamentals, software architecture, numerics, and coupling. IEEE Ind. Electron. Mag. **11**(1), 34–50 (2017)
26. Palmieri, M., Bernardeschi, C., Masci, P.: A flexible framework for FMI-based co-simulation of human-centred cyber-physical systems. In: Software Technologies: Applications and Foundations - STAF 2018 Collocated Workshops, Toulouse, June 25–29 France 2018, Revised Selected Papers, pp. 21–33 (2018)
27. Pnueli, A.: The temporal logic of programs. In: 18th Annual Symposium on Foundations of Computer Science (sfcs 1977), pp. 46–57, October 1977
28. Pulle, D., Darnell, P., Veltman, A.: Applied Control of Electrical Drives: Real Time Embedded and Sensorless Control Using VisSimTM and PLECSTM. Power Systems. Springer, Cham (2015). https://doi.org/10.1007/978-3-319-20043-9
29. Tudorache, T., Trifu, I., Ghita, C., Bostan, V.: Improved mathematical model of PMSM taking into account cogging torque oscillations. Adv. Electr. Comput. Eng. **12**(3), 59–64 (2012)

Challenges for Integrating Humans into Vehicular Cyber-Physical Systems

Sulayman K. Sowe[1]($\boxtimes$), Martin Fränzle[1], Jan-Patrick Osterloh[2],
Alexander Trende[2], Lars Weber[2], and Andreas Lüdtke[2]

[1] Department of Computer Science, Carl von Ossietzky University of Oldenburg,
26129 Oldenburg, Germany
{sulayman.sowe,martin.fraenzle}@uni-oldenburg.de
[2] Institute for Information Technology, Escherweg 2, 26121 Oldenburg, Germany
{osterloh,trende,lars.weber,luedtke}@offis.de

Abstract. Advances in Vehicular Cyber-Physical Systems (VCPS) are
the primary enablers of the shift from no automation to fully autonomous
vehicles (AVs). One of the impacts of this shift is to develop safe AVs in
which most or all of the functions of the human driver are replaced with
an intelligent system. However, while some progress has been made in
equipping AVs with advanced AI capabilities, VCPS designers are still
faced with the challenge of designing trustworthy AVs that are in sync
with the unpredictable behaviours of humans. In order to address this
challenge, we present a model that describes how a Human Ambassador
component can be integrated into the overall design of a new generation
of VCPS. A scenario is presented to demonstrate how the model can
work in practice. Formalisation and co-simulation challenges associated
with integrating the Human Ambassador component and future work we
are undertaking are also discussed.

Keywords: Human-Centered Cyber Physical Systems · Vehicular
Cyber-Physical Systems · Human Ambassador Component ·
Autonomous vehicles · Co-simulation · Formal methods

1 Introduction

Research and anecdotal evidence indicates that over a million of people die
in traffic accidents each year, and that 94% of these deaths are the result of
human error [4]. The current approach of the automotive industry to decrease
these fatalities is to reduce, and eventually eliminate, the human from the control
task of the car, by adding more and more automation. It is predicted that in
less than a decade this will be possible when fully autonomous vehicles (AVs)
become a reality. The AVs global market has responded to the hype and is
expected to reach USD 126.8 billion by 2027. Automakers (e.g. BMW, Tesla),

Research supported by the German Research Foundation grant FR 2715/4-1 and LU
1880/2-1.

J. Camara and M. Steffen (Eds.): SEFM 2019 Workshops, LNCS 12226, pp. 20–26, 2020.
https://doi.org/10.1007/978-3-030-57506-9_2

service providers (e.g. Uber, Lyft), and companies (e.g. Google, Amazon) are all actively involved in developing AVs prototypes that fall within the Society of Automotive Engineers (SAE) automation levels four to five classification. The hope is that with the advent of fully-autonomous cars, car sharing will bring about cheap and fast mode of transportation, thus reducing traffic congestion, and road accidents.

AVs can be seen as Human-centered Cyber Physical System (HCPS) [13] that integrate human capabilities (e.g. situation and context awareness, adaptability, reasoning) [12] with physical and computational processes. The application of HCPS can be found in all societal-scale autonomous systems where control is dynamically shifting between humans and machines. A Vehicular Cyber-Physical Systems (VCPS) is a special type of HCPS that have vehicles and road networks as physical systems and computing and communication as cyber systems [11].

In order to increase societal trust and confidence, and to ensure that AVs can adapt or deal with the unpredictable behaviours of humans, VCPS designers have to find better ways of integrating the human into the overall design of VCPS. As argued by [1], AVs will not only have to resolve interactions with humans, but also with other human driven vehicles, pedestrians, cyclists, etc. Furthermore, [10] commented that AVs are more likely to be accepted by the general public if they "behave like human drivers". [5] emphasised that it is important to develop a comprehensive model that will help us understand how to integrate the human into VCPS, understand what humans can and cannot do in autonomous vehicles, and how they can amicable work with these systems to meet societal expectations.

A lot of research has been undertaken to accommodate the human in some way in AVs. For example, the Audi Fit Driver feature uses vehicle sensors to provide real-time evaluation of the driver's health condition. Ford is experimenting with features for detecting driver's fatigue, diabetes, cardiac condition, and stress [7]. [2] presented a neuro-physiological study in which they detected drivers' frustration with oncoming traffic and adapting their driving strategy accordingly. Thus, we will continue to have complex VCPS, where human driven cars have to interact with semi-autonomous and fully-autonomous vehicles. In addition, in semi-autonomous cars there will be hand-over situations, where control is shifted from the car to the driver, and vice versa. Each of the features or services provides added value for the AV user.

As a precursor to our ongoing research research project on Human-centered Cyber-Phyiscal Systems [9], the goal of this research is to develop, formalise and validate (using co-simulations where appropriate) a model for integrating humans into VCPS. The the current version of the model describes how six basic aspects of the human (e.g. personal information, tasks he/she can perform, his/her medical and psychological states, etc.) can be encoded into what we call a Human Ambassador component (HAC). However, the model is extensible and the possibility to add more modules is denoted by H^{n+1}. The HAC represents and has the characteristics of a human drive. It can communicate with the vehicular physical sensors, actuators, and data stores. The component can then be integrated with other VCPS components. One potential value of this component is to provide a kind of template for representing certain human characteristics as modules in the component early in the VCPS design process. These modules can be modified, reused and customised to meet the needs of the AV user. We will call a VCPS with an integrated HAC a Vehicular Human Cyber-Physical System or VHCPS (VCPS + Human Ambassador Component).

In what follows we present an overview of the model for integrating the HAC in VHCP in Sect. 2. A scenario to show how this model can work in practice is discussed in Sect. 3. Challenges associated with integrating the Human Ambassador component and future work we are undertaking are presented in Sect. 4. Section 5 concludes the paper.

2   Model for Integrating Humans into VCPS

A schematic representation of the model is shown in Fig. 1. The Human Ambassador component can dynamically exchange data with the sensors, actuators, and the Data stores and Information Processing Units of the vehicle. This data can then be used by other components in the vehicle to make smart decisions and alert or enter into dialogue with the person in the vehicle. The Human Ambassador component contains six basic modules as described in Table 1. Each of these modules can have several sub-modules which can be adapted for different users or AV situations. Depending on the situation or scenario being addressed, more modules can be added, as denoted by H^{n+1}.

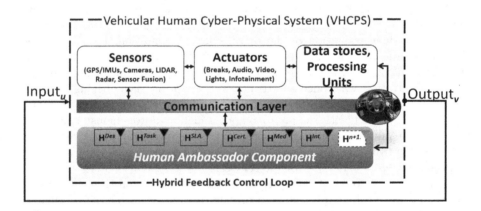

Fig. 1. Human Ambassador component module integration into VHCPS

3   Vehicular Human Cyber-Physical Systems Scenario

The goal of the model in Fig. 1 is to illustrate how other AV components can work with the Human Ambassador component to provide added value for the

Table 1. Human Ambassador component modules

Module	Description	Examples
	Use case	
$H^{Des.}$	Human personal info.	Name, address, location
	An AV sharing company can match users with their AV preference	
H^{Task}	Specific task the human can perform in the AV	Driving licence, freeways or urban traffic driving experience
	An AV drives in a traffic environment it is not capable of navigating. The H^{Task} module can verify if the user is able take over control and perform the required driving task	
H^{SLA}	Service Level Agreement between the human and the AV component manufacturer	Legal binding information regarding the storage and use of the data and information in the Human Ambassador component
	The Human Ambassador component wants to share personal information with the user's medical advisor. H^{SLA} assures that the user agreed sharing this info.	
$H^{Cert.}$	Certification of user qualifications for the specific task	Validates driving licence, address, qualifications, etc.
	An AV wants to hand over the control to the user because it is in a situation that it is not capable of navigating. $H^{Cert.}$ assures that the user has the correct driving licence and experience, to operate the vehicle safely	
$H^{Med.}$	Human health and behavioural states	Heart condition, psychological, neuro-physiological [2], and behavioural states
	$H^{Med.}$ monitors the health state of the user and takes actions in an emergency (e.g. heart attack). A good example involving the Tesla Model X car is presented by [7]	
$H^{Int.}$	User and car Human-machine interface	Mobile device, voice command, an app, direct touch, biometric recognition, etc.
	Because of a traffic jam, an AV communicates changes to a planned route to the user via an interface defined in $H^{Int.}$	

person/s in the vehicle. An event location scenario is a prime example to show how the model can work in practice to achieve this goal.

In an event location scenario, the owner of an autonomous car activates the Human Ambassador component and uses her/his car from Monday to Thursday to go from home to office, and back to home. Almost every Friday, after work, the car owner passes through a supermarket to do shopping, and then goes back home. Occasionally, after shopping, the car owner goes to a pub for some beers, and then goes home at 2 am. The Human Ambassador component records and learns these habitual errands.

Subsequently, the car can "ask" the owner whether she/he wants to pass through the usual supermarket. If affirmative, a command is issued to other (sensor) components to scan the usual route for possible traffic congestion, availability of parking slots at or near the supermarket. The car then "reports back" to the owner about (a) the favourable traffic conditions and availability of parking, and reconfirm whether "they" (car + owner) are ready to go for shopping, or (b) congested traffic and unavailable parking nearby, and advise or confirm with the owner whether she/he still wants to proceed with the shopping trip or wait for the car to check and update the parking and traffic situation later.

In this scenario, the most active human capabilities involved are stored in $H^{Des.}$ (e.g. geo-location data), as well as the component's capabilities to learn and recognise the car owner's habitual errands. The $H^{Med.}$ module can also play a role in this scenario. For example, giving the neurophysiological and behavioural states of the owner, the $H^{Med.}$ might determine that the driver is too drunk and unfit to drive back home when he leaves the pub drunk at 2 am. The $H^{Med.}$ module can then recommend to the routing module of the system and subsequently the actuators that the car should drive itself home.

4   Research Challenges and Future Work

Vehicular Human Cyber-Physical Systems (VHCPS) are pervasive and ubiquitous hybrid systems comprising of hundreds to thousands of embedded components. Modelling and simulation techniques are often used to guarantee that these complex systems will perform as expected. However, whether these techniques are applicable or will scale in VHCPS with an embedded Human Ambassador component is an open research question. The beauty of co-simulation, as noted by [6], is that a global simulation of a system such as a VHCPS can be achieved by composing the simulations of its parts. Thus, we can take out the Human Ambassador component from the VHCPS, simulate it, gain some insight, and put it back again without interfering with the other VCPS components. However, as each system is unique, the fundamental challenge we have is in finding best practice guidelines and tools that we can use to simulate the Human Ambassador component or what aspect or modules of the component is possible to simulate.

Other issues we are trying to address in this model includes:

- *Data security, privacy, legislations and data sharing*: The fact that the car can be driven across borders and regions, the security and privacy concerns, as well as the different legislation governing AVs needs to be clarified in the modules (e.g. $H^{Des.}$, $H^{Med.}$). Data dissemination and sharing across vehicular networks also needs addressing.
- *Interoperability*: The embedded systems-of-systems characteristics of VHCPS means that various components must operate and communicate across standards and protocols. Where many vehicle manufactures, OEMs, Vehicular

Ad-Hoc Network providers are involved, how can a Human Ambassador component inter-operate with other VCPS components remains an open issue.

Parts of the proposed model namely a subset of the modules $H^{Med.}$, H^{Task} and $H^{Des.}$ are currently being investigated in the *AutoAkzept* [3,14] project. One of the goals is to investigate user profiles for VHCPS that account for the individual user's preferences regarding driving style and to adapt the vehicles behaviour according to these preferences and the current human state. Furthermore, we are planning to combine integrated human behaviour models [2,8] into the $H^{Med.}$ module to come up with a unified human integration model for VHCPS.

5   Concluding Remarks

In this paper, we presented our ongoing work and initial concept of Human Vehicular Cyber-Physical System model to describe one possible way of integrating the human into the overall design of Vehicular Cyber-Physical Systems. An autonomous vehicle event location scenario was used to demonstrate how the model can work in practice. Some research challenges and work we are currently undertaking to improve the model were also highlighted.

The modules described in this model shows that a multidisciplinary approach is needed to advance the development of the new generation of vehicular cyber-physical system, and autonomous vehicles in particular. For instance, knowledge from medicine and psychology is needed for the $H^{Med.}$ module, legal and privacy for modules $H^{Cert.}$ and H^{SLA}, and engineering. Finally, it is envisaged that this kind of model will be useful in helping autonomous vehicle testing teams and the co-simulation community test many variables that may influence human-Vehicular interactions which are not possible test today's simulators environments.

References

1. Bartl, M., Rosenzweig, J.: The voice of the crowd - an innovation mining study on autonomous driving. In: Revolution of Innovation Management - The Digital Breakthrough. Brem, Alexander, Viardot, Eric, Palgrave Macmillan (2016)
2. Damm, W., Fränzle, M., Lüdtke, A., Rieger, J.W., Trende, A., Unni, A.: Integrating neurophysiological sensors and driver models for safe and performant automated vehicle control in mixed traffic. In: The IEEE Workshop on Human Factors in Intelligent Vehicles (HFIV 2019) abs/1902.0 (2019). http://arxiv.org/abs/1902.04929
3. Drewitz, U., et al.: Automation ohne Unsicherheit: Vorstellung des Förderprojekts AutoAkzept zur Erhöhung der Akzeptanz automatisierten Fahrens. Accepted for 10. VDI-Tagung Mensch-Maschine-Mobilität (2019)
4. Favarò, F.M., Nader, N., Eurich, S.O., Tripp, M., Varadaraju, N.: Examining accident reports involving autonomous vehicles in California. PLoS ONE **12**(9), 1–20 (2017)

5. Fridman, L., et al.: MIT autonomous vehicle technology study: large-scale deep learning based analysis of driver behavior and interaction with automation. CoRR 1711.06976 (2019). https://arxiv.org/abs/1711.06976

6. Gomes, C., Thule, C., Broman, D., Larsen, P.G., Vangheluwe, H.: Co-simulation: a survey. ACM Comput. Surv. **51**(3), 49:1–49:33 (2018). https://doi.org/10.1145/3179993. http://doi.acm.org/10.1145/3179993

7. Grifantini, K.: Self driving and self diagnosing: with emerging technology, your car may soon serve not only as personal chauffeur and entertainment center but as a health advisor too. IEEE Pulse **9**(4), 4–7 (2018)

8. Kacianka, S., Ibrahim, A., Pretschner, A., Trende, A., Luedtke, A.: Extending causal models from machines into humans. In: CREST 2019 4th Workshop on Formal Reasoning About Causation, Responsibility, and Explanations in Science and Technology, 7 April 2019

9. Kyriakidis, M., et al.: A human factors perspective on automated driving. Theoret. Issues Ergon. Sci. **20**(3), 223–249 (2019)

10. Li, A., Jiang, H., Zhou, J., Zhou, X.: Learning human-like trajectory planning on urban two-lane curved roads from experienced drivers. IEEE Access **7**, 65828–65838 (2019). https://doi.org/10.1109/ACCESS.2019.2918728

11. Rawat, D.B., Bajracharya, C.: Adaptive connectivity for spectrum agile VANETs in fading channels. In: Vehicular Cyber Physical Systems, pp. 25–40. Springer, Cham (2017). https://doi.org/10.1007/978-3-319-44494-9_3

12. Sowe, S.K., Simmon, E., Zettsu, K., de Vaulx, F., Bojanova, I.: Cyber-physical-human systems: putting people in the loop. IT Prof. **18**(1), 10–13 (2016). https://doi.org/10.1109/MITP.2016.14

13. Sztipanovits, J., et al.: Science of design for societal-scale cyber-physical systems: challenges and opportunities. Cyber-Phys. Syst. **5**(3), 145–172 (2019). https://doi.org/10.1080/23335777.2019.1624619

14. Trende, A., Gräfing, D., Weber, L.: Personalized user profiles for autonomous vehicles. In: Accepted for AutomotiveUI 2019 Adjunct, Utrecht, Netherlands, 21–25 September 2019. ACM, Netherlands, September 2019. https://doi.org/10.1145/3349263.3351315

Automatic Generation of Functional Mock-Up Units from Formal Specifications

Maurizio Palmieri[1,2(✉)] and Hugo Daniel Macedo[3]

[1] DINFO, Department of Engineering, University of Florence, Florence, Italy
[2] DII, Department of Information Engineering, University of Pisa, Pisa, Italy
`maurizio.palmieri@ing.unipi.it`
[3] DIGIT, Department of Engineering, Aarhus University,
Finlandsgade 22, 8200 Aarhus N, Denmark
`hdm@eng.au.dk`

Abstract. This paper reports on the approach used to augment a transition system tool with automatic Functional Mock-up Units (FMU) generation. To verify the FMU properties, the same transition system can be translated into a formal language. Among intrinsic system properties, transition systems are associated with the following two: the disjointedness and the coverage, which assert that the controller is deterministic and defined for every possible input. This paper shows how both properties are enforced when proving the type checking conditions derived by the PVS theorem prover.

1 Introduction

Co-simulation enables a compositional approach to system simulation, where each of the system's components is simulated by an FMU [1], and a co-simulation environment (e.g. [2]) can be used to couple FMUs and perform joint simulations.

Depending on the criticality of the simulated component, some FMUs may demand formal verification. As formal verification involves modelling the component behaviour, it makes sense to re-use such models in the derivation of the respective FMUs. In this paper we apply such reasoning to the PVSio-web toolkit.

PVSio-web [3] simplifies and enhances the usage of formal methods by exploiting a graphical editor, which allows users to define models of reactive systems as an Emuchart diagram, a subset of the Statechart diagrams, and then verify the models by translating the Emuchart model into a PVS [5] model/theory on which the theorem prover of PVS can be applied.

PVSio-web provides an automatic procedure to translate the Emuchart diagram into a MISRA C code program [4] that can be exploited to generate an FMU. The properties verified on the PVS model derived from an Emuchart can be assumed for free in the behaviour of FMU generated from the same Emuchart, assuming that the translations are well defined. An example of such properties

© Springer Nature Switzerland AG 2020
J. Camara and M. Steffen (Eds.): SEFM 2019 Workshops, LNCS 12226, pp. 27–33, 2020.
https://doi.org/10.1007/978-3-030-57506-9_3

is the deterministic behaviour of the system, which is often required in many cases (e.g. critical cyber-physical systems).

Contribution. We extended PVSio-web to generate standalone FMU components using a graphical editor. We show that the translation into MISRA C code used for the FMU generation has some common elements with the translation into PVS model, pointing to the possibility of using the PVS model to prove properties of the FMU. Finally we describe how two general properties are dealt with in the PVS theorem prover in Subsect. 3.2.

Related Work. Our work departs from previous results [6,7] where PVSio-web is successfully used to generate tool-wrapper FMUs which communicate with GUIs via websockets. This work adds a new support to the previous work by showing that the generation of standalone FMUs for discrete event reactive system controllers is possible.

2   Background

PVSio-web is a toolkit for prototyping and analysis of interactive (human-centred) systems. Each PVSio-web prototype consists of two parts: a back-end defining the behaviour of the system (for instance using Emuchart diagrams, see Fig. 1); and a graphical front-end defining the visual appearance of the system. The front-end (See Fig. 1 in [3]) is not an object of this work.

Emuchart Diagrams. An Emuchart diagram is an automaton representation of a system containing the following elements:

– a collection of different operational **states** in which the system operates,
– a collection of all the possible **transitions** among the states,
– a collection of all the **variables** of the system.

In every diagram there is an initial transition pointing to the state where the Emuchart execution starts from. We show an Emuchart diagram in Fig. 1 with one state and one reentrant transition (i.e. a transition where the source state is also the destination state).

Emuchart **transitions** are graphically depicted as arrows between a source and a destination state, and are annotated with the following triples:

$$label\ [condition]\{action\}$$

where **label** is the name of the transition, **condition** is a Boolean expression which guards the firing of the transition, and **action** is an operation which is executed when the transition

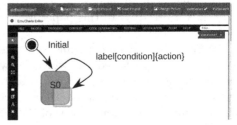

Fig. 1. Emuchart example

is taken. There can be more transitions with the same `label`, but with different `condition` and `action` definitions.

For PVSio-web model animation, it is mandatory to have at least one transition with label `tick` that represents the time advancement of the model. To animate a model, the simulation engine of PVSio-web periodically fires the transition `tick`, and all the other transitions are fired on demand, when an event occurs on the front-end (e.g. the user presses a button on the UI).

```
State* l(State* st) {
        if (st->mode == source1 && ( t_condition1 )) {
                leave(source1, st);
                t_action1;
                enter(dest1, st);
        }
        ...
        else if (st->mode == sourceN && ( t_conditionN )) {
                leave(sourceN, st);
                t_actionN;
                enter(destN, st);
        }
        return st;
}
```

Listing 1.1. MISRA C translation of transition

2.1 Emuchart Translation into MISRA C

As defined in [4], the MISRA C generated code includes:

- an enumeration type called `Mode` with all the names of the states as values,
- a structure type called `State` with all the variables of the model as fields plus two fields termed `mode` and `previous_mode` of type `Mode`, used to save the current and the previous state respectively, during the simulation runtime,
- a void function *enter* : *Mode* × *State*∗ that updates the value of the `mode` field in the input `State*` with the current state in the simulation,
- a void function *leave* : *Mode* × *State*∗ that updates the value of the field `previous_mode` in the input `State*` with the previous state in the simulation.

Then, for each label `l` of transitions a function $l : State* \rightarrow State*$ is created. The template body of the function `l` is shown in Listing 1.1, where there are N transitions with label `l`, `st` is a variable of type `State*`, and `t_conditionX`/`t_actionX` are the condition/action of transition X translated into the MISRA C syntax.

2.2 Emuchart Translation into PVS

The types `Mode` and `State`, and the functions `enter` and `leave` created for MISRA C are also created in the PVS theory with the same meaning.

The transitions in the Emuchart models are translated with the PVS COND statement in the following way:

1. For each transition with label 1 in the Emuchart, a PVS function named 1 is created and its body is a COND statement.
2. Each `condition` in transitions with label 1 is translated into a PVS `Boolean expression` (be) inside the COND statement generated for 1 and is joined with the requirement that the current state (called mode of `State`) of the simulation is the source state.
3. The `action` is translated into a `LET IN expression` that consists of three operations: An invocation of the `leave` function with the source state as argument, the performance of the action, and a call to the `enter` function with the destination state as argument.

For the example in Fig. 1 the condition in Listing 1.2 is generated.

```
1 (st: State): State =
COND
  [be] AND mode(st) = S0
    -> LET st = leave(S0)(st)
       st = st WITH [action]
       IN enter(S0)(st)
ENDCOND
```

Listing 1.2. PVS translation of transition

3   Emuchart Translation into FMU

In this work, PVSio-web has been extended with a new feature to generate an FMU package from an Emuchart model. Figure 2 shows the dataflow for the generation of an FMU. Starting from the `Emuchart Diagram` and two Handlebars [1] templates, we generate the `MISRA C Code` which contains the behaviour of the model, and the `FMU Shared Library Code` which contains the implementation of the FMI standard. Then we compile the `MISRA C Code` with the `FMU Shared Library Code` to generate a `FMU Shared Library`, which is then zipped with the joint files (modelDescription.xml, etc.), to generate the FMU.

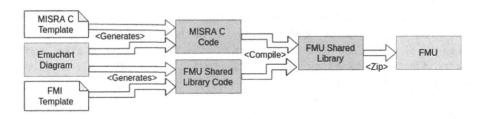

Fig. 2. FMU generation dataflow

---

[1] https://handlebarsjs.com.

3.1   FMU Adaptation

In order to create an FMU of the Emuchart model, the generated MISRA C code is invoked by the implementation of the FMI shared library. The FMI implementation creates a variable st of type State to keep track of the state of the system and a structure named fmiBuffer that can be accessed by the master algorithm to get/set variables.

An example of the FMI function that performs a co-simulation step is shown in Listing 1.3, where lines 2 and 3 move the values of the input variables from the fmiBuffer to the state st, line 4 invokes the function tick, which is written in the MISRA C code, using the address of st as parameter (pass by reference). After line 4 the output variables of state st have been updated and lines 5 and 6 move the new values computed by tick from the state st to the fmiBuffer.

The scope of the variables is written in the Emuchart Diagram and known to the master algorithm (with reference to Listing 1.3 the master algorithm knows that variable with index 4 and 5 are input variables and variables 9 and 10 are output variables). The FMI master algorithm does not directly access st.

```
1  void doStep() {
2      st.lfLeftVal = fmiBuffer.realBuffer[4];
3      st.lfRightVal = fmiBuffer.realBuffer[5];
4      tick(&st);
5      fmiBuffer.realBuffer[9] = st.servoLeftVal;
6      fmiBuffer.realBuffer[10] = st.servoRightVal;
```

Listing 1.3. Snippet of FMI step function

3.2   Checking Disjointedness of Conditions and Coverage Properties

Here we show how to use PVS to ensure that an Emuchart diagram is deterministic and defined for every input, and how, by construction, the FMU is also deterministic and defined. The result is a corollary of the conjunction of the following disjointedness of conditions and coverage properties and a lemma:

Lemma. Because the transitions are translated into a COND expression in the PVS language with the Emuchart conditions as Boolean expressions (be)s (see Sect. 2.2). The translation defined in Sect. 2.2 equates the following:

– Emuchart: The set of conditions of all the transitions with the same label and same source state name.
– PVS: The set of all the bes in the relative COND expression for the label.

Disjointedness of Conditions. This property guarantees that when a transition is fired there is no more than one action to be executed; i.e., for each state, it is never possible to have more than one outgoing edge with both guards satisfied.

As PVS checks if all the bes are pairwise disjoint, e.g.: for the set be_1, be_2 and be_3 the expression $\neg(be_1 \wedge be_2) \wedge \neg(be_1 \wedge be_3) \wedge \neg(be_2 \wedge be_3)$ is valid, then it is not possible to have two different actions for the same transition. That would imply that two conditions were satisfied and provide a pair of non-disjoint bes.

Coverage. This property guarantees that when a transition is fired, at least one action is executed, i.e. there is no state where the transition is not defined. As PVS checks that the generalized union of the bes is a tautology, thus covering the whole subtype, if there is a state where a transition leads to no action, then none of the conditions defined for the transition is satisfied which means there is an element of the subtype that is not covered by the generalized union of the boolean conditions, thus the union is not a tautology.

The PVS theorem prover can automatically (no human input needed) generate and discharge type checking conditions to ensure both these properties are verified (see [5] p. 53). When the generated type check conditions are verified, the **Coverage** and **Disjointedness of conditions** together guarantee that when a transition is fired then there is one and only one action executed, which implies the Emuchart is deterministic and defined for every possible input.

According to the PVS language reference (see again [5] p. 53) the COND expression is an abbreviation (polymorphic version) of nested IF-THEN-ELSE statements, which is the strategy used in the MISRA C translation, thus the properties of the PVS COND statement are also verified for the MISRA C nested IF-THEN-ELSE statements.

4   Discussion and Future Work

The generation of the FMUs from Emucharts is now automatic thanks to the adaptation proposed in this work. It is worth noticing that the verification of the type checking conditions is automatic thus we provide an automatic procedure to generate a formally verified FMU without requiring PVS knowledge.

The claim that properties proved in PVS are also applied on the FMU is based on reasoning at a high-level, and a mechanised proof is needed to ensure the equivalence in the triangulation we propose: Emuchart-PVS-FMU. The similarities between the MISRA C and the PVS generation and the polymorphism between the COND and the IF-THEN-ELSE suggest that the equivalence between the three elements is indeed verifiable (an approach has been suggested in Appendix of [4]).

In addition, our work is in a standpoint to provide the initial step towards thoroughly defining the semantics of the translation of Emucharts into PVS, which is a much needed future work possibility.

Acknowledgements. We would like to thank Peter Gorm Larsen for feedback, and Paolo Masci for input on this paper and for his seminal work on the PVSio-web.

References

1. Blochwitz, T., et al.: Functional mockup interface 2.0: the standard for tool independent exchange of simulation models. In: Proceedings of the 9th International Modelica Conference, pp. 173–184. The Modelica Association (2012)
2. Larsen, P.G., et al.: The INtegrated TOolchain for Cyber-Physical Systems (INTO-CPS): a Guide. Technical report, INTO-CPS Association, October 2018. www.into-cps.org
3. Masci, P., Oladimeji, P., Mallozzi, P., Curzon, P., Thimbleby, H.: PVSio-web: mathematically based tool support for the design of interactive and interoperable medical systems. In: Proceedings of the 5th EAI International Conference on Wireless Mobile Communication and Healthcare, pp. 42–45. ICST (Institute for Computer Sciences, Social-Informatics and Telecommunications Engineering) (2015)
4. Mauro, G., Thimbleby, H., Domenici, A., Bernardeschi, C.: Extending a user interface prototyping tool with automatic MISRA C code generation. In: Proceedings of the Third Workshop on Formal Integrated Development Environment (2016)
5. Owre, S., Shankar, N., Rushby, J.M., Stringer-Calvert, D.W.: PVS Language Reference. Computer Science Laboratory, SRI International, Menlo Park, vol. 1, no. 2, p. 21 (1999)
6. Palmieri, M., Bernardeschi, C., Masci, P.: Co-simulation of semi-autonomous systems: the line follower robot case study. In: Cerone, A., Roveri, M. (eds.) SEFM 2017. LNCS, vol. 10729, pp. 423–437. Springer, Cham (2018). https://doi.org/10.1007/978-3-319-74781-1_29
7. Palmieri, M., Bernardeschi, C., Masci, P.: A flexible framework for FMI-based co-simulation of human-centred cyber-physical systems. In: Mazzara, M., Ober, I., Salaün, G. (eds.) STAF 2018. LNCS, vol. 11176, pp. 21–33. Springer, Cham (2018). https://doi.org/10.1007/978-3-030-04771-9_2

Generation of Co-simulation Algorithms Subject to Simulator Contracts

Cláudio Gomes[1]([✉]), Casper Thule[2], Levi Lúcio[3], Hans Vangheluwe[1], and Peter Gorm Larsen[2]

[1] University of Antwerp, Flanders Make, Antwerp, Belgium
{claudio.gomes,hans.vangheluwe}@uantwerp.be
[2] Aarhus University, Aarhus, Denmark
casper.thule@eng.au.dk
[3] fortiss, Munich, Germany
lucio@fortiss.org

Abstract. Correct co-simulation results require a careful consideration of how the interacting simulators are implemented. In version 2.0 of the FMI Standard, input handling implementation is left implicit, which leads to the situation where a simulator can be interacted with in a manner that its implementation does not expect, yielding incorrect results.

In this paper, we build on prior work to make information about each simulator implementation explicit, in order to derive correct interactions with it. The formalization we use is specific to two kinds of contracts, but could serve as a basis to a general approach to black box co-simulation. The algorithm we propose generates a co-simulation execution plan in linear time. It has been successfully applied to an industrial case study, and the results are available online.

Keywords: Co-simulation · Prolog · Contract-based code generation · Constraint solving

1 Introduction

Correct co-simulation results require a careful consideration of how the interacting simulators are implemented (e.g., see [12,14,19], and references thereof). Co-simulation is a technique to combine multiple black-box simulators, each responsible for a model, in order to compute the behavior of the combined models over time [16]. The simulators, often developed independently from each other, are coupled using a master algorithm, also often developed independently, that communicates with each simulator via its interface. This interface comprises functions for setting/getting inputs/outputs, and computing the associated model behavior over a given interval of time. An example of such interface,

---

C. G. is a FWO Research Fellow, at the University of Antwerp, supported by the Research Foundation - Flanders (File Number 1S06316N). We thank the organizers of the CAMPaM workshop for providing a platform where the ideas described here flourished. Finally, we thank the reviewers for the thorough feedback.

© Springer Nature Switzerland AG 2020
J. Camara and M. Steffen (Eds.): SEFM 2019 Workshops, LNCS 12226, pp. 34–49, 2020.
https://doi.org/10.1007/978-3-030-57506-9_4

the terminology of which we adopt here, is the Functional Mockup Interface (FMI) Standard [3,4]. In the FMI Standard, the simulators are called Functional Mockup Units (FMUs).

The widespread adoption of co-simulation is hindered by the lack of guarantees on the correctness of the results [14]. Indeed, a recent empirical survey has shown that practitioners still experience difficulties in the configuration of co-simulations [17,18]. Version 2.0 of the FMI Standard does not impose a single way of interacting with an FMU (see Sect. 2.1). However, different interaction protocols with an FMU lead to assumptions on the implementation of that FMU. Recent work [12] shows that one of the reasons for these difficulties is the lack of information about the implementation of each FMU.

Contribution. In this paper, we propose a way to model simulator capabilities, which we denote as contracts, and automatically generate fixed-step master algorithms that satisfy those contracts. While our long term research goal is to consider arbitrary contracts, in this paper, we restrict our attention to input approximation and output calculation contracts. These contracts correspond to a partial view of how the FMUs implement their input approximation schemes and the algebraic dependencies used to calculate the outputs. Hence, they do not expose intellectual property. As we argue next, respecting these contracts is a necessary condition to obtaining correct results. In the future, more advanced master algorithms can be generated if simulators expose more capabilities (Sect. 5 discusses some of these).

Prior Work. The need for these contracts has been identified in prior work [11] and an incomplete solution is advanced in [12]. The solution proposed in [11] works under the assumptions that FMUs have the same contract for every input (because it assumes FMUs have a single input/output vector), and the solution described in [12] neglects how the outputs are computed [12, Assumption 2]. The submitted manuscript [10] addresses these omissions and describes the semantics of a master algorithm that satisfies such contracts. Since that formalization is defined in pure Prolog, it can be used to generate master algorithms as well. However, this process takes exponential time in the size of the co-simulation scenario (which, for long running co-simulation, becomes negligible). With the current manuscript, we propose a linear time algorithm to perform such generations.

Structure. The next section recalls the formalization proposed in [10], shows why different contracts require different FMU implementations, and formalizes our research problem. Then, Sect. 3 describes our contribution and application results. Section 4 describes related work and Sect. 5 concludes.

2   Background

In this section, we provide a formalization of FMI co-simulation with a restricted set of contracts. We show, through a simple but representative example, that minimizing the error in the co-simulation involves a careful consideration of both master and FMU implementations of such contracts. Such formalization has been implemented in Prolog, presented in [10], and available online[1].

2.1 FMUs and Contracts

Definition 1. *An FMU with identifier c is represented by the tuple*

$$\langle S_c, U_c, Y_c, \texttt{set}_c, \texttt{get}_c, \texttt{doStep}_c \rangle,$$

where: – S_c represents the state space; – U_c and Y_c the set of input and output variables, respectively; – $\texttt{set}_c : S_c \times U_c \times V \to S_c$ and $\texttt{get}_c : S_c \times Y_c \to V$ are functions to set the inputs and get the outputs, respectively (we abstract the set of values that each input/output variable can take as V); and – $\texttt{doStep}_c : S_c \times \mathbb{R}_{\geq 0} \to S_c$ is a function that instructs the FMU to compute its state after a given time step.

If an FMU is in state $s_c^{(n)}$ at time t, $\texttt{doStep}_c(s_c^{(n)}, H)$ approximates the state of the corresponding model at time $t + H$. The result of this approximation is encoded in state $s_c^{(n+1)}$. If the model is continuous, the FMU will internally approx-

Fig. 1. Running example.

imate the evolution in the interval $[t, t + H]$, using an approximation function to estimate the values of the inputs in that interval. In this formalization, we leave this function implicit in the $\texttt{doStep}_c$, as reflected in the version 2.0 of the FMI Standard.

Definition 2 (Scenario). *A scenario is a structure $\langle C, L \rangle$ where each identifier $c \in C$ is associated with an FMU, as defined in Definition 1, and $L(u) = y$ means that the output y is connected to input u. Let $U = \bigcup_{c \in C} U_c$ and $Y = \bigcup_{c \in C} Y_c$, then $L : U \to Y$. It is common to represent a co-simulation scenario as a diagram. For example, Fig. 1 shows an example scenario with two FMUs, connected in a feedback loop.*

The following definitions correspond to the operations that are permitted in a co-simulation, and are correlated later in Definitions 8 to 10.

Definition 3 (Step). *Given a scenario $\langle C, L \rangle$, a co-simulation step, or just step, is a finite ordered sequence of FMU function calls $(f_i)_{i \in \mathbb{N}} = f_0, f_1, \ldots$ with $f_i \in F = \bigcup_{c \in C} \{\texttt{set}_c, \texttt{get}_c, \texttt{doStep}_c\}$, and i denoting the order of the function call.*

Definition 4 (Initialization). *Given a scenario $\langle C, L \rangle$, we define the initialization procedure $(I_i)_{i \in \mathbb{N}}$ in the same way as a step, with $I_i \in F$.*

Definition 5 (Master). *Given a scenario $\langle C, L \rangle$, a step size H, a step $(f_i)_{i \in \mathbb{N}}$, and an initialization procedure $(I_i)_{i \in \mathbb{N}}$, a master algorithm is a structure defined as $\mathcal{A} = \langle C, L, H, (I_i)_{i \in \mathbb{N}}, (f_i)_{i \in \mathbb{N}} \rangle$.*

[1] http://msdl.cs.mcgill.ca/people/claudio/projs/PrologCosimGeneration.zip.

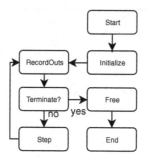

Fig. 2. Generic master.

Figure 2 shows the main steps of any master algorithm, and sheds light on the relationship between the initialization and step procedures.

Algorithms 1 to 3 are possible step procedures for the scenario introduced in Fig. 1. We use the notation $s_c^{(0)}, s_c^{(1)}, \dots$ to stress the transformations on the internal state of the FMU. The index is independent of the co-simulation time, so the state can undergo multiple transformations at the same co-simulation time.

Version 2.0 of the FMI standard [4] is not sufficiently rigorous to conclude whether any of the three algorithms is not a valid step. In fact, page 104 contains "There is the additional restriction in 'slaveInitialized' state that it is not allowed to call fmi2GetXXX functions after fmi2SetXXX functions without an fmi2DoStep call in between"[2], invalidating Algorithms 2 and 3. However, this is contradicted by the fact that the standard supports *feed-through* dependencies, which induce algebraic dependencies between inputs and outputs. To quote the standard:

- "'output': The variable value can be used by another model or slave. The algebraic relationship to the inputs is defined via the dependencies attribute of `<fmiModelDescription><ModelStructure><Outputs><Unknown>`.", page 45.
- "Attribute dependencies defines the dependencies of the outputs from the knowns [...] at the current Communication Point (CoSimulation).", page 58.

The need for feed-through is also described in the scientific literature by the founders of the standard (e.g., [1, Fig. 3]). Since even the simplest mechanical systems, such as mass-spring-dampers, when coupled in a co-simulation, exhibit such feed-through effect [13], we are convinced that the statement on page 104 is incorrect. Therefore, Algorithms 1 to 3 satisfy the standard.

If the designers of the standard did not intend for feed-through to be supported, and our conclusion is wrong, then we can easily work around this limitation by asking the FMU to take a very small step whenever an input is set that needs to be propagated to the output (Fig. 3).

---

[2] An equivalent conclusion can be drawn from the mathematical description of FMU for co-simulation in Table 2, in page 99.

Algorithm 1	Algorithm 2	Algorithm 3
1: $s_a^{(1)} \leftarrow \texttt{doStep}_a(s_a^{(0)}, H)$	1: $s_b^{(1)} \leftarrow \texttt{doStep}_b(s_b^{(0)}, H)$	1: $s_b^{(1)} \leftarrow \texttt{doStep}_b(s_b^{(0)}, H)$
2: $s_b^{(1)} \leftarrow \texttt{doStep}_b(s_b^{(0)}, H)$	2: $s_a^{(1)} \leftarrow \texttt{doStep}_a(s_a^{(0)}, H)$	2: $v \leftarrow \texttt{get}_b(s_b^{(1)}, y_b)$
3: $v_a \leftarrow \texttt{get}_a(s_a^{(1)}, y_a)$	3: $v \leftarrow \texttt{get}_b(s_b^{(1)}, y_b)$	3: $s_a^{(1)} \leftarrow \texttt{set}_a(s_a^{(0)}, u_a, v)$
4: $v_b \leftarrow \texttt{get}_b(s_b^{(1)}, y_b)$	4: $s_a^{(2)} \leftarrow \texttt{set}_a(s_a^{(1)}, u_a, v)$	4: $v \leftarrow \texttt{get}_a(s_a^{(1)}, y_a)$
5: $s_b^{(2)} \leftarrow \texttt{set}_b(s_b^{(1)}, u_b, v_a)$	5: $v \leftarrow \texttt{get}_a(s_a^{(2)}, y_a)$	5: $s_b^{(2)} \leftarrow \texttt{set}_b(s_b^{(1)}, u_b, v)$
6: $s_a^{(2)} \leftarrow \texttt{set}_a(s_a^{(1)}, u_a, v_b)$	6: $s_b^{(2)} \leftarrow \texttt{set}_b(s_b^{(1)}, u_b, v)$	6: $s_a^{(2)} \leftarrow \texttt{doStep}_a(s_a^{(1)}, H)$
7: $s_a^{(0)} \leftarrow s_a^{(2)}$	7: $s_a^{(0)} \leftarrow s_a^{(2)}$	7: $s_a^{(0)} \leftarrow s_a^{(2)}$
8: $s_b^{(0)} \leftarrow s_b^{(2)}$	8: $s_b^{(0)} \leftarrow s_b^{(2)}$	8: $s_b^{(0)} \leftarrow s_b^{(2)}$

Fig. 3. Three algorithms conforming to the FMI Standard (version 2.0). The last two lines represent the assignment of the new state to the state to be used in the next co-simulation step.

We now show that the results produced by each of these algorithms depend on the implementation of the FMUs. Regarding the feed-through of each FMU, assume that the output y_a depends instantaneously on, or has a feed-through from, the input u_a, and that the output y_b does not depend instantaneously on u_b. The instantaneously dependency condition can be expressed formally as: $\exists v, v' \in \mathcal{V}$, such that $s_a^{(1)} = \texttt{set}_a(s_a^{(0)}, u_a, v), s_a^{(2)} = \texttt{set}_a(s_a^{(0)}, u_a, v')$, and $\texttt{get}_a(s_a^{(1)}, y_a) \neq \texttt{get}_a(s_a^{(2)}, y_a)$. With these suppositions, Algorithm 1 is inadequate, because the value of y_a can only be computed after the value of u_a is known.

The feed-through information is a piece of information about the implementation of the FMU that allows us to code master algorithms that produce better results. It is natural to wonder whether there are other aspects that we can use to distinguish Algorithms 2 and 3.

Comparing Algorithms 2 and 3, one notices that, in Algorithms 3, the input u_a is set after $\texttt{doStep}_b$ is invoked. This means that, FMU b advances in time, produces an input to FMU a, and only after does FMU a catch up to the time that b is in. Indeed, this is the main difference between a Gauss-Seidel master algorithm, and a Jacobi one. These are well known algorithms in the literature, and accepted as being compatible with the FMI Standard [2].

However, the implementation of FMU a in Algorithm 3 must differ from the implementation of FMU a in Algorithm 2. To see why, suppose that a does a linear *interpolation* of its inputs. An interpolation formula between two given inputs v_t and v_{t+H}, expected at times t and $t + H$, respectively, is given by $\tilde{u}_a(t + \Delta t) = v_t + \frac{v_{t+H} - v_t}{H} \Delta t$. In contrast, an extrapolation between two given inputs v_{t-H} and v_t, expected at times $t - H$ and t, is given by $\tilde{u}_a(t + \Delta t) = v_t + \frac{v_t - v_{t-H}}{H} \Delta t$. Note the difference between the two formulas and the expected timestamps of the inputs. Since the timestamps of the inputs are implicit in the FMI Standard, the same FMU will either implement an interpolation, or an extrapolation, but cannot implement both.

If FMU a implements an interpolation, and is used in Algorithm 2, then the result will be a delayed input approximation of u_a. This is because an interpolation will given the wrong inputs, for instance, with timestamps $t-H$ and t, instead of t and $t + H$. The delayed input is illustrated Fig. 4. For purely continuous systems, this delay may not introduce substantial errors. However, as has been shown in [20], in systems with discontinuities, the delay can propagate to trigger abrupt changes in the systems' behavior.

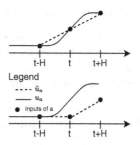

Fig. 4. Application of an interpolation formula to inputs with the right timestamps (above) and the wrong timestamps (below). The dashed curve below shows the delayed input effect.

We now formalize the contracts over the outputs of the FMU (input/output feedthrough), and the contracts over the inputs (interpolation or extrapolation). We use the more generic term *reactivity* to the contracts over the inputs because it can be used for purposes other than input approximation implementations. For example, a software FMU may not implement a linear input interpolation, but still be reactive to reflect the fact that it runs with a very short sampling interval (short relative to co-simulation step size).

Definition 6 (Feed-through). *The input $u_c \in U_c$ feeds through to output $y_c \in Y_c$, that is, $(u_c, y_c) \in D_c$, when there exists $v_1, v_2 \in V$ and $s_c \in S_c$, such that* $\text{get}_c(\text{set}_c(s_c, u_c, v_1), y_c) \neq \text{get}_c(\text{set}_c(s_c, u_c, v_2), y_c)$.

Definition 7 (Reactivity). *For a given FMU c with input $u_c \in U_c$, $R_c(u_c) = true$ if the function doStep_c assumes that the input u_c comes from a FMU that has advanced forward relative to FMU c.*

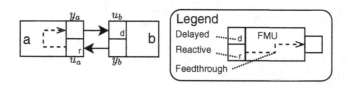

Fig. 5. Contracts notation.

The feed-through and reactivity information for the scenario introduced in Fig. 1 can be represented visually as in Fig. 5, i.e., FMU a is reactive and has feed-through, whereas FMU b is delayed. An FMU is delayed when it is not reactive.

2.2 Master Algorithms

In order to determine whether a given master algorithm satisfies a given scenario and contracts, we need to formalize the constraints that the contracts impose on the valid master algorithms. For that, we need to formalize the run-time state of each FMU, and how the invocation of each co-simulation operation evolves this state.

Definition 8 (Run-time State). *Given an FMU c as defined in Definition 1, the run-time state of c is a member of the set $S_c^R = \mathbb{R}_{\geq 0} \times S_{U_c}^R \times S_{Y_c}^R$, where $\mathbb{R}_{\geq 0}$ is the time base, $S_{U_c}^R = \prod_{u_c \in U_c} S_{u_c}^R$ represents the aggregated state set of the input ports, $S_{u_c}^R = \mathbb{R}_{\geq 0} \times \{defined, undefined\}$ represents the set of states of an input port $u_c \in U_c$, $S_{Y_c}^R = \prod_{y_c \in Y_c} S_{y_c}^R$ represents the aggregated state set of the output ports, and $S_{y_c}^R = \mathbb{R}_{\geq 0} \times \{defined, undefined\}$.*

Note that the run-time state of an FMU c differs from the state of the FMU. The later belongs to the state space S_c, while the former is defined next. Moreover, note that each port has its own timestamp, the reason of which will become clear when we define how each co-simulation operation changes the run-time state of the co-simulation.

Definition 9 (Co-simulation State). *Given a co-simulation scenario $\langle C, L \rangle$, as defined in Definition 2, the co-simulation state is a member of the set $S_C^R = \prod_{c \in C} S_c^R$.*

For the scenario introduced in Fig. 1, the run-time state set is $S_a^R \times S_b^R$, with $S_a^R = \mathbb{R}_{\geq 0} \times S_{u_a}^R \times S_{y_a}^R$, and $S_b^R = \mathbb{R}_{\geq 0} \times S_{u_b}^R \times S_{y_b}^R$. Before initialization (recall Fig. 2), every port has not yet been defined, and the timestamp of the ports and FMUs is 0. To improve readability, we will use a visual notation to represent the state, as illustrated in Fig. 6.

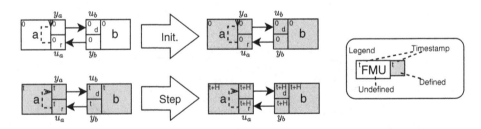

Fig. 6. Visual representation of the state before and after initialization/step.

Definition 10 (Consistent State). *A co-simulation run-time state S_C^R is consistent when all FMUs and ports have the same timestamp, and all ports are either defined, or undefined. We shall use the notation Consistent(S_C^R) = (defined, t) or Consistent(S_C^R) = (undefined, t), when such is the case, respectively.*

Using these definitions and notation, we can summarize the purpose of the initialization process, depicted in Fig. 2, and defined in Definition 4: to take a run-time state S_C^R where $Consistent(S_C^R) = (undefined, 0)$, and transform it into a run-time state $S_C^{R'}$ where $Consistent(S_C^{R'}) = (defined, 0)$. Similarly, one can summarize the purpose of the step process, defined in Definition 3: to take a run-time state S_C^R where $Consistent(S_C^R) = (defined, t)$, and transform it into a run-time state $S_C^{R'}$ where $Consistent(S_C^{R'}) = (defined, t + H)$. Figure 6 illustrates this for the example in Fig. 1.

We use structural operational semantics (SOS) notation to represent the run-time state evolution rules.

Definition 11. *Given a scenario $\langle C, L \rangle$, a set of contracts $\mathcal{C} = \bigcup_{c \in C} \{(R_c, D_c)\}$ a finite sequence of operations $(f_i)_{i \in \mathbb{N}} = f_0, f_1, \ldots$, with $f_i \in F$ as used in Definitions 3 and 4, and a run-time state S_C^R as in Definitions 9, we define the application of (f_i) to S_C^R in SOS as*

$$\frac{\langle C; L; \mathcal{C}; S_C^R; f_0 \rangle \Rightarrow S_C^{R'}}{\langle C; L; \mathcal{C}; S_C^R; f_0, f_1, \ldots \rangle \rightarrow \langle C; L; \mathcal{C}; S_C^{R'}; f_1, \ldots \rangle}$$

$$\frac{\langle C; L; \mathcal{C}; S_C^R; f \rangle \Rightarrow S_C^{R'}}{\langle C; L; \mathcal{C}; S_C^R; f \rangle \rightarrow \langle C; L; \mathcal{C}; S_C^{R'}; \emptyset \rangle}$$

The following definitions detail the $\Rightarrow$ reduction (not to be confused with the application operation $\rightarrow$, specified in Definition 11). Examples of this reduction are shown in Fig. 7. We will use the notation $\_$ for variables that need not be named.

Definition 12 (Output Computation). *The reduction*

$$\langle C; L; \mathcal{C}; S_C^R; \mathsf{get}_c(\_, y_c) \rangle \Rightarrow S_C^{R'}$$

represents the effect on the run-time state of operation $\mathsf{get}_c(\_, y_c)$. The reduction is valid if, in S_C^R, all inputs that feed-through to y_c are defined and have the same timestamp t. In that case, $S_C^{R'}$ is obtained by setting the run-time state of y_c in S_C^R to defined with timestamp t.

Definition 13 (Input Computation). *The reduction*

$$\langle C; L; \mathcal{C}; S_C^R; \mathsf{set}_c(\_, u_c, v) \rangle \Rightarrow S_C^{R'}$$

represents the effect on the run-time state of operation $\mathsf{set}_c(\_, u_c, v)$. The reduction is valid if, in S_C^R, all outputs connected to u_c are defined and have the same timestamp t. In that case, $S_C^{R'}$ is obtained by setting the run-time state of u_c in S_C^R to defined with timestamp t.

Definition 14 (Step Computation). *The reduction*

$$\langle C; L; \mathcal{C}; S_C^R; \texttt{doStep}_c(\_, H) \rangle \Rightarrow S_C^{R'}$$

represents the effect on the run-time state of operation $\texttt{doStep}_c(\_, H)$. *Let* t *denote the timestamp of* c *in* S_C^R. *The success of this reduction depends on satisfying all the following conditions:*

- *For every input port* u_c *that has a non-reactive contract in* $\mathcal{C}$, S_C^R *must contain the state of* u_c *as defined at timestamp* t.
- *For every input port* u_c *that has a reactive contract in* $\mathcal{C}$, S_C^R *must contain the state of* u_c *as defined at timestamp* $t + H$.

If such conditions hold, then $S_C^{R'}$ *is obtained by setting the run-time state of* c, *and all its output ports, to timestamp* $t + H$, *and by setting all the output ports to undefined.*

Figure 7 shows the application of the first three operations of Algorithm 3 on the run-time state of the co-simulation at the beginning of a step.

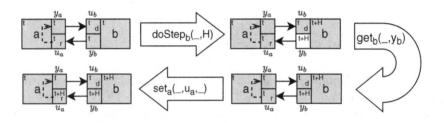

Fig. 7. Example application of operations on the run-time state.

Our problem can now be formalized.

Problem 1. Given a scenario $\langle C, L \rangle$, and the set of contracts $\mathcal{C} = \bigcup_{c \in C} \{(R_c, D_c)\}$, generate a master algorithm

$$\mathcal{A} = \langle C, L, H, (I_i)_{i \in \mathbb{N}}, (f_i)_{i \in \mathbb{N}} \rangle,$$

such that:

$$\langle C; L; \mathcal{C}; S_C^R; (I_i)_{i \in \mathbb{N}} \rangle \rightarrow^* \langle C; L; \mathcal{C}; S_C^{R^{(0)}}; \emptyset \rangle \text{ and}$$

$$\langle C; L; \mathcal{C}; S_C^{R^{(j)}}; (f_i)_{i \in \mathbb{N}} \rangle \rightarrow^* \langle C; L; \mathcal{C}; S_C^{R^{(j+1)}}; \emptyset \rangle,$$

where S_C^R, $S_C^{R^{(0)}}$, $S_C^{R^{(j)}}$, and $S_C^{R^{(j+1)}}$, are such that

$$Consistent(S_C^R) = (undefined, 0), \quad Consistent(S_C^{R^{(0)}}) = (defined, 0),$$

$$Consistent(S_C^{R^{(j)}}) = (defined, t), \quad Consistent(S_C^{R^{(j+1)}}) = (defined, t + H).$$

3 Generation of Co-simulation Algorithms

In this section, we propose a graph-based master generation algorithm, with complexity that is linear in the number of ports and FMUs in a given co-simulation scenario. We will focus on the generation of the step procedure, as the generation of the initialization procedure can be easily derived. The key insight in our contribution is the following.

Proposition 1. *For each* $c \in C$ *of a given co-simulation scenario:* $\mathtt{doStep}_c(\_, H)$ *needs to be executed once, and only once; for each* $y_c \in Y_c$, $\mathtt{get}_c(\_, y_c)$ *needs to be executed once; and for each* $u_c \in U_c$, $\mathtt{set}_c(\_, u_c, \_)$ *needs to be executed once.*

Proposition 1 allows us to build a graph representing every operation that might be executed in a step procedure. The edges of this graph represent precedence constraints, and a topological sorting of the graph yields a valid step procedure. We provide a proof sketch of this claim in Sect. 3.1.

Definition 15 (Step Operation Graph). *Given a co-simulation scenario* $\langle C, L \rangle$, *and a set of contracts* $\mathcal{C} = \bigcup_{c \in C} \{(R_c, D_c)\}$, *we define the step operation graph where each node represents an operation* $\mathtt{set}_c(\_, u_c, \_)$, $\mathtt{doStep}_c(\_, H)$, *or* $\mathtt{get}_c(\_, y_c)$, *of some fmu* $c \in C$, $y_c \in Y_c$, *and* $u_c \in U_c$. *The edges are created according to the following rules:*

1. *For each* $c \in C$ *and* $u_c \in U_c$, *if* $L(u_c) = y_d$, *add an edge* $\mathtt{get}_d(\_, y_d) \rightarrow \mathtt{set}_c(\_, u_c, \_)$;
2. *For each* $c \in C$ *and* $y_c \in Y_c$, *add an edge* $\mathtt{doStep}_c(\_, H) \rightarrow \mathtt{get}_c(\_, y_c)$;
3. *For each* $c \in C$ *and* $u_c \in U_c$, *if* $R_c(u_c) = true$, *add an edge* $\mathtt{set}_c(\_, u_c, \_) \rightarrow \mathtt{doStep}_c(\_, H)$;
4. *For each* $c \in C$ *and* $u_c \in U_c$, *if* $R_c(u_c) = false$, *add an edge* $\mathtt{doStep}_c(\_, H) \rightarrow \mathtt{set}_c(\_, u_c, \_)$;
5. *For each* $c \in C$ *and* $(u_c, y_c) \in D_c$, *add an edge* $\mathtt{set}_c(\_, u_c, \_) \rightarrow \mathtt{get}_c(\_, y_c)$.

Figure 8 shows an example graph, constructed from the example in Fig. 5.

3.1 Correctness

We now provide a proof sketch of the claim that a topological sorting of the above defined graph will yield a valid step procedure. The proof is divided into two parts. The first part proves that each operation is invoked in the correct order, with respect the conditions for its execution, detailed in Definitions 12 to 14. The second part proves Proposition 1, which essentially means that the graph is complete. The proof sketch also establishes that the successive application

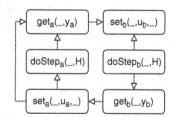

Fig. 8. Example step operation graph.

of the operations, in the topological order, satisfy the conditions in problem 1, thereby transforming a consistently defined run-time state with timestamp t into a consistently defined run-time state at time $t + H$.

We will assume a given non-trivial co-simulation scenario. A non-trivial scenario contains at least two fmus, every input is connected to an output, there are no self-connections, and it is possible to construct a topological ordering of the step operation graph.

Ordering. We now sketch the proof that each operation in the topological ordering satisfies the conditions for its execution, as detailed in Definitions 12 to 14.

Given a non-trivial scenario $\langle C, L \rangle$, and a set of contracts $\mathcal{C}$, consider a topological ordering $(f_i)_{i \in \mathbb{N}}$ of the graph constructed as in Definitions 15, and let us prove the correct ordering by induction on i. Let S_C^R be the given run-time state before the step procedure is executed. It satisfies $Consistent(S_C^R) = (defined, t)$ for some t.

$i = 1$. Let us now consider the form of f_1:

- $f_1 = \text{get}_c(\_, y_c)$, for some $c \in C$ and $y_c \in Y_c$. This case is impossible, as every output operation in c must be preceded by a step operation of c.
- $f_1 = \text{set}_c(\_, u_c, \_)$, for some $c \in C$ and $u_c \in U_c$. This case is impossible as every input operation is preceded by at least one output operation.
- $f_1 = \text{doStep}_c(\_, H)$, for some $c \in C$. This case is possible, and every input of c is delayed (otherwise there would be no topological sort). Since every input u_c is delayed, and since $Consistent(S_C^R) = (defined, t)$, the conditions in Definition 14 hold.

$i > 1$. Let $S_C^{R(i-1)}$ denote the run-time state after the (successful) invocation of operations $f_1, \ldots, f_{i-1}$ in the topological order. Let us now consider the form of f_i:

- $f_i = \text{get}_c(\_, y_c)$, for some $c \in C$ and $y_c \in Y_c$. In this case, according to Definition 15, it must be the case that: $\text{doStep}_c(\_, H)$ has been invoked successfully; $\text{set}_c(\_, u_c, \_)$ has been invoked successfully, for each $(u_c, y_c) \in D_c$; and, the timestamp of y_c in $S_C^{R(i-1)}$ is $t + H$. Since S_C^R contains all inputs defined at timestamp t, the only reason to invoke $\text{set}_c(\_, u_c, \_)$ on any input u_c is to set its timestamp to $t + H$. Therefore, every $(u_c, y_c) \in D_c$ has the same timestamp $t + H$. This satisfies the conditions in Definition 12.
- $f_i = \text{set}_c(\_, u_c, \_)$, for some $c \in C$ and $u_c \in U_c$. With a similar argument to the previous case, we conclude that every y_d connected to u_c is defined and has the same timestamp $t + H$.
- $f_i = \text{doStep}_c(\_, H)$, for some $c \in C$. In this case, according to Definition 15, we know that: $\text{set}_c(\_, u_c, \_)$ has been invoked successfully, for each $u_c \in U_c$ such that $R_c(u_c) = true$; and, $\text{set}_c(\_, u_c, \_)$ has not been invoked yet, for each $u_c \in U_c$ such that $R_c(u_c) = false$. Therefore, for every $u_c \in U_c$, if $R_c(u_c) = true$, then its timestamp is $t + H$, and if $R_c(u_c) = false$ then its timestamp is t. This satisfies the conditions in Definition 14.

Since all possible options are satisfied, the topological ordering is correct.

Completeness (Proof of Proposition 1). Given a non-trivial scenario $\langle C, L \rangle$, and a set of contracts C, consider a topological ordering $(f_i)_{i \in \mathbb{N}} = f_1, \ldots, f_N$ of the graph constructed as in Definition 15. Let S_C^R be the given run-time state before the step procedure is executed. It satisfies $Consistent(S_C^R) = (defined, t)$ for some t. Let us define a function that assigns a natural number to each run-time state: $Remaining(x, t)$ is the number of ports and fmus whose timestamp is less than t. For example, $Remaining(S_C^R, t + H)$ denotes the number of ports and the number of FMUs in the scenario $\langle C, L \rangle$, and $Remaining(S_C^R, t) = 0$. Let $S_C^{R^{(i-1)}}$ denote the run-time state after the (successful) invocation of operations $f_1, \ldots, f_{i-1}$ in the topological order. Now we show by induction on i that $Remaining(S_C^{R^{(i)}}, t + H) = N - i$. This will establish that $Remaining(S_C^{R^{(N)}}, t + H) = 0$, which implies that $Consistent(S_C^{R^{(N)}}) = (defined, t + H)$.

$i = 1$. As established in Sect. 3.1, $f_1 = \mathtt{doStep}_c(\_, H)$, and the conditions in Definition 14 hold. Therefore, the operation is executed and the timestamp of c becomes $t + H$ in $S_C^{R^{(1)}}$.

$i > 1$. Assume that $Remaining(S_C^{R^{(i-1)}}, t + H) = N - (i - 1)$. As in Sect. 3.1, every possible form of f_i can be executed. Hence, let us consider the effects of each execution in turn:

- $f_i = \mathtt{get}_c(\_, y_c)$, for some $c \in C$ and $y_c \in Y_c$. In this case, it is easy to see that the $\mathtt{get}_c(\_, y_c)$ operation has not been executed before, therefore the timestamp of y_c in $S_C^{R^{(i-1)}}$ is t. After execution, the timestamp of y_c in $S_C^{R^{(i)}}$ is $t + H$. Therefore, $Remaining(S_C^{R^{(i)}}, t + H) = Remaining(S_C^{R^{(i-1)}}, t + H) + 1 = N - i$.
- $f_i = \mathtt{set}_c(\_, u_c, \_)$, for some $c \in C$ and $u_c \in U_c$. The argument is similar to above.
- $f_i = \mathtt{doStep}_c(\_, H)$, for some $c \in C$. The argument is similar to above.

This concludes our proof sketch for the completeness of the graph based approach to generating master algorithms.

3.2   Optimization

In this section, we describe a simple optimization to the topological ordering that leverages the fact that the FMI standard allows multiple ports to be set and get in bulk. Essentially, we have modified the topological ordering procedure to group operations that can be executed *in parallel*. If multiple set or get operations on the same FMU belong to the same group, then these can be merged into a single operation.

The correctness of this optimization can be established by noting that this grouping procedure amounts to representing all possible topological orderings, and Sect. 3.1 establishes that each ordering is correct. The next section shows an example application of this procedure.

3.3 Application

Our contribution has been implemented in Prolog and is available online (See footnote 1). Consider the scenario in Fig. 9. The optimized generated step procedure is shown in Algorithm 4.

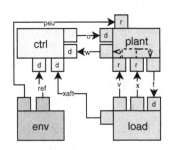

Fig. 9. Case study scenario. Based on [12].

Algorithm 4

1: $s_{load}^{(1)} \leftarrow \mathtt{doStep}_{load}(s_{load}^{(0)}, H)$

2: $s_{env}^{(1)} \leftarrow \mathtt{doStep}_{env}(s_{env}^{(0)}, H)$

3: $[v_x, v_v, v_{xaft}] \leftarrow \mathtt{get}_{load}(s_{load}^{(1)}, [x, v, xaft])$

4: $[v_{psu}, v_{ref}] \leftarrow \mathtt{get}_{env}(s_{env}^{(1)}, [psu, ref])$

5: $s_{plant}^{(1)} \leftarrow \mathtt{set}_{plant}(s_{plant}^{(0)}, [psu, x, v], [v_{psu},] v_x, v_v),$

6: $s_{plant}^{(2)} \leftarrow \mathtt{doStep}_{plant}(s_{plant}^{(1)}, H),$

7: $[v_w, v_f] \leftarrow \mathtt{get}_{plant}(s_{plant}^{(2)}, [w, f]),$

8: $s_{ctrl}^{(1)} \leftarrow \mathtt{set}_{ctrl}(s_{ctrl}^{(0)}, w, v_w)$

9: $s_{load}^{(2)} \leftarrow \mathtt{set}_{load}(s_{load}^{(1)}, f, v_f),$

10: $s_{ctrl}^{(2)} \leftarrow \mathtt{doStep}_{ctrl}(s_{ctrl}^{(1)}, H),$

11: $v_o \leftarrow \mathtt{get}_{ctrl}(s_{ctrl}^{(2)}, o)$

12: $s_{ctrl}^{(3)} \leftarrow \mathtt{set}_{ctrl}(s_{ctrl}^{(2)}, [ref, xaft]),$

13: $s_{plant}^{(3)} \leftarrow \mathtt{set}_{plant}(s_{plant}^{(2)}, o, v_o),$

14: $s_{plant}^{(0)} \leftarrow s_{plant}^{(3)}, s_{load}^{(0)} \leftarrow s_{load}^{(2)}$

15: $s_{env}^{(0)} \leftarrow s_{env}^{(1)}, s_{ctrl}^{(0)} \leftarrow s_{ctrl}^{(3)}$

---

4 Related Work

The closest work to our own is reported in [21], where a formalization of the semantics of FMI is proposed. However, our work differs in two key aspects: first, the objective of [21] is to prove properties about the system being co-simulated, whereas our goal is to guarantee certain basic properties of the co-simulation; second, the aforementioned work does not accommodate for simulator contracts, but includes the rollback operation. Ongoing work is revising the contracts and semantics in order to accommodate the rollback operation.

Prior work [5–8,15] is focused on the correct synchronization of a discrete event simulator with a continuous one. This seminal work assumes a standard synchronization algorithm, where, in the presence of possible state events, the discrete simulator is always one step behind the continuous simulator, to avoid rollbacks. This is an example of reactive simulator contract. Ongoing work is exploring how to accommodate step rejection in the simulator contracts, to allow for hybrid co-simulation master algorithms.

Instead of enforcing a correct synchronization, some work has focused on finding the maximum allowed delay in the event detection. For instance, the work in [9] explores how the energy of a hybrid system can be increased when state events are not accurately reproduced by the co-simulation. It presents a way to find the largest co-simulation step that prevents this from happening.

5   Conclusion

Driven by the need to make explicit information regarding the implementation of black box simulators, we have built on a prior formalization of the FMI standard to derive a procedure that generates master algorithms that respect such implementations. This algorithm consists of constructing a topological ordering of a precedence graph. An optimization, whereby input/output operations on the same simulator are clustered together, was proposed.

The key insight that makes this algorithm possible is the fact that each co-simulation operation on each port and fmu needs to be executed only once. In the future, when we consider more complex master algorithms, such as the ones supporting rollback and step size adaptation operations, this will no longer be true, and more research will be required to efficiently derive these master algorithms.

Note that, as one reviewer pointed out, we have not considered the accuracy of the master algorithm, beyond the satisfaction of the contracts. When there are multiple possible topological orderings of the co-simulation step, it would be interesting to know which one leads to less error.

Nevertheless, our algorithm was applied successfully to an industrial case, developed in prior work [12]. The code to reproduce the experiments in this paper is available for download (See footnote 1).

References

1. Arnold, M., Clauss, C., Schierz, T.: Error analysis and error estimates for co-simulation in FMI for model exchange and co-simulation V2.0. Arch. Mech. Eng. **LX**(1), 75 (2013). https://doi.org/10.2478/meceng-2013-0005
2. Bastian, J., Clauß, C., Wolf, S., Schneider, P.: Master for co-simulation using FMI. In: 8th International Modelica Conference, pp. 115–120. Linköping University Electronic Press, Linköpings universitet (2011). https://doi.org/10.3384/ecp11063115
3. Blockwitz, T., et al.: Functional mockup interface 2.0: the standard for tool independent exchange of simulation models. In: 9th International Modelica Conference, pp. 173–184. Linköping University Electronic Press (2012). https://doi.org/10.3384/ecp12076173
4. FMI: Functional Mock-up Interface for Model Exchange and Co-Simulation (2014). https://fmi-standard.org/downloads/
5. Gheorghe, L., Bouchhima, F., Nicolescu, G., Boucheneb, H.: Formal definitions of simulation interfaces in a continuous/discrete co-simulation tool. In: 2006 Seventeenth IEEE International Workshop on Rapid System Prototyping, pp. 186–192 (2006). https://doi.org/10.1109/RSP.2006.18

6. Gheorghe, L., Bouchhima, F., Nicolescu, G., Boucheneb, H.: A formalization of global simulation models for continuous/discrete systems. In: Summer Computer Simulation Conference, pp. 559–566. Society for Computer Simulation International San Diego, CA, USA (2007). Series Title: SCSC '07

7. Gheorghe, L., Bouchhima, F., Nicolescu, G., Boucheneb, H.: Semantics for model-based validation of continuous/discrete systems. In: Design, Automation and Test in Europe, pp. 498–503. ACM (2008). https://doi.org/10.1145/1403375.1403493, series Title: DATE '08

8. Gheorghe, L., Nicolescu, G., Boucheneb, H.: Semantics for rollback-based continuous/discrete simulation. In: IEEE International Behavioral Modeling and Simulation Workshop, BMAS 2008, pp. 106–111 (2008). https://doi.org/10.1109/BMAS.2008.4751250

9. Gomes, C., Karalis, P., Navarro-López, E.M., Vangheluwe, H.: Approximated stability analysis of bi-modal hybrid co-simulation scenarios. In: Cerone, A., Roveri, M. (eds.) SEFM 2017. LNCS, vol. 10729, pp. 345–360. Springer, Cham (2018). https://doi.org/10.1007/978-3-319-74781-1_24

10. Gomes, C., Lucio, L., Vangheluwe, H.: Semantics of co-simulation algorithms with simulator contracts. In: First International Workshop on Multi-Paradigm Modelling for Cyber-Physical Systems (2019, submitted)

11. Gomes, C., et al.: Semantic adaptation for FMI co-simulation with hierarchical simulators. Simulation 95(3), 1–29 (2018). https://doi.org/10.1177/0037549718759775

12. Gomes, C., et al.: HintCO - hint-based configuration of co-simulations. In: International Conference on Simulation and Modeling Methodologies, Technologies and Applications, pp. 57–68 (2019). https://doi.org/10.5220/0007830000570068

13. Gomes, C., Thule, C., Broman, D., Larsen, P.G., Vangheluwe, H.: Co-simulation: state of the art. Technical report, University of Antwerp (2017). http://arxiv.org/abs/1702.00686

14. Gomes, C., Thule, C., Broman, D., Larsen, P.G., Vangheluwe, H.: Co-simulation: a survey. ACM Comput. Surv. 51(3), Article 49 (2018). https://doi.org/10.1145/3179993

15. Iugan, L.G., Boucheneb, H., Nicolescu, G.: A generic conceptual framework based on formal representation for the design of continuous/discrete co-simulation tools. Des. Autom. Embedded Syst. 19(3), 243–275 (2015). https://doi.org/10.1007/s10617-014-9156-3

16. Kübler, R., Schiehlen, W.: Two methods of simulator coupling. Math. Comput. Modelling Dyn. Syst. 6(2), 93–113 (2000). https://doi.org/10.1076/1387-3954(200006)6:2;1-M;FT093

17. Schweiger, G., et al.: Functional mock-up interface: an empirical survey identifies research challenges and current barriers. In: Proceedings of the American Modelica Conference, pp. 138–146. Linköping University Electronic Press, Linköpings Universitet (2018). https://doi.org/10.3384/ecp18154138

18. Schweiger, G., et al.: An empirical survey on co-simulation: promising standards, challenges and research needs. Simul. Modelling Practice Theory 95, 148–163 (2019). https://doi.org/10.1016/j.simpat.2019.05.001

19. Schweizer, B., Li, P., Lu, D.: Explicit and implicit cosimulation methods: stability and convergence analysis for different solver coupling approaches. J. Comput. Nonlinear Dyn. 10(5), 051007 (2015). https://doi.org/10.1115/1.4028503

20. Thule, C., Gomes, C., Deantoni, J., Larsen, P.G., Brauer, J., Vangheluwe, H.: Towards the verification of hybrid co-simulation algorithms. In: Mazzara, M., Ober, I., Salaün, G. (eds.) STAF 2018. LNCS, vol. 11176, pp. 5–20. Springer, Cham (2018). https://doi.org/10.1007/978-3-030-04771-9_1

21. Zeyda, F., Ouy, J., Foster, S., Cavalcanti, A.: Formalising cosimulation models. In: Cerone, A., Roveri, M. (eds.) Software Engineering and Formal Methods, vol. 10729, pp. 453–468. Springer, Heidelberg (2018). https://doi.org/10.1007/978-3-319-74781-1_31

Towards Reuse of Synchronization Algorithms in Co-simulation Frameworks

Casper Thule[1], Maurizio Palmieri[2,3], Cláudio Gomes[4(✉)], Kenneth Lausdahl[5], Hugo Daniel Macedo[1], Nick Battle[6], and Peter Gorm Larsen[1]

[1] DIGIT, Department of Engineering, Aarhus University, Finlandsgade 22, 8200 Aarhus N, Denmark
{casper.thule,hdm,pgl}@eng.au.dk
[2] University of Florence, Florence, Italy
[3] Pisa University, Pisa, Italy
maurizio.palmieri@ing.unipi.it
[4] University of Antwerpen, Antwerp, Belgium
claudio.gomes@uantwerp.be
[5] Mjølner Informatics A/S, Aarhus N, Denmark
kgl@mjolner.dk
[6] Newcastle upon Tyne, UK
nick.battle@acm.org
http://digit.au.dk

Abstract. An immediate industry challenge is to fashion a co-simulation that replicates real-systems behaviour with high fidelity. To achieve this goal, developers rely on frameworks to enhance the creation and analysis of the co-simulation. One major problem is that new co-simulation frameworks require extensive development, most of which resides in non-essential functionalities, before they can be used in practice. Additionally, existing co-simulations demand a thorough understanding before they can be extended.

Our vision is a modular co-simulation framework architecture, that is easily extensible by researchers, and can integrate existing and legacy co-simulation approaches. The architecture we propose permits extension at three levels, each providing different degrees of flexibility. The most flexible integration level involves the specification of a Domain Specific Language (DSL) for Master Algorithms (MAs), and this paper sketc.hes such a DSL, and illustrates how it is expressive enough to describe well-known MAs.

Keywords: Co-simulation · Functional Mock-up Interface · Co-simulation framework

This work has been supported by the Poul Due Jensen Foundation. C. G. is a FWO Research Fellow, at the University of Antwerp, supported by the Research Foundation - Flanders (File Number 1S06316N). Furthermore, this work is carried out in the context of INTO-CPS Association and the results are provided under the INTO-CPS Association Public License Version 1. See https://into-cps.org for details.
N. Battle—Independent.

J. Camara and M. Steffen (Eds.): SEFM 2019 Workshops, LNCS 12226, pp. 50–66, 2020.
https://doi.org/10.1007/978-3-030-57506-9_5

1 Introduction

Co-simulation frameworks require extensive development before they can become usable in practice. A co-simulation following the Functional Mock-up Interface (FMI) Standard is a collaborative simulation carried out by combining multiple simulators called Functional Mock-up Units (FMUs), each representing a constituent of a system [7]. The algorithm describing how the coupling of FMUs is carried out is referred to as the Master Algorithm (MA), and the FMUs are denoted as slaves. A scenario is the configuration of FMUs to use, how the FMUs are coupled, and which MA to use[1].

A co-simulation framework provides the foundations that implement the elements above, allowing users to run co-simulations, and execute other simulation activities such as optimization, sensitivity analysis, etc. In essence, such a framework is what makes co-simulation an integral part of a development process. To be usable, therefore, a co-simulation framework needs to seamlessly integrate with existing design processes. For that, its users ought not worry about:

1. how to establish communication with the FMUs; or
2. how to configure the MA and FMUs, to achieve reliable co-simulation results.

Fortunately, co-simulation standards such as the FMI [5] have largely relieved practitioners from having to worry about (1). As for (2), however, recent surveys [7,14,17,21,22] indicate that the configuration of an MA is still an open challenge. For instance, the configuration of co-simulation scenarios is one of the immediate industry challenges [21], and there is evidence that reliable co-simulation results might not be, in general, attainable without a custom combination of existing MAs [9,18].

To research and develop novel co-simulation approaches, it is necessary to equip researchers with proper foundations to conduct their research on. This means relieving them from the need for extensive development efforts that are not directly related to co-simulation configuration and execution. In fact, the development team of the INTO-CPS application [15] has reported that the development of the features surrounding the execution of an MA (e.g., simulator loading, Graphical User Interface (GUI), setup and deployment, etc.) far exceed the effort of coding such MA. This development took place over three years, from 2015 to 2017, and the approximate time percentage spent on common functionality is shown in Fig. 1.

Researchers seeking to have an impact with their novel co-simulation approaches may never achieve it if they cannot afford such development efforts. At the same time, existing co-simulation frameworks cannot keep up with the new developments in MAs, making the adoption of novel techniques slow.

Therefore, there is a need to modularize the architecture of a co-simulation framework, in order to maximise reuse, and combination, of mature and industry-proven features common to every MA, in the deployment of novel MAs.

---

[1] We adopt the terminology in [10].

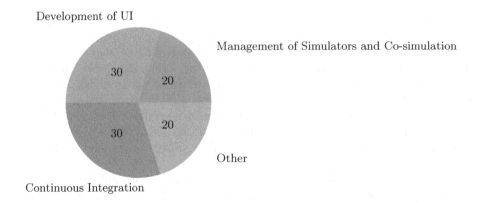

Fig. 1. Time (%) spent on developing common functionality.

Contribution. In this paper, we propose an architecture to promote easy integration of novel MAs into a co-simulation framework. This architecture enables researchers to contribute with custom MAs with three different levels of integration, each providing increasing levels of flexibility. The most flexible integration level involves the specification of a Domain Specific Language (DSL) for MA and this paper proposes a preliminary analysis of requirements for such a DSL. We invite and welcome interested parties to contribute to the future development of the DSL and its semantics.

The proposed DSL is under development in context of the INTO-CPS Association[2] and therefore free of charge for non-commercial benefits[3]. Furthermore, the reader will encounter several references to INTO-CPS technology throughout the paper, as the proposed DSL will engage in the open tool-chain of INTO-CPS.

2 Problem Statement

This section exposes the problem that we are trying to solve. We assume that the reader is familiar with co-simulation (see, e.g., [10,12] for an introduction and tutorial), and the FMI standard (see, e.g., [3] for an introduction, and [5] for the specification). We will adopt the following definitions:

FMU Runtime denotes the set of libraries that allows one to load, instantiate, and communicate with FMUs. Examples are: INTO-CPS FMI library[4] (Java), the FMPy library[5] (Python), PyFMI[6] (Python), or the FMI Library[7] (C).

---

[2] https://into-cps.org.
[3] https://into-cps.org/membership/.
[4] https://github.com/INTO-CPS-Association/org.intocps.maestro.fmi.
[5] https://github.com/CATIA-Systems/FMPy.
[6] https://jmodelica.org/pyfmi/.
[7] https://jmodelica.org/fmil/FMILibrary-2.0.3-htmldoc/index.html.

MA denotes the procedure that coordinates the time synchronization between FMUs. It relies on the FMU Application Programming Interface (API) to communicate with the FMUs. Examples are the Jacobi or Gauss Seidel algorithms [3,11]. Maestro [24], the co-simulation framework from the INTO-CPS project, is based on the Jacobi algorithm.

GUI, Command Line Interface (CLI), API denote the interfaces that enable a users to describe the co-simulation scenario, to configure the MA, and to run co-simulations. Examples include the INTO-CPS Application[8] [2,20].

Simulation Activities denotes any activity that is part of a development process and relies on the GUI/CLI/API to be completed. For example, optimization/Design Space Exploration (DSE), sensitivity analysis, or X-in-the-loop co-simulation.

Figure 2 summarizes the layered relationship of these concepts, and distinguishes a co-simulation framework from co-simulation application.

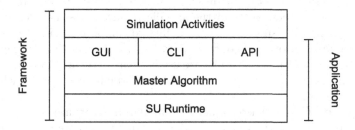

Fig. 2. Main definitions used.

Traditionally, co-simulation has been applied to mostly two simulators, with custom built MAs [11]. This worked well because the people who built those MAs were, or worked closely with, domain experts. However, this approach does not scale in the number of simulators involved, and the FMI standard was developed to address this need. As a result, many practitioners expect to use FMI co-simulation without having co-simulation expertise, and the black box nature of this standard (where the models being simulated, and solvers used, are kept hidden) does not make it easier to understand the details of the simulators that are being coupled.

In fact, there is evidence that version 2.0 of the standard is insufficient to ensure that a co-simulation can be configured correctly, and that more information about the FMUs is required[9]: a clear indication that research in co-simulation will continue, and that researchers will have to code new co-simulation

---

[8] https://github.com/INTO-CPS-Association/into-cps-application.

[9] See [6,9,18] for example co-simulations that cannot be configured correctly without information that is not covered in the standard. Work has commenced on FMI 3.0, see http://fmi-standard.org/faq for more information.

frameworks. We want to minimize the effort required for these researchers to produce usable frameworks.

Just as with simulation, it is instructive to run multiple co-simulations with different MAs, to measure the degree of sensitivity of the results with respect to the MA and simulator configuration. Therefore, we also want to be able to produce a unified front-end to users who want to run such exploratory co-simulations, similar to what was carried out in the INTO-CPS Application [2].

Figure 3 shows the space of simulator information that can be used to configure co-simulations, and the space of capabilities currently covered by the FMI standard (version 2.0). Our goal is that co-simulations taking advantage of these extra capabilities, even the ones not covered by the standard, can be developed. Moreover, in the long term, we aim at improving the co-simulation support for the following simulation activities, each imposing specific requirements to co-simulation frameworks:

Optimization/DSE: Co-simulations are run as part of an optimization loop. This includes decision support systems, used, for example, in a digital twin [13] setting, where a modelled system is updated based on the operating realised system. Some of the specific requirements include: ability to define co-simulation stop conditions, ability to compute sensitivity, high performance, fully automated configuration, faster than real-time computation.

Certification: Co-simulation results are used as part of certification endeavours. Requirements include fully transparent, and formally certified, synchronization algorithms.

X-in-the-loop: Co-simulations include simulators that are constrained to progress in sync with the wall-clock time, because they represent human operators or physical subsystems.

3 Envisioned Architecture

Our goal is to conceive an architecture which can be evolved to accommodate a wide variety of co-simulation research activities and applications of co-simulation. Figure 4 summarizes the proposed architecture to facilitate the three levels of integration introduced in Sect. 1, and will be used as reference in the rationale and explanation below.

3.1 Legacy Integration

The legacy integration, to the left of Fig. 4, involves the improvement of the existing interface between the INTO-CPS application, so that existing MAs can be integrated. Under this approach, a legacy MA, along with its own simulator runtime libraries, uses the Master API to communicate with the INTO-CPS Application.

Legacy integration is already partially supported by the MA API that has been developed within the INTO-CPS project [23]. The Master API is detailed

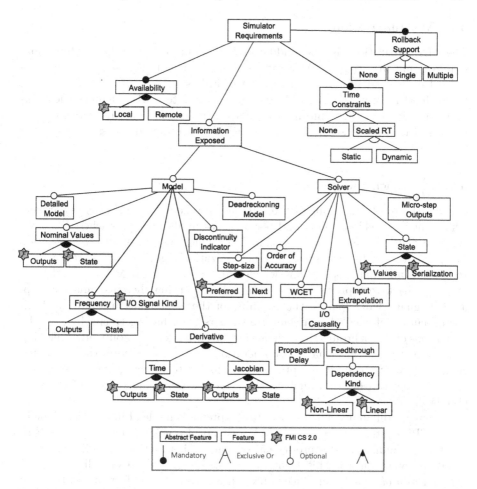

Fig. 3. Simulator capabilities adapted from [11]. The FMI standard capabilities represent only a subset, and many of these are optional.

in [19]. Any new MA needs to implement such an API. The following are some of the operations.

Status which allows the Application to query the status of the MA.

Initialize which allows new co-simulation sessions to be created. A JSON payload details the co-simulation scenario and other configuration parameters.

Simulate which instructs the MA to start the co-simulation based on provided experiment parameters.

Result which queries the MA for the simulation results.

Destroy which instructs the MA to clear the resources of a co-simulation session.

Reset which instructs the MA to reset a session.

3.2   MA Integration

The MA integration, in the middle of Fig. 4, unlike the legacy integration, requires only that the new MA implements the Master API, and uses the provided Runtime API for the management of FMUs.

Such API allows the new MA to easily instantiate FMUs, manage their life-cycle, and inspect their information. For example, the new MA will not need to parse the static description within an FMU in order to access the available variables.

3.3   Approach Integration

Finally, the most ambitious of the integration schemes is aimed at researchers who want to quickly develop and test new co-simulation approaches. We envision the development of an extensible DSL, which we call *Master Specification Language*, that aims at expressing synchronization algorithms. The rationale is that there are many operations which are common to all MAs, e.g., the act of rolling back to a previous time point, or of retrying the co-simulation step. This language will separate the planning of the co-simulation approach, from the execution of such plan, freeing researchers from having to specify how the operations of a synchronisation scheme are executed, focusing only on developing algorithms to describe what those operations are. Furthermore, the developed APIs will allow for analysis/optimisation plugins to be integrated as well. For example, one can have an analysis that enforces a specific version of the FMI standard.

The main difference with respect to the previous mode of integration done in INTO-CPS context is that a new MA, instead of invoking the runtime API to run the co-simulation, will produce a sequence of instructions detailing how the simulator synchronises. This sequence of instructions, which we call *Synchronisation Protocol*, will be produced through a series of transformations that are applied to the given co-simulation scenario.

More details are given in Sect. 4.

4   MA Specification Language

In this section, we provide a preliminary specification of the DSL proposed in the previous section. The language is comprised of three main parts: synchronization protocols; scenario and adaptations; and transformations (which describe how a co-simulation scenario is transformed into a MA). Each part is now described. We conclude this section with a discussion on extensibility of the DSL.

4.1   Synchronization Protocols

We start by giving examples of how known co-simulation algorithms can be implemented in this framework, and then we generalize to the specification of the language.

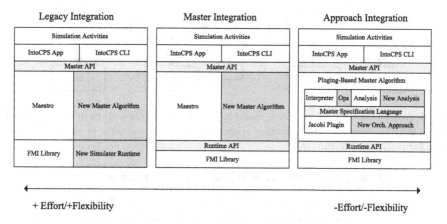

Fig. 4. The three planned integration approaches from the view of external researchers. Each approach is represented as a layered architecture, and an example of a newly integrated component is given (in orange). In green, we represent the key interfaces that enable the integration. Components below the API implement it, while the ones above, use it. Maestro is the MA from the INTO-CPS project. (Color figure online)

Example 1 (Running Example). We will use, as running example, the co-simulation scenario illustrated in Fig. 5.

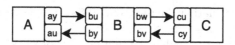

Fig. 5. Running example. The rectangles define FMUs and the round boxes denote inputs/outputs.

A generic co-simulation algorithm has a predictable structure, shown in Fig. 6, and variations in the implementation of each of the stages shown will yield different MAs. Our DSL allows one to describe the structure of the Step and Initialize stages of Fig. 6. We focus on the Step stage, as it is the richest in terms of variability, and the Initialize activity can be seen as a special case of the Step stage since the operations are roughly the same, but the order might be different.

Simpler MAs are those with fixed step-sizes and well known examples are the Jacobi and the Gauss-Seidel algorithms. The Jacobi MA, applied to Example 1, is shown in Fig. 7. Each operation is translated to the corresponding FMI function call, with the DSL implementation filling in the missing arguments: the simulated time, used in the FMI stepping operation, is automatically computed; the values computed by the GetOut operations are stored in variables that are then used to compute the correct value for the SetIn operations. The management of values

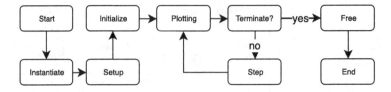

Fig. 6. Generic MA structure. Each round rectangle represents a stage in the execution of the MA. For instance, the plotting stage will query the outputs of the FMUs and record them in a CSV file.

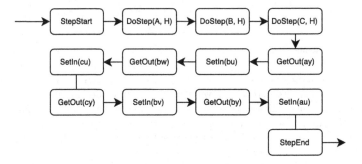

Fig. 7. Jacobi Step specification, applied to Example 1. DoStep operation calls are not constrained to a certain order. The same holds for SetIn and GetOut, although outputs shall be retrieved before the corresponding input.

is implemented by translating the GetOut and SetIn operations to their refined counterparts, as is shown in Fig. 8.

The MA in Fig. 8 can be enhanced in a number of ways:

- Parallelisation of i.e. DoStep operation calls.
- Automate the choice of step size to use at each step to control the error, rolling back when the error is deemed too large.
- Dealing with an FMU that refuses a given step.
- Apply fixed point iteration of algebraic conditions and/or the co-simulation step.

The insight of our contribution is that the above items can be orthogonally combined by refinements of the Step specification (e.g., the one shown in Fig. 7). An example for each of the above enhancements is provided in the following, by showing the resulting refinement.

Figure 9 shows an example of a pessimistic adaptive step-size control scheme. The implementation of the UpdateStep operation can be defined in a plugin (see Sect. 4.4). The Transaction, Commit, and Rollback operations are implemented in the DSL.

Figure 10 shows an example that handles step-size rejections, and Fig. 11 an example of fixed-point iteration with convergence testing on one signal (multiple

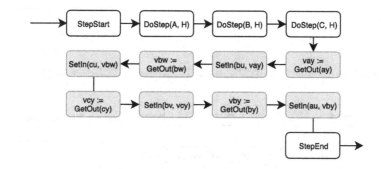

Fig. 8. Explicit memory refinement of Fig. 7.

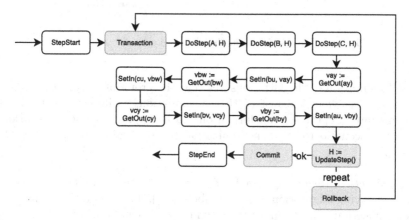

Fig. 9. Pessimistic adaptive step size MA.

signals can be supported, but its implementation is a straightforward extension of Fig. 11).

4.2 Scenarios and Adaptations

The synchronization protocol sub-language allows one to describe a wide range of co-simulation algorithms. However, it is not expressive enough to describe the following MAs: multi-rate; signal corrective; waveform relaxation; MAs that spawn new co-simulations (e.g., for each step of an FMU, an entire co-simulation is run to calculate some result). We now describe how the use of semantic adaptations which, when carefully combined with the synchronization protocol sub-language, can be used to implement the above algorithms.

Multi-rate. A semantic adaptation is a transformation that rewrites a co-simulation scenario by either changing a group of, or adding more, FMUs (see [8] for examples of semantic adaptations). For instance, a multi-rate adaptation consists of grouping a given set of FMUs into one hierarchical FMU, where

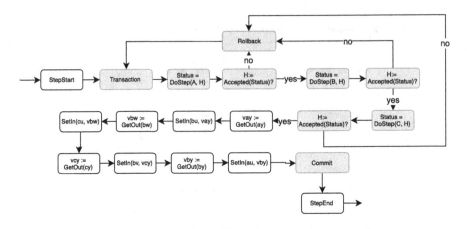

Fig. 10. Step specification that handles step size rejection.

the implementation of the latter ensures that the group of FMUs communicate at a higher rate than the rest of the co-simulation, as illustrated in Fig. 12. The multi-rate adaptation transformation can be applied to a scenario prior to passing the scenario to the synchronization protocol generation, explained in Sect. 4.1.

Signal-Corrective. Regarding signal corrective adaptations, we describe here the energy preserving adaptation, first described in [4]. The adaptation applies to a pair of connections that form a power bond (see [1, Chapter 9] for an introduction). Whenever a value is propagated in those connections, it gets corrected to account for approximation errors made in the receiving FMU. Hence, the adaptation replaces the ports connected by the power bond to apply that correction whenever an input is set. Alternatively, a new FMU that performs the correction can be inserted in place of the power bond connections. These are illustrated in Fig. 13.

The application of the energy preserving adaptation depends on the implementation of the synchronization protocol. As such the resulting scenario (after applying the adaptation) cannot be given to any synchronization protocol generator.

Waveform Relaxation. A waveform relaxation algorithm is an iterative co-simulation synchronization protocol that, instead of applying a fixed point iteration of point values (as the iterative Jacobi described in Fig. 11 does), it applies a fixed point iteration on functions. There are multiple ways to check for equality of two functions. One of those ways is to perform a point-wise comparison, and return the maximum of such comparisons. Two functions are then considered equal if that value is within some given threshold.

The waveform relaxation is a kind of multi-rate adaptation that is combined with an iterative synchronization protocol (see [16] for an introduction). First, as

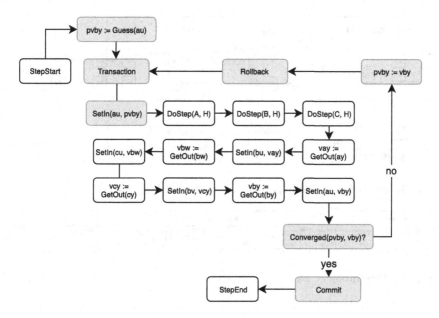

Fig. 11. Iterative refinement of the Jacobi step specification, with convergence test on one signal.

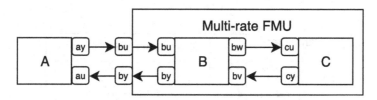

Fig. 12. Example multi-rate adaptation created by rewriting the scenario introduced in Fig. 5. FMUs B and C communicate at a higher rate.

illustrated in Fig. 14, each FMU is grouped into a multi-rate FMU, along with new FMUs that represent proxies of their environment. The multi-rate FMU will run a complete co-simulation each time it is invoked. When running this co-simulation, the Proxy FMUs will record the outputs of the non proxy FMU, and construct a function with these. The proxy FMUs also "replays" the input function they have in their storage. When this co-simulation is completed, it means that the multi-rate FMU has completed a step. At that moment, the multi-rate FMUs will exchange input and output values. These values are complete functions, which are tested for convergence (recall Fig. 11). If they have converged, the co-simulation is completed. Otherwise, the process is repeated, with the proxies having exchanged the recorded functions.

Sub-co-simulations. Finally, co-simulation scenarios that have FMUs that may spawn a new co-simulation are constructed with a Hierarchical Cosim FMU.

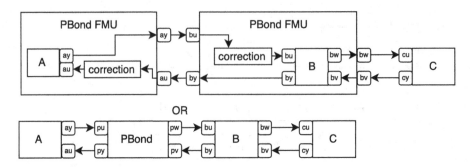

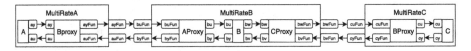

Fig. 13. Illustration of two implementations of the energy correction adaptation.

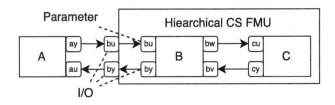

Fig. 14. Illustration of waveform relaxation adaptation, applied to Example 1.

Figure 15 illustrates an example of this. At each DoStep of the hierarchical cosim, a new co-simulation is run, with the parameters defined by the input value bu.

Fig. 15. Illustrations of the use of a hierarchical FMU to run a co-simulation between B and C, for each step in the co-simulation of A.

4.3   Transformations

The application of semantic adaptations, as introduced in Sect. 4.2, require careful coordination with the application of synchronization protocols, introduced in Sect. 4.1. Attempting to automatically derive the rules of such compositions is a tremendous challenge, and subject for future work. Instead, we support a library of transformations that can be composed manually to generate a MA. Such transformations operate on models described in our DSL.

A model contains a scenario, adaptations, and an MA, as illustrated in Fig. 16. A particular co-simulation approach is then a sequence of transformations applied to a model that yield an executable co-simulation algorithm.

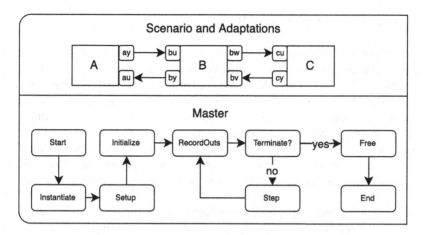

Fig. 16. Example model.

A composition of transformations describes how the model is refined until it can be executed. For example, a multi-rate composition would first apply the multi-rate adaptation to rewrite the scenario in Fig. 16 to the scenario in Fig. 12, and then would apply the Jacobi algorithm transformation to refine the step operation in Fig. 16 and Fig. 7. Different sequences of transformations will yield potentially different MAs.

4.4 Extensibility

There are several ways to extend the DSL:

Protocol Operation. New synchronization operations can be declared. Our interpreter will then load the declared plugins and execute them. For example, the UpdateStep operation, in Fig. 9, could be implemented in a plugin.

Virtual FMUs. Virtual FMUs, implemented in Scala or Java, can be declared. These will be loaded and executed by the interpreter as any other FMUs, with the difference that they do not need to be represented as FMUs in the FMI standard. The main use case for virtual FMUs is researching co-simulation, and not necessarily aiming for a full FMI co-simulation.

Transformation Rules. New transformation rules that manipulate the co-simulation scenario, and/or the synchronization protocol, can be declared.

Transformation Compositions. New transformation compositions can be declared.

We envision these extensions to be done in the form of plugins, without the need to recompile the tool. The rationale for these requirements are that researchers experimenting with novel master algorithms need not be proficient with building and deploying the DSL.

5   Prospect and Future Work

We have sketc.hed an architecture to support multiple levels of integration, in order to maximize the reuse of existing co-simulation algorithms, and facilitate the development of new ones. Our main contribution is a DSL that allows novel co-simulation algorithms to be developed, by refining a given scenario and a generic master algorithm. A preliminary prototype[10] has been built defining the semantics of simple synchronization protocols. Ongoing work is formalizing the language and contributions are welcomed. A general goal is that the language and extension interfaces shall consistently be in a stable and usable state once the initial plugins and native functionality to conduct a co-simulation have been realized.

An interesting research opportunity is to devise analyses that ensure the validity of arbitrary transformation compositions. Such analyses would be a first step towards deriving rules for automated enhancement of master algorithms provided by researchers (for example, the addition of step size rejection handlers). The final goal that we foresee is a free marketplace where plugins are selected and composed to produce MAs addressing specific needs.

We expect to validate the DSL by developing master algorithms that make use of vendor-specific information in FMUs to achieve better results, and enable co-simulation within the digital twin context. This will require the use of the multi-rate and hierarchical co-simulation adaptations, plus custom synchronisation operations.

Furthermore, FMI 3.0 is currently being developed, and this process is followed closely, and the DSL is expected to support FMI 3.0 in a later phase.

Finally, we would like to give our thanks to the anonymous reviewers for their comments that helped to improve this paper.

References

1. van Amerongen, J.: Dynamical Systems for Creative Technology. Controllab Products B.V. http://doc.utwente.nl/75219/
2. Bandur, V., et al.: INTO-CPS tool chain user manual. Technical report, INTO-CPS Deliverable, D4.3a, December 2017
3. Bastian, J., Clauß, C., Wolf, S., Schneider, P.: Master for co-simulation using FMI. In: 8th International Modelica Conference, pp. 115–120. Linköping University Electronic Press, Linköpings Universitet. https://doi.org/10.3384/ecp11063115
4. Benedikt, M., Watzenig, D., Zehetner, J., Hofer, A.: NEPCE-a nearly energy preserving coupling element for weak-coupled problems and co-simulation. In: IV International Conference on Computational Methods for Coupled Problems in Science and Engineering, Coupled Problems, pp. 1–12 (2013)
5. Blochwitz, T., et al.: Functional mockup interface 2.0: the standard for tool independent exchange of simulation models. In: Proceedings of the 9th International Modelica Conference, pp. 173–184. The Modelica Association (2012). https://doi.org/10.3384/ecp12076173,key=blo+12mcproject=LCCC-modeling

---

[10] https://github.com/into-cps-association/maestrov2.

6. Cremona, F., Lohstroh, M., Broman, D., Lee, E.A., Masin, M., Tripakis, S.: Hybrid co-simulation: it's about time 10270. https://doi.org/10.1007/s10270-017-0633-6
7. Gomes, C., Thule, C., Broman, D., Larsen, P.G., Vangheluwe, H.: Co-simulation: a survey. ACM Comput. Surv. **51**(3), 49:1–49:33 (2018)
8. Gomes, C., et al.: Semantic adaptation for FMI co-simulation with hierarchical simulators **95**(3), 1–29. https://doi.org/10.1177/0037549718759775
9. Gomes, C., et al.: HintCO - hint-based configuration of co-simulations. In: International Conference on Simulation and Modeling Methodologies, Technologies and Applications, pp. 57–68. https://doi.org/10.5220/0007830000570068
10. Gomes, C., Thule, C., Broman, D., Larsen, P.G., Vangheluwe, H.: Co-simulation: a survey **51**(3), Article 49. https://doi.org/10.1145/3179993
11. Gomes, C., Thule, C., Broman, D., Larsen, P.G., Vangheluwe, H.: Co-simulation: state of the art. http://arxiv.org/abs/1702.00686
12. Gomes, C., Thule, C., Larsen, P.G., Denil, J., Vangheluwe, H.: Co-simulation of continuous systems: a tutorial. http://arxiv.org/abs/1809.08463
13. Grieves, M.: Origins of the digital twin concept. Florida Institute of Technology (2016)
14. Hafner, I., Popper, N.: On the terminology and structuring of co-simulation methods. In: Zimmer, D., Bachmann, B. (eds.) Proceedings of the 8th International Workshop on Equation-Based Object-Oriented Modeling Languages and Tools, pp. 67–76. ACM Press. https://doi.org/10.1145/3158191.3158203
15. Larsen, P.G., et al.: Integrated tool chain for model-based design of Cyber-Physical Systems: the INTO-CPS project. In: 2016 2nd International Workshop on Modelling, Analysis, and Control of Complex CPS (CPS Data), Vienna, Austria. IEEE, April 2016. http://ieeexplore.ieee.org/document/7496424/
16. Li, L., Seymour, R.M., Baigent, S.: Integrating biosystem models using waveform relaxation (2008). 308
17. Palensky, P., Van Der Meer, A.A., Lopez, C.D., Joseph, A., Pan, K.: Cosimulation of intelligent power systems: fundamentals, software architecture, numerics, and coupling **11**(1), 34–50. https://doi.org/10.1109/MIE.2016.2639825
18. Pedersen, N., Lausdahl, K., Sanchez, E.V., Thule, C., Larsen, P.G., Madsen, J.: Distributed co-simulation of embedded control software using INTO-CPS. In: Obaidat, M.S., Ören, T., Rango, F.D. (eds.) SIMULTECH 2017. AISC, vol. 873, pp. 33–54. Springer, Cham (2019). https://doi.org/10.1007/978-3-030-01470-4_3
19. Pop, A., Bandur, V., Lausdahl, K., Groothuis, M., Bokhove, T.: Final Integration of Simulators in the INTO-CPS Platform
20. Rasmussen, M.B., Thule, C., Macedo, H.D., Larsen, P.G.: Moving the INTO-CPS application to the cloud. In: The 17th Overture Workshop, Porto, Portugal, October 2019
21. Schweiger, G., et al.: Functional mock-up interface: an empirical survey identifies research challenges and current barriers. In: The American Modelica Conference, Cambridge, MA, USA, pp. 138–146. Linköping University Electronic Press, Linköpings Universitet (2018). https://doi.org/10.3384/ecp18154138
22. Schweiger, G., et al.: An empirical survey on co-simulation: promising standards, challenges and research needs **95**, 148–163. https://doi.org/10.1016/j.simpat.2019.05.001

23. Thule, C., Lausdahl, K., Gomes, C., Meisl, G., Larsen, P.G.: Maestro: the INTO-CPS co-simulation framework **92**, 45–61. https://doi.org/10.1016/j.simpat.2018.12.005

24. Thule, C., Lausdahl, K., Gomes, C., Meisl, G., Larsen, P.G.: Maestro: the INTO-CPS co-simulation framework. Simul. Model. Pract. Theory **92**, 45 – 61 (2019). https://doi.org/10.1016/j.simpat.2018.12.005. http://www.sciencedirect.com/science/article/pii/S1569190X1830193X

ASYDE 2019

Organization

ASYDE 2019 – Workshop Chairs

Farhad Arbab	Centre for Mathematics and Computer Science (CWI)
Marco Autili	University of L'Aquila
Federico Ciccozzi	Malardalen University
Pascal Poizat	Sorbonne Université
Massimo Tivoli	University of L'Aquila

ASYDE 2019 – Program Committee

Luciano Baresi	Politecnico di Milano
Steffen Becker	University of Stuttgart
Domenico Bianculli	SnT Centre – University of Luxembourg
Antonio Brogi	University of Pisa
Radu Calinescu	University of York
Antinisca Di Marco	University of L'Aquila
Amleto Di Salle	University of L'Aqula
Schahram Dustdar	Vienna University of Technology
Nikolaos Georgantas	Inria
Marina Mongiello	Politecnico di Bari
Cristina Seceleanu	Mälardalen University
Meng Sun	Peking University
Apostolos Zarras	University of Ioannina

Towards a Continuous Model-Based Engineering Process for QoS-Aware Self-adaptive Systems

Mirko D'Angelo[1]([⊠]), Lorenzo Pagliari[2], Mauro Caporuscio[1],
Raffaela Mirandola[3], and Catia Trubiani[2]

[1] Linnaeus University, Växjö, Sweden
{mirko.dangelo,mauro.caporuscio}@lnu.se
[2] Gran Sasso Science Institute, L'Aquila, Italy
{lorenzo.pagliari,catia.trubiani}@gssi.it
[3] Politecnico di Milano, Milan, Italy
raffaela.mirandola@polimi.it

Abstract. Modern information systems connecting software, physical systems, and people, are usually characterized by high dynamism. These dynamics introduce uncertainties, which in turn may harm the quality of service and lead to incomplete, inaccurate, and unreliable results. In this context, self-adaptation is considered as an effective approach for managing run-time uncertainty. However, classical approaches for quality engineering are not suitable to deal with run-time adaptation, as they are mainly used to derive the steady-state solutions of a system at design-time. In this paper, we envision a Continuous Model-based Engineering Process that makes use of architectural analysis in conjunction with experimentation to have a wider understanding of the system under development. These two activities are performed incrementally, and jointly used in a feedback loop to provide insights about the quality of the system-to-be.

1 Introduction

Digitalization of industry, by many considered as the fourth industrial revolution, is changing the competitive landscape in several business domains. The connectivity between software and physical systems opens up for new innovative business or mission critical services responsible for a vast part of the value chain. Indeed, modern information systems (e.g., intelligent transportation systems, smart power grids, network infrastructures and robotics) usually connect software, physical systems, and people [18], who either interact with or are part of the system itself. This means that systems should be designed and developed to explicitly include operational processes and people (e.g., the operators).

Such modern systems are usually characterized by high dynamism, as participating and interacting entities are heterogeneous and autonomous, and unexpected/uncontrolled conditions may arise within the environment. These dynamics introduce uncertainties, which in turn may harm the quality of service and

© Springer Nature Switzerland AG 2020
J. Camara and M. Steffen (Eds.): SEFM 2019 Workshops, LNCS 12226, pp. 69–76, 2020.
https://doi.org/10.1007/978-3-030-57506-9_6

lead to incomplete, inaccurate, and unreliable results [12]. Managing run-time uncertainty is then crucial to operate modern and complex interacting systems and satisfy their quality requirements. To this end, self-adaptation is considered as an effective approach to manage dynamic interacting systems. In fact, self-adaptive systems are able to adjust their behavior, by hence operating autonomously, in response to their perception of the environment and of the system itself by addressing run-time uncertainties [10].

Engineering modern complex systems exhibiting self-adaptive behavior is challenging, as engineers are required to deal with many different aspects: (i) does the type and scale of the system requires for centralized or decentralized adaptation control schemes? (e.g., in terms of coordination among interacting components), (ii) does the decisions concerned with the designed behavior introduce overhead? (e.g., in terms of number of exchanged messages), (iii) how to validate the quality of different adaptation decisions before putting the system into operation (e.g., in terms of specific quality indicators, such as the system response time, resource utilization, service throughput, etc.)?

To this end, the main research question addressed by this position paper is: "*How to engineer QoS-aware self-adaptive systems by jointly taking into account all the aforementioned challenges?*".

Classical engineering approaches for quality engineering are not suitable to deal with quality-based adaptation of complex interacting systems, as they mainly employ techniques to derive the steady state solutions of a system at design-time [4].

Therefore, we envision an engineering approach that builds a knowledge-based repository from the continuous and combined use of analytical and experimentation results. This knowledge is built incrementally and used in a continuous model-based engineering process with the aim of providing reasoning support based on the relative costs and benefits for individual design choices.

In our approach the engineer: (i) executes the architectural analysis, (ii) exploits obtained results for deriving and driving the experimentation phase (e.g., by running only the configurations validated via the architectural analysis), (iii) uses the experimentation results to refine/revise the architectural analysis outcome (e.g., some configurations validated by the architectural analysis could be not valid in the experimentation), (iv) iterates the process by using the new results as a baseline for the next cycle. Indeed, the overall idea is to combine the benefits of architectural analysis techniques, which are fast but inaccurate for predicting complex states, with experimental results, which on the other hand are accurate but require detailed information on the solution to experiment with.

The paper is organized as follows. Section 2 overviews the overall approach and explains the different phases, namely *design*, *experimentation*, and *feedback*. Therefore, In Sect. 3 we discuss related work. Finally, Sect. 4 concludes the paper with hints for future research.

2   The Continuous Model-Based Engineering Process

The main idea of the *Continuous Model-based Engineering Process* is to use architectural analysis in conjunction with experimental analysis to have a wider understanding of the system under development. Indeed, the overall objective is to provide insights about the quality of the system-to-be: the architectural and experimental analyses are performed incrementally and used in the continuous system engineering development process. This supports the system engineers in the process of making informed design decisions on the system under investigation by potentially cutting out or exploring in detail those designed solutions that show either bad or good level of quality.

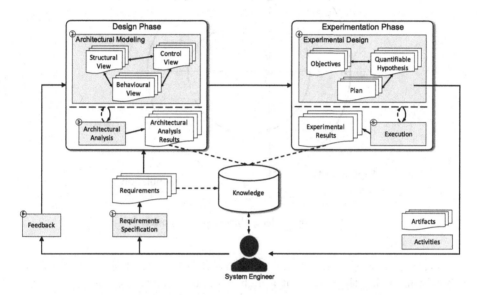

Fig. 1. Continuous model-based engineering process

To this end, the proposed process leverages on the model-based systems engineering paradigm [17], and refers to the systematic use of models as primary artifacts for engineering self-adaptive systems. As shown in Fig. 1, the *Continuous Model-based Engineering Process* comprises two different development phases, namely *Design Phase* and *Experimentation Phase*. Specifically: *Requirements Specification* (①) is devoted to eliciting and formally specifying functional and extra-functional requirements for the system, which in turn drive the following phases, as well as the specification and (iterative) evolution of the *Knowledge*. Indeed, the *Knowledge* plays a key role in the envisioned development process as it allows for (iteratively) merging the outcomes of the two phases and providing the System Engineer with a wider view of the system's development. In particular, the knowledge is in charge of linking requirements to design decisions, so that the System Engineer can continuously check and evaluate the different design alternatives with respect to the requirements to be fulfilled. To this end, the knowledge shall be designed as an *Architectural Knowledge* [15] consisting of many different aspects, including (but non limited to): requirements, assumptions, constraints, hypotheses, architecture design decisions, as well as other factors – e.g., the design as built so far, the available technology, best practices, and past experience in the reference domain.

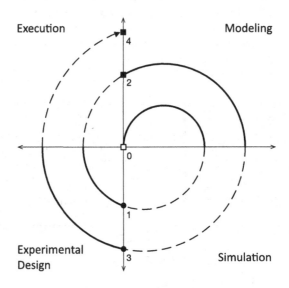

Fig. 2. Knowledge-based spiral model

Once the requirements are specified, the *Architectural Modeling* (②) is in charge of modeling the system at a high level of abstraction by means of three different views: (*i*) the *Structural* view defines the system's structure and composition, (*ii*) the *Control* view defines the self-adaptive architecture (e.g., MAPE [20]), and (*iii*) the *Behavioral* view defines the behavior of the system's entities. *Architectural Analysis* (③) performs the model-based analysis of the overall system and checks whether the requirements are satisfied or not. The *Architectural Analysis Results* are then stored into the knowledge for further comparison with the run-time measurements obtained from the experimentation. In fact, jointly considering both design and run-time system's properties allows software engineers to better identify discrepancies between predictions (i.e., architectural analysis results) and measurements (i.e., experimental results) [7].

According to Model-based System Engineering, design-time models might be used to generate (either manually or automatically) the system to be executed. As self-adaptive systems are hard to test in real operational settings, experimentation should be performed in a closed and fully controlled execution environment. To this end, *Experimental Design* (④) aims at deriving, from general objectives, the set of assumptions, constraints, quantifiable hypothesis and phenomenons to be observed and examined during the *Execution* ((5)) of experiments [14]. *Experimental Results* are stored in the knowledge and merged with *Architectural Analysis Results*. The System Engineer can now compare the results and possibly solve observed discrepancies by *feeding back* ((6)) into the *Design Phase*. This leads towards a new *Design-Experimentation-Feedback* iteration over the refined/revised system's specification.

Figure 2 shows how the four activities occur in each iteration of the spiral and how they use the knowledge: (*i*) at *Point* 0 the knowledge includes requirements, assumptions, constraints, hypotheses and any other general aspect related to the system context, e.g., best practices, and design patterns; (*ii*) at *Point* 1, at the end of the first Architectural Modeling and Analysis, the knowledge also contains the design decisions taken during the modeling activity and the result of their evaluation against the requirements; (*iii*) all the information contained in the knowledge (e.g., requirements, assumptions, constraints, hypotheses, architectural models, and evaluation results) is used to devise and run the experiments, which in turn enriches the knowledge by providing new results; (*iv*) finally, the knowledge obtained as result of each iteration (*Points* 2 and 4) is used as baseline for the next cycle, where the system specification is further refined/revised and evaluated.

3   Related Work

During the system engineering life-cycle it is fundamental to analyze the behavior of the system under investigation. In particular, it is of key relevance to understand how the designed software alternatives impact the QoS requirements. Two types of analysis can be performed: one which is driven by analytical models, and one emulating the actual system behavior through simulation. The former is typically performed at design time and aims at quantifying as early as possible the QoS characteristics of the systems with analytical and/or QoS-based analysis techniques [5]. The latter is usually used when the resulting system behavior is too complex to be captured by theoretical techniques and more detailed models of the system are introduced to get meaningful QoS-based results.

For the majority of modern systems a satisfactory and omni-comprehensive analysis is highly impractical or even impossible to perform at design time. In fact, in this stage, the system engineer has to verify a complex system with respect to a set of requirements, and there is often no need to consider the precise structure of the system and the details of its elements [16]. When the QoS requirements are not tied to the concrete behavior/execution of the system, high-level QoS models can be selected to preliminarily assess the designed system. Analytical models can be adopted in this phase depending on the specific domain of the system under investigation and the type of QoS requirements to validate. When analyzing QoS characteristics of software systems, many approaches have been proposed to optimize different quality indicators [1]. The main quality attributes that have been evaluated in literature are: performance [19], cost [6], reliability [3], availability [13], but also trade-off analysis among multiple quality attributes has been pursued [11].

When the system exhibits complex behaviors, experimentation-based analysis is usually used to collect results that are otherwise impossible to gather.

Experimentation has been used in software engineering from the 80s [2,14,21] and include (but is not limited to) controlled experiments as well as open-ended exploration. The different methods require for rigorous study design and empirical data analysis to derive insightful and indisputable conclusions from obtained results. In particular, *controlled experiments* relies on: (*i*) the manipulation of the input parameters, (*ii*) the observation of the system's state and output, and (*iii*) an accurate cause-effect analysis.

Experimentation may be considered at different levels. At the system level, experimentation may be used for selecting a specific feature out of a set of alternatives (e.g., A/B testing), whereas at the technical level, experimentation may be used to verify and then optimize a given property (e.g., either functional or non-functional). To this extent, experimentation should be considered as a systemic activity driving the whole development process, from requirement elicitation to verification and validation. This would allow for carefully analyzing the domain hypotheses and assumptions, as well as experimenting the uncertainties. Obtained results would then be turn into knowledge to be incorporated within the decision-making process.

The research landscape on performing design-time and run-time analysis and interpreting the obtained results is less broad, and this is the first factor influencing our research in such a direction. In our previous work [7] we proposed a QoS-based approach that jointly considers design-time and run-time results as complementary aspects of systems. However, the self-adaptation was not considered at all, and there was no interaction by humans in the process. In this position paper we present an approach that deals with these challenges and provides an actual integration of analysis and experimental results in a continuous software engineering life-cycle.

Summarizing, differently from the aforementioned approaches for design-time and/or run-time QoS analysis, our idea is to jointly use architectural analysis and experimental results to provide a continuous knowledge-based engineering process. This way, we aim to support system engineers in the development of QoS-aware self-adaptive systems.

4   Conclusion and Future Work

Modern information systems are characterized by high dynamism, which may introduce uncertainties leading to inaccurate and unreliable results. In this context, employing self-adaptive mechanisms is considered as an effective approach to make a system able to adjust its behavior in response to changes perceived in the environment. However, engineering self-adaptive systems is challenging, as many crosscutting concerns must be jointly accounted during the development process.

In this position paper we envisioned a *Continuous Model-based Engineering Process*, which provides insights about the quality of the system-to-be by incrementally building a knowledge-based repository from the continuous and combined use of analytical and experimental results.

In order to achieve the systematic application of the envisioned process, current and future work is towards two different and complementary research directions. On the one hand, we aim at validating and evaluating the process in real-world industrial settings. To this end, we plan to validate the approach applicability in different domains, by employing it in ongoing and future research projects (e.g., Smart Power Grid [8]). We also plan to conduct a controlled experiment with engineers and practitioners from industrial partners, which will design and develop a real fully-featured application in the context of an ongoing research project. Such application will be used to evaluate the efficacy of the process and derive meaningful descriptive statistics.

Further, to fully engineer and (partially) automatize the process, we aim at empowering model-to-code transformations to automatically derive experiments from design artifacts. In the same line of research, we aim at formally specifying the meta-model of the knowledge (e.g., as Architectural Knowledge [9]) to facilitate its instantiation and run-time evolution.

Acknowledgment. This research has received funding from the Swedish Knowledge Foundation, Grants No. 20150088 and No. 20170232. This work has been also partially supported by the PRIN 2017TWRCNB SEDUCE (Designing Spatially Distributed Cyber-Physical Systems under Uncertainty).

References

1. Aleti, A., Buhnova, B., Grunske, L., Koziolek, A., Meedeniya, I.: Software architecture optimization methods: a systematic literature review. IEEE Trans. Software Eng. **39**(5), 658–683 (2013)
2. Basili, V.R., Selby, R.W., Hutchens, D.H.: Experimentation in software engineering. IEEE Trans. Software Eng. **SE–12**(7), 733–743 (1986)
3. Bhunia, A.K., Sahoo, L., Roy, D.: Reliability stochastic optimization for a series system with interval component reliability via genetic algorithm. Appl. Math. Comput. **216**(3), 929–939 (2010)
4. Bocciarelli, P., D'Ambrogio, A.: A model-driven method for enacting the design-time QoS analysis of business processes. Softw. Syst. Model. **13**(2), 573–598 (2013). https://doi.org/10.1007/s10270-013-0345-5
5. Calinescu, R., Grunske, L., Kwiatkowska, M.Z., Mirandola, R., Tamburrelli, G.: Dynamic QoS management and optimization in service-based systems. IEEE Trans. Software Eng. **37**(3), 387–409 (2011)
6. Cao, L., Cao, J., Li, M.: Genetic algorithm utilized in cost-reduction driven web service selection. In: Hao, Y., et al. (eds.) CIS 2005. LNCS (LNAI), vol. 3802, pp. 679–686. Springer, Heidelberg (2005). https://doi.org/10.1007/11596981_100
7. Caporuscio, M., Mirandola, R., Trubiani, C.: Building design-time and run-time knowledge for QoS-based component assembly. Softw. Pract. Exp. **47**(12), 1905–1922 (2017)
8. D'Angelo, M., Napolitano, A., Caporuscio, M.: CyPhEF: a model-driven engineering framework for self-adaptive cyber-physical systems. In: Proceedings of the International Conference on Software Engineering (2018)

9. de Boer, R.C., Farenhorst, R., Lago, P., van Vliet, H., Clerc, V., Jansen, A.: Architectural knowledge: getting to the core. In: Overhage, S., Szyperski, C.A., Reussner, R., Stafford, J.A. (eds.) QoSA 2007. LNCS, vol. 4880, pp. 197–214. Springer, Heidelberg (2007). https://doi.org/10.1007/978-3-540-77619-2_12

10. de Lemos, R.: Software engineering for self-adaptive systems: a second research roadmap. In: de Lemos, R., Giese, H., Müller, H.A., Shaw, M. (eds.) Software Engineering for Self-Adaptive Systems II. LNCS, vol. 7475, pp. 1–32. Springer, Heidelberg (2013). https://doi.org/10.1007/978-3-642-35813-5_1

11. Doğan, A., Özgüner, F.: Biobjective scheduling algorithms for execution time-reliability trade-off in heterogeneous computing systems. Comput. J. 48(3), 300–314 (2005)

12. Garlan, D.: Software engineering in an uncertain world. In Proceedings of the International Workshop on Future of software engineering research (2010)

13. Guo, H., Huai, J., Li, H., Deng, T., Li, Y., Du, Z.: ANGEL: optimal configuration for high available service composition. In Proceedings of the International Conference on Web Services, pp. 280–287 (2007)

14. Juristo, N., Moreno, A.M.: Basics of Software Engineering Experimentation, 1st edn. Springer, HEidelberg (2010)

15. Kruchten, P., Lago, P., van Vliet, H.: Building up and reasoning about architectural knowledge. In: Hofmeister, C., Crnkovic, I., Reussner, R. (eds.) QoSA 2006. LNCS, vol. 4214, pp. 43–58. Springer, Heidelberg (2006). https://doi.org/10.1007/11921998_8

16. Marchiori, M.: Light analysis of complex systems. In: Proceedings of the ACM Symposium on Applied Computing, pp. 18–22. ACM, New York (1998)

17. Mellor, S.J., Clark, A.N., Futagami, T.: Model-driven development. IEEE Softw. 20(5), 14–18 (2003)

18. Rajkumar, R., Lee, I., Sha, L., Stankovic, J.: Cyber-physical systems: the next computing revolution. In: Proceedings of the International Conference on Design Automation, pp. 731–736 (2010)

19. Sharma, V.S., Jalote, P.: Deploying software components for performance. In: Chaudron, M.R.V., Szyperski, C., Reussner, R. (eds.) CBSE 2008. LNCS, vol. 5282, pp. 32–47. Springer, Heidelberg (2008). https://doi.org/10.1007/978-3-540-87891-9_3

20. Weyns, D., et al.: On patterns for decentralized control in self-adaptive systems. In: de Lemos, R., Giese, H., Müller, H.A., Shaw, M. (eds.) Software Engineering for Self-Adaptive Systems II. LNCS, vol. 7475, pp. 76–107. Springer, Heidelberg (2013). https://doi.org/10.1007/978-3-642-35813-5_4

21. Wohlin, C., Runeson, P., Höst, M., Ohlsson, M.C., Regnell, B.: Experimentation in Software Engineering. Springer, Heidelberg (2012). https://doi.org/10.1007/978-3-642-29044-2

Automated Feature Identification
for Android Apps

Gian Luca Scoccia[✉]

Gran Sasso Science Institute, L'Aquila, Italy
gianluca.scoccia@gssi.it

Abstract. Mobile apps are becoming increasingly complex, as nowadays a growing amount of apps no longer focuses on being a "specialized utility" but acts as an "all-around" app that offers assorted features (e.g., news feed, messaging, weather, map, and navigation, etc.). In this paper, we argue that being able to automatically and precisely identify the features offered by an app would allow researchers to investigate new technical solutions, that in turn would benefit both end-users, developers and, researchers. As a stepping stone in this direction, we describe an automated technique to identify features within Android apps. Our approach performs the identification of the features by extracting information from the app user interface and grouping together semantically similar concepts thanks to knowledge-base aided natural text processing and machine learning.

Keywords: Mobile apps · Features · Android

1 Introduction

Mobile apps are experiencing explosive growth in the last years. New mobile applications (apps for short) are developed and released at a dramatic speed. Represented by the well known Google Play Store, the Android apps market now counts more than two millions apps, downloaded billions of times per year [17]. At the same time, mobile apps are becoming increasingly complex, as many apps act as "all-around" applications, including more and more functionalities not to be considered as their main one, such as news feed, messaging, weather, map, and navigation, etc. Users interact with Android apps through user interfaces (UI) whose wealth of detail and articulation is growing hand in hand with the complexity of the apps. Building on the definition provided in the Software Engineering Body of Knowledge [3], in the following we will identify with the term feature a functionality offered by the app to the user.

We believe that being able to automatically and precisely identify app features would enable the design of new systems and technological solutions that would, in turn, impact multiple actors of the mobile app ecosystem: end-users, developers and researchers. For users, it enables the creation of systems able to reason and take action on a per-feature basis. As an example, in our own

© Springer Nature Switzerland AG 2020
J. Camara and M. Steffen (Eds.): SEFM 2019 Workshops, LNCS 12226, pp. 77–84, 2020.
https://doi.org/10.1007/978-3-030-57506-9_7

work [14], a mapping between app features and their implementation is used as a basis to implement finer-grained app permissions: end-users no longer have to grant permissions monolithically to the whole app, but can specify them on a per-feature basis. Moreover, it would enable the development of new app search engines that would help in finding apps with desired features without the need of trying them out first. Conversely, it can be used as a vetting mechanism, as apps with undesired features (such as storage of data in the cloud) can more easily be identified and discarded.

Concerning developers, they can benefit from the development of new tools and techniques aimed at assisting them in the course of the different tasks they perform during software maintenance and evolution. Major benefits would be reaped in *Feature location*, i.e., the process of identifying the initial location in the source code that corresponds to specific functionality, when coupled with source code mining. Feature location is one of the most important and common activities performed by programmers [4]. Other potential applications are in the (semi-)automation of activities such as the creation of app descriptions, generation of documentation, and feature removal [13].

Being able to identify app features would also represent a new useful tool for researchers themselves. One of its possible applications is in app store mining studies [7], where it can open up a new dimension for researchers to explore. Indeed, while investigating apps' technical, customer and business aspects no longer they would be restricted to coarse-grained groupings of apps (e.g., apps belonging to the same app store category or with similar users rating) but would be able to group apps that offer similar functionalities. Likewise, they would be enabled with a tool to investigate how the presence (absence) of a feature impacts users' perception of the app. Another possible application is in the context of repackaged apps [19] and malware detection. While carrying out the former, obviously, identifying an app that possesses features identical to a second one is a strong indication of potential repackaging. While performing the latter, apps with seemingly "out of place" features can be flagged for further inspection.

In this paper, we propose an automated technique to identify features within Android apps. Our approach performs the identification of the features by extracting information from the app user interface and grouping together semantically similar concepts thanks to knowledge-base aided Natural Text Processing (NLP) and machine learning.

2 Proposed Solution

The contribution of this work is the definition of an automated technique for the identification of features within Android apps. At the heart of our approach lies the intuition that text contained in the user interface of an Android application exposes a wealth of information about the app functionalities. Thus, by extracting, refining and reasoning on it we can identify app features.

Figure 1 provides an overview of the sequential steps that compose our method. As common with all techniques that rely on machine learning, our approach is divided in two phases: *training* and *prediction*. During the former, the system is provided with training data to learn from. A *dataset of Android apps* (e.g., [1]) is used as training data in our approach. For each app in the dataset, the following steps are sequentially performed:

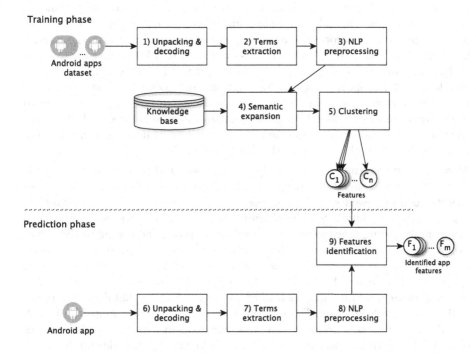

Fig. 1. Composition of the process of feature identification

1) Unpacking & decoding: An Android app UI is mostly defined via means of XML files. All the strings used in the layout definition, are stored in a `strings.xml` file (refer to Fig. 2(a) for an example). During this step, this file is extracted and decoded into a human-readable format, suitable for processing in subsequent steps. Off-the-shelf tools such as `dex2jar`[1] and `apktool`[2] can be leveraged to implement this step.

2) Terms extraction: Inside the `strings.xml` file, strings are stored as key-value pairs. Keys are short definitions of each string, which reflect the developers' perspective of the UI. Values are what will be presented in the UI, i.e., what users will see. Both keys and values are extracted and are supplied as input to the following step.

---

[1] https://github.com/pxb1988/dex2jar.
[2] https://ibotpeaches.github.io/Apktool/.

3) NLP preprocessing: In this step, some refinements are applied to refine extracted terms for subsequent processing. First, heuristics are used to split identifiers with camel case and underscore-connected naming to proper words. Considering the example of Fig. 2(a), the string "`shoppingCartConfirm`" cannot be used directly. Rather, it is divided into the embedded words "`shopping`", "`cart`" and "`confirm`". Afterward, well-known natural language processing techniques such as *stopwords removal, stemming* and *lemmatization* are applied [2]. Stopwords removal is the process of removing words commonly used in the English language (e.g., "as", "it", "so") which do not greatly affect the semantics of a sentence. Stemming is the process of reducing inflected or derived words to their root form. For instance, the words "connection" and "connected" are reduced to the same base word "connect". Lemmatization is the process of reducing a word to its canonical form named lemma. Lemmatization is performed with the aid of dictionaries and takes the linguistic context of the term into consideration. For instance, "good" is the lemma of the word "better".

4) Semantic expansion: To identify features, we need to abstract from words to their related semantic concept, that represents real-world attributes like objects, actions, events, etc. [12]. For instance, referring to the example of Fig. 2, the words "buy", "purchase" and "shop" all refer to the same concept of acquiring by giving in exchange an equivalent in money (according to the definition provided by the Oxford English Dictionary[3]). For this purpose, we employ knowledge-base aided *semantic expansion*. Semantic expansion is the process of adding words to a set of words to better represent an object or a meaning [15]. In our approach, we augment each word with its definition contained in a previously built knowledge-base. To build the knowledge-base, definitions can be collected from different sources: dictionaries, encyclopedias and answering engines (e.g., Wolfram|Alpha[4]) to collect open-domain knowledge; mobile and developer specific resources (e.g., Stack Overflow[5]) to collect domain specific knowledge. Hence, for each word given as input, a textual document containing its expanded definition is outputted and fed to the following step.

5) Clustering: In this step, machine learning techniques are employed to group together semantically similar concepts contained in input documents. For this purpose, inputs must first be transformed into a representation suitable for the application of machine learning techniques. In our methodology, we select the popular *bag-of-words* model coupled with *tf-idf* normalization [2]. Bag-of-words is a simplifying representation in which a document is represented as the multiset of its words, disregarding grammar and word order, but keeping multiplicity. Tf-idf (term frequency-inverse document frequency) is a normalization procedure that weights with diminishing importance terms that occur in more frequently in the corpus of all documents.

---

[3] https://public.oed.com/about/.
[4] https://www.wolframalpha.com.
[5] https://stackoverflow.com.

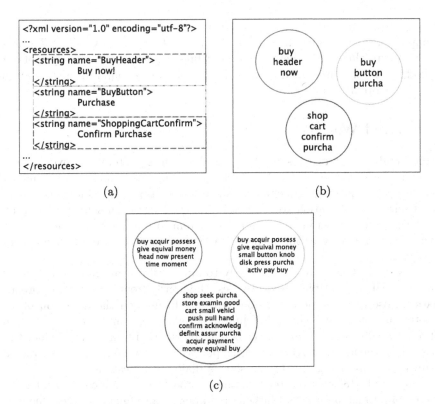

(a)   (b)

(c)

Fig. 2. An example of terms collected: in XML documents that define the user interface (a), after extraction and refinements through NLP techniques (b), and after semantic expansion according to definitions in the knowledge base (c)

After the transformation, a *density-based clustering* algorithm is applied. Clustering refers to the task of identifying groups (clusters) in a data set. In density-based clustering, a cluster is a set of data objects spread in the data space over a contiguous region of high density of objects. Density-based clusters are separated from each other by contiguous regions of low density of objects [10]. Since, as seen in the previous step, words that refer to the same concept have similar definitions, these are grouped together by the clustering algorithm. Thus, the output of this step is a set of clusters C_1–C_n, each representing a feature. Considering the example of Fig. 2, definitions for the words "buy", "purchase" and "shop" are all grouped into a single cluster, that represents the "Selling of products/services" feature.

After the training is completed, the system is ready for the *prediction* phase. Given as input a previously unseen Android app for which we want to identify features, unpacking, decoding, extraction of terms and their refinement are executed for it as in the training phase (steps 6 through 8 from Fig. 1), thus obtaining a word set from the UI text. Afterward, we verify whether each of the extracted words belongs to any of the clusters C_1–C_n identified during training. An app is considered as having feature C if its word set contains at least T words that belong to cluster C, where T is a predefined threshold. Final output of our method is the set of identified features F_1–F_m that were found in the app given as input for prediction.

3   Related Works

A considerable body of work has been produced in the literature investigating techniques for feature location. Approaches targeting traditional software mainly make use of text processing techniques such as Latent Semantic Indexing [9] and Latent Dirichlet Allocation [16] to determine the features in software based on the textual information in code. As these systems are ultimately built to assist developers during software maintenance tasks, they require a user provided query to operate.

The work of Guo et al. [6], similarly to ours, utilizes information extracted from apps' UI to identify offered features. Differently from ours, their approach makes no use of semantic expansion and only focuses on the detection of six predetermined features frequently found in mobile apps. Kanda et al. [8] instead utilize API calls mined from source code as information from which deduct features. Given the fact that API calls often perform low-level operations, extracted features are more fine-grained (e.g., show a dialog, get location).

Wang et al. [18] utilize a text mining approach on source code to infer the purpose of permission usages. Rather than infer all app functionalities, the output of their approach is a short description of those functionalities that requires access to some sensitive resource. For instance, a functionality that requires the user' location could be labeled, among others, as "search nearby places" or "geotagging".

CHABADA [5] uses descriptions collected from app markets to extrapolate app functionalities. These are then compared to API usage to identify possible anomalies in app behavior. Evaluated on a set of 172 malware apps, CHABADA was effective in flagging 56% of them as malware, without prior built-in knowledge of their behavior.

PerRec [11] leverages mining-based techniques to recommend permissions for given apps according to their used APIs. Similarly to our approach, semantic expansion is employed, as API descriptions are used in place of API names, to abstract from specific terms and cluster together APIs with similar purposes.

4   Roadmap and Future Works

At the time of writing, we are concluding our prototype implementation of the proposed approach. Afterward, we are planning to demonstrate its precision and usefulness. First, we will assess the quality of obtained clusters C_1–C_n, employing metrics commonly used to evaluate density-based clustering algorithms [10]. This step will also be useful to refine the different steps that compose our approach and tune clustering algorithm parameters. Thereupon, we will directly engage with Android developers to perform a more in-depth assessment of the approach precision and usefulness by i) asking them to evaluate the precision of identified features for apps they developed and ii) designing a set of experiments in which they will be asked to complete a set of software maintenance tasks with the assistance of our prototype tool.

Currently our approach provides limited traceability between a feature and the corresponding source code files that implement it. To make it more helpful in feature location tasks, we are planning on extending it with information extracted from apps decompiled source code, in addition to the one coming from the user interface files. Currently our approach also requires to be trained multiple times in order to be able to identify features in a dataset with mixed languages. In the future we plan on investigating more advanced representations than bag-of-words to overcome this limitation.

References

1. Allix, K., Bissyandé, T.F., Klein, J., Le Traon, Y.: AndroZoo: collecting millions of android apps for the research community. In: 2016 IEEE/ACM 13th Working Conference on Mining Software Repositories (MSR), pp. 468–471. IEEE (2016)
2. Bird, S., Klein, E., Loper, E.: Natural language processing with Python: analyzing text with the natural language toolkit. O'Reilly Media Inc., Sebastopol (2009)
3. Bourque, P., Fairley, R.E., et al.: Guide to the software engineering body of knowledge (SWEBOK (R)): version 3.0. IEEE Computer Society Press (2014)
4. Dit, B., Revelle, M., Gethers, M., Poshyvanyk, D.: Feature location in source code: a taxonomy and survey. J. Softw. Evol. Process. 25(1), 53–95 (2013)
5. Gorla, A., Tavecchia, I., Gross, F., Zeller, A.: Checking app behavior against app descriptions. In: Proceedings of the 36th International Conference on Software Engineering, pp. 1025–1035. ACM (2014)
6. Guo, Y., Li, Y., Yang, Z., Chen, X.: What's inside my app?: understanding feature redundancy in mobile apps. In: Proceedings of the 26th Conference on Program Comprehension. pp. 266–276. ACM (2018)
7. Harman, M., Jia, Y., Zhang, Y.: App store mining and analysis: MSR for app stores. In: Proceedings of the 9th IEEE Working Conference on Mining Software Repositories, pp. 108–111. IEEE Press (2012)
8. Kanda, T., Manabe, Y., Ishio, T., Matsushita, M., Inoue, K.: Semi-automatically extracting features from source code of android applications. IEICE Trans. Inf. Syst. 96(12), 2857–2859 (2013)
9. Kawaguchi, S., Garg, P.K., Matsushita, M., Inoue, K.: MUDABlue: an automatic categorization system for open source repositories. J. Syst. Softw. 79(7), 939–953 (2006)
10. Kriegel, H.P., Kröger, P., Sander, J., Zimek, A.: Density-based clustering. Wiley Interdiscip. Rev. Data Min. Knowl. Discov. 1(3), 231–240 (2011)
11. Liu, Z., Xia, X., Lo, D., Grundy, J.: Automatic, highly accurate app permission recommendation. Autom. Softw. Eng., 1–34 (2019)
12. Loh, S., Wives, L.K., de Oliveira, J.P.M.: Concept-based knowledge discovery in texts extracted from the web. ACM SIGKDD Explor. Newsl. 2(1), 29–39 (2000)

13. Pascarella, L., Geiger, F.X., Palomba, F., Di Nucci, D., Malavolta, I., Bacchelli, A.: Self-reported activities of android developers. In: 2018 IEEE/ACM 5th International Conference on Mobile Software Engineering and Systems (MOBILESoft), pp. 144–155. IEEE (2018)
14. Scoccia, G.L., Malavolta, I., Autili, M., Di Salle, A., Inverardi, P.: User-centric android flexible permissions. In: Proceedings of the 39th International Conference on Software Engineering Companion, pp. 365–367. IEEE Press (2017)
15. Song, M.: Handbook of Research on Text and Web Mining Technologies. IGI Global, Pennsylvania (2008)
16. Tian, K., Revelle, M., Poshyvanyk, D.: Using latent Dirichlet allocation for automatic categorization of software. In: 2009 6th IEEE International Working Conference on Mining Software Repositories, pp. 163–166. IEEE (2009)
17. University of Alabama at Birmingham Online Masters in Management Information Systems: The Future of Mobile Application (2014). http://businessdegrees.uab.edu/resources/infographic/the-future-of-mobile-application/
18. Wang, H., Li, Y., Guo, Y., Agarwal, Y., Hong, J.I.: Understanding the purpose of permission use in mobile apps. ACM Trans. Inf. Syst. (TOIS) 35(4), 43 (2017)
19. Zhou, W., Zhou, Y., Jiang, X., Ning, P.: Detecting repackaged smartphone applications in third-party android marketplaces. In: Proceedings of the second ACM conference on Data and Application Security and Privacy, pp. 317–326. ACM (2012)

Mapping BPMN2 Service Choreographies to Colored Petri Nets

Tala Najem[(✉)] and Alexander Perucci

University of L'Aquila, L'Aquila, Italy
tala.najem@graduate.univaq.it, alexander.perucci@univaq.it

Abstract. Nowadays, software systems are often built by reusing and integrating existing services distributed over the Internet. Service choreography is a service engineering approach to compose together and coordinate services by specifying their external interactions in terms of flows of peer-to-peer message exchanges, given from a global perspective. BPMN2 offers a dedicated notation, called Choreography Diagrams, to specify service choreographies. However, BPMN2 specifications lack formal semantics causing some misinterpretations by practitioners and researchers. Colored Petri Net (CPN) is a formally proved notation with mathematical semantics and tool support for different analysis techniques. In this paper, we present a mapping to transform BPMN2 Choreography Diagrams into Colored Choreography Nets (CCNs). The latter is a CPN for enabling simulation and analysis of service choreographies.

1 Introduction

Nowadays, we are surrounded by a rapidly increasing number of software systems that provide different services in various domains. To fulfill the needs of this new reality, software systems are often built by reusing and integrating existing services distributed over the Internet. The ability to automatically *compose* and *coordinate* services enables the modular construction of both business and commercial systems [2,15]. Most of the existing service composition approaches are based on orchestration [17]. Service Orchestration is a centralized composition approach in which an orchestrator forwards requests to the other participant services in order to fulfill the overall composition's goal. Differently from orchestration, Service Choreography [3,6,15] is a decentralized approach that describes the interactions among the participant services from a global perspective. A service choreography models peer-to-peer communication by defining a multiparty protocol that, when put in place by the cooperating services, allows for reaching the overall choreography goal in a fully distributed way. The involved services are active and aware entities that communicate with each other to make decisions and perform tasks. In this sense, service choreographies are significantly different from service orchestrations in which a single stakeholder (i.e., the orchestrator) centrally plans and decides how an objective should be reached through the cooperation with other services. Contrariwise, service choreography does not rely on a

© Springer Nature Switzerland AG 2020
J. Camara and M. Steffen (Eds.): SEFM 2019 Workshops, LNCS 12226, pp. 85–100, 2020.
https://doi.org/10.1007/978-3-030-57506-9_8

central coordinator since each involved service knows precisely when to execute its operations and which other services to interact with. However, composing different existing services, as third-party participants being reused, might not follow the desired collaboration prescribed by the choreography specification.

In the literature, there are many valuable works that, in different forms and for different purposes, deal with the foundational problems of choreographies, e.g., checking choreography realizability, analyzing repairability of the choreography specification, verifying conformance, and enforcing realizability. Specifically, the works in [7,9,20] tackle the problems of deciding and enforcing choreography realizability, and checking choreography conformance. They are based on different interpretations of the choreography interaction semantics, concerning both the subset of considered choreography constructs and the used formal notations (e.g., process algebra, Labelled Transition Systems (LTS), and automata), which were not specifically born for distributed systems. On the other hand, other works [12–14], use Petri Nets notations, which has proven its efficiency in modeling and simulating parallel and distributed systems.

The need for practical approaches to the realization of choreographies was recognized in the OMG's Business Process Modeling Notation version 2.0[1] (BPMN2), which introduces dedicated *Choreography Diagrams*, a practical notation for specifying choreographies. By following the pioneering BPMN process and collaboration diagrams, choreography diagrams are amenable to be automatically treated and transformed into actual code. Nonetheless, BPMN2 specification is only defined as a textual description and lacks formal semantics which causes some misinterpretations by practitioners and researchers. This aspect makes it harder to design, verify and analyze choreographies. To this end, the works in [15,18] deal with conformance verification and realizability checking of BPMN2 Choreography Diagrams. While, the work in [10] propose an approach for checking the conformance of BPMN2 collaboration diagrams with respect to choreography diagrams. These works still use the intermediate formal notations, which are not dedicated for distributed system. An extension of traditional Petri Nets are Colored Petri Nets (CPNs) [16], which are a formally proved notation with mathematical semantics and tool support for different analysis techniques. CPNs were developed for concurrent and distributed systems and thus are considered a good dedicated notation to adopt when modeling choreographies. To the best of our knowledge, the latest work in the literature that considered dealing with BPMN2 notations using CPN-based approach is introduced in [11] to solve the state space explosion problem resulted by large-scale BPMN models. However, in this approach, the authors provide a clear algorithm and transformation of BPMN2 Collaboration Diagrams into Colored Petri Nets, without an explicit treatment of BPMN2 Choreography Diagrams.

In this paper, we provide a preliminary mapping of a subset BPMN2 Choreography Diagrams constructs into Colored Choreography Nets (CCNs). A CCN is a CPN enabling simulation and different types of analysis such as state space, deadlocks and performance analysis. These analysis, among others, provide

---

[1] www.omg.org/spec/BPMN/2.0.

insights regarding choreographies that are not evident from a BPMN2 Choreography Diagram. The interpretations of the considered BPMN2 choreography
interaction semantics is complementary to the one proposed in [11].

The rest of the paper is structured as follows. Section 2 introduces a simple
example of BPMN2 Choreography Diagram, highlights the considered choreography constructs and interaction semantics, and gives the definition of CCN.
Section 3 describes the mapping of BPMN2 choreography constructs into CCNs.
Section 4 describes the deadlock analysis conducted with the CCN of the example. Section 5 discusses related work, and Sect. 6 concludes the paper and discusses future directions.

2 Background Notions

This section describes the considered choreography constructs and their interaction semantic (Sect. 2.1), and gives the formal definition of CCN (Sect. 2.2).

2.1 BPMN2 Choreography Diagrams

As already mentioned, BPMN2 Choreography Diagrams are a practical notation
to realize choreographies and focus on specifying the message exchanges among
the participants from a global point of view. Figure 1 depicts a simple example
of BPMN2 Choreography Diagram. Specifically, Choreography Diagrams use
rounded-corner boxes to denote tasks.

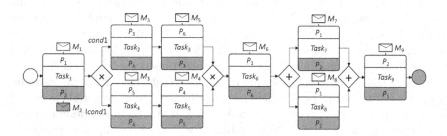

Fig. 1. A BPMN2 Choreography Diagram

Each task is labeled with the roles of the two involved participants (e.g., P_1
and P_2 in Fig. 1), and the name of the task (e.g., $Task_1$). By referring to $Task_1$
in the figure, a task is performed by the initiating participant (P_1) by sending
a message (M_1) to the receiving participant (P_2) and, optionally, receiving a
reply message (M_2) afterwards, upon task accomplishment. A role contained
in the white box denotes the initiating participant. Messages are specified by
using XML schema[2]. Moreover, the BPMN2 specification employs the theoretical concept of a token that, traversing the sequence flows and passing through

---

[2] www.w3.org/XML/Schema.

the elements in a process, aids to define its behavior. The start event generates the token that must eventually be consumed at an end event. Referring to Fig. 1, the circle with no incoming arrows denotes the start event (see the white circle), and the circle with no outgoing arrows denotes the end event (see the gray circle). The remaining elements are used to create and merge exclusive (see the × rhombus) and parallel flows (see the + rhombus). A diverging exclusive gateway (see the × rhombus with two outgoing arrows) is used to create alternative flows based on conditional expressions (see $cond1$ and $cond2$). These alternative flows are merged at the corresponding converging exclusive gateway (see the × rhombus with two incoming arrows). Similarly to the exclusive gateway, a converging parallel gateway (see the + rhombus with two outgoing arrows) creates parallel flows without checking any conditional expression. These parallel flows are synchronized at the corresponding converging parallel gateway (see the + rhombus with two incoming arrows).

The possible interactions prescribed by the choreography in Fig. 1 are such that P_1 sends the message M_1 to P_2 that, in turn, replies to P_1 with the message M_2 ($Task_1$). Then, when in the diverging exclusive gateway, two alternatives can be undertaken. One alternative (i.e., $cond1$ is evaluated to $true$) accounts for P_3 sending M_3 to P_4, followed by P_6 sending M_5 to P_3 ($Task_2$ followed by $Task_3$). The other alternative (i.e., $!cond1$ is evaluated to $true$) accounts for P_5 sending M_3 to P_4, followed by P_4 sending M_4 to P_5 ($Task_4$ followed by $Task_5$). Then, the two alternative paths lead to the converging exclusive gateway, from where the interaction continues with P_1 which sends M_6 to P_6 ($Task_6$). Then, when in the diverging parallel gateway, two parallel flows are undertaken. One flow accounts for P_1 sending M_7 to P_2 ($Task_7$) and the second one accounts for P_1 sending M_8 to P_2 ($Task_8$). When $Task_7$ and $Task_8$ are both accomplished, the two parallel flows are synchronized at the converging parallel gateway, from where the interaction continues with P_2 that sends M_9 to P_1 ($Task_9$) and finally leads to the end event, from where no more outgoing transitions can be undertaken.

Some of the above interactions are unrealizable with respect to the realizability notion formalized in [8]. Furthermore, as discussed in more details in Sect. 4, the choreographed system might go in deadlock at run-time. For designing realizable choreographies, the BPMN2 standard specification imposes constraints which must be taken into account, and strictly concerning the choreography in Fig. 1 the constraints that were not met are:

1. **for a choreography task:** the initiating participant of a task must be an initiating or receiving participant of the task that precedes it (e.g., $Task_3$ violates this constraint since P_6 is not involved in $Task_2$);
2. **for an exclusive gateway:** the initiating participant of each task that follows the gateway must be an initiating or receiving participant of the task that precedes the gateway (e.g., $Task_2$ and $Task_4$ violate this constraint since P_3 and P_5 are not involved in $Task_1$).

Although we can design choreographies by following the BPMN2 constraints, when third-party participants are involved as black-box services to be reused, the choreography might still

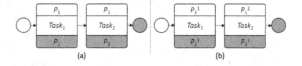

Fig. 2. A choreography with reused services

be unrealizable. With reference to Fig. 2.(a) the choreography prescribes the collaboration of participants P_1, P_2, and P_3 performing $Task_1$ and $Task_2$. At first glance, this choreography seems to be realizable since the initiating participant (P_1) of $Task_2$ is also involved in $Task_1$ (that is the task that precedes $Task_2$), and no other constraints are violated. In order to realize this choreography, black-box services might be involved to play the role of participants P_1, P_2, and P_3. Figure 2.(b) depicts the equivalent choreography of (a), in which third-party participants P_1^1 and P_1^2 play the role of P_1 performing tasks $Task_1$ and $Task_2$, respectively, and P_2^1 (resp., P_3^1) plays the role of P_2 (resp., P_3). Since P_1^1 and P_1^2 are two different reused services, the choreography depicted in (b) is now unrealizable violating the above BPMN2 constraint regarding choreography tasks. Specifically, when third-party participants are involved, the following problem must be considered: "given a choreography specification and a set of existing services, how to externally coordinate their interaction so to fulfill the collaboration prescribed by the specification?". To address this problem, possible coordination issues must be solved [3–5]. The realizability enforcement of choreographies is out of the scope of this paper and the interested reader can refer to [1–5].

2.2   Colored Choreography Nets

Colored Petri Nets (CPNs) [16] are a formally proved notation for designing and analyzing concurrent and distributed systems. CPNs extend the traditional Petri nets model with support for modeling data preserving their useful properties as well as extending them. CPNs allow the distinction of tokens by attaching data values (i.e., colors) to them and adds some constraints and functions to the net. Constraints and functions are specified by adding guards on transitions or by defining expressions on arcs. Thus, providing more flexibility in system modeling and validation. CPNs are formally defined as follows:

Definition 1 (CPN).   *A Colored Petri Net is a nine-tuple $CPN = \{P, T, A, \Sigma, V, C, G, E, I\}$, where:*

- *P, T and A are each a finite set of **places,transitions** and directed **arcs**, respectively. Such that $P \cap T = \emptyset$ and $A \subseteq P \times T \cup T \times P$.*
- *Σ is a finite set of non-empty **colour sets**.*
- *V is a finite set of **typed variables** such that $Type[v] \in \Sigma$ for all $v \in V$.*
- *$C : P \to \Sigma$ is a **colour set function** that assigns a colour set to each place.*
- *$G : T \to EXPR_V$ is a **guard function** that assigns a guard to each transition t such that $Type[G(t)] = Bool$, where $EXPR_V$ is the set of expressions in which the variables of each expression form a subset of V.*

- $E : A \to EXPR_V$ is an **arc expression function** that assigns an arc expression to each arc a such that $Type[E(a)] = C(p)_{MS}$, where p is the place connected to the arc a, and $EXPR_V$ is the set of expressions in which the variables of each expression form a subset of V.
- $I : P \to EXPR_\emptyset$ is an **initialization function** that assigns an initialization expression to each place p such that $Type[I(p)] = C(p)_{MS}$, where $EXPR_\emptyset$ is the set of closed expressions in which the variables of each expression cannot have any free variables.

In CPNs, a marking M of a net is the assignment of tokens to the places. According to the transition semantics of CPN, a transition is enabled (i.e., can fire) if there are enough tokens in its input places for the consumption to be possible and if its guard $G(t)$ is evaluated to *true* (called a binding). Firing a transition t changes the marking of the net from M to M', in which, tokens from the preceding places of t are removed and new tokens are generated in the successive ones by evaluating the guard $G(t)$) and the arcs' expressions connecting from and to t.

A Colored Choreography Net (CCN), is a CPN that describes the message flow among the choreography participants and expresses the ordered interactions among them from a global perspective.

Definition 2 (CCN). *A Colored Choreography Net is a CPN where:*

- $\Sigma = CP \cup CM \cup L$, where:
  - CP is the color set that represents all **participants** involved in the choreography.
  - CM is the color set that represents all **messages** exchanged among the choreography participants.
  - $L = \{(cp, m, cp') | cp, cp' \in CP \wedge m \in CM\}$ is the color set representing the participant cp that sends the message m to the participant cp'.
- E is the universal set of **Boolean expressions** (i.e., propositional formulae) plus **specific expressions** of the form internal, $send_m$ or $receive_m$, where m can be any message.
- I is the initialization function that assigns the color $l \in L$ to each $p \in P$.

By referring to Fig. 1 $CP = \{P_1, P_2, P_3, P_4, P_5, P_6\}$, $CM = \{M_1, M_2, M_3, M_4, M_5, M_6, M_7, M_8, M_9\}$, and $L = \{(P_1, M_1, P_2), (P_2, M_2, P_1), (P_3, M_3, P_4), (P_5, M_3, P_4), (P_6, M_5, P_3), (P_4, M_4, P_5), (P_1, M_6, P_6), (P_1, M_7, P_2), (P_1, M_8, P_2), (P_2, M_9, P_1)\}$.

As it will be detailed in Sect. 4, a CCN provides insights regarding choreographies that are not evident from a BPMN2 Choreography Diagram, and it can be analyzed to check the presence of deadlocks in a service choreography.

3   BPMN2 to CCN

This section describes the mapping of BPMN2 Choreography Diagrams into CCNs. Specifically, the mapping can be adopted as a base for implementing an automatic BPMN2-to-CCN transformation. The transformation can be done in different manners including the adoption of general-purpose programming languages. It takes as input one or more models conforming to the BPMN2 metamodel and generates one or more models conforming to the CCN metamodel. Thus, to develop the BPMN2-to-CCN transformation, both the BPMN2 and CCN metamodels are required. The former is available in the Eclipse ecosystem; the latter (see Fig. 3) consists of an arbitrary number of *Transitions*, *Places*, *Arcs*, *Participants*, *Messages*, and *Tokens*. Each place contains zero or more tokens and each transition has one guard associated to it. A token represents a message to be exchanged between an initiating participant (i.e., the one sending the message) and a receiving participant (i.e., the one receiving the message).

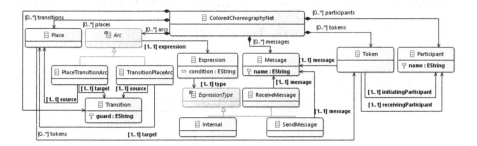

Fig. 3. Colored Choreography Nets metamodel

Places and transitions serve as sources and/or targets for arcs. Each arc is concretized as *PlaceTransitionArc* or *TransitionPlaceArc* to express the flow relation from a place to a transition, or vice versa. Moreover, each arc has an *Expression* that models the action of either sending or receiving a message (observable actions), or an internal action (not observable from outside). The *Expression* contains also an enabling condition for the arcs; if the condition holds, a token can traverse the arc.

In the remaining of the section, we present a mapping of a subset of BPMN2 Choreography Diagrams constructs into CCNs. The discussion is based on the representative cases shown in Table 1, Table 2, and Table 3. In each table, the left column reports the BPMN2 Choreography Diagrams constructs and the right column reports the corresponding CCN models.

Task exchanging one message (a) – a task in which the initiating participant P_1 sends the message M_1 to the receiving participant P_2 is mapped into a CCN with two places, one transition, and two arcs. The arc connecting the first place with the transition (i.e., *PalceTransitionArc* in the CCN metamodel) represents the sending of the message M_1 (see the expression $send_{M1}$ in Table 1.(a)). While, the arc connecting the transition to the second place (i.e., *TransitionPalceArc* in the CCN metamodel) represents the receiving of M_1 by P_2 (see the expression $receive_{M1}$ in Table 1.(a)). The guard $[M_1]$ of the transition indicates that only tokens with a color value that contains M_1 can fire this transition. The place immediately preceding the transition holds the token te_1 with the value (P_1, M_1, P_2). Thus, when the transition is fired, it simulates both the sending of M_1 from P_1 and the receiving of M_1 by P_2.

Task exchanging two messages (b) – for a task in which the initiating participant P_1 sends the message M_1 to the receiving participant P_2, followed by P_2 that replies to P_1 with M_2, each message exchange is mapped by following the mapping **(a)**. Specifically, two different nets are used. The first one represents the exchange of M_1 from P_1 to P_2 and the second one represents the exchange of M_2 from P_2 to P_1. Then, these two nets are connected together with an arc from the place of the *TransitionPalceArc* of the first net to the transition of the *PalceTransitionArc* of the second net. The guard $[M_1 \& M_2]$ of the second net makes the use of the logical *AND* operator indicating that the transition can be enabled only when the token te_1 (i.e., the token with the color value that contains M_1) reaches the place before the transition. This transition ensures that the sending of M_2 contained in te_2, happens only after P_2 receives M_1.

Table 1. Mapping of Choreography Tasks into CCNs

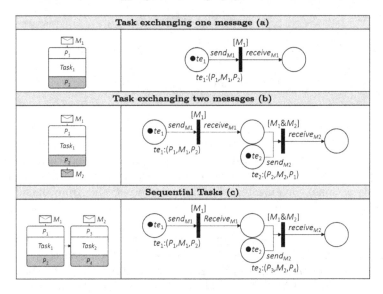

Sequential Tasks (c) – form the BPMN2 specification, the sequential tasks flow defines the ordering in which Choreography Tasks must be executed. Referring to the BPMN2 Choreography Diagram in Table 1.(c), $Task_1$ must be executed before $Task_2$. By performing $Task_1$, P_1 sends M_1 to P_2, and only when the $Task_1$ is accomplished P_3 sends M_2 to P_4. In order to fulfill the execution order of $Task_1$ and $Task_2$ the mapping of sequential tasks is equivalent to the one described in **(b)**. $Task_1$ and $Task_2$ are mapped with two sequentially connected nets, and the guard $[M_1 \& M_2]$ ensures that $Task_1$ is executed before $Task_2$.

Diverging Parallel Gateway (d) – it creates parallel flows without checking any condition. Following the mapping in Table 1.(a), $Task_1$, $Task_2$, and $Task_3$ are mapped with three different nets. As shown in Table 2.(d), the place immediately preceding the transitions of the nets related to $Task_2$ and $Task_3$ are merged into a single place forming a single net. The merged place holds both tokens te_2 and te_3. Finally, the net related to $Task_1$ is connected to the new net with two *PlaceTransitionArc*; from the place reachable after firing the transition with guard $[M_1]$ to the two transitions with guard $[M_1\&M_2]$ and $[M_1\&M_3]$, respectively. Thus, when $Task_1$ is accomplished the tokens te_2 and te_3 can be both fired simulating the parallel sending of M_2 (from P_2) and M_3 (from P_1).

Table 2. Mapping of Parallel Gateways into CCNs

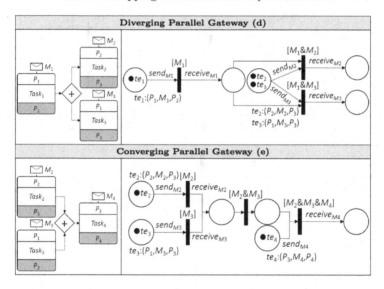

Converging Parallel Gateway (e) – it synchronizes parallel flows. Similarly to the mapping in (d), $Task_2$, $Task_3$, and $Task_4$ are mapped with three different nets. These nets are then connected by merging the places of the *TransitionPalceArc* of the nets related to $Task_2$ and $Task_3$ in a single place, which in turn is connected to a new transition with guard $[M_2\&M_3]$ (see Table 2.(e)). Finally, the place that follows this transition is connected to the transition of the net related to $Task_4$ (i.e., the transition with guard $[M_2\&M_3\&M_4]$). It is worthwhile noticing that, the guard $[M_2\&M_3]$ ensures the synchronization of the parallel flows, and the guard $[M_2\&M_3\&M_4]$ ensures that $Task_4$ must be executed only when $Task_2$ and $Task_3$ are both accomplished.

Diverging Exclusive Gateway (f) – it creates alternative flows based on conditional expressions. As shown in Table 3.(f) the mapping of a Diverging Exclusive Gateway is similar to the mapping in Table 2.(d) with the difference that the arcs representing the sending of M_2 ($send_{M2}$) and M_3 ($send_{M3}$) are labeled with the conditional expression *cond* and !*cond*, respectively. According to the BPMN2 standard specification, P_1 and P_2 must have sent or received the message that provided the data upon which the conditional decision is made. In addition, the message that provides the data for the gateway conditional decision may be in any choreography task prior to the gateway. It is worthwhile noticing that, differently from the mapping in (**d**), depending on the evaluation of the conditions only one token (either te_2 or te_3) can be passed, and hence, only the transition with the guard $[M_1\&M_2]$ or $[M_1\&M_3]$ can be enabled.

Table 3. Mapping of Exclusive Gateways into CCNs

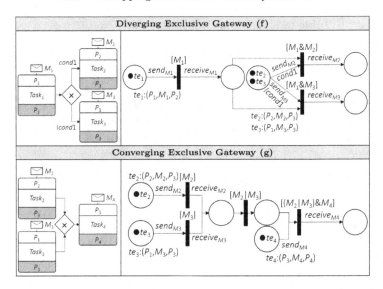

Converging Exclusive Gateway (g) – it merges alternative flows. The mapping of a Converging Exclusive Gateway is similar to the mapping in (**e**) with the difference that the transition with guard $[M_2|M_3]$ is the merging point of the alternative flows incoming to the gateway (see Table 2.(**g**)). The use of the logical OR operator indicates that only the message M_2 or M_3 is exchanged, i.e., only the token te_2 (that contains M_2) or te_3 (that contains M_3) reaches the place before the transition. Similarly, the transition with guard $[(M_2|M_3)\&M_4]$ also considers that either M_2 or M_3 is exchanged. Thus, only when the transition $[M_2|M_3]$ is enabled the token te_4 can be passed fulfilling the execution order of tasks as prescribed by the BPMN2 Choreography Diagrams.

4   Deadlock Analysis of CCN

This section describes the deadlock analysis conducted on the CCN in Fig. 4 generated from the mapping of the choreography in Fig. 1. A CCN model can be simulated, verified and analyzed using various tools (e.g., CPN Tools[3]) and approaches provided in the literature [11,13,14,19,21] that are dedicated to CPNs. Validation, verification, state space analysis, performance analysis, and deadlock analysis among others, are different analysis techniques that can be carried out on CCNs to check the soundness, and gain insights regarding different systems, including concurrent and distributed ones. In order to detect deadlocks, our approach takes as input the CCN generated out of the BPMN2 Choreography Diagrams and generates, via projection, a sub-CCN for each participant involved in the choreography. A sub-CCN describes the interaction protocol of a single participant. It is a partial view of the global CCN since it only concerns the flows where the considered participant is involved.

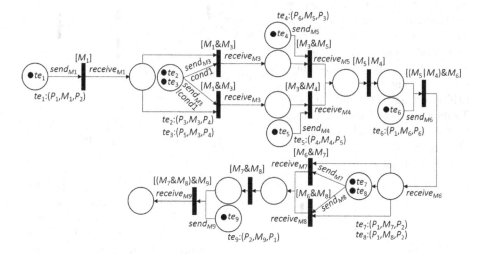

Fig. 4. CCN of the Choreography Diagram in Fig. 1

Table 4. Projection of participants P_3, P_4, P_5, and P_6

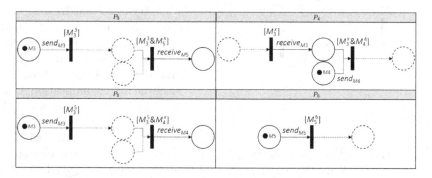

Then, the sub-CCNs are parallelly composed such that the resulting CCN models the synchronous communication between them. In the CCN in Fig. 4, a deadlock occurs in the alternative flows. For the sake of readability, Fig. 5 shows an excerpt of the CCN in Fig. 4, which depicts these alternative flows. Table 4 reports only the sub-CCNs of the participants P_3, P_4, P_5, and P_6. By referring to the CCN in Figure 5, P_3 sends the message M_3 (see token te_2) and then, receives the message M_5 afterwards (see token te_4). The projection of P_3 is shown in Table 4.P_3. The related sub-CCN is constructed in a way that P_3 sends M_3 to a participant that is different from P_3 and, hence, unknown to P_3.

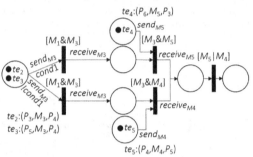

Then, P_3 receives M_5 from an unknown participant. For the sake of presentation, sending and receiving of messages by unknown participants are graphically represented with dotted arcs and places. A transition guard $[M_y^x]$ indicates that message y is sent by participant x. Still referring to the sub-CCN in Table 4.P_3, guard $[M_3^3]$ indicates that M_3 is sent by P_3, and guard $[M_5^x]$ indicates that M_5 is sent by an unknown participant x.

Fig. 5. A CCN excerpt of Fig. 4

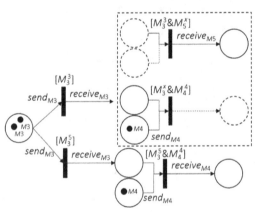

Fig. 6. CCN of the composed system

In order to model the synchronous communication between P_3, P_4, P_5, and P_6, the sub-CCNs given in Table 4 are composed in parallel as follows. Basically, the idea is to merge dotted elements with non-dotted ones of the sub-CCNs, while trying to match/unify message values of the guards then instantiating the unknown participants with all the possible known participants established after the match/unification. Concerning the projections of P_3, P_4, and P_5, the participant P_4 is expected to receive M_3, which is sent by other participants (see guard $[M_3^x]$ and the related dotted elements). Instead, P_3 and P_5 are the participants that send M_3, which is received by other participants (see guards $[M_3^3]$ and $[M_3^5]$, and the related dotted elements). By composing the projections of P_3, P_4, and P_5, the resulting net models the sending of M_3 by both P_3 and P_5. Therefore, as shown in Fig. 6 the place holding the two M_3 tokens creates two alternative flows as prescribed by the choreography. One flow occurs from the composition of P_4 with P_3 (see guards $[M_3^3]$), while the second flow occurs from the composition of P_4 with P_5 (see guards $[M_3^5]$). The sub-CCNs of P_4 and P_5 can be fully composed, while the composition of P_4 and P_3 cannot be fulfilled since the guard $[M_3^3 \& M_5^x]$ of P_3 does not match with the guard $[M_3^x \& M_4^4]$ of P_4. This means that the CCN goes in deadlock due to the synchronous communication between the participants P_3 and P_4. In fact, P_4 sends the message M_4, whereas P_3 is expecting to receive M_5. It is noteworthy that, the participant that sends M_5 is P_6 (see Table 4.P_6), but this participant cannot be composed with P_3 since the guards do not match. As it is clear from the composition, deadlocks might occur in the choreographed system due to the synchronous communication among the participants, which is not evident in Fig. 1.

5 Related Work

There exists various approaches, related to ours, that transform different kinds of choreography notations into more formal specifications. In [11], the authors propose an approach to transform BPMN models into CPN models that support hierarchical verification. They aim to address the state space explosion problem caused by large-scale BPMN models. The proposed approach is to partition and transform the BPMN models into CPN sub-nets and provide an algorithm of state space construction, which is implemented as a BPMN verification framework. The BPMN partitioning technique can be adopted in our work for dealing with large-scale BPMN2 choreography models. Moreover, in our work, the interpretations of the BPMN interaction semantics are complementary to the ones considered in [11]. However, our approach adds explicit treatment to the BPMN2 Choreography Diagrams by mapping the choreography constructs into CCN models. Our approach aims to perform different analysis techniques on BPMN2 Choreography Diagrams. Specifically, concerning deadlock analysis, our approach leverages the concept of projection from the work done in [8,9].

In [13], the authors propose an approach to model web service choreographies and service orchestrations with colored Petri nets. Differently from our approach, the flows of messages exchanged by involved participants in the composition are defined by using the Web Service Choreography Interface (WSCI). They distinguish between different types of flow structure in the CPNs including sequence, alternative and parallel flows to manage different type of message flows. Our mapping, as well, considers these flows as specified by the interaction semantics of BPMN2 choreography constructs. Moreover, the approach in [13] generates a Message Sequence Chart (MSC) out of CPN models in order to check and validate whether the model of the composed system corresponds to the logic structure and the exchanged messages as prescribed by WSCI.

In [14], the authors propose a CPN-based approach for service composition, and "similar" to our work, they extend the CPN model. The authors define a model called Colored PetriNet for Service Composition (CPSC) to represent the behavioral aspects of the conceptual constructs of service interfaces and different composition aspects of the constituent services. Specifically, the CPSC provides an efficient way for service composition and validation, and enables scalability, reusability of services to facilitate frequent changes in user requirements. Moreover, simulation and analysis of CPSC models are carried out using CPN Tools.

In [10], the authors propose a formal approach for directly checking the conformance of BPMN2 collaborations with respect to BPMN2 choreography models without using any intermediate languages. The authors provide a formal operational semantics for modeling collaborations and choreographies for checking the conformance between them. They develop the C^4 Supporting Tool, which takes as input both BPMN Collaboration and Choreography Diagrams, and generates the corresponding Labelled Transition System (LTS) for both diagrams. Out of LTSs, a Bisimulation-Based and Trace-Based Conformance are performed. Specifically, the Trace-Based Conformance relation guarantees that the collaboration is able to produce the same sequences of messages of the choreography, and vice versa, without controlling the presence of deadlock states and distinguishing different decision points and non-determinism forms.

Most of the previous approaches consider as input choreographies specified by using different notations and formalisms. Only a few use BPMN2 Choreography Diagrams, notably in [10,11]. Depending on their purposes, these approaches transform the choreography into different (formal) representations such as Petri Net, and state machines. However, these approaches are based on diverse interpretations of the choreography interaction semantics and consider different subsets of choreography constructs.

6   Conclusions and Future Work

This paper presents a first attempt to map BPMN2 Choreography Diagrams into Colored Choreography Nets (CCNs). The latter is a CPN for enabling simulation and analysis of service choreographies. BPMN2 lacks formal semantics which makes it harder to design, verify and analyze service choreographies. While, the expressiveness of the CCN metamodel allows us to fully automate the approach and to transform complex choreography specifications into rigorous descriptions to provide insights regarding choreographies that are not evident from a BPMN2 Choreography Diagram. Specifically, this paper proposes an approach to detect deadlocks in service choreography-based distributed systems. As future work, we plan to develop an automatic BPMN2-to-CCN transformation in order to provide automatic support for deadlock analysis. Also, we plan to extend the proposed mapping to include the rest of the BPMN2 choreography constructs.

Acknowledgments. This work was supported by the following projects: (i) INCIPICT (INnovating CIty Planning through Information and Communication Technologies) – Italian MEF, cipe resolution n. 135/2012, (ii) GAUSS (Governing Adaptive and Unplanned Systems of Systems) – Italian MIUR, PRIN 2015 program, contract n. 2015KWREMX, and (iii) ConnectPA (Connect Public Administration) – Italian POR FESR Abruzzo 2014–2020 program, CAR n. 2617 - COR n. 538508.

References

1. Autili, M., Di Ruscio, D., Di Salle, A., Perucci, A.: CHOReOSynt: enforcing chore-ography realizability in the future internet. In: Proceedings of the 22nd International Symposium on Foundations of Software Engineering, pp. 723–726 (2014)
2. Autili, M., Inverardi, P., Tivoli, M.: Automated synthesis of service choreographies. IEEE Softw. **32**(1), 50–57 (2015)
3. Autili, M., Inverardi, P., Tivoli, M.: Choreography realizability enforcement through the automatic synthesis of distributed coordination delegates. Sci. Comput. Program. **160**, 3–29 (2018)
4. Autili, M., Di Ruscio, D., Di Salle, A., Inverardi, P., Tivoli, M.: A model-based synthesis process for choreography realizability enforcement. In: Proceedings of the 16th FASE, pp. 37–52 (2013)
5. Autili, M., Di Salle, A., Perucci, A., Tivoli, M.: On the automated synthesis of enterprise integration patterns to adapt choreography-based distributed systems. In: Proceedings of the 14th International Workshop on Foundations of Coordination Languages and Self-Adaptive Systems, pp. 33–47 (2015)
6. Barker, A., Walton, C.D., Robertson, D.: Choreographing web services. IEEE TSC **2**(2), 152–166 (2009)
7. Basu, S., Bultan, T.: Choreography conformance via synchronizability. In: Proceedings of the 20th International Conference on World Wide Web, pp. 795–804 (2011)
8. Basu, S., Bultan, T.: Automated choreography repair. In: Stevens, P., Wąsowski, A. (eds.) FASE 2016. LNCS, vol. 9633, pp. 13–30. Springer, Heidelberg (2016). https://doi.org/10.1007/978-3-662-49665-7_2
9. Basu, S., Bultan, T., Ouederni, M.: Deciding choreography realizability. In: Proceedings of the 39th Symposium on Principles of Programming Languages, pp. 191–202. ACM (2012)
10. Corradini, F., Morichetta, A., Polini, A., Re, B., Tiezzi, F.: Collaboration vs. choreography conformance in BPMN 2.0: from theory to practice. In: 22nd IEEE International Enterprise Distributed Object Computing Conference, pp. 95–104, October 2018
11. Dechsupa, C., Vatanawood, W., Thongtak, A.: Hierarchical verification for the BPMN design model using state space analysis. IEEE Access **7**, 16795–16815 (2019)
12. Decker, G., Weske, M.: Local enforceability in interaction Petri nets. In: Alonso, G., Dadam, P., Rosemann, M. (eds.) BPM 2007. LNCS, vol. 4714, pp. 305–319. Springer, Heidelberg (2007). https://doi.org/10.1007/978-3-540-75183-0_22
13. Deng, X., Lin, Z., Cheng, W., Xiao, R., Fang, L., Li, L.: Modeling web service choreography and orchestration with colored Petri nets. In: Proceedings of the 8th International Conference on Software Engineering, Artificial Intelligence, Networking and Parallel/Distributed Computing, vol. 2, pp. 838–843 (2007)
14. Gaur, M., Mandal, A.K., Sarkar, A., Debnath, N.C.: Interface driven service composition: a highlevel colored PetriNet based approach. In: 2017 International Conference on Recent Advances in Signal Processing, Telecommunications Computing, pp. 59–64, January 2017
15. Güdemann, M., Poizat, P., Salaün, G., Ye, L.: VerChor: a framework for the design and verification of choreographies. IEEE TSC **9**(4), 647–660 (2016)
16. Jensen, K., Kristensen, L.M.: Coloured Petri Nets. Springer, Heidelberg (2009). https://doi.org/10.1007/b95112

17. Lemos, A.L., Daniel, F., Benatallah, B.: Web service composition: a survey of techniques and tools. ACM Comput. Surv. **48**(3), 33:1–33:41 (2016)
18. Poizat, P., Salaün, G.: Checking the realizability of BPMN 2.0 choreographies. In: Proceedings of the 27th Annual ACM Symposium on Applied Computing, pp. 1927–1934. ACM (2012)
19. Ratzer, A.V., et al.: CPN tools for editing, simulating, and analysing coloured Petri nets. In: van der Aalst, W.M.P., Best, E. (eds.) ICATPN 2003. LNCS, vol. 2679, pp. 450–462. Springer, Heidelberg (2003). https://doi.org/10.1007/3-540-44919-1_28
20. Salaün, G., Bultan, T., Roohi, N.: Realizability of choreographies using process algebra encodings. IEEE TSC **5**(3), 290–304 (2012)
21. Westergaard, M.: CPN tools 4: multi-formalism and extensibility. In: Colom, J.-M., Desel, J. (eds.) PETRI NETS 2013. LNCS, vol. 7927, pp. 400–409. Springer, Heidelberg (2013). https://doi.org/10.1007/978-3-642-38697-8_22

CIFMA 2019

Organization

CIFMA 2019 – Workshop Chairs

Antonio Cerone   Department of Computer Science, Nazarbayev University
Alan Dix   Computational Foundry, Swansea University

CIFMA 2019 – Program Committee

Oana Andrei	University of Glascow, UK
Luca Andrighetto	University of Genoa, Italy
Giovanna Broccia	Institute for Information Science and Technologies (CNT-ISTI), Italy
Ana Cavalcanti	University of York, UK
Antonio Cerone (Co-chair)	Nazarbayev University, Kazakhstan
Peter Chapman	Edinburgh Napier University, UK
Anke Dittmar	Rostock University, Germany
Alan Dix (Co-chair)	Swansea University, UK
Filippo Domaneschi	University of Genoa, Italy
Siamac Fazli	Nazarbayev University, Kazakhstan
Andrey Filchenko	Nazarbayev University, Kazakhstan
Roberta Gori	University of Pisa, Italy
Guido Governatori	Data61, CSIRO, Australia
Pierluigi Graziani	University of Urbino, Italy
Per Ola Kristensson	University of Cambridge, UK
Karl Lermer	Safety Critical Systems Research Lab, ZHAW, Switzerland
Kathy L. Malone	Nazarbayev University, Kazakhstan
Paolo Masci	US National Institute of Aerospace (NIA), USA
Mieke Massink	Institute of Information Science and Technologies (CNR-ISTI), Italy
Paolo Milazzo	University of Pisa, Italy
Marcello Passarelli	Institute for Educational Technologies (CNT-ITD), Italy
Ahti-Veikko Pietarinen	Nazarbayev University, Kazakhstan
Peter Ölveczky	University of Oslo, Norway
Ka I. Pun	Western Norway University of Applied Sciences, Norway
Anara Sandygulova	Nazarbayev University, Kazakhstan
Volker Stolz	Western Norway University of Applied Sciences, Norway
Jim Tørresen	University of Oslo, Norway

Interdisciplinary Aspects of Cognition

Antonio Cerone[1,4]([✉]), Siamac Fazli[1], Kathy L. Malone[2],
and Ahti-Veikko Pietarinen[3,4]

[1] Department of Computer Science, Nazarbayev University, Nur-Sultan, Kazakhstan
{antonio.cerone,siamac.fazli}
[2] Graduate School of Education, Nazarbayev University, Nur-Sultan, Kazakhstan
kathy.malone@nu.edu.kz
[3] Department of History, Philosophy and Religious Studies, Nazarbayev University,
Nur-Sultan, Kazakhstan
ahtiveikko.pietarinen@nu.edu.kz
[4] Intelligence, Robotics and Cognition Cluster, Nazarbayev University,
Nur-Sultan, Kazakhstan

Abstract. This position paper analyses the multidisciplinarity of cognitive research and its challenges from three perspective: the *foundations* of cognitive science, which draw from logic and neuroscience and their interconnections in studying human logic; *computation* as a means to identify mathematical patterns in human cognition, represent them symbolically and use such representations in computer emulations of human cognitive activities and possibly verify properties of such activities; *education*, devising and implementing learning models that exploit as well as address human cognition.

Keywords: Cognitive science · Logic · Human-computer interaction · Neuroscience · Cognitive learning · Formal methods

1 Introduction

The online Oxford Dictionary [43] defines cognition as "The mental action or process of acquiring knowledge and understanding through thought, experience, and the senses." This is the definition of the *mass* or *uncountable* noun, which denotes the abstract concept. There is also a countable meaning of the word cognition, which the Oxford Dictionary defines as "A perception, sensation, idea, or intuition resulting from the process of cognition". The English word "cognition" comes from the Latin verb "cognoscere", which means "to get to know". The English mass noun accurately describes how the action expressed by the Latin verb takes effect in the human mind in the form of a process. The English count noun refers to all possible entities that are the result of such a process. The wide range of these possible cognition outcomes, which may belong to the external world, experienced through the human capabilities (e.g. perception, sensation), but may also originate within the mind itself (e.g. idea, intuition), makes cognition an intrinsically interdisciplinary discipline of study.

J. Camara and M. Steffen (Eds.): SEFM 2019 Workshops, LNCS 12226, pp. 103–118, 2020.
https://doi.org/10.1007/978-3-030-57506-9_9

Although cognitive science is quite a recent discipline of study, nevertheless the deep interest in understanding and explaining cognition goes back to the origin of western philosophy, with Plato focussing on the ideas and Aristotle on the experiences. Plato's distinction between perfect *ideas*, or *forms*, and their imperfect copies in the experienceable world evolved through the centuries and found a turning point in Descartes' mind-body dualism. This turning point can be seen as the origin of a new discipline, which had to wait for over two centuries to find a name, psychology, and even more to have a recognition as a science. It is, in fact, the double intent to study both mind and behaviour, that made it difficult for psychology to acquire its own identity as a science. And when this started to happen, around the end of the 19th century and the beginning of the 20th century, psychology was split into two main schools, *structuralism*, whose object of study was the human mind, observed through introspection, and *functionalism*, which later evolved to *behaviourism*, whose object of study was the observed human behaviour. This opposition went on for several decades until in the mid 20th century. The building of the first computers and the development of its theoretical bases in terms of logic and computability theories offered an alternative way of looking at cognition, namely as a mental process similar to a computer process. This is the *computer analogy* or *computer metaphor*, in which the human mind is compared to a computer with processing unit, input and output "devices" and different kinds of memories for short-term and long-term storage. This way of understanding the human mind went beyond scientific circles and, with popular publications of eclectic scientists like Noam Chomsky and Douglas R. Hofstadter, also captivated ordinary people. Hofstadter's 800-page bestseller [25] shows how cognition is related to mathematics, logic, computer science, biology and art, specifically Escher's figurative art and Bach's music. Interestingly, Hofstadter manages to do this without even using the word 'cognition'.

Furthermore, the relation between cognition and computer science actually goes both ways. Not only can cognition be modelled in a computer-science fashion but is also largely affected by the way computer science has spread throughout the human living environment. The increasing complexity of this environment is no longer restricted to its natural components and the humans populating it, but is permeated by the ubiquitous presence of technology, which includes physical systems, computational systems, virtual worlds and robots. Such an extended human environment has modified the way humans live, work, interact with each other and learn.

Although the study of cognition split from philosophy almost two centuries ago, there are philosophical foundations of cognition which are still actual nowadays. In Sect. 2 we start from such philosophical foundations and we introduce a fundamental dilemma, which is also a first rule underlying human reasoning and logic. Then we explore some foundational challenges relating human logic and neuroscience and we illustrate future research applications. In Sect. 3, we move from the notions of symbolic manipulation and recursion and their use in mathematical proofs as the basis for modelling cognitions to an overview of cognitive architectures and their application. Then we discuss how to enrich cognitive architectures with findings from research in human logic and enable them to perform formal verification in order to tackle the most recent challenges encountered in human-computer interaction (HCI). In Sect. 4 we show how new learning environments, inspired by cognitive science, improve knowledge development and produce cognitive skills in students fostering their transition to adulthood and their involvement in lifelong learning. Finally, in Sect. 5 we draw some conclusions on the interrelation among the considered perspectives.

2 Foundations: From Logic to Neuroscience

Cognition is both a theoretical and natural phenomenon. We humans have evolved as the only species in the observable universe known to be capable of reasoning at its highest levels: we make abstractions, place thoughts as subjects of other thoughts, erect in our own minds a higher-order theory of other minds, and have evolved to communicate with the most expressive of human innovations: natural language. As the result we are able, at least in principle, to constantly improve our own mental instruments of thought, repair reasoning when it is ill, and elevate levels of critical and innovative thinking to new, unprecedented heights.

Yet the enormous complexity of the human brain and the mind gives rise to a fundamental dilemma. We fail to be sufficiently cautious when the task at hand is not to fool those who are the easiest ones to be fooled: ourselves. This fact—that we should not take it for granted that we are proficient enough when exercising our own critical faculties—is *the First Rule of Reason*. It is also the first rule of logic in human mind and cognition to be expected to be able to re-invent self-controlled thoughts and to implement long-lasting solutions.

What does the future of intelligent cognition look like in the world? Abject failures of this rule are evident in today's world: we meet irrational and inconsistent behavior that discounts the future; biases that have led to collective erosion of reason such as in-group favouritism, out-group prejudice, deindividuation and group narratives that only advance causes no different from self-serving attitudes; overconfidence boosted by ignorance, and widespread resistance to radical solutions when they clash with uncriticised appeals to the Precautionary Principle. Such feats are trumped only by the abundance of Type I errors we make when our apophenic neural relics kick in. Acts that harm others simply because of the possession of different belief systems are just some examples of dire consequences of uncriticised reasoning among many.

Various and well-documented logical, behavioural, economic, sociological, philosophical, psychological and cognitive theories can be adduced to explain extreme wrongdoings of human cognition and reason. These include *game theory*, *social dilemmas*, incomplete *evolutionary developments* such as the work-in-progress status of the evolution of our mammalian neuroendocrinological system, *inter-group conflict theories*, *dual-process theories of cognition*, and the intrinsically confusing mechanisms that *natural language* has created, churning *paradoxes* out of its system of propositional meaning and reference. Add the frailty and intractability of the consistency-maintenance of our belief systems and a living time-nuke may be ticking around the corner.

Section 2.1 illustrates how these issues can be studied logically. Section 2.2 briefly highlights how technology and techniques used in neuroscience can support and complement the such logic studies.

2.1   Logics for Cognition

What is needed are future-oriented logical and formal representations and models appropriate for the study of general intelligence and cognition. This has to be done by resetting the scope of logic and reasoning and to have it incorporate the full spectrum not only of the integrated human, machine and algorithmic *deductive* reasoning, but also the integrated *inductive* and *abductive* modes of inference modelling intelligent interactive systems [14,18,60]. But here is where the future looks promising: in the experimental world of cognitive neuroscience, one might expect to find much new and interesting neural and behavioural correlates to those expanded and interconnected logical modes and modalities.

The aims and challenges in the future studies of logic in cognition are thus three-fold:

- *Develop new forms of logic as the basis of cognitive and substrate-independent studies of intelligent interaction.* One needs an integrated logical, cognitive, algorithmic and philosophical perspective to understand human reasoning, (ir)rational action and generalized computational thought. New notational innovations, such as diagrams and icons, have to occur in information production and in rational acts of signification, independently of systems of linguistic meaning and reference. Such innovations are likely to impact how we perceive both the scope and the formal and mathematical structures of logic in ways that apply to cognitive theories of reasoning and mind.
- *Achieve new theoretical insights to human reasoning and decision-making.* Game-theoretical studies of behaviour and reasoning are common, but need a sea change: human strategic reasoning is after all at bottom an abductive, not a deductive, undertaking. Players deliberate on possible future histories and take positions that according to standard common belief of rationality approaches will never actually be reached as 'the surprising facts'. Prompted to reason to antedating actions under which such positions would be rendered comprehensible, less surprising, or utterly facile and natural, the change in view to abductive reasoning means to imaginatively look for where those perturbations, such as trembles or quantal responses, could take place. The conclusion is a conjecture about such perturbations [47].
- *Study experimental validations of the above.* Different forms of reasoning, pragmatic and naturalized logics may be exposed through the advice of neurocognitive studies. In particular, one could predict that various novel brain measurement methods such as fNIRS (functional near-infrared spectroscopy) produce data providing important insights into issues such as

- the performance of linear vs. non-linear (iconic, diagrammatic and visual) reasoning tasks;
- optimal logical representation tasks in different areas of pre-frontal cortex;
- how inventions of new solutions come about (abduction and anticipation);
- verifications of cognitive economy of reasoning;
- how particular formal systems (such as negation-free conditional logic [6]) could explain a host of cognitive biases without resorting to dual-process theories.

Three observations can be made from these desiderata:

1. The advent of modern logic has made the study of reasoning and higher executive tasks a remarkably *platform-independent* endeavor not limited to traditional theories of rational behavior.
2. A key benefit of the application of logic in cognitive science is that we can now study the *non-deductive* and *imagistic* sides of such reasoning better than before [2, 3, 12, 28, 36, 46], including modes of reasoning encountered in automatized decision-making systems, to reset the bounds of logic. This is not to hasten to deny that all good reasoning is justified, at bottom, by deductive patterns of inference.
3. *New experimental analyses* promise to reveal a cortical differentiation between the three major reasoning modes (deduction, induction and abduction). Measurements by fNIRS can reveal biological differences between these three modalities, in which case differences in solving various reasoning tasks have neural correlates in the prefrontal cortex. A hypothesis yet to be tested is that *frontal lobes are most active in deduction, occipital lobes in abduction, and there is increased activation in parietal lobes in induction.* Also, one can study symbolic vs. iconic representations of logical tasks (such as graphical logics) and observe to what extent the latter excites increased activities in the right hemisphere and occipital lobes.

Future applications of research in logic and cognition are valuable not only in cognitive sciences but also in general artificial intelligence. For example, computations in various important hierarchies are non-monotonic, and are commonly used in logic, mathematics and their applications. Known examples are neural networks and expert systems, where information recovered during computations increases non-monotonically with time, as information previously obtained may later be defeated and strategies of computation need reflect those changes. In mathematical logic, such processes are known as "trial and error" processes. Interestingly, they are related to abduction in ways not yet fully understood.

The future harbours new notational and empirical distinctions concerning integrated human and artificial reasoning both at their theoretical and neurophysiological levels. This, if successful, will in turn result in improved methods that apply such distinctions to creation of artificial models of cognition and computational structures that reflect those distinction and could hence become inventive, ampliative and generalisable when confronted with various critical reasoning tasks independently of the particularities of the human, social, mathematical or machine contexts.

Future insights may also include why conspiracy 'theories' have become so widespread and what symptoms, factors and theoretical explanations, such as hyper-rationalisability, they correlate with, namely exactly where and why certain executive areas in the prefrontal cortex assume abnormal functions. Theoretical activities and findings in logic and cognition are thus expected to have translational and clinical impacts.

2.2   Brain-Computer Interfaces

A brain-computer interfaces (BCI) is a direct communication pathway between an enhanced or wired brain and an external device. Since the early prototypes in the 70's [57], the field of BCI has witnessed a rapid growth, and a large number of neuroimaging technologies have been employed, such as Electroencephalography (EEG) [5], Magnetoencephalography (MEG) [58], Electrocorticography (ECoG) [7], functional magnetic resonance imaging (fMRI) [34], near-infrared spectroscopy (NIRS) [56] as well as combinations thereof [15,16]. Early BCI systems were based on operand conditioning [4], where the subject had to adapt to the BCI in order to give meaningful commands. However, these types of systems required weeks of adaptation on the subject side. More recently, a machine learning approach has been adopted by the community in order to reduce setup times of real-time feedback sessions [5,17]. While BCIs have originally been proposed as a communication tool for patients with disabilities, such as paraplegia or locked-in syndrome [4], a whole range of other applications have been proposed, which use BCI decoding techniques such as gaming, biometrics [13], workload detection and driver fatigue [21].

The field of BCIs can play an important role for further advances in cognitive sciences, since a number of technologies that have been developed are applicable beyond this field of research. A recent BCI study that employed multi-modal neuroimaging for intention decoding found that EEG and NIRS can lead to higher decoding accuracy when combined and more importantly, that their information is complementary [16]. In another study, a machine learning approach of mental state decoding was applied to the Libet experiment [51]. Generally, BCI techniques are tools for decoding mental states and intentions in real time. Clearly, these mental states underlie higher order cognitive processes, which can be disseminated further by careful experimental design.

3   Computation: From Mathematics to Computer Science

Hofstadter's 800-page bestseller [25] aims to show how *self-reference*, which essentially corresponds to the mathematical notion of *recursion*, is the basis of *self-awareness*. Hofstadter considers the diagonal argument used by Kurt Gödel to prove his two incompleteness theorems: the use of a property that refers to itself to prove that (1) there is no axiomatic system capable to prove all properties of the arithmetic and (2) no consistent axiomatic system which includes Peano arithmetic can prove its own consistency.

Gödel's results may be seen as an evidence that there is no objective reality and that there are questions that cannot have an answer. Hofstadter writes in the preface to the 20th-anniversary edition of his book: 'Something very strange thus emerges from the Gödelian loop: the revelation of the causal power of meaning in a rule-bound but meaning-free universe. [...] When and only when such a loop arises in a brain or in any other substrate, is a *person*—a unique new "I"— brought into being.' This means that symbolic computation, especially through recursion, potentially allows meaning to emerge from the manipulation of meaningless symbols, up to the complexity of human reasoning. The fact that recursion is the fundamental mathematical tool in mechanising reasoning is not a surprise for a computer scientist. After all, programming languages used in artificial intelligence, either Lisp-like functional languages or Prolog-like declarative languages, heavily exploit recursion.

3.1   A Philosphical Digression

It is interesting to note that Gödel's results inspired, on the one hand, Penrose's claim that *human consciousness* is non-algorithmic, and thus is not capable of being modeled by a conventional Turing machine, which includes a digital computer [45] and, on the other hand, Hofstadter's identification of what emerges from Gödel's diagonalisation, i.e. from an algorithmic process, as self-awareness [25,26]. If we put the two things together, then it may be true that, as Penrose believes, human consciousness cannot be modelled algorithmically, but, following Hofstadter, self-awareness, i.e. the recognition of that consciousness and its limitations, emerges from a recursive algorithm. Although, this may appear as a paradox, in reality, Gödel's proving procedure uses self-reference, i.e. a recursive algorithm to understand the limitations of highly expressive formal systems. And this "understanding process" is nothing else than *cognition*.

We can then conclude this philosophical digression by stating that symbolic manipulation, i.e. algorithms, may potentially be used to model human cognition. However, a first important question is whether this potential power of symbolic manipulation together with the high performance of today's computers can effectively be used to emulate human cognition. Then, if this is possible, a second question is what would be the purpose and the real-life usage of a computational emulation of human cognition. We will look for answers to these questions in Sects. 3.2–3.3.

3.2   Cognitive Architectures

A cognitive architecture has to be intended as a comprehensive model of the human mind, with a computational power that supports the in silico replication of experiments carried out in cognitive psychology as well as some form of prediction and analysis. A cognitive architecture is based on and implements a theory of cognition, which conceptualises the structure of mind in terms of its processing and storage components and the way such components work together to produce human thinking and behaviour [1]. Cognitive architectures originated from the research carried out in artificial intelligence during the 1950s with the aim of creating computer programs that could solve a wide range of problems across several domains and adapt themselves to new contexts and new situations and, finally, in line with the Hofstadter's Gödelian loop, to reason about themselves.

A number of cognitive architectures have been proposed since the 1970s [33,50], following three approaches: *symbolic* (or *cognitivist*), such as Soar, which are based on a set of predefined general rules to manipulate symbols, *connectionist* (or *emergent*), such as DAC, which count on emergent properties of connected processing components (e.g. nodes of a neural network), and *hybrid*, such as CLARION, which combine the two previous approaches. However, there is no clear agreement on the categorisation of specific architecture in this taxonomy. For example, ACT-R [1] is often classified as symbolic but, in fact, explicitly self-identifies as hybrid.

Kotseruba and Tsotsos [33] note that most cognitive architectures have been developed for research purposes rather than for real-life usage. Nevertheless, they consider several major categories of application:

- *Psychological experiments* is the largest category comprising more than one third of the architectures and supports the replication of a large number of psychophysiological, fMRI and EEG experiments with the aim of demonstrating the capability of adequately modelling and possibly explaining psychological and physiological phenomena.
- *Robotics* includes nearly one quarter of the architectures and mostly involves relatively simple forms of behaviour, such as navigation, obstacle avoidance and object search and manipulation, but, in some instances, incorporates multiple skills to perform a complex behaviour.
- *Human performance modelling (HPM)* to perform a quantitative analysis of the human behaviour in carrying out specific tasks.
- *Human-robot interaction (HRI) and human-computer interaction (HCI)* to analyse the interaction process in which the human is assisted by a robot or machine.
- *Natural language processing (NLP)* to model various processing aspect from low-level auditory perception to high-level conversation, though the latter only in limited domains.
- *Categorisation and Clustering* comprises mostly connectionist architectures and aims at processing noisy sensory data.
- *Computer vision* comprises most of connectionist architectures and aim at solving computer vision problems.
- *Games and puzzles* to demonstrate reasoning and learning ability.
- *Virtual agents* to model human behaviour in a domain in which experiments might have lethal consequence such as military and counter-terrorism.

3.3   Human-Computer Interaction and Cognitive Errors

Human-computer interaction is the study, planning, and design of the interaction between humans (users) and computers. A system that involves such an interaction is called *interactive system*. Interactive systems may appear to work correctly and safely when analysed in isolation from the human environment in which they are supposed to work. In fact, the same cognitive skills that enable humans to perform complex tasks may also become the source of critical errors in the interaction with systems and devices designed as supports for such tasks [27].

These kinds of errors are called *cognitive errors*. Normally, cognitive errors occur when a mental process aiming at optimising the execution of a task causes instead the failure of the task itself. The existence of a cognitive cause in human errors started to be understood already at the beginning of the 20th century, when Mach stated that "knowledge and error flow from the same mental sources, only success can tell the one from the other" [37]. In fact, human errors in interacting with machines have started to be studied at the beginning of the 20th century. However, we had to wait until the 1990's to clearly understand that "correct performance and systematic errors are two sides of the same coin" [48].

The systematic analysis of human errors in interactive systems has its roots in Human Reliability Assessment (HRA) techniques [31], which mostly emerged in the 1980's. However, these first attempts in the safety assessment of interactive systems were typically based on *ad hoc* techniques [35], with no efforts to incorporate a representation of human cognitive processes within the model of the interaction. With the increasing use of computers in safety-critical domains, such as avionics, aerospace, transportation and medicine, during the second half of the 20th century, the increased complexity of overall systems consisting of both computer and human components made it difficult to predict the range of possible human errors that could be observed (*phenotype errors*) and even more difficult to relate them to their cognitive causes (*genotype errors*).

3.4 Using Formal Methods in Human-Computer Interaction

In the critical contexts considered in Sect. 3.3 it is thus essential to verify the desired properties of an interactive system using a model that not only includes a user-centered description of the task, but also incorporates a representation of human cognitive processes within the task execution. However, although cognitive architectures can mimic many aspects of human cognitive behaviour and learning, including some aspects of human interaction with machines, they could never be really incorporated in the system and software verification process.

In contrast, the important role played by formal methods in the modelling and verification of computer systems in general, and of safety and security systems in particular, cannot be questioned. In fact, in safety-critical domains, it is explicitly dictated by standards that verification of critical modules must be formal. However, the use of formal methods in HCI has often been restricted to specific domains or applications, with the unfounded hope to be able to identify most human errors which may occur.

Nonetheless, the way the validity of both functional and non-functional properties is affected by the user behaviour is quite intricate. It may seem obvious for functional properties that an interactive system can deploy its functionalities only if it is highly usable. However, usability may actually be in conflict with functional correctness, especially in applications developed for learning or entertainment purpose. More in general, high usability may be in conflict with user experience, whereby the user expects some challenges in order to test personal skills and knowledge, enjoy the interaction and avoid boredom.

Usability is also strictly related to critical non-functional properties such as safety [27] and security [11]. Moreover, safety and security are two critical context in which human error may lead to catastrophic consequences, in term of loss of properties, injuries and even loss of life.

The relationship between usability and critical non-functional properties is actually two ways. On one side improving usability increases safety and/or security. On the other side introducing mechanisms to increase safety and/or security may reduce usability and, as a result, may lead to an unexpected global decrease in safety [27] and/or security [11]. Although in an ideal world human errors may be avoided through a rigorous user-centred design, in the real world humans have to frequently deal with inappropriate operating environments [9,27], constraining social contexts [11,27] and cultural differences [23], thus building up experiences that may then produce expectation failures and result adverse in the interaction with "correctly" designed systems [9]. Moreover, the individual analysis of different aspects of cognition, such as specific cognitive errors [30], patterns of behaviour [9], specific cognitive processes such as automatism and attention [8,53] and social interaction [11] fails to capture failures that may emerge from the combination of these aspects [27]. Furthermore, the context in which the interaction occurs and its effect on the human behaviour are often unpredictable; thus they cannot be modelled a priori. This complex situation determines a number of important research challenges in developing a methodology for the modelling and analysis of interactive systems:

1. non-functional properties that are in conflict with each other or with functional properties must be "cognitively weighted";
2. the correctness of a system depends also on the effect that previous environments or context have on human cognition and human learning;
3. system failures depend on multiple aspects of cognition, which need to be dealt with during analysis in a holistic way;
4. the intrinsic unpredictability of human behaviour requires the validation of any a priori model on real data;
5. the use of formal methods for system modelling and analysis requires high expertise in mathematics and logic, which is not common among interaction design and usability experts as well as psychologists and other social scientists.

We believe that these challenges can only be tackled through an interdisciplinary approach in which computer scientists cooperate with logicians, neuroscientists, cognitive scientists and social scientists. Cognitive architectures are already the result of interdisciplinary efforts, but additional efforts are needed to make them usable not just for emulating aspects of the human behaviour but also to prove properties of the human behaviour and its interaction with machines. That is, to reason about the same behaviour they model or, in the spirit of Hofstadter's "golden braid", to reason about themselves.

In this respect, the new forms of logic discussed in Sect. 2 would provide expressive, appropriate languages to describe properties that, on the one hand, have visual characteristic fostering human intuition and, on the other hand, are also apt to the symbolic manipulation needed for formal analysis. We claim that the realisation of cognitive architectures able to carry out formal analysis is a promising way to tackle the five challenges above [10].

4 Education: Cognitive Learning

The field of cognitive science has greatly enhanced our understanding of many areas of human thought processing including but not limited to memory, intelligence, brain research, problem solving, expert-novice continuum, information processing and pattern recognition. This in turn has greatly affected education and its practices. Cognitive learning (i.e., cognitive education) could be defined as an educational approach that has its basis in cognitive science research and is focused on the teaching and learning of the cognitive processes and skills connected to reasoning [22,54]. Thus, the subsequent instruction engages students in learning and helps them to make connections between new and older concepts in order to make learning more meaningful.

In the previous sections we have already very much emphasised the multidisciplinary nature of cognitive science and its subdisciplines. The field of cognitive learning is no exception. It is multidisciplinary and draws from the findings in a number of fields (e.g., human computer interaction, cognitive linguistics, neuroscience and cognitive psychology) in order to design learning environments that produce the most effective learning possible so that learning occurs not only more effectively but in a deeper fashion. These cognitive processes or skills are mechanisms used by everyone to navigate their everyday lives. Which means that these redesigned learning environments will allow for not only increases in understanding in specific fields but also allow for the production of lifelong learners and thinkers in all areas of life. While a traditional learning environment is teacher directed and centered on knowledge transmission, memorisation, based in facts and usually competitive in nature, a cognitive approach is student centered and focused on knowledge construction, development of reasoning skills, collaborative and practical in nature.

4.1 Learning Environments for Multiple Disciplines

The findings from these multiple fields have led to numerous new, effective learning environments. Drawing from HCI, cognitive tutors have been shown to be highly effective in mathematical classes [49]. Cognitive tutors make use of findings drawn from interactions that include just in time scaffolding to assist students as they construct their knowledge of arithmetic. Other approaches have been developed that have been successfully used in multiple disciplines to teach reasoning skills such as problem-based learning [59] and project-based learning [32]. Project-based learning has been shown to be highly effective and makes use of student-led projects. These projects are tasks that are highly challenging, which allows students to engage in activities such as problem solving and decision making while allowing students to work independently for extended periods of time [55]. Tan and Chapman [55] found that this learning method encouraged students to learn to work collaboratively while gaining cognitive skills in problem solving.

4.2 Modelling in Science—A Cognitive Learning Environment

One learning environment that has been utilised in the field of science education and has its base in cognitive science is the use of models in science classrooms [24,44]. These methods make use of the work done by cognitive psychologists to discover the cognitive activities and tools that practicing scientists make use of on a daily basis. Giere [20] postulated that the tools used by scientists to make sense of the world cannot be much different from those used by people in everyday life. Nersessian [42] studied historical and contemporary scientists to determine that the construction and use of science models was at the center of scientific thought.

Mental models are constructions in each individual brain which they can encode into multiple representations to share with others thus producing what Hestenes calls a conceptual model [24]. These conceptual models consist of multiple reprehensions that can take many forms such as that of diagrams, algebraic equations or graphical depictions of reality. The conceptual models can then become shared within a group of individuals to make predictions and refinements in thinking. The use of mental models for meaning making is also quite well known in cognitive linguistics [19]. Modelling in science is basically model-based reasoning. It is the production of models from empirical data and the use of these models to produce predictions whose failure leads to refinements of the original model. Thus, it is an iterative cycle [52]. It has been shown to be highly effective at producing conceptual gains in physics [29] and biology [40] as well as gains in student understanding of models [61].

The problem solving of students has been shown to become more expert like and allow students the ability to undertake productive error analysis [38]. In addition, in some fields it is difficult to produce empirical data within the context of classrooms simply because there is not enough time. In these cases, computer modeling has been used to produce simulations that help students 'collect' data on which to base their initial models [39,41]. These simulations then allow for further analysis of the strategies used by students by cognitive psychologists. Finally, modelling in science has been shown to increase student fascination with science over that of traditionally taught students [41].

In conclusion, cognitive learning in the educational field has produced gains in knowledge development as well as producing students with the cognitive skills to become effective reasoning adults no matter what path they take in life.

5   Conclusion

We have considered cognitive research and its challenges from three perspectives: *foundations, computation* and *education*. Within each of these perspectives. We have identified important relations and complementarity among different disciplines.

Foundations of cognition can be in terms of either logic description of high-level reasoning modalities or low-level neurological signals. We have proposed the use of new experimental analyses to map reasoning modes to areas of the prefrontal cortex. From a computational perspective, cognitive architectures can be enriched with formal analysis mechanisms to carry out the verification of the overall interactive system. Furthermore, as a transversal relation across foundations and computation, symbolic and visual aspects of new logics for human cognition may be exploited to enable formal analysis and facilitate user understanding, respectively.

Finally education is a perspective in which research in cognition can be applied to any discipline by defining the appropriate learning environment.

Acknowledgments. The authors would like to thank the four anonymous reviewers whose comments and suggestions greatly contributed to improve the paper.

References

1. Anderson, J.R.: The Architecture of Cognition. Psychology Press (1983)
2. Bellucci, F., Chiffi, D., Pietarinen, A.-V.: Assertive graphs. J. Appl. Non Cl. Log. **28**(1), 72–91 (2017)
3. Bellucci, F., Pietarinen, A.-V.: Two dogmas of diagrammatic reasoning: a view from existential graphs. In: Hull, K., Atkins, R. (eds.) Peirce on Perception and Reasoning: From Icons to Logic, pp. 174–196. Routledge, Abingdon (2017)
4. Birbaumer, N., et al.: A spelling device for the paralysed. Nature **398**(6725), 297 (1999)
5. Blankertz, B., Dornhege, G., Krauledat, M., Müller, K.-R., Curio, G.: The non-invasive Berlin brain-computer interface: fast acquisition of effective performance in untrained subjects. NeuroImage **37**(2), 539–550 (2007)
6. Bobrova, A., Pietarinen, A.-V.: Logical guidance and the dual-process theories of reasoning. In: Shafiei, M., Pietarinen, A.-V. (eds.) Peirce and Husserl: Mutual Insights on Logic, Mathematics and Cognition. Springer, New York (2019)
7. Brunner, P., Ritaccio, A.L., Emrich, J.F., Bischof, H., Schalk, G.: Rapid communication with a "P300" matrix speller using electrocorticographic signals (ECoG). Front. Neurosci. **5**, 5 (2011)
8. Cerone, A.: Closure and attention activation in human automatic behaviour: a framework for the formal analysis of interactive systems. In: Proceedings of FMIS 2011. Electronic Communications of the EASST, vol. 45 (2011)
9. Cerone, A.: A cognitive framework based on rewriting logic for the analysis of interactive systems. In: De Nicola, R., Kühn, E. (eds.) SEFM 2016. LNCS, vol. 9763, pp. 287–303. Springer, Cham (2016). https://doi.org/10.1007/978-3-319-41591-8_20

10. Cerone, A.: Towards a cognitive architecture for the formal analysis of human behaviour and learning. In: Mazzara, M., Ober, I., Salaün, G. (eds.) STAF 2018. LNCS, vol. 11176, pp. 216–232. Springer, Cham (2018). https://doi.org/10.1007/978-3-030-04771-9_17

11. Cerone, A., Elbegbayan, N.:. Model-checking driven design of interactive systems. In: Proceedings of FMIS 2006. Electronic Notes in Theoretical Computer Science, vol. 183, pp. 3–20. Elevier (2007)

12. Champagne, M., Pietarinen, A.-V.: Images as arguments? Towards a clearer picture of the role of pictures in arguments. Argumentation (2019, in Press)

13. Chen, Y., et al.: A high-security EEG-based login system with RSVP stimuli and dry electrodes. IEEE Trans. Inf. Forensics Secur. 11(12), 2635–2647 (2016)

14. Chiffi, D., Pietarinen, A.-V.: Abductive inference within a pragmatic framework. Synthese (2018). https://doi.org/10.1007/s11229-018-1824-6

15. Fazli, S., Dähne, S., Samek, W., Bießmann, F., Müller, K.-R.: Learning from more than one data source: data fusion techniques for sensorimotor rhythm-based brain-computer interfaces. Proc. IEEE 103(6), 891–906 (2015)

16. Fazli, S., et al.: Enhanced performance by a hybrid NIRS-EEG brain computer interface. NeuroImage 59(1), 519–529 (2012)

17. Fazli, S., Popescu, F., Danóczy, M., Blankertz, B., Müller, K.-R., Grozea, C.: Subject-independent mental state classification in single trials. Neural Netw. 22(9), 1305–1312 (2009)

18. Gabbay, D., Woods, J.: The Reach of Abduction. A Practical Logic of Cognitive Systems, vol. 2. North-Holland, Amsterdam (2005)

19. Geeraerts, D., Kristiansen, G., Peirsman, Y. (eds.): Advances in Cognitive Sociolinguistics, vol. 45. Walter de Gruyter, Berlin (2010)

20. Giere, R.N.: Explaining Science: A Cognitive Approach. University of Chicago Press, Chicago (1988)

21. Haufe, S., Treder, M.S., Gugler, M.F., Sagebaum, M., Curio, G., Blankertz, B.: EEG potentials predict upcoming emergency brakings during simulated driving. J. Neural Eng. 8(5), 056001 (2011)

22. Haywood, H.C.: Thinking in, around, and about the curriculum: the role of cognitive education. Int. J. Disabil. Dev. Educ. 51, 231–252 (2004)

23. Heimgärtner, R.: Ultural differences in human computer interaction: results from two online surveys. In: Open Innovation. Proceedings of 10th International Symposium for Information Science, pp. 145–157 (2007)

24. Hestenes, D.: Modeling theory for math and science education. In: Lesh, R., Galbraith, P., Haines, C., Hurford, A. (eds.) Modeling Students' Mathematical Modeling Competencies, pp. 13–41. Springer, Boston (2010). https://doi.org/10.1007/978-1-4419-0561-1_3

25. Hofstadter, D.R.: Gödel, Escher, Bach: and Eternal Golden Braid, 20th-Annuversary edn. Penguin, London (2000)

26. Hofstadter, D.R.: I Am a Strange Loop. Basic Books, New York (2007)

27. Iacovides, I., Blandford, A., Cox, A., Back, J.: How external and internal resources influence user action: the case of infusion devices. Cogn. Technol. Work. 18(4), 793–805 (2016)

28. Issayeva, J., Pietarinen, A.-V.: The heterogenous and dynamic nature of mental images: an empirical study. Belgrade J. Philos. 31, 57–83 (2018)

29. Jackson, J., Dukerich, L., Hestenes, D.: Modeling instruction: an effective model for science education. Sci. Educ. 17, 10–17 (2008)

30. Johnson, C.: Reasoning about human error and system failure for accident analysis. In: Proceedings of INTERACT 1997, pp. 331–338. Chapman and Hall (1997)

31. Kirwan, B.: Human reliability assessment. In: Evaluation of Human Work, Chap. 28. Taylor and Francis (1990)
32. Kokotsaki, D., Menzies, V., Wiggins, A.: Project-based learning: a review of the literature. Improv. Sch. **19**, 267–277 (2016)
33. Kotseruba, I., Tsotsos, J.K.: 40 years of cognitive architectures: core cognitive abilities and practical applications. Artif. Intell. Rev. (2018). https://doi.org/10.1007/s10462-018-9646-y
34. Lee, J.H., Ryu, J., Jolesz, F.A., Cho, Z.H., Yoo, S.S.: Brain-machine interface via real-time fMRI: preliminary study on thought-controlled robotic arm. Neurosci. Lett. **450**, 1–6 (2009)
35. Leveson, N.G.: Safeware: System Safety and Computers. Addison-Wesley, Boston (1995)
36. Ma, M., Pietarinen, A.-V.: A weakening of alpha graphs: quasi-boolean algebras. In: Chapman, P., Stapleton, G., Moktefi, A., Perez-Kriz, S., Bellucci, F. (eds.) Diagrams 2018. LNCS (LNAI), vol. 10871, pp. 549–564. Springer, Cham (2018). https://doi.org/10.1007/978-3-319-91376-6_50
37. Mach, C.: Knowledge and Error. Reidel, London (1905). English translation, 1976
38. Malone, K.L.: Correlations among knowledge structures, force concept inventory, and problem-solving behaviors. Phys. Rev. Spec. Top. Phys. Educ. Res. **4**(2), 020107 (2008)
39. Malone, K.L., Schuchardt, A.: Improving students' performance through the use of simulations and modelling: the case of population growth. In: Lane, H., Zvacek, S., Uhomoibhi, J. (eds.) Proceedings of the 11th International Conference on Computer Supported Education, vol. 1, pp. 220–230. SCITEPRES, Setú bal (2019)
40. Malone, K.L., Schuchardt, A.M., Sabree, Z.: Models and modeling in evolution. In: Harms, U., Reiss, M.J. (eds.) Evolution Education Re-considered, pp. 207–226. Springer, Cham (2019). https://doi.org/10.1007/978-3-030-14698-6_12
41. Malone, K.L., Schunn, C.D., Schuchardt, A.M.: Improving conceptual understanding and representation skills through excel-based modeling. J. Sci. Educ. Technol. **27**, 30–44 (2018)
42. Nersessian, N.J.: The cognitive basis of model-based reasoning. In: The Cognitive Basis of Science, pp. 133–153. Cambridge University Press (2002)
43. Online Oxford Dictionary. https://www.lexico.com/en/definition/cognition
44. Passmore, C., Gouvea, J.S., Giere, R.: Models in science and in learning science: focusing scientific practice on sense-making. In: Matthews, M.R. (ed.) International Handbook of Research in History, Philosophy and Science Teaching, pp. 1171–1202. Springer, Dordrecht (2014). https://doi.org/10.1007/978-94-007-7654-8_36
45. Penrose, R.: The Emperor's New Mind. Oxford University Press, Oxford (1983)
46. Pietarinen, A.-V.: Peirce and the logic of image. Semiotica **192**, 251–261 (2011)
47. Pietarinen, A.-V.: Conjectures and abductive reasoning in games. J. Appl. Log. IfCoLog J. Log. Appl. **5**(5), 1121–1144 (2018)
48. Reason, J.: Human Error. Cambridge University Press, Cambridge (1990)
49. Ritter, S., Anderson, J.R., Koedinger, K.R., Corbett, A.: Cognitive tutor: applied research in mathematics education. Psychon. Bull. Rev. **14**, 249–255 (2007)
50. Samsonovich, A.V.: Towards a unified catalog of implemented cognitive architectures. In: Biologically Inspired Cognitive Architectures (BICA 2010), pp. 195–244. IOS Press (2010)
51. Schultze-Kraft, M., et al.: The point of no return in vetoing self-initiated movements. Proc. Natl. Acad. Sci. **113**(4), 1080–1085 (2016)

52. Stammen, A., Malone, K., Irving, K.: Effects of modeling instruction professional development on biology teachers' scientific reasoning skills. Educ. Sci. Spec. Issue Biol. Educ. (8) (2018). https://doi.org/10.3390/educsci8030119

53. Su, L., Bowman, H., Barnard, P., Wyble, B.: Process algebraic model of attentional capture and human electrophysiology in interactive systems. Form. Asp. Comput. **21**(6), 512–539 (2009)

54. Talkhabi, M., Nouri, A.: Foundations of cognitive education: issues and opportunities. Procedia Soc. Behav. Sci. **32**, 385–390 (2012)

55. Tan, J.C., Chapman, A.: Project-based Learning for Academically-able Students: Hwa Chong Institution in Singapore. Springer, Singapore (2016). https://doi.org/10.1007/978-94-6300-732-0

56. Tsubone, T., Muroga, T., Wada, Y.: Application to robot control using brain function measurement by near-infrared spectroscopy. In: International Conference of the IEEE Engineering in Medicine and Biology Society, 2007, pp. 5342–5345 (2007)

57. Vidal, J.J.: Toward direct brain-computer communication. Annu. Rev. Biophys. Bioeng. **2**(1), 157–180 (1973)

58. Waldert, S., et al.: Hand movement direction decoded from MEG and EEG. J. Neurosci. **28**, 1000–1008 (2008)

59. Walker, A.E., Leary, H., Hmelo-Silver, C.E., Ertmer, P.A. (eds.): Essential Readings in Problem-Based Learning. Purdue University Press, West Lafayette (2015)

60. Woods, J.: Reorienting the logic of abduction. In: Magnani, L., Bertolotti, T. (eds.) Springer Handbook of Model-Based Science. SH, pp. 137–150. Springer, Cham (2017). https://doi.org/10.1007/978-3-319-30526-4_6

61. Xiang, L., Passmore, C.: A framework for model-based inquiry through agent-based programming. J. Sci. Educ. Technol. **24**, 311–329 (2015)

A Trust Logic for the Varieties of Trust

Mirko Tagliaferri[ID] and Alessandro Aldini[(✉)][ID]

University of Urbino, 61029 Urbino, Italy
{mirko.tagliaferri,alessandro.aldini}@uniurb.it

Abstract. In his paper *Varieties of Trust*, Eric Uslaner presents a conceptual analysis of trust with the aim of capturing the multiple dimensions that can characterize various notions of trust. While Uslaner's analysis is theoretically very useful to better understand the phenomenon of trust, his account is rarely considered when formal conceptions of trust are built. This is often due to the fact that formal frameworks concentrate on specific aspects of phenomena rather than general features and, thus, there is little space for omni-comprehensive considerations about concepts. However, building formal languages that can describe trust generally are extremely important, since they can provide basic accounts employable as starting points for further investigations on trust. This paper addresses exactly this issue by providing a logical language expressive enough to describe all the varieties of trust derivable from Uslaner's conceptual analysis. Specifically, Uslaner's analysis is transformed into a conceptual map of trust, by strengthening his analysis with further reflections on the nature of trust. Then, a logical language for trust is introduced and it is shown how the validity classes of such language can characterize all the varieties of trust derivable from the conceptual map previously built.

Keywords: Computational trust · Trust logic · Conceptual analysis of trust

1 Introduction

The social and economic research on trust conducted over the last few decades have created an abundance of different theoretical notions of trust [8,23,26]. Each of those theoretical notions can be employed to model trusting behaviours in various contexts and for different purposes. However, the existence of various approaches with their specific technical languages and their subject-oriented goals produced an ever increasing number of different and often incompatible definitions for trust. This makes the task of providing a proper and omnicomprehensive definition of trust hardly achievable, if not straightforwardly impossible. Moreover, despite what might be expected, moving to formal evaluations of the notion of trust made the matter even worse; various and distinct formal notions of trust have been developed in the last few decades to cope with the ever increasing necessity of implementing soft-security mechanisms in digital

© Springer Nature Switzerland AG 2020
J. Camara and M. Steffen (Eds.): SEFM 2019 Workshops, LNCS 12226, pp. 119–136, 2020.
https://doi.org/10.1007/978-3-030-57506-9_10

environments [16]. As a final concern, little attention is paid to crossover analyses of trust between socio-economical studies, on the one side, and computer science on the other. The lack of those crossover analyses is explained by two phenomena that characterize the literature on trust in computer science. First, computer scientists, given the highly complex nature of trust, prefer to analyse and employ reputation systems rather than pure trust systems (often, and mistakenly, conflating the two), where reputation is a property possessed by a specific individual/object that determines how the individual/object is perceived by the whole community of which the individual/object is part of. On the other hand, trust is generally seen as an attitude of an individual towards another individual/object [17], thus a private and subjective phenomenon. Second, the few authors that deal directly with trust [15], build systems focused more on trust manipulation rather than trust computing, i.e., they build formal frameworks that can produce new trust values starting from previously computed trust values, but seldom provide tools to compute initial primitive trust values that can be fed into their models. Those phenomena lead to the fact that the various formal notions of trust employed in computer science have little resemblance to the ones that are typical of social or economical environments (either because reputation is modeled instead of trust or because the model doesn't provide any insight on how to generate trust in the first place). Thus, not only there seem to be a failure of both classical and formal analyses to provide unified accounts of trust, but there is also little affinity between the two typologies of analysis. This is highly problematic, since it is thought that formal notions of trust are useful in digital environments to the extent that they can produce benefits similar to the ones trust produces in ordinary society. It is thus necessary to recognize the importance of the socio-economical analyses of trust first and then employ those analyses to guide the evaluation of trust models employed in formal frameworks. This paper is an attempt to provide a partial solution to the problem of bridging socio-economical analyses of trust and formal ones. In order to achieve this goal the paper is structured as follows: in section two, Uslaner's analysis of trust is introduced and additional criteria employable to conceptualize trust are investigated. Those new criteria are taken from [25] and are assessed by looking at customary forms of trust that can be found in the philosophical literature on trust. Thanks to those criteria (Uslaner's and the added ones) a conceptual map for trust is built; in section three, a logical language for trust, dubbed Modal Logic for Trust (MLT), is introduced through the definition of its syntax and semantics. The language introduced in this paper is inspired by an already existing modal logic for trust presented in [28–30]. Differently from those previous versions, the language here presented: i) provides a slightly cleaner semantical structure; ii) eliminates some redundant functions; iii) introduces some theoretical clarifications on the functions employed to compute the trust values; iv) adds the definitions of the validity classes for the language. Finally, in section four, the validity classes for the language are discussed with reference to the conceptual map introduced in section two. Concluding remarks will follow.

2   The Conceptual Map of Trust

Navigating through the various definitions of trust given in the different disciplines can be a burdensome task. First of all, disciplines as diverse as sociology [1,5,8,20], economics [6,7,27,35], political science [10,11,19] and evolutionary biology [2,31,32] dedicated some of their attention to trust, obviously prioritizing their specific needs and using their typical examination techniques. This produced many theoretical definitions of trust which diverge on the technical language employed to express their definitions and the principal features that are highlighted about the phenomenon. This section is aimed at producing a conceptual map which can help the novice reader in his navigation of the diverse literatures on trust. The map (which can be seen in Fig. 1) is constructed around three dimensions which characterize trust and it is claimed that all definitions of trust (at least already existing ones) fall under a specific quadrant of the map. The conceptual idea of the map is taken from [25] which is a theoretical improvement of the ideas given by Uslaner in [34].

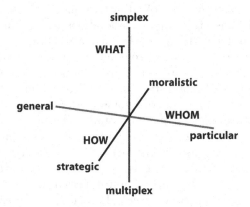

Fig. 1. Conceptual map of trust dimensions.

In his paper *Varieties of Trust* [34], Uslaner identifies two core dimensions which can characterize trust. To the dimensions he identifies, another will be added, to take into consideration also aspects of the situations in which trust arises. The first dimension characterizes the core nature of trust and distinguishes between *strategic* and *moralistic* notions of trust. The second dimension characterizes the nature of the trustees, distinguishing between trust directed towards individuals and trust directed towards institutions or larger groups of individuals. The third, and final dimension, characterizes the nature of the situation in which trust must be assessed. All the dimensions of the map will be discussed in order to provide a clear understanding of their role in possible definitions of trust. Specifically, the three dimensions regard *the nature of the actual trust relation; who is trusted by the trustor* and, finally, *what is the context in which to trust.*

The first dimension, indicated in [25] as the *how* dimension, characterizes the core nature of trust and distinguishes between trust definitions that are *strategic* and those that are *moralistic*. A *strategic* definition [5,10,11] of trust identifies the phenomenon of trusting as one depending on explicit knowledge and explicit computations about the interacting party's trustworthiness, intentions and capacities. On the other hand, a *moralistic* definition [21,33] of trust identifies the phenomenon of trusting as a by-product of an agent's moral and ethical upbringing and consequently it depends on his psychological predispositions as defined by social norms and the values of the agent's culture. Where strategic trust can be described by the motto: *Agent A trusts agent B to do X, because of Y*; moralistic trust is simply described by saying that: *agent A trusts agent B to do X*. This dimension of trust is absolutely important to discussions concerning the notion, insofar as strategic definitions of trust presuppose that, for agent A to trust agent B, repeated encounters between the agents are necessary and, moreover, agent A must posses the computational powers to compute trustworthiness values based on information acquired during those encounters. Even though plausible, those assumptions are suited only for small communities and apply to a small number of situations and thus, strategic trust can't account for *all* the transactions and collaborations that occur in ordinary life. Moralistic versions of trust are designed to overcome this downside of strategic trust. If trust is produced as a moral commandment (similar in spirit to Kant's *categorical imperative* [18]), then even complete strangers might initiate a trust relationship. In the case of moralistic trust, it is the culture of the trustor that determines whether or not he will trust someone else and past experiences with the trustee are neither required nor important. The fact that this dimension really captures the core ideas behind the nature of trust is supported by the fact that all major accounts of trust are instances of either the strategic view of trust or the moralistic view of trust. In particular, *risk-assessment views* [6,10,22] and *will-based views* [14] of trust are both instances of strategic trust as defined by Uslaner, while *participant stance views* [12] and *virtue-based accounts* [13] of trust are both instances of moralistic trust.

The second dimension, indicated in [25] as the *whom* dimension, distinguishes between trust definitions that are particular and those that are general. A *particular* definition of trust identifies the phenomenon of trusting as a one-to-one relation, where trust can only be placed on specific individuals. In particular, the individuals that are considered to be trust bearers are those on whom the trustor has a fair amount of information, such as, e.g., family members, friends or colleagues. On the other hand, a *general* definition of trust identifies the phenomenon of trusting as a one-to-many relation, where trust can be placed also on anonymous individuals or strangers and such that there is no specific task or context of evaluation. In such a case, it might be said that trust is considered as an omnicomprehensive attitude towards a specific group of individuals (often those attitudes are determined by stereotypical categories). This dimension has an obvious relation with the first one: moralistic trust seem to lend well to general trust, while strategic trust is strictly tied to particular trust. However, those links are not absolute, leaving open the possibility for strategic general trust and moralistic particular trust. The former case is typical of views in which trust is seen as a stereotype: specific information about a given group of agents, i.e., the stereotyped group under consideration, is taken into consideration to determine whether the group falls indeed under the category at the base of the stereotype; then, this information is used to compute a trust value on the whole group. The latter case identifies views for which agents are morally inclined to cooperate with (and therefore trust) close relatives and known others and base their decisions to trust only on those moral values and not on specific information about the person they must interact with. As it was the case for the *how* dimension, also in the case of the *whom* dimension it is possible to find support for the relevance of this dimension by looking at major accounts of trust. In particular, the trust literature is divided between accounts that treat trust as an interpersonal phenomenon (which are the dominant paradigms of trust) and what is labelled as "institutional trust", i.e., the trust that agents place on specific institutions. In the former case, there is an obvious relation to particular definitions of trust, while the latter represent obvious instances of general definitions of trust.

The third, and final, dimension, indicated in [25] as the *what* dimension, is not directly presented in Uslaner's paper, but seems to capture a distinctive feature of trust conceptions. According to such dimension, it is possible to distinguish between trust definitions that are simplex and those that are multiplex. A *simplex* definition of trust identifies the phenomenon of trusting as being highly context-specific, where trust is granted according to a very narrow and clearly identifiable task. On the other hand, a *multiplex* definition of trust identifies trust as an extended phenomenon, which might either take into consideration various contexts at the same time or consider no contexts at all. In the former case, trust is evaluated on a case-by-case basis and the same two agents might trust each other in specific contexts and refuse to do so in different situations. Given the variety of different scenarios that might happen in the real world, the assumption that trust is context-specific seem to be a suitable one for a good definition of trust. However, it is important to note that there are times in which an agent trusts others blindly or in different (and multiple) situations. For instance, a child trusts his parents blindly[1]. Moreover, even admitting that context-free multiplex phenomena of trust are impossible (independently from how much you trust someone, that someone might not be able to perform given actions, e.g., flying a plane, and thus he shall not be trusted in such contexts), it is still plausible that mild-versions of multiplex trust exist, where trust is granted with respect to a set of contexts sharing some core features, rather than a single one.

Given the three dimensions introduced, it is possible to allocate trust definitions into eight different categories (in Fig. 1 each quadrant represents a category). Each category corresponds to a given idea of what trust is. This said, not all of them will find an adequate corresponding phenomenon in the real world (e.g. strategic general multiplex trust), but, it is argued, most, if not all,

---

[1] Note that some authors might claim that the child isn't actually trusting the parents, since he has no choice other than relying on them.

definitions of trust that can be found in the literature can be redescribed through the conceptual map that is given here.

This conceptual map will help all further discussion on trust, by allowing the indication of a specific class which can be placed into correspondence with the formal evaluations that will be made in subsequent sections.

In the next section, the syntax and semantics of a logical language for trust will be introduced. This language will provide a proper formal framework to model all the distinct notions of trust identified in this section.

3   Modal Logic for Trust

The core idea behind the language is to describe the information possessed by an agent and then transform this knowledge into a trust value about a given proposition. In MLT, propositions substitute direct relationships between agents (or between an agent and an object). The reason is straightforward: a propositional language (rather than a predicative one) makes it easier to think about implementations of the language in computational environment, while, at the same time, retaining an expressivity which is sufficient to describe trust and its relationship to knowledge. The idea is that the relationship between the trustor and the trustee can be expressed through the use of a proposition, which is then assessed by the trustor for trust. Furthermore, while employing a predicative language might allow to express some subtleties related to trust, it also makes it infeasible to obtain positive results for decision-problems, which are, again, desirable results when building a language that is thought as a starting point for practical implementations.

Basically, the language is a modal language augmented with a trust operator, interpreted in a monotonic neighborhood semantics structure[2].

3.1   Syntax

In our language $\mathcal{L}(At)$ (for short $\mathcal{L}$) of logic formulas (which are ranged over by $\phi, \psi, \dots$), we start with a finite set At of atomic propositions representing basic pieces of information. Given $p \in At$ our language is defined by the following grammar, given in BNF form:

$$\phi := p \mid \neg\phi \mid \phi \wedge \phi \mid K(\phi) \mid T(\phi)$$

All other Boolean connectives are defined in the standard way and we allow for a dual operator for knowledge and for trust (expressing possible knowledge and possible trust).

Formula $K(\phi)$ should be intuitively read as "formula ϕ is known"; we will call such formulas *knowledge formulas*. Formula $T(\phi)$ should be intuitively read

---

[2] See [4,9] for a general introduction to modal logics and monotonic neighborhood structures. Moreover, see [29] for an approach that interprets the same language in a standard relational structure.

as "formula ϕ is trusted"; we will call such formulas *trust formulas*. The degree to which a formula can be trusted goes from 0, complete distrust, to 1, complete trust; the point of transition from distrust to trust will strictly depend on the semantic structure we will now introduce.

3.2   Semantics

The semantics we will provide in this paper is in truth theoretical form and depends on a structure that is a combination of an augmented neighborhood structure for the modal part [24] and an added component to assign weights to formulas for the trust part. The added component is novel in the literature about computational trust and forms the core of the novelties this paper introduces to formalize trust.

We will interpret the above presented language in the following structure:

Definition 1 (Contextual Trust Model). *A **contextual trust model** is a tuple* $M = (S, C, \pi, N, \mathcal{T}, \Theta)$, *where*

- S *is a finite set of possible states of the system* $s, s', \ldots$.
- C *is a finite set of primitive evaluation scenarios* $c, c', \ldots$.
- π *is a valuation function, assigning set of states to atomic propositions.*
- N *is an augmented neighborhood function.*
- $\mathcal{T} = \{\langle \omega_c, \mu_{c,\phi} \rangle \mid c \in C \text{ and } \phi \in \mathcal{L}\}$ *is a trust relevance structure.*
- $\Theta = \{\theta_c \mid c \in C\}$ *is a family of trustworthiness threshold functions.*

Intuitively, a possible state $s \in S$ represents a way in which the system can be specified; hence, two states differ from one another by what propositions hold in such states. It is assumed that states are *maximally consistent* descriptions of the system. They are maximal insofar as the truth value of each proposition is specified. They are consistent insofar as a proposition and its negation can't both be true in the same state.

Set C is a finite set of primitive scenarios. Intuitively, a scenario is a situation in which trust must be assessed. The main reason to include such a set in the semantical structure comes from the consideration that most conceptions of trust see the phenomenon as a context-dependent phenomenon [8,20] (other authors also use terms as, e.g., "scope", "purpose", "aim", and so on). Thus, in order to achieve a properly general formal system for trust, it is necessary to include in the system a component dealing with the (possible) contextuality of the phenomenon. For instance, someone might trust his mechanic when it comes to fixing cars, but might not trust him for financial advice. In the previous example, "fixing cars" and "giving financial advice" are to be considered two separate contexts of evaluation. Informally, contexts could be seen as labels assigned to states of the system, where each context is a different label that can be assigned to the same state. Thus, the whole evaluation space of formulas is equivalent to the cartesian product between the set of states S and the set of contexts C.

Function π is a valuation function that assigns to each proposition $p \in At$ a set of states, i.e., $\pi : At \rightarrow \wp(S)$; a state is included in the set if, and only if, the proposition holds in the given state.

Function N is an augmented neighborhood function that assigns to each state $s \in S$ a finite set of subsets of S, i.e., $N : S \rightarrow \wp(\wp(S))$; the set of subsets obtained by applying N is closed under superset, i.e., for each $X \subseteq S$ and each $s \in S$, if $X \in N(s)$ and $X \subseteq Y \subseteq S$, then $Y \in N(s)$. Moreover, N contains its core, i.e., $\cap N(s) \in N(s)$. Intuitively, function N assigns to each state the sets of states *corresponding to the known* propositions in such state[3]. The neighborhood function is employed to interpret the knowledge operators of the language. Note that using neighborhood functions knowledge is defined directly: thus, the informative content of a proposition is determined (in the specific case of this language by applying function π or, as it will be shown later, an extension of such a function), and the function N assigns to each state of the system a set containing all those contents corresponding to the known propositions. The closure under superset condition expresses the intuitive idea that when something is known, weakened pieces of information derived from the knowledge possessed are also known[4]. The closure under core, on the other hand, indicates that an agent is always aware of the conjunction of the information he possesses.

$\mathcal{T}$ is a trust relevance structure, where for each $\phi \in \mathcal{L}$ and each $c \in C$, there is an ordered couple $\langle \omega_c, \mu_{c,\phi} \rangle$. ω_c is a function that assigns to each formula $\phi \in \mathcal{L}$ a consistent[5] set of subsets of S, i.e., $\omega_c : \mathcal{L} \rightarrow (\wp(\wp(S)) - \emptyset)$ (the consistency condition expresses the informal idea that contradictions should never be considered relevant for trust formulas). This consistent set, which we call $\Omega_{c,\phi}$, contains the sets of states corresponding to the formulas relevant for trust in ϕ. $\mu_{c,\phi}$ is a trust weight function, assigning to elements in $\Omega_{c,\phi}$ rational numbers in the range $[0, 1]$ according to their relevance for trust in the formula, i.e. $\mu_{c,\phi} : \Omega_{c,\phi} \rightarrow [0,1] \in \mathbb{Q}$. 0 represents no trust relevance and 1 represents full trust relevance. It is assumed that the weights assigned are subadditive to 1, i.e., $\sum_{X \in \Omega_{c,\phi}} \mu_{c,\phi}(X) \leq 1$, guaranteeing that it is never possible to exceed full trust (i.e. the value 1). Intuitively, the functions $\mu_{c,\phi}$ assign to the trust relevant formulas a specific weight for trust, with respect to a given formula ϕ, which is evaluated for trust and a context of evaluation c. The notion of relevance employed here is an intuitive one: an information related to a formula is relevant for trust, if knowing such information would modify the trust assessment made towards that formula. Obviously, having no trust relevance means that whether or not the information is known, the trust assessment would be the same; on the

---

[3] To make the exposition simpler during the course of the paper, elements of $\wp(S)$ will be indicated with letters from the end of the alphabet capitalized and with eventual superscripts and subscripts, i.e., $X, X_2, Y, X', X_2', Y' \ldots$.

[4] For instance, if a proposition p is known at a state s, i.e., $\pi(p) \in N(s)$, then also $p \vee q$ is known at s, i.e., $\pi(p \vee q) \in N(s)$.

[5] $\mathcal{U}$ is **consistent**, if $\emptyset \notin \mathcal{U}$.

other hand, full trust relevance means that knowing the information is the only way it is possible to modify the trust assessment.

Finally, Θ is a trustworthiness threshold structure, where, for each context $c \in C$, θ_c assigns to each formula $\phi \in \mathcal{L}$ a rational number between 0 and 1^6, i.e. $\theta_c : \mathcal{L}(At) \rightarrow [0,1] \in \mathbb{Q}$. This rational number indicates the minimum threshold needed to trust the given formula.

Before providing the truth definition for a formula in a model, we must add some further functions; those functions will help us in defining the truth of knowledge and trust formulas.

First note that a neighborhood function N can induce a map m_N, which is a function that associates to each element $X \in \wp(S)$ another element $Y \in \wp(S)$, according to the neighborhood function N, i.e. given $N : S \rightarrow \wp(\wp(S))$, there is a map $m_N : \wp(S) \rightarrow \wp(S)$. The function m_N is defined formally as follows:

$$m_N(X) = \{s \mid X \in N(s)\} \tag{1}$$

Intuitively, m_N returns, for each set of states corresponding to a formula (i.e. the formulas informative content), a set of states such that a state is in the set if, and only if, the formula is known in the state. The function m_N will help in defining the truth of knowledge formulas.

A second and important derived element of the semantic structure is the family of functions $\Lambda = \{\tau_{c,\phi} \mid c \in C \text{ and } \phi \in \mathcal{L}\}$, which contains functions that assign ideal trust values to formulas in states of the system, and in a given context. Intuitively, a function $\tau_{c,\phi}$ ($\tau_{c,\phi} : S \rightarrow [0,1] \in \mathbb{Q}$) indicates how much trust an agent has in the formula ϕ (representing the parameter of $\mu_{c,\phi}$) in the given state and context denoting the argument of $\tau_{c,\phi}$, provided that the agent is aware, in such a state, of all the relevant basic information related to ϕ, i.e., the agent knows all the relevant propositions which are true in that state. Another way to put it is the following: if an agent knows exactly which one is the current state of the system (thus possessing all possible knowledge regarding the system), then $\tau_{c,\phi}$ will specify the amount of trust the agent has towards ϕ. Therefore, $\tau_{c,\phi}$ represents an ideal measurement of trust. Note that, even though ideal, this is a trust measure indicating how much an agent trusts the proposition ϕ in the given state and it still remains a subjective measurement.

Functions $\tau_{c,\phi}{}^7$ are defined as follows:

$$\tau_{c,\phi}(s) = \sum_{X \in \Omega_{c,\phi}:s\in X} \mu_{c,\phi}(X) \tag{2}$$

It is assumed that if in Eq. 2 there is no X such that $s \in X$ then $\tau_{c,\phi}(s) = 0$. Moreover, the subadditivity criterion on $\mu_{c,\phi}$ guarantees that $\tau_{c,\phi}$ itself never exceeds 1 (this is to be expected, since trust, even in an ideal setting might

---

[6] Real numbers could have been employed. However, it is believed that density is sufficient to capture the different grades of trust and continuity is not required. For this reason, the choice to use rational numbers is made.

[7] Again, one for each $\phi \in \mathcal{L}$.

never exceed the maximum value of 1, i.e., full trust). Note that it is possible that $\tau_{c,\phi}(s) = 0$ and $\tau_{c,\neg\phi}(s) < 1$, thus the functions do not complement each other. This is perfectly reasonable, given the fact that trust, especially in ideal settings, might not be closed under complementation. In fact, it is perfectly acceptable that an agent does not trust a given proposition at all and, at the same time, he does not fully trust the negation of such proposition.

Given the family of functions $\tau_{c,\phi}$, it is possible to define a trust value for each $X \in \wp(S)$. The functions performing such task will be defined as $\tau_{c,\phi}^{ext}$ and are formally specified as follows:

$$\tau_{c,\phi}^{ext}(X) = min_{s \in X}\{\tau_{c,\phi}(s)\} \tag{3}$$

Intuitively, the function $\tau_{c,\phi}^{ext}$ looks at all states in the set X under analysis and selects the worst-case scenario, i.e., that in which the trust value is the lowest. This choice models the behaviour of a cautious agent, who will only consider the information he possesses to make an evaluation on trust and will not, therefore, make any other assumption on the trustworthiness of the formula under analysis. However, other possibilities for the definition of $\tau_{c,\phi}^{ext}$ are possible, such as taking the maximum (which would model the behaviour of an optimistic agent) or the average value between all the $\tau_{c,\phi}(s)$ (which would model the behaviour of an agent which is neither cautious nor optimistic).

Specifically, such definition would be formalized as follows.

For the maximum (optimistic agent):

$$\tau_{c,\phi}^{ext}(X) = max_{s \in X}\{\tau_{c,\phi}(s)\} \tag{4}$$

For the average (neutral agent):

$$\tau_{c,\phi}^{ext}(X) = \frac{\sum_{s \in X}\{\tau_{c,\phi}(s)\}}{|X|} \tag{5}$$

Where $|X|$ stands for the cardinality of X.

The various $\tau_{c,\phi}^{ext}$ equations return the ideal trust value of the set under consideration given a specific attitude of the trusting agent. The equations just given identify the trust value of a formula when the states (worlds) compatible with an agent's knowledge are selected.

It is interesting to observe that if the formula is applied to a singleton set containing only a single state s (i.e., $X = \{s\}$), then the value of the function $\tau_{c,\phi}^{ext}(X)$ is equal to the value of $\tau_{c,\phi}(s)$. This proves that $\tau_{c,\phi}^{ext}$ is indeed a proper extension of $\tau_{c,\phi}$.

To improve the readability of the truth theoretical definition for the formulas, a definition of truth set is given for each formula of the language.

Definition 2 (Extension of the Valuation Function). *Given a contextual trust model $M = (S, C, \pi, N, \mathcal{T}, \Theta)$, then the truth set of a formula, denoted π_M^{ext} (M will be omitted when the model is clear in the discussion), is defined recursively as follows:*

- $\pi_M^{ext}(p) = \pi(p)$ *for all* $p \in At;$
- $\pi_M^{ext}(\neg\phi) = S - \pi_M^{ext}(\phi);$
- $\pi_M^{ext}(\phi \wedge \psi) = \pi_M^{ext}(\phi) \cap \pi_M^{ext}(\psi);$
- $\pi_M^{ext}(K(\phi)) = m_N(\pi_M^{ext}(\phi));$
- $\pi_M^{ext}(T(\phi)) = \{s \mid \tau_{c,\phi}^{ext}(\bigcap_{X \in N(s)} X) \geq \theta_c(\phi)\}.$

Two things that characterize the truth sets of trust formulas are: $\bigcap_{X \in N(s)} X$, which can also be indicated with $\bigcap N(s)$, is the core of $N(s)$ and indicates the minimal set of states which are compatible with all the knowledge of the agent; to compute the π^{ext} of $T(\phi)$, it must be checked whether in a given state the trust value of the core of N in such state is greater than or equal to the trustworthiness threshold for the formula.

Now that we introduced all the elements of our semantical structure, we can provide the truth definition of a formula ϕ at a contextual pointed model (M, s, c):

Definition 3. *Given a contextual trust model* $M = (S, C, \pi, N, T, \Theta)$, *a state* $s \in S$ *and a context* $c \in C$, *then a formula* ϕ *is satisfied at a contextual pointed model* (M, s, c) *if:*
$(M, s, c) \models p$ *iff* $s \in \pi(p), \forall p \in At;$
$(M, s, c) \models \phi$ *iff* $s \in \pi^{ext}(\phi).$

Given the above satisfiability conditions, it is possible to define some slightly more complicated satisfiability conditions. Those will help in defining the validity classes for MLT.

Definition 4. *Given a contextual trust model* $M = (S, C, \pi, N, T, \Theta)$, *a state* $s \in S$ *and a set of contexts* $A \subseteq C$, *then the following holds:*
$(M, s, A) \models \phi$ *iff* $\forall c \in A, (M, s, c) \models \phi.$

All the above definitions allow to identify four different validity concepts.

Definition 5. *Given a contextual trust model* $M = (S, C, \pi, N, T, \Theta)$, *a formula* ϕ *is context-valid with respect to a set of contexts* $A \subseteq C$ *if:*

$$\forall s \in S : (M, s, A) \models \phi \tag{6}$$

A formula ϕ *is state-valid with respect to a state* $s \in S$ *if:*

$$\forall c \in C : (M, s, c) \models \phi \tag{7}$$

A formula ϕ *is model-valid if:*

$$\forall s \in S \; \forall c \in C : (M, s, c) \models \phi \tag{8}$$

Finally, a formula ϕ *is valid* $(\models \phi)$ *if it is model-valid for every model* M.

Those validity concepts will be analysed, one at a time, in the next section.

3.3   Example

In this subsection, a partial example of how the language just introduced works will be given. The example will be short and won't show the true potential of the language, but can still play an important role as a facilitator for the understanding of all the components of the language.

Four atomic propositions will be employed[8]: p_1 = Mario has provided valid credentials. p_2 = Mario has a positive past history as a user. p_3 = Mario lives in a country where copyright infringments are severely punished. q = Mario won't break the terms and conditions of the website.

Two contexts of evaluation will be considered: c_1 = Material on the website will be shown to the user. c_2 = Material on the website will be made available for download.

It will be assumed that there are eight possible states of the system $S = \{s_1, s_2, s_3, s_4, s_5, s_6, s_7, s_8\}$. The π function is the following:

$$\pi(p_1) = \{s_1, s_2, s_3, s_4\};$$
$$\pi(p_2) = \{s_1, s_2, s_5, s_6\};$$
$$\pi(p_3) = \{s_1, s_3, s_5, s_7\}.$$

The valuation of proposition q is not required, since what must be assessed is not whether the proposition is true or not, but if it is trusted or not.

Only two states will be checked for satisfiability of $T(q)$, namely s_1 and s_2. The neighbourhood function is the following:

$$N(s_1) = \{(s_1, s_2, s_3, s_4)\};$$
$$N(s_2) = \{(s_1, s_2, s_3, s_4), (s_1, s_2, s_5, s_6), (s_2, s_4, s_6, s_8)\}.$$

Intuitively, the neighbourhood function sets that the evaluator knows only p_1 in s_1 and knows p_1, p_2 and $\neg p_3$ in s_2.

Given this neighbourhood function, the core of s_1 ($\bigcap N(s_1)$) is the following: (s_1, s_2, s_3, s_4). On the other hand, the core of s_2 ($\bigcap N(s_2)$) is the following: (s_2). The threshold functions for the proposition q are the following:

$$\theta_{c_1}(q) = 0.5;$$
$$\theta_{c_2}(q) = 0.8.$$

Finally, the trust relevance structure is the following:

$$\omega_{c_1}(q) = \{(s_1, s_2, s_3, s_4), (s_1, s_2, s_5, s_6)\};$$
$$\mu_{c_1,q}(s_1, s_2, s_3, s_4) = 0.5;$$
$$\mu_{c_1,q}(s_1, s_2, s_5, s_6) = 0.5;$$
$$\omega_{c_2}(q) = \{(s_1, s_2, s_3, s_4), (s_1, s_2, s_5, s_6), (s_1, s_3, s_5, s_7)\};$$
$$\mu_{c_2,q}(s_1, s_2, s_3, s_4) = 0.5;$$
$$\mu_{c_2,q}(s_1, s_2, s_5, s_6) = 0.3;$$
$$\mu_{c_2,q}(s_1, s_3, s_5, s_7) = 0.2.$$

---

[8] Only atomic propositions will be employed in order to keep the example short.

It is now possible to evaluate whether $T(q)$ is satisfied in either s_1 or s_2 for the two contexts c_1 and c_2. What is needed to do so is the ideal trust values for q in all the members of the cores $\bigcap N(s_1)$ and $\bigcap N(s_2)$, again for the two contexts. For c_1, the ideal trust values are the following:

$$\tau_{c_1,q}(s_1) = 1;$$
$$\tau_{c_1,q}(s_2) = 1;$$
$$\tau_{c_1,q}(s_3) = 0.5;$$
$$\tau_{c_1,q}(s_4) = 0.5.$$

Similarly, for c_2:

$$\tau_{c_2,q}(s_1) = 1;$$
$$\tau_{c_2,q}(s_2) = 0.8;$$
$$\tau_{c_2,q}(s_3) = 0.7;$$
$$\tau_{c_2,q}(s_4) = 0.5.$$

It is finally possible to evaluate q for satisfiability. Once all the numbers are computed, it is easy to check that q is satisfied in the contextual pointed models (M, s_1, c_1); (M, s_2, c_1) and (M, s_2, c_2), but it is not satisfied in the contextual pointed model (M, s_1, c_2).

4   Validity Classes for MLT

When assessing trust formulas according to the validity principles introduced at the end of the last section, nice considerations about trust might be derived. Those considerations will also be made with respect to the conceptual map introduced in section two. It will be shown that the logical language introduced in this paper is expressive enough to talk about all varieties of trust indicated by the conceptual map. Before proceeding to the discussion, it is important to notice that in the model introduced in the previous section to interpret the language $\mathcal{L}$, the contexts of evaluation are employed to identify what are the issues for which trust must be assessed for trust, while the states of the system define how the system under analysis is structured (which is not directly impactful on trust) and, moreover, what is known (which greatly influences trust). Therefore, a context-valid formula, w.r.t. a context $c \in C$, might be seen as a formula that is always considered trustworthy, in that specific context $c \in C$, independently from what is known. Furthermore, a state-valid formula, w.r.t. a state $s \in S$, might be seen as a formula that is always considered trustworthy, given a specific set of known facts (i.e., the facts known in s), independently from what is the issue for which the formula must be assessed for trust. Finally, a model-valid formula is a formula that is always considered trustworthy, independently from what is known and what is the issue. With those small clarifications in hand, it is now possible to compare the semantical expressivity of the language MLT with the dimensions of trust introduced in Sect. 2.

4.1   Context-Validity

If a trust formula is context-valid with respect to a set A of contexts, then the notion of trust analysed is one for which, in the given set of context A, what might be known by the trustor is irrelevant for the attribution of trust. Thus, whatever the state of the system is, in that set of contexts trust will be granted. This kind of trust is typical of situations in which there is little choice other than trusting and no matter what is the level of knowledge, trust is always the best decision. A possible example could be a situation where the cost of not trusting and therefore not collaborating with (or not relying on) another agent/object can be so high that even if the other agent will defect the collaboration (or the object won't serve the purpose for which is was trusted), the loss is still less than or equal to the cost of not trusting. Take as an example a worn rope which an agent must choose whether to use or not to escape his house during a fire[9]. Assuming that the cost for the agent of not using the rope is death, no matter what he knows about the rope, he will trust it and use it as a possible escaping tool. This is because, even if the rope breaks (defects the trusting relationship), the worse that can happen to the agent is that he breaks his leg falling, while if he refuses to use the rope, he might face death.

Note that context-validity allows a modeller to move along the *how* dimension of trust. A formula that is context-valid w.r.t. a class of contexts can represent well moralistic versions of trust. Recall that moralistic trust is indeed based on the ethical and moral values of the trustor and, thus, specific knowledge about the trustee or, in the case of MLT, about the formula to be trusted seldom enter the picture in this typology of trust. When a trust formula is context-valid with respect to a class of contexts (or a single context), the only important factor is *that* specific class of contexts in which the formula is evaluated. Those contexts determine the exact situations in which the moral evaluations of the trustor condition him to trust the proposition under analysis. Note that trust formulas that are not context-valid represent (at least partially) strategic conceptions of trust. This is due to the fact that non-context-valid formulas distinguish between states of the system in order to assess trust and, therefore, the way the system (or world) is represented and what is known in each state matters. This can only be the case if some specific information about the proposition under evaluation is relevant for trust and, thus, knowing such information can change the trust assessment concerning the proposition. As said in section two, this kind of interaction between knowledge and trust is typical of strategic conceptions of trust, as was claimed above. Therefore, purely strategic versions of trust can be modelled using trust formulas for which there is no context making them

---

[9] In this case, there is only one element in the set A of contexts, i.e., escaping a burning house.

context-valid, while it is possible to gradually move towards moralistic versions
of trust by looking at trust formulas that are context valid with respect to bigger
and bigger sets of contexts.

4.2   State-Validity

If a trust formula is state-valid with respect to a state $s \in S$, then the notion of
trust analysed is one for which, in the given state s, the context of evaluation is
irrelevant for the attribution of trust. This means that the knowledge possessed
is sufficient to have trust in the formula independently from the scenario in which
trust must be assessed. This might be the case when an agent evaluates some
general factors as relevant for trust independently from the contexts or where
contexts have no impact on trust at all (e.g., trusting that Charlie has blond
hair). For example, he might believe that, independently from the situation, a
Buddhist monk would never fail to collaborate or maintain his word, therefore,
knowing that someone is a Buddhist monk is sufficient to trust him, no matter
the context.

Note that state-validity allows a modeller to move along the *what* dimension
of trust. A formula that is state-valid w.r.t. a given state can represent well
multiplex versions of trust, when the contextual model that is built contains
various contexts. However, by looking at sub-contextual models for MLT that
contain only a subclass of all the possible contexts or by simply looking at
formulas that are not state-valid, it is possible to move towards the simplex
vertex of the what-dimension. In particular, the fewer the contexts taken into
consideration in the contextual model or the fewer contexts for which a formula
is satisfied in a state, the closer the notion of trust taken into consideration is
to the simplex notion of trust. In fact, all non state-valid formulas cover the
whole length of the what dimension, while trust formulas that are state-valid in
contextual model represent only multiple versions of trust.

4.3   Whom-Dimension: A Matter of Modelling

Note that there seems to be no class of validities that can capture the *whom*
dimension of trust, i.e., no references have been made to the distinction between
particular and general conceptions of trust. This is due to the fact that this
dimension is not captured by validity principles but, instead, by the choice of
trusting formulas that are evaluated. Recall that in MLT propositions substitute
the relationship between agents or between an agent and an object. Thus, in case
the modeller wants to capture a *particular* notion of trust, he will employ formalization that highlight only one-to-one relations, e.g., Alice will help me. On
the other hand, if the modeller wants to focus on *general* notions of trust, he will
employ formalizations that express a relation between the trustor and a bigger
group of agents (or an institution), e.g., Microsoft will sell me a non-defective
product. The language here proposed leaves complete freedom to the modeller to
evaluate all the formulas he considers important. Such formulas might express
propositions about single agents or multitudes of those. Therefore, the whom

dimension enters the language a step before the other dimensions and is characterized by the appropriate choice of propositions to evaluate. Obviously, this dimension of trust can be integrated with the others by evaluating the specific trust proposition in the model(s) and determining the other two dimensions according to the previously presented validity principles.

This concludes the comparison between the dimension of trust as introduced in Sect. 2 and the way MLT identifies, through its characteristics and its validity classes, different conceptions of trust.

5   Conclusion and Future Works

It has been shown in the paper that different conceptions of trust are possible. Those conceptions have been categorized according to a conceptual map, which might aid in understanding the important features of all the different conceptions of trust. Then, a novel formal language to reason about trust has been introduced. Moreover, it has been shown that such a formal language is capable of representing all the different conceptions of trust by just employing the formal tools present in it. The comparison proved to be successful insofar as the language is expressive enough to talk about various conceptions of trust.

However, the language still requires a syntactic representation of the validity classes, in order to determine which rules of inference and which axioms are necessary to obtain the various validity principles. Having such a representation might help in the future to understand which are the rational mechanisms that produce trust in social and economical environment. This is a great improvement for computer science, since knowing how trust is fostered in social communities might help in reproducing the same mechanisms in digital communities, thus fostering digital versions of trust. Moreover, it might be interesting to understand if the core ideas of the formal language here introduced can be employed to improve the quality of already existing computational trust models, providing them with the tools that allow the representation of other conceptions of trust over and above the ones considered for the specific applications those models are applied to.

References

1. Barber, B.: The Logic and Limits of Trust. Rutgers University Press, New Brunswick (1983)
2. Bateson, P.: The biological evolution of cooperation and trust. In: Gambetta, D. (ed.) Trust: Making and Breaking Cooperative Relations, pp. 31–48. Blackwell (1988)
3. van Benthem, J., Fernández-Duque, D., Pacuit, E.: Evidence logic: a new look at neighborhood structures. Adv. Modal Logic 9, 97–118 (2012)
4. Chellas, B.L.: Modal Logic: An Introduction. Cambridge University Press, Cambridge (1980)
5. Coleman, J.: Foundations of Social Theory. Harvard University Press, Cambridge (1990)

6. Dasgupta, P.: Trust as a commodity. In: Gambetta, D. (ed.) Trust: Making and Breaking Cooperative Relations, pp. 49–72. Blackwell (1988)
7. Fehr, E.: On the economics and biology of trust. J. Eur. Econ. Assoc. **7**, 235–266 (2009)
8. Gambetta, D. (ed.): Trust: Making and Breaking Cooperative Relations. Blackwell, Hoboken (1988)
9. Hansen, H.H.: Monotonic modal logic. Master's thesis (2003)
10. Hardin, R.: Trust and Trustworthiness. Russell Sage Foundation, New York (2002)
11. Hardin, R.: The street-level epistemology of trust. Polit. Soc. **21**, 505–529 (1993)
12. Holton, R.: Deciding to trust, coming to believe. Australas. J. Philos. **72**(1), 63–76 (1994)
13. Jones, K.: Trustworthiness. Ethics **123**(1), 61–85 (2012)
14. Jones, K.: Second-hand moral knowledge. J. Philos. **96**(2), 55–78 (1999)
15. Jøsang, A.: Subjective Logic. Springer, Cham (2016). https://doi.org/10.1007/978-3-319-42337-1
16. Jøsang, A.: Trust and reputation system. In: Aldini, A., Gorrieri, R. (eds.) Foundations of Security Analysis and Design IV, pp. 209–245 (2007)
17. Jøsang, A., Ismail, R., Boyd, C.: A survey of trust and reputation systems for online service provision. Decis. Support Syst. **43**(2), 618–644 (2007)
18. Kant, I.: Groundwork of the Mataphysic of Morals. Cambridge University Press, Cambridge (1785)
19. Levi, M.: A state of trust. In: Braithwaite, V., Levi, M., Cook, K.S., Hardin, R. (eds.) Trust and Governance, pp. 77–101. Russell Sage Foundation (1998)
20. Luhmann, N.: Trust and Power. Wiley, Hoboken (1979)
21. Mansbridge, J.: Altruistic trust. In: Warren, M.E. (ed.) Democracy and Trust. Cambridge University Press, pp. 290–309 (1999)
22. O'Neill, O.: Autonomy and Trust in Bioethics. Cambridge University Press, Cambridge (2002)
23. Ostrom, E., James, W. (eds.) Trust and Reciprocity. In: Russell Sage Foundation Series on Trust, vol. VI (2005)
24. Pacuit, E.: Neighborhood Semantics for Modal Logic. Springer, Cham (2017). https://doi.org/10.1007/978-3-319-67149-9
25. Robbins, B.G.: What is trust? A multidisciplinary review, critique, and synthesis. Sociol. Compass **10**(10), 972–986 (2016)
26. Robbins, B.G.: On the origins of trust. Ph.D. thesis, University of Washington (2014)
27. Schelling, T.: The Strategy of Conflict. Harvard University Press, Cambridge (1960)
28. Tagliaferri, M.: A logical language for computational trust. Ph.D. thesis, University of Urbino (2019)
29. Tagliaferri, M., Aldini, A.: From knowledge to trust: a logical framework for pre-trust computations. In: Gal-Oz, N., Lewis, P.R. (eds.) IFIPTM 2018. IAICT, vol. 528, pp. 107–123. Springer, Cham (2018). https://doi.org/10.1007/978-3-319-95276-5_8
30. Tagliaferri, M., Aldini, A.: A trust logic for pre-trust computations. In: Proceedings of the 21th International Conference on Information Fusion (Fusion 2018), pp. 2010–2016. IEEE (2018)
31. Trivers, R.L.: The evolution of reciprocal altruism. Q. Rev. Biol. **46**(1), 35–57 (1971)
32. Trivers, R.L.: Natural Selection and Social Theory: Selected Papers of Robert Trivers. Oxford University Press, Oxford (2002)

33. Uslaner, E.M.: Who do you trust? In: Shockley, E., Neal, T.M.S., PytlikZillig, L.M., Bornstein, B.H. (eds.) Interdisciplinary Perspectives on Trust, pp. 71–83. Springer, Cham (2016). https://doi.org/10.1007/978-3-319-22261-5_4

34. Uslaner, E.M.: Varieties of trust. Eur. Polit. Sci. **2**, 43–49 (2003). https://doi.org/10.1057/eps.2003.18

35. Williamson, O.: Calculativeness, trust, and economic organization. J. Law Econ. **36**(2), 453–486 (1993)

Behaviour and Reasoning Description Language (BRDL)

Antonio Cerone[✉]

Department of Computer Science, Nazarbayev University, Nur-Sultan, Kazakhstan
`antonio.cerone@nu.edu.kz`

Abstract. In this paper we present a basic language for describing human behaviour and reasoning and present the cognitive architecture underlying the semantics of the language. The language is illustrated through a number of examples showing its ability to model human reasoning, problem solving, deliberate behaviour and automatic behaviour. We expect that the simple notation and its intuitive semantics may address the needs of practitioners from non matematical backgrounds, in particular psychologists, linguists and other social scientists. The language usage is twofold, aiming at the formal modelling and analysis of interactive systems and the comparison and validation of alternative models of memory and cognition.

Keywords: Cognitive science · Human reasoning · Problem solving · Human behavior · Formal methods

1 Introduction

Research in modelling human cognition has resulted in the development of a large number of *cognitive architectures* over the last decades [9,17]. However, we are still very far from having a unified approach to modelling cognition. In fact, cognitive architectures are based on three different modelling approaches, *symbolic* (or *cognitivist*), such as Soar [10], which are based on a set of predefined general rules to manipulate symbols, *connectionist* (or *emergent*), such as DAC [19], which count on emergent properties of connected processing components (e.g. nodes of a neural network), and *hybrid*, such as CLARION [18], which combine the two previous approaches. Moreover, there is no clear agreement on the categorisation of specific architecture in this taxonomy. For example, ACT-R [1] is often classified as symbolic but, in fact, explicitly self-identifies as hybrid. Furthermore, most architectures have been developped for research purposes and are fairly specialised in one or more of the following areas: psychological experiments, cognitive robotics, human performance modelling, human-robot interaction, human-computer interaction, natural language processing, categorisation and clustering, computer vision games and puzzles, and virtual agents [9].

The complexity of these cognitive architectures makes it difficult to fully understand their semantics and requires high expertise in programming them.

J. Camara and M. Steffen (Eds.): SEFM 2019 Workshops, LNCS 12226, pp. 137–153, 2020.
https://doi.org/10.1007/978-3-030-57506-9_11

Moreover, although cognitive architectures can mimic many aspects of human behaviour and learning, they never really managed to be easily incorporated in the system and software verification process.

In this paper we propose a notation, the *Behaviour and Reasoning Description Language (BRDL)*, for describing human behaviour and reasoning. The semantics of the language is based on a basic model of human memory and memory processes and is adaptable to different cognitive theories. This allows us, on the one hand, to keep the syntax of the language to a minimum, thus making it easy to learn and understand and, on the other hand, to use alternative semantic variations to compare alternative theories of memory and cognition. The latter can be easily achieved by replacing implementation modules and, on a finer grain, varying the values of a number of semantic parameters.

BRDL originated from and extends the *Human Behaviour Description Language (HBDL)* introduced in our previous work [2,3]. HBDL focuses on the modelling of automatic and deliberate behaviour. However, it requires reasoning and problem solving aspects to be modelled explicitly in a procedural way, whereby the reasoning process and the problem solution are explicitly described with the language. BRDL, instead, is equipped with the linguistic constructs to specify reasoning goals (e.g. questions), inference rules and unsolved problems. The cognitive engine implementing the language then emulates the reasoning and problem solving processes. In our previous work [2,3], HBDL has been implemented using the Maude rewrite language and system [11,16]. In our recent work [4] we started implementing BRDL using the real-time extension of Maude [15]. The use of formal methods, specifically Maude, to implement the languages allows us to combine human components and system components and perform formal verification. This is carried out by exploiting the model checking capability of Maude and Real-time Maude.

This paper aims at addressing a broad community of researchers from different backgrounds but all interested in cognition. For this reason, rather than listing formal definitions, we start from small, practical examples and then generalise them as semi-formal definitions or algorithmic descriptions in which we avoid jargon and keep the formal notation to a minimum. Formality is introduced, usually in term of elementary set theory, only when is needed to avoid ambiguity, but is avoided whenever a textual explanation is sufficient.

Section 2 introduces the underlying memory and cognitive model, inspired by the information processing approach. Section 3 describes the notation used for knowledge representation and presents the algorithm used for knowledge retrieval. Section 4 presents how to model deliberate behaviour in term of reasoning, interaction and problem solving. In particular, it illustrates how inference rule are used in reasoning and interaction and how knowledge drives the decomposition of the problem goal into subgoals. Section 5 presents how to model automatic behaviour and how this evolves from deliberate behaviour through skill acquisition. Finally, Sect. 6 concludes the paper and discusses the ongoing BRDL implementation as well as future work.

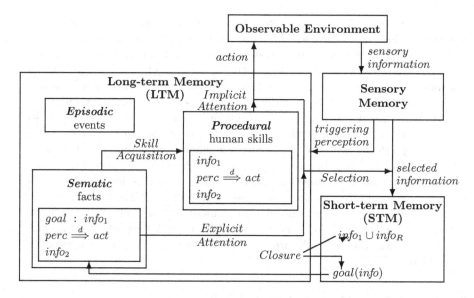

Fig. 1. Human memory architecture underlying BRDL semantics

2   Human Memory Architecture

Following the *information processing* approach normally used in cognitive psychology, we model human cognitive processes as processing activities that make use of input-output channels, to interact with the external environment, and three main kinds of memory, to store information. Input and output occur through the senses and the motor system. We give a general representation of input channels in term of *sensory information*, possibly abstracting away from the specific senses that are used. We represent output channels in term of *actions* performed on the observable environment.

Figure 1 describes the human memory architecture we will use to provide the semantics of BRDL. The notational details of the figure will be explained in Sects. 4 and 5. The memory consists of the following components:

sensory memory
  where information perceived through the senses persists for a very short time [13];
short-term memory (STM)
  which has a limited capacity and where the information that is needed for processing activities is temporarily stored with rapid access and rapid decay [6,7,13];
long-term memory (LTM)
  which has a virtually unlimited capacity and where information is organised in structured ways, with slow access but little or no decay [5,8].

We must note that the term STM indicates a mere, short-term storage of information, whereas the term *working memory* is used for a short-term buffer that also supports processing and manipulation of information [6,7]. Although some neuropsychological studies show evidences supporting this distinction, which correspond to two different neural subsystems within the prefrontal cortex [7], in our work we do not associate processing with memory directly. In fact, we consider the short-term storage aspects as a whole and express them in the BRDL syntax, while all processing aspects are delegated to the semantics of the language.

As shown in Fig. 1, we consider a human memory architecture in which, depending on the content of the LTM, some *perception* (*perc*) selected among the *sensory information* stored in sensory memory, in combination with information (*info*$_1$) and possibly a goal (*goal*) stored in STM, *triggers* some human *action* (*act*) on the observable environment and/or the transfer of the (possibly processed) selected information from sensory memory to STM (*info*$_2$).

A usual practice to keep information in memory is *rehearsal*. In particular, *maintenance rehearsal* allows us to extend the time during which information is kept in STM, whereas *elaborative rehearsal* allows us to transfer information from STM to LTM.

2.1   Short-Term Memory (STM) Model

The limited capacity of the STM has been measured using experiments in which the subjects had to recall items presented in sequence. By presenting sequences of digits, Miller [12] found that the average person can remember 7 ± 2 digits. However, when digits are grouped in *chunks*, as it happens when we memorise phone numbers, it is actually possible to remember larger numbers of digits. Therefore, Miller's 7 ± 2 rule applies to chunks of information and the ability to form chunks can increase people's STM actual capacity.

We assume that the STM may contain pieces of information, which may describe cognitive information, possibly retrieved from the LTM, goals, recent perceptions or planned actions. Therefore we can denote the set of pieces of information that may be in STM as

$$\Theta = \Pi \cup \Sigma \cup \Delta \cup \Gamma,$$

where Π is a set of perceptions, Σ is a set of mental representations of human actions, Δ is a set of pieces of cognitive information and Γ is a set of goals. Moreover, each piece of information is associated with a *life time*, which is initialised as the *STM decay time* when the information is first stored in the STM and then decremented as time passes. A piece of information disappears from the STM once its life time has decreased to 0.

The limited capacity of short-term memory requires the presence of a mechanism to empty it when the stored information is no longer needed. When we produce a chunk, the information concerning the chunk components is removed from the STM. For example, when we chunk digits, only the representation of the chunk stays in the STM, while the component digits are removed and can no longer be directly remembered as separate digits. Generally, every time a task is completed, there may be a subconscious removal of information from STM, a process called *closure*: the information used to complete the task is likely to be removed from the STM, since it is no longer needed. Therefore, when closure occurs, a piece of information may disappear from the STM even before its life time has decrease to 0. Furthermore, a piece of information may disappear from the STM also when the STM has reached its maximum capacity and it is needed to make space for the storage of needed information. Conversely, *maintenance rehearsal* resets the life time to the value of the decay time.

2.2   Long-Term Memory (LTM) Model

Long term memory is divided into two types

***declarative* or *explicit* memory**
> refers to our knowledge of the world ("knowing what") and consists of the *events* and *facts* that can be *consciously* recalled:
> - our experiences and specific events in time stored in a serial form (*episodic memory*);
> - structured record of facts, meanings, concepts and knowledge about the external world, which we have acquired and organised through association and abstraction (*semantic memory*).

***procedural* or *implicit* memory**
> refers to our skills ("knowing how") and consists of *rules* and *procedures* that we *unconsciously* use to carry out tasks, particularly at the motor level.

Emotions and specific contexts and environments are factors that affect the storage of experiences and events in episodic memory. Information can be transferred from episodic to semantic memory by making abstractions and building associations, whereas *elaborative rehearsal* facilitates the transfer of information from STM to semantic memory in an organised form.

Note that also declarative memory can be used to carry out tasks, but in a very inefficient way, which requires a large mental effort in using the STM (*high cognitive load*) and a consequent high energy consumption. In fact, declarative memory is heavily used while learning new skills. For example, while we are learning to drive, ride a bike, play a musical instrument or even when we are learning to do apparently trivial things, such as tying a shoelace, we consciously retrieve a large number of facts from the semantic memory and store a lot of information in the STM. Skill acquisition typically occurs through repetition and practice and consists in the creation in the procedural memory of rules and procedures (*proceduralisation*), which can be then unconsciously used in an automatic way with limited involvement of declarative memory and STM.

2.3   Memory Processes and Cognitive Control

We have mentioned in Sect. 2.2 that skill acquisition results in the creation in procedural memory of the appropriate rules to automatically perform the task, thus reducing the accesses to declarative memory and the use of STM, and, as a result, optimising the task performance.

As shown in Fig. 1, sensory information is briefly stored in the sensory memory and only relevant information is transferred, possibly after some kind of processing, to the STM using *attention*, a selective processing activity that aims to focus on one aspect of the environment while ignoring others. *Explicit attention* is associated with our goal in performing a task and is activated by the content of the semantic memory. It focusses on goal-relevant stimuli in the environment. *Implicit attention* is grabbed by sudden stimuli that are associated with the current mental state or carry emotional significance. It is activated by the content of the procedural memory.

Inspired by Norman and Shallice [14], we consider two levels of cognitive control:

automatic control
: fast processing activity that requires only *implicit attention* and is carried out outside awareness with no conscious effort implicitly, using rules and procedures stored in the procedural memory;

deliberate control
: processing activity triggered and focussed by *explicit attention* and carried out under the intentional control of the individual, who makes explicit use of facts and experiences stored in the declarative memory and is aware and conscious of the effort required in doing so.

For example, automatic control is essential in properly driving a car and, in such a context, it develops throughout a learning process based on deliberate control. During the learning process the driver has to make a conscious effort that requires explicit attention to use gear, indicators, etc. in the right way (deliberate control). In fact, the driver would not be able to carry out such an effort while talking or listening to the radio, since the deliberate control is entirely devoted to the driving task. Once automaticity in driving is acquired, the driver is no longer aware of low-level details and resorts to implicit attention to perform them (automatic control), while deliberate control and explicit attention may be devoted to other tasks such as talking or listening to the radio.

One of the uses of BRDL is the analysis and comparison of different architectural models of human memory and cognitions. In this sense the semantics of the language depends on the values assigned to a number of parameters, such as:

STM maximum capacity the maximum number of pieces of information (possibly chuncks) that can be stored in STM;

STM decay time the maximum time that information may persist in STM in absence of maintenance rehearsal;

lower closure threshold the minimum STM load to enable closure;

upper closure threshold the minimum STM load to force closure;

LTM retrieval maximum time the maximum time that can be used to retrieve information from LTM before a retrieval failure occurs.

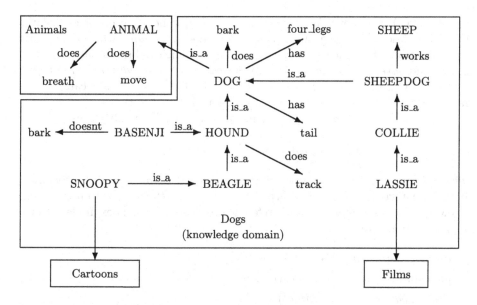

Fig. 2. Example of semantic network (adapted from Dix' work [8]).

3   Knowledge Representation

Semantic networks are a simple, effective way to describe how we represent and structure information in semantic memory. We call *category* any item that is the object of our knowledge. An association between two categories is described by a labelled arrow. A label is used to specify the nature of the association. For example, an arrow labelled with "is_a" denotes a *generalisation*: the arrow goes from the more specific to the more generic category. Additionally, a category may have *attributes*, which may also be categories. The arrow from the category to one of its attribute is labelled with a *type* characterising the relationship between the attribute and the category. In the case of generalisation, the more specific category inherits all attributes of the more generic category unless the attribute is redefined at the more specific category level.

For example, Fig. 2 shows a semantic network for the *knowledge domain dogs*. Note that in Fig. 2 we have used words entirely in upper-case letters for categories and capitalised words for knowledge domains for readability purposes. However, this convention is not used in BRDL. Note that the *bark* attribute is duplicated only for better readability of the semantic network. In fact, a single *bark* attribute should occur as the target of two arrows, one with source *dog* and label *does* and on with source *basenji* and label *doesnt*.

Associations are described in BRDL either in terms of the application of the label *is_a* to a category (*generalisation*) or in terms of the application of a type to an attribute (*typed attribute*). For example, the *dog* category is generalised as the more generic category *animal* (*is_a(animal)*) at a higher level and has the following typed attributes with obvious meaning: *does(bark)*, *has(four_legs)* and $has(tail)$. Category *dog* is also the $is\_a(dog)$ generalisation of lower-level categories describing dog groups, such as *sheepdog* and *hound*, which are in turn generalisations of even lower-level categories describing dog breeds, such as *collie*, *beagle* and *basenji*. Furthermore, category *basenji* has the $doesnt(bark)$ typed attribute, which redefines the $does(bark)$ typed attribute of the *dog* category. In fact, a basenji is an exceptional dog breed that does not bark.

A *fact representation* in semantic memory is modelled in BRDL as

$$domain : category \mid \xrightarrow{delay} \mid type(attribute)$$

where *delay* is the mental processing time needed to retrieve the association between category *category* and type attribute *type(attribute)* within the given knowledge domain *domain*. With reference to Fig. 2, obvious examples of fact representations are:

1. $animals : animal \mid \xrightarrow{d_1} \mid does(breath)$,
2. $animals : animal \mid \xrightarrow{d_2} \mid does(move)$,
3. $dogs : dog \mid \xrightarrow{d_3} \mid is\_a(animal)$,
4. $dogs : dog \mid \xrightarrow{d_4} \mid does(bark)$,
5. $dogs : hound \mid \xrightarrow{d_5} \mid is\_a(dog)$,
6. $dogs : basenji \mid \xrightarrow{d_6} \mid is\_a(hound)$,
7. $dogs : hound \mid \xrightarrow{d_7} \mid does(track)$,
8. $dogs : basenji \mid \xrightarrow{d_8} \mid doesnt(bark)$.

There are some relations between attribute types. For instance, *doesnt* is the negation of *does* and $isnt\_a$ is the negation of is_a.

3.1   Knowledge Retrieval

Knowledge retrieval occurs deliberately, driven by specific goals we have in mind. Our working memory is the STM, so our current goals are stored in STM. Within a given knowledge *domain*, we model the goal of retrieving the *attributes* of a given *type* that are associated with a given *category* as

$$goal(domain, type\_what?(category)).$$

The presence of such a goal in STM triggers the retrieval of one specific *attribute* so that a new piece of *cognitive information*, either fact *type(category, attribute)* or its negation is added to the STM, unless it is already there, while the goal is removed from the STM. If the fact is already in STM, then other attributes will be retrieved until we have a fact that is not in STM yet, and can thus added to it. If there are more facts matching the goal that are not in STM yet, then the one whose representation in LTM has the least mental processing time is retrieved. One of the memory parameters introduced in Sect. 2.3, the *LTM retrieval maximum time*, defines the maximum time for such a search, after which the *dontknow(domain, type_what?(category))* fact replaces the goal in STM.

Suppose that we want to find out what an animal does. Our goal is

$$goal(animals, does\_what?(animal)).$$

This goal immediately matches fact representations 1 and 2 in LTM introduced in the example in Sect. 3. Thus the goal is replaced in STM by *does(animal, breath)* after time d_1, if $d_1 < d_2$, or by *does(animal, move)* after time d_2, if $d_2 < d_1$. If $d_1 = d_2$, then the choice is nondeterministic.

Other possible goals are:

goal(domain, type_which?(attribute)) for retrieving the *category* with which *type(attribute)* is associated;

goal(domain, type?(category, attribute)) for answering the question on whether *category* is associated with *type(attribute)* and, if the answer is positive, adding fact *type(category, attribute)* to the STM, otherwise adding its negation to the STM.

We want now to find out whether a basenji breaths. Our goal is

$$goal(dogs, does?(basenji, breath)).$$

Since none of the attributes of *basenji* matches our question we need to climb the hierarchy of categories described in Sect. 3 and go through *hound* (fact representation 6) and *dog* (fact representation 5) until we reach *animal* (fact representation 3) and find out that our question matches fact representation 1. The time for such a retrieval is the sum of the retrieval times of all *is_a* fact representations for all categories we have gone through (d_6, d_5 and d_3) plus the sum of the retrieval times of all *does* facts associated with each of these categories that do not match the goal (d_7) plus the retrieval time of the fact representation that matches the goal (d_1): $d_6 + d_5 + d_3 + d_7 + d_1$, which is obviously greater than time d_1 needed to find out whether an animal breaths. This is consistent with Collins and Quillian's experiments on retrieval time from semantic memory [5].

Finally, we want to find out whether a basenji barks. Our goal is

$$goal(dogs, does?(basenji, bark)).$$

This goal immediately matches fact representation 8 in LTM introduced in the example in Sect. 3. Thus the goal is replaced in STM by *doesnt(basenjil, bark)* after time d_7.

In general, given goal $g(c) = goal(dom, type\_what?(c))$ and an LTM retrieval maximum time d_{max}, the fact $f(g, c)$ that replaces the goal in STM after time $t(g, c)$ is defined as follows:

1. $f(g, c) = type(c, a)$ with $t(g, c) = d$
   if $dom : c \mid \xrightarrow{d} \mid type(a)$ is in LTM;

2. $f(g,c) = f(g,c')$ with $t(g,c) = s(type,c) + d' + t(g,c')$

   if there is no attribute a such that $dom : c \mid \xrightarrow{d} \mid type(a)$ is in LTM
   and $t(g,c) < d_{max}$ and there is a knowledge domain dom' such that
   $dom' : c \mid \xrightarrow{d'} \mid is\_a(c')$ is in LTM;

3. $f(g,c) = \overline{type}(c,a)$ with $t(g,c) = d_{max}$

   if there is no fact in LTM that can be retrieved within time d_{max}

where $\overline{type}$ is the negation of $type$ and $s(type,c)$ is the sum of the retrieval times
of all fact representations in LTM with the given category c and type $type$. The
attribute a associated with category c may be retrived without climbing the
hierarchy of categories (1) or may be required to climb the hierarchy (iteration
of 2) or may not be found at all (3).

Similar algorithms can be given for goals $goal(dom, type\_which?(a))$ and
$goal(dom, type?(c,a))$. Note that $goal(dogs, does?(basenji, bark))$ would retrieve
the fact $does(bark, dog)$ without considering the exception $basenji$, which is at
a lower level than dog in the hierarchy. This is consistent with the fact that we
normally neglect exceptions when we make general cosiderations.

We conclude this section with a clarification about the role of the knowledge
domain. Although retrieval goes across knowledge domains, it is the existence of
a specific knowledge domain to enable it. For example, with reference to Fig. 2,
knowledge domain 'Dogs' allows us to retrieve information on 'SNOOPY' as a
dog, but not as a cartoon character. That is, we can find out that SNOOPY
tracks but not that SNOOPY thinks. This last piece of information, instead,
could be retrieved within the 'Cartoon' knowledge domain.

4   Deliberate Basic Activities

Fact representations in semantic memory not only describe the *static knowledge*
of the world but also the *dynamic knowledge* on how to deliberately manipulate
our own internal knowledge and understand the external world (*reasoning* and
problem solving) and how to use knowledge to perceive and manipulate the
external world (*interaction* and *problem solving*).

The general structure of a deliberate basic activity is

$$goal : info_1 \uparrow perc \xrightarrow{d} act \downarrow info_2$$

where

- $goal \in \Gamma$ is a goal, which may be structured in different ways;
- $perc \in \Pi$ is a perception on which the human *explicitly* focusses;
- $info_1 \subseteq \Theta \backslash \Gamma$ is the information retrieved and removed from the STM;
- $info_2 \subseteq \Theta$ is the information stored in the STM;
- $act \in \Sigma$ is the mental representation of a human action;
- d is the mental processing time (up to the moment action act starts, but not
  including act duration).

The upward arrow denotes that $info_1$ is removed from the STM and the downward arrow denotes that $info_2$ is added to the STM. In case $info_1$ must not be removed from the STM we can use the following derived notation:

$$goal : info_1 \,|\, perc \xRightarrow{d} act \downarrow info_2$$

where the '|' instead of '↑' denotes that $info_1$ is not removed from the STM. This derived notation is equivalent to $goal : info_1 \uparrow perc \xRightarrow{d} act \downarrow info_1 \cup info_2$. Special cases are:

$goal : info_1 \uparrow\xRightarrow{d} act \downarrow info_2$ and $goal : info_1 \,| \xRightarrow{d} act \downarrow info_2$
   if there is no perception;
$goal : info_1 \uparrow perc \xRightarrow{d}\downarrow info_2$ and $goal : info_1 \,|\, perc \xRightarrow{d}\downarrow info_2$
   if there is no action;
$goal : info_1 \uparrow\xRightarrow{d}\downarrow info_2$ and $goal : info_1 \,| \xRightarrow{d}\downarrow info_2$
   if there is neither perception nor action.

4.1 Goals

We have seen in Sect. 3.1 that a goal $goal(dom, q)$ for knowledge retrieval means that we deliberately look for an answer to question q within knowledge domain dom. Once the answer is found or the ignorance of the answer is established, the goal is achieved and is removed from STM.

In more complex deliberate activities the knowledge domain might be related to the underlying *purpose* in our behaviour or represent a specific *task* to carry out. Thus goal $goal(dom, info)$ means that we deliberately want to achieve the information given by a non-empty set $info \subseteq \Theta\backslash\Gamma$, which may comprise one experienced perception, one performed action and some of the information stored in the STM except goals. Therefore, a goal $goal(dom, info)$ in STM is achieved when

- the human experiences $perc \in info$ or $\Pi \cap info = \emptyset$, and
- the human performs $act \in info$ or $\Sigma \cap info = \emptyset$, and
- $info\backslash\Pi\backslash\Sigma$ is included in STM,

where set difference '\' is left associative.

4.2 Reasoning

One way to manipulate our internal knowledge is to infer new facts from other facts whose representations are in our LTM. The inferred facts are added to the STM and may be preserved for the future either by transferring them to LTM through elaborative rehearsal or by recording them in the external environment in some way, e.g. through writing.

The LTM contains inference rules that we have learned throughout our life and are applied deliberately. For example, consider a person who is learning to drive. At some point throughout the learning process, the person learns the following rule:

A driver has to give way to pedestrians ready to walk across the road on a zebra crossing.

The premises of this rule are

zebra—there is a zebra crossing, and
ped—there are pedestrians ready to walk across the road.

The consequences is

goal($driving, gw$)—the driver's goal is to give way to the pedestrians,

where gw is the fact that the driver has given way to the pedestrians, which has to be achieved.

Inference rule

$$infer(driving) : \{zebra, ped\} \mid \stackrel{d}{\Longrightarrow}\downarrow \{goal(driving, gw)\},$$

models the fact that from the set of premises $\{zebra, ped\}$ we can infer the set of consequences $\{goal(driving, gw)\}$ in knowledge domain *driving*. The premises are not removed from the STM after applying the inference.

The general structure of an inference rule is

$$infer(dom) : premises \uparrow\stackrel{d}{\Longrightarrow}\downarrow consequences.$$

The rule is enabled when special goal *infer* and the *premises* are in STM. The application of the rule requires time d and removes both special goal *infer* and the *premises* from STM and add the *consequences* to it. Since normally premises are not removed after applying the inference, it is common to use derived rule

$$infer(dom) : premises \mid \stackrel{d}{\Longrightarrow}\downarrow consequences,$$

which is equivalent to $infer(dom) : premises \uparrow\stackrel{d}{\Longrightarrow}\downarrow premises \cup consequences$.

Reasoning inference rules support all three main human reasoning modes: *deduction*, *abduction* and *induction*. The rule for giving way to pedestrian presented above is an example of *deduction*.

The following example of *abduction*

A train that does not arrive at the scheduled time is late.

can be modelled as

$$infer(railway) : \{arrivalTimePassed, noTrain\} \mid \stackrel{d}{\Longrightarrow}\downarrow \{trainLate\}.$$

In this case the inference goes from the *events*, i.e. the arrival time is passed and the train has not arrived yet, to the *cause*, i.e. the train is late. In reality, the train might have been cancelled rather than being late.

Finally, the following example of *induction* or *generalisation*

if three trains in a row arrive late then all trains arrive late.

can be modelled as

$$infer(railway) : \{train1Late, train2Late, train3Late\} \mid \stackrel{d}{\Longrightarrow}\downarrow \{allTrainsLate\}.$$

4.3   Interaction

Interaction concerns the perception and the manipulation of the external world making use of internal knowledge. Consider again a person who is learning to drive and has to deal with a zebra crossing. Normally the explicit attention of a learner who is driving a car tries to focus on a large number of perceptions. If we restrict the driving task (*driving*) to just a zebra crossing, explicit attention involves only two perceptions, *zebra* and *ped*, and is driven by two goals, *driving*, {*zebra*} and *driving*, {*ped*}, which are simultaneously in STM.

This restricted driving task may be modelled in BRDL as:

1. $goal(driving, \{zebra\}) : \emptyset \mid zebra \overset{d_1}{\Longrightarrow} \downarrow \{zebra\}$,
2. $goal(driving, \{ped\}) : \emptyset \mid ped \overset{d_2}{\Longrightarrow} \downarrow \{ped\}$,
3. $goal(driving, \{ped\}) : \{zebra\} \mid ped \overset{d_3}{\Longrightarrow} \downarrow \{ped, infer(driving)\}$,
4. $goal(driving, \{zebra\}) : \{ped\} \mid zebra \overset{d_4}{\Longrightarrow} \downarrow \{zebra, infer(driving)\}$,
5. $goal(driving, \{gw\}) : \emptyset \mid \overset{d_5}{\Longrightarrow} stop \downarrow \{gw\}$.

After the driver has perceived the presence of zebra crossing and pedestrians and stored *zebra* and *perc* in the STM (basic activities 1 and 3 or 2 and 4), an inference rule enabled by the content of the STM is searched. This is the rule defined in Sect. 4.2, which store *gw* in the STM, thus informing the driver about the need to give way to the pedestrian. The driver complies with the rule by performing action *stop* to stop the car (basic activity 5).

4.4   Problem Solving

Problem solving is the process of finding a solution to an unfamiliar task. In BRDL problems to be solved are modelled by goals stored in STM. We illustrate with an example how the knowledge stored in LTM may lead to the solution.

Consider the task of moving a box full of items. The STM contains

– goal *goal*(*boxes*, {*moved*, *full*});
– pieces of information *notMoved* and *full*.

Suppose to have the following obvious knowledge stored in LTM:

1. $goal(boxes, \{full\}) : \mid full \overset{d_1}{\Longrightarrow} \downarrow \{full\}$
2. $goal(boxes, \{empty\}) : \mid empty \overset{d_2}{\Longrightarrow} \downarrow \{empty\}$
3. $goal(boxes, \{moved\}) : \{empty, notMoved\} \uparrow \overset{d_3}{\Longrightarrow} move \downarrow \{empty, moved\}$
4. $goal(boxes, \{empty\}) : \{full\} \uparrow \overset{d_4}{\Longrightarrow} remove \downarrow \{empty\}$
5. $goal(boxes, \{full\}) : \{empty\} \uparrow \overset{d_5}{\Longrightarrow} fill \downarrow \{full\}$

Basic activities 1 and 2 model the explicit attention on whether the box is full or empty. Basic activities 3 models the moving of an empty box. Basic activities 4 models the filling of an empty box. Basic activities 5 models the removal of all items from a full box. We assume that the box may be filled or emptied with just a single action.

None of the basic activities in LTM is enabled by the contents of the STM. Therefore, first goal $goal(boxes, \{moved, full\})$ is decomposed into two goals of knowledge domain $boxes$ that control basic activities in LTM

$$goal(boxes, \{moved\}) \text{ and } goal(boxes, \{full\})$$

and is replaced by them after time $d_1 + d_2 + d_3 + d_4 + d_5$, which is needed to explore all basic activities within the knowledge domain. Then, the contents of the STM are removed from information $\{empty, notMoved\}$, which enables the basic activities that are controlled by the two goals but not triggered by perceptions. The resultant information $\{empty\}$ is what is missing from the STM to make progress in solving the problem. Therefore, a goal $goal(boxes, \{empty\})$ is added to the STM after a further $d_3 + d_5$ time.

Goal $goal(boxes, \{empty\})$ is considered first, since it is the last one that was added to the STM, and is achieved by performing basic activity 4. This makes the box empty, thus enabling basic activities 3 and 5. Between the two, basic activity 3 is chosen first since it is enabled by a larger amount of information ($\{empty, notMoved\}$ versus $\{empty\}$), thus moving the box and achieving goal $goal(boxes, \{moved\})$. Finally, basic activity 5 is performed and also goal $goal(boxes, \{full\})$ is achieved.

5   Automatic Basic Activities

Automatic basic activities are performed independently from the goals in the STM. The general structure of an automatic basic activity is

$$dom : info_1 \uparrow perc \overset{d}{\Longrightarrow} act \downarrow info_2$$

where

- dom is a knowledge domain, possibly a task;
- $perc \in \Pi$ is a perception on which the human *implicitly* focusses;
- $info_1 \subseteq \Theta \backslash \Gamma$ is the information retrieved and removed from the STM;
- $info_2 \subseteq \Theta$ is the information stored in the STM;
- $act \in \Sigma$ is the mental representation of a human action;
- d is the mental processing time (up to the moment action act starts, but not including act duration).

Also for automatic basic activities, perception and/or action may be absent.

Automatic basic activities originate from the proceduralisation in procedural memory of repeatedly used deliberate activities in semantic memory. Consider the example of the behaviour of a driving learner at a zebra crossing, which was introduced in Sect. 4.3. After a lot of driving experience, the driver's behaviour will become automatic. From the five deliberate basic activity in semantic memory the following new automatic activity are created in procedural memory:

1. $driving : \emptyset \mid zebra \xrightarrow{d'_1} \downarrow \{zebra\}$,
2. $driving : \{zebra\} \mid ped \xrightarrow{d'_2} stop \downarrow \{ped\}$.

Automatic basic activity 1 models the skill driver's implicit attention focussing on the zebra crossing, whose presence is unconsciously noted while approaching it, either though direct sight or indirectly via a warning signal. With such an automatic behaviour, the mental processing time of a skilled drivers, who is aware of the presence of a zebra crossing, from the moment of the perception of the pedestrians to the moment the *stop* action starts is d'_2. Taking into account that the application of the zebra crossing inference rule introduced in Sect. 4.2 requires d mental processing time, with the learner's deliberate behaviour modelled in Sect. 4.3 such a mental processing time is either $d_3 + d + d_5$, if the driver notices the zebra crossing first (deliberate basic activities 1 and 3), or $d_4 + d + d_5$, if the driver notices the pedestrians first (deliberate basic activities 2 and 4), which are both expected to be greater than d'_2. In this sense the skilled driver's behaviour is safer than the lerner's behaviour.

6　Conclusion and Future Work

We have introduced the Behaviour and Reasoning Description Language (BRDL) for describing human behaviour and reasoning as an extension of the Human Behaviour Description Language (HBDL) presented in our previous work [2,3]. BRDL semantics has been provided on-the-fly in terms of a basic model of human memory and memory processes. We are currently implementing BRDL [4] using Real-time Maude [15] as part of a formal modelling and analysis environment that includes both human components and system components [3].

The object-oriented nature of Real-time Maude supports a highly modular implementation with separate modules describing alternative theories of cognition. Moreover, the use of a number of parameters as the ones listed at the end of Sect. 2.3 supports a fine-grain control of the applicability of Maude rewrite rules. In our future work, we will use this feature to compare in-silico experiments that use different combinations of parameter values with the data collected from real-life observations and experiments. This is expected to provide a calibration of the cognitive architecture underlying BRDL and, hopefully, important insights into alternative cognitive theories.

Finally, BRDL is a basic language, easy to extend and adapt to new contexts. This important characteristic is matched at the implementation level by exploiting Maude equational logic to construct new, complex data types.

Acknowledgments. The author would like to thank the four anonymous reviewers whose comments and suggestions greatly contributed to improve the paper.

References

1. Anderson, J.R.: The Architecture of Cognition. Psychology Press, East Sussex (1983)

2. Cerone, A.: A cognitive framework based on rewriting logic for the analysis of interactive systems. In: De Nicola, R., Kühn, E. (eds.) SEFM 2016. LNCS, vol. 9763, pp. 287–303. Springer, Cham (2016). https://doi.org/10.1007/978-3-319-41591-8_20

3. Cerone, A.: Towards a cognitive architecture for the formal analysis of human behaviour and learning. In: Mazzara, M., Ober, I., Salaün, G. (eds.) STAF 2018. LNCS, vol. 11176, pp. 216–232. Springer, Cham (2018). https://doi.org/10.1007/978-3-030-04771-9_17

4. Cerone, A., Ölveczky, P.: Modelling human reasoning in practical behavioural contexts using Real-time Maude. In: FM Collocated Workshops 2018 (FMIS). Lecture Notes in Computer Science, vol. 12025. Springer (2019). https://doi.org/10.1007/978-3-030-54994-7_32, In press

5. Collins, A.M., Quillian, M.R.: Retrieval time from semantic memory. J. Verbal Learn. Verbal Behav. **8**, 240–247 (1969)

6. Cowan, N.: What are the differences between long-term, short-term, and working memory? Prog. Brain Res. **169**, 223–238 (2008)

7. Diamond, A.: Executive functions. Annu. Rev. Psychol. **64**, 135–168 (2013)

8. Dix, A., Finlay, J., Abowd, G., Beale, R.: Human-Computer Interaction, 3rd edn. Pearson Education, London (2004)

9. Kotseruba, I., Tsotsos, J.K.: 40 years of cognitive architectures: core cognitive abilities and practical applications. Artif. Intell. Rev. **53**(1), 17–94 (2018). https://doi.org/10.1007/s10462-018-9646-y

10. Laird, J.A.: The Soar Cognitive Architecture. MIT Press, Cambridge (2012)

11. Martí-Oliet, N., Meseguer, J.: Rewriting logic: roadmap and bibliography. Theor. Comput. Sci. **285**(2), 121–154 (2002)

12. Miller, G.A.: The magical number seven, plus or minus two: some limits on our capacity to process information. Psychol. Rev. **63**(2), 81–97 (1956)

13. Nairne, J.S., Neath, I.: Sensory and working memory, volume 4, experimental psychology, chapter 15. In: Handbook of Psychology, 2nd edn., pp. 419–446 (2012)

14. Norman, D.A., Shallice, T.: Attention to action: willed and automatic control of behaviour. In: Consciousness and Self-Regulation. Advances in Research and Theory, vol. 4. Plenum Press (1986)

15. Ölveczky, P.C.: Real-time Maude and its applications. In: Escobar, S. (ed.) WRLA 2014. LNCS, vol. 8663, pp. 42–79. Springer, Cham (2014). https://doi.org/10.1007/978-3-319-12904-4_3

16. Ölveczky, P.C.: Designing Reliable Distributed Systems. UTCS. Springer, London (2017). https://doi.org/10.1007/978-1-4471-6687-0

17. Samsonovich, A.V.: Towards a unified catalog of implemented cognitive architectures. In: Biologically Inspired Cognitive Architectures (BICA 2010), pp. 195–244. IOS Press (2010)

18. Sun, R., Slusarz, P., Terry, C.: The interaction of the explicit and implicit in skill learning: A dual-process approach. Psychol. Rev. **112**, 159–192 (2005)

19. Verschure, P.: Distributed adaptive control: a theory of the mind, brain, body nexus. Biol. Inspired Cogn. Architect. **1**, 55–72 (2012)

Cognitive Learning with a Robot: The Case of Script Acquisition

Anara Sandygulova[1]($\boxtimes$), Anna CohenMiller[1], Nurziya Oralbayeva[1],
Wafa Johal[2,3], Thibault Asselborn[3], and Pierre Dillenbourg[3]

[1] Nazarbayev University, Nur-Sultan, Kazakhstan
anara.sandygulova@nu.edu.kz
[2] University of New South Wales, Sydney, Australia
[3] CHILI Lab, EPFL, Lausanne, Switzerland

Abstract. This research is situated in a specialized context offering a rarely occurring opportunity for research questions and technical objectives about language acquisition. The Kazakh language transition from Cyrillic to Latin alphabet in Kazakhstan raises challenges to teach the whole population to write and read in the new script. We propose an unique interdisciplinary approach by integrating innovative solutions from robotics, computer vision fields and pedagogical strategies from education, linguistics and cognitive sciences that will assist various demographic groups in this challenging endeavor. This paper presents the proposed system—a human-robot interaction application designed to assist primary school children in learning a new script and its associated handwriting. The system was deployed in a series of experiments where children increase their knowledge of the new script when practicing handwriting with a robot.

Keywords: Human-robot interaction · Child learning · Language learning · Social robot—Cognitive learning theory—Interdisciplinarity

1 Introduction

Kazakhstan's recent decision on the transfer of the Kazakh writing system from Cyrillic into the Latin alphabet was approved by the Kazakh authorities in October 2017 [1]. While there are clear reasons and goals for this reform addressing all levels of society, attention should be paid to educating all generations to read and write in the Latin script. Although it is believed that learning will not cause difficulties due to the exposure to English or other foreign languages sharing the Latin-based script, there are numerous risks facing the transfer, including risks to cause disinterest and lack of motivation to learn to write and read the Latin-based Kazakh among children and adults [2].

While there are clear reasons for many language reforms, the potential effects on literacy [3], identity [4], and education more broadly, need to be considered.

© Springer Nature Switzerland AG 2020
J. Camara and M. Steffen (Eds.): SEFM 2019 Workshops, LNCS 12226, pp. 154–162, 2020.
https://doi.org/10.1007/978-3-030-57506-9_12

As transition to the Latin alphabet requires the learning of the script, effective strategies and tools might be necessary in the process of teaching and learning. Various technologies are increasingly being used in the application of education [5] for language and handwriting learning [6]. Sysoev et al. (2017) [7] introduced SpeechBlocks application that helps children learn spelling principles by listening to the correct pronunciation of the letters' various arrangements. The application facilitates children's engagement, self-efficacy, and sense of authorship. Moreover, Dewi et al. (2018) implemented a Javanese script learning application for elementary school children in Indonesia which allowed learning of the script in an intuitive and engaging way [8]. Also working with elementary school children, Yanikoglu et al. (2017) [9] found that first-grade children preferred tablet-based learning (that included handwriting recognition and automatic assessment) in comparison to paper-based approach. Recent years have seen the increase in the amount of work investigating the topic of language learning using social robots [10,11] making human-robot interaction a fast growing research area [5] demonstrating potential for integrating social robots into educational systems. Since 2014, the CoWriter project has explored how robotic technologies can help children with the training of handwriting via an original paradigm known as learning by teaching (LbT) [12–14]. Since then, other research have successfully applied the robot-enhanced LbT learning methodology to other domains the curriculum [15,16].

The proposed CoWriting Kazakh system integrates a humanoid robot, NAO, and a tablet with stylus, where the robot plays a unique social role when interacting with learners. The robot is programmed to demonstrate a desire to learn Kazakh language. Yet, since it can not read Cyrillic script, a child becomes the robot's teacher. The child engages in writing words in Latin to help the robot read and learn Kazakh. The robot then asks the child to translate simple words from English to Kazakh (e.g., "hello") and to demonstrate how to write them using Latin script. In other words, the child is positioned as a "more knowledge-able other" guiding the learning as a teacher and peer [17,18] even though in actuality, the child is not yet an expert.

The CoWriter system can recognize children's handwritten letters in Cyrillic and convert them to Latin letters. The handwriting recognition was developed based upon our collection of the first-ever Cyrillic-MNIST dataset. Apart from automatically converting the spellings of words for the user, the system is intended to motivate children to learn and memorize the new alphabet. To investigate whether this approach would cause children to learn more letters in Latin-based Kazakh, we conducted two studies in a primary school in Kazakhstan with different vocabulary choices: an exploratory study with 48 children and a main study with 67 children. Children were asked to complete both a pre-test prior to interacting with the robot and also a post-test to calculate the number of learned letters in Latin-based Kazakh. Children interacted with the robot, showing it how to write Kazakh words using either a Cyrillic script or a Latin script. The robot then repeated the child's demonstration using the Latin-based Kazakh script while correcting for any misspelled words. In this way, the child had the opportunity to see the correct spelling in the Latin script and learn from their mistakes through a type of error analysis [19]. We hypothesize

Latin demonstration by the child (in contrast to Cyrillic demonstration) is more effective for learning a new script. Results demonstrate a gender bias with this learning strategy being more effective for girls. In contrast, boys learned significantly more when they spelled the words using Cyrillic and then observed the robot's correct spelling of the Latin-based Kazakh words.

In this paper, we discuss other scenarios that might be more effective at learning a new script. Since the CoWriter Kazakh learning activity relies upon a multidisciplinary approach including education, linguistics, and cognitive science, there is a need to explore and compare other theories to find alternative learning scenarios that might maximize children's learning gains. Thus, this paper also explores existing theories in multiple research domains (e.g., education, linguistics, cognitive science) to integrate into the system and measured by their impact on children's learning process. In purposefully integrating multiple disciplinary perspectives, an expanded understanding of a complex issue can be achieved [20,21]. Through human-robot interaction user studies, the CoWriting Kazakh activity will build upon the evolution of the research.

2 HRI System

This section presents the human-robot interaction system, namely CoWriting Kazakh, and details the scenario that was designed using the system.

2.1 Software and Hardware Components

The hardware components of the system include the Wacom Cintiq Pro tablet, its pen, and a humanoid robot NAO. The tablet serves as the second monitor when connected to a laptop. Its pen has 8,192 levels of pressure sensitivity and tilt recognition. This allows to acquire not only the trajectory of the handwriting, but also the pressure and tilt at every point. A humanoid robot, NAO, is a programmable autonomous robot developed by SoftBank Robotics. It is widely used in human-robot interaction research, in particular, educational and robot-assisted therapy applications. A humanoid robot's height is 58 cm which makes it comfortable to transport, also its appearance is appealing for children. Furthermore, it has 25 degrees of freedom and 7 tactile sensors. CoWriting Kazakh is an extension of the original CoWriter system[1]. In contrast to the original CoWriter's Learning by Teaching paradigm where robot's handwriting improved gradually via several demonstrations by the child, the CoWriting Kazakh does not have a handwriting improvement component. In the presented system, the robot and a child engage in co-operative learning where the robot learns from the child the new vocabulary in Kazakh, while the child learns from the robot the spelling in the new script. Thus, they take turns in writing words in Kazakh (see Fig. 1 [23]). In addition, the CoWriting Kazakh system integrates handwriting recognition in Cyrillic that was trained on over 120,000 samples of the Cyrillic-MNIST

---

[1] https://github.com/chili-epfl/cowriter.

dataset[2], collected for the first time for the Cyrillic-based languages. In order to dynamically adapt to each child's individual handwriting style and to provide an alternative to the default robot font, trajectories of human handwriting collected in real time are used in Learning by Demonstration (LbD) and Reinforcement Learning approaches[3]

2.2   Scenario

The scenario is designed for the robot to play the role of a peer. The robot is introduced to a child as a native English speaker of approximately his or her age who wants to learn Kazakh. The robot asks the child for help, in particular, to demonstrate how to write Kazakh words using the new Latin-based alphabet because it is convenient for the robot to read. In a control condition, the robot does not ask to write explicitly in Latin script, which means the child writes words in their preferred script (i.e., Cyrillic script as that is what they are used to).

The interaction takes approximately 20–30 min depending on how long children take to write. The speech utterances programmed on a robot are presented below:

NAO: -Hello. I am a robot. My name is Mimi. [Waves his hand]
Child: -...
NAO: -I study Kazakh language. Can you help me?
Child: -...
NAO: -How do you say "Hello" in Kazakh?
Child: -Sálem
NAO: - How do you write it? [In Latin-to-Latin case: Please write it using Latin letters so that I can read it.]
Child: -[Writes on a tablet the word in one of the scripts]
NAO: -Let me try to write it too [gesticulates]. This is a correct writing using Latin letters.

... repeated for another 12 words

NAO: - You are a great teacher. Thank you very much! Goodbye! [waves]

3   Experiments

This research was approved by the Ethical committee of Nazarbayev University. We conducted the studies in a primary school in the capital of Kazakhstan with a few classes of different age groups. First, an introductory session was conducted to provide a brief description of the research. Consent forms were distributed and children were able to ask questions. Teachers then collected assents and consent forms for us in the next few days.

---

[2] https://github.com/HRI-lab-NU/Cyrillic-MNIST.
[3] https://github.com/HRI-lab-NU/CoWriting-Kazakh.

3.1 Conditions

In order to investigate whether it is more effective for the child to perform conversion mentally and observe correctly written Latin spelling by the robot, we distinguish two conditions that are different in who performs the conversion:

- Latin-to-Latin: the child does the conversion mentally and writes directly in Latin.
- Cyrillic-to-Latin: the robot does the conversion. The child writes in Cyrillic and observes the Latin writing provided by the robot.

During the interaction, the researchers did not help children in writing and did not correct their mistakes. Instead, we only help to clarify what the robot said.

3.2 Preliminary Study

The first study was conducted with 48 children (24 females) aged 8–10 years old. Exactly half of the participants interacted in a Latin-to-Latin case with a random selection and counterbalancing for gender and age groups (see Kim et al. (2019) [27] for more details about the study). The average number of new learned letters is 3.73 (SD = 2.15, Max = 9, Min = 0). Strong learning gains were not observed as the pre- and post-tests asked for a subset of all letters (23 out of 42 letters). Children performed significantly differently in two robot conditions: on average children spent 1.21 ± 0.41 min vs 1.83 ± 0.69 min on each word in Cyrillic-to-Latin vs Latin-to-Latin case while on average the total time to complete the task was 11.88 ± 2.54 min vs 15.96 ± 3.43 min in both conditions respectively. These significant findings of time differences are expected as it was easier for children to write using a script which they use every day.

3.3 Main Study

Due to a major limitation in the way the pre-test was conducted in the preliminary study, we replicated the study with the same system design, interaction scenario, and the two experimental conditions, but with a different execution of the pre- and post-tests (with a preference for paper-based tests), which included all 42 letters without showing the correct answers in cases of mistakes or hesitations. There were 67 children (32 females) aged 8–11 years old. In general, children improved their knowledge of Latin alphabet during the experiment. The average number of new learned letters is 4.35 (SD = 3.7, Max = 18, Min = 0). Significant effect between gender group and robot condition was found: boys learned more in Cyrillic-to-Latin condition (5.06 ± 3.28 vs 3.59 ± 2.89) while girls learned more in Latin-to-Latin condition (3.00 ± 2.87 vs 6.07 ± 5.31). We can conclude the learning strategy of performing mental conversion was more effective for girls, in contrast to boys who learned more when the robot performed the conversion for them. More details of the study are presented in [23].

4 Discussion

We plan to further refine the scenarios in search of best strategies for learning a new script. For example, it might be effective to enable children to use their knowledge of foreign language vocabulary to advance their foreign script learning. Contrary to this strategy, it might be more effective to use unknown/non-existing words in languages children know in order to avoid confusions with prior knowledge. We believe it is important to study various strategies to find the most effective cognitive learning scenario as the robot is situated in the physical world, interactions with a social robot can be multimodal (e.g., verbal, visual, tactile) and be adapted according to all perceptual modalities, including events on the tablet, its stylus data and child's feedback. Through the lens of multimodality, children's language acquisition with the robot could be explored through multiliteracies [25,26].

Based on the results suggested by the study, the CoWriting Kazakh System seems to entail the cognitive learning character due to two-way human-robot interaction activity. This means the learning happens in both ends of the continua with a child at one end and the robot at the other end, involving the handwriting, script conversion and vocabulary selection tasks.

In general, this process can be explained through a constructivist view of cognitive learning, which implies that instead of passively receiving knowledge, children construct it on their own [27]. Therefore a direct relationship can be seen connecting cognitive learning to constructivism. As Schunk notes, "Cognitive constructivist perspectives emphasize that learners are not passive recipients of information but rather actively seek, construct, and adapt their knowledge, skills, strategies, and beliefs" (p. iv) [28]. Moreover, cognitive learning, as Shuell (1986) states, includes several mental activities. Some examples of those can be "generation and organization of appropriate response" and the "use of various learning strategies" [35]. In the context of the present research involving 67 children, the underlying premise is that during the selected two conditions (Latin-to-Latin versus Cyrillic-to-Latin), children perform the above-stated mental activities. In particular, they perform the mental selection of words from their existing vocabulary in two languages, as well as refer to their orthographic knowledge and knowledge of alphabets in order to choose the appropriate one. These activities consequently can be perceived by children as an entertaining learning strategy.

It is thus through handwriting that benefits are being shown. Research from multiple fields support the idea of handwriting as an asset for learning. For instance, handwriting can be seen as a scaffolding tool for children's cognitive development. Li and James (2016) confirm that handwriting facilitates learning of letters and their perception, "supporting the notion of developmental change though brain-body-environment interactions" (p. 298) [29]. Similarly, researchers studying at the intersection of neuroscience, psychology and education have shown the use of handwriting as a means of increasing cognitive activity and literacy [30–32]. These studies show a link between cognitive learning, language acquisition and motor learning.

Furthermore, perception's role within mental responses is significant for language and learning [34]. By perceiving the visual discrimination of letters, children become able to differentiate scripts according to a particular language. In a bilingual or multilingual setting, where two or more scripts co-exist, the primary stage of language learning (i.e. alphabet and orthography learning) can be handled through transliteration, which in turn enables cognitive development [23,24]. According to Al-Azami et al. (2010), transliteration is an asset for reaching and using one's linguistic repertoire to its fullest [24].

Thus, as Carrow-Woolfolk (1981) suggested, in the process of creating associations with words and formation of perceptions of concepts, the cognitive role of visual memory is tremendous [34]. Taken collectively, the literature suggests there is a chain reaction between handwriting, script conversion, and vocabulary selection. Thus, the overall framing of the CoWriting Kazakh System can be conceptualized through the lens of cognitive learning as means for facilitating learning and language acquisition.

5 Conclusion

This paper describes the CoWriting Kazakh system and the created scenario that allows to perform conversion of letters themselves/seeing the results having conversion performed by the robot. Future work will include creating and refining learning scenarios allowing children to choose which words to teach the robot. Additionally, integrating the original CoWriter's handwriting learning to have the robot exposed to several demonstrations of the same word warrants investigation as a means to explore long-term commitment to an interaction.

Acknowledgments. This work was supported by the Nazarbayev University Collaborative Research Program grant (award number is 091019CRP2107). This research was also funded by the Swiss State Secretariat for Education, Research and Innovation (SERI) as parts of the CIS Region Seeding Grants (Project SFG 1038), and the NCCR Robotics (SNSF).

References

1. Altynsarina, E.: Kazakhstan adopts new version of Latin-based Kazakh alphabet (2018). https://astanatimes.com/2018/02/kazakhstan-adopts-new-version-of-latin-based-kazakh-alphabet/
2. Kadirova, R.B.: The Sociolinguistic Attitudes of Kazakhs Towards the Latin Alphabet and Orthography Reform in Kazakh (2018). https://cdr.lib.unc.edu/concern/dissertations/br86b405f
3. Crisp, S.: Soviet language planning 1917–53. In: Kirkwood, M. (ed.) Language Planning in the Soviet Union. Palgrave Macmillan, London (1990). https://doi.org/10.1007/978-1-349-20301-7_2
4. Hatcher, L.: Script change in Azerbaijan: acts of identity. Int. J. Soc. Lang. **2008**(192), 105–116 (2008). https://doi.org/10.1515/IJSL.2008.038

5. Mubin, O., Shahid, C.J., Al Mahmud, A., Dong, J.J.: A review of the applicability of robots in education. Technol. Educ. Learn. **1**(209), 13 (2013). https://doi.org/10.2316/journal.209.2013.1.209-0015
6. Balkibekov, K., Meiirbekov, S., Tazhigaliyeva, N., Sandygulova, A.: Should robots win or lose? robot's losing playing strategy positively affects child learning.: In Robot and Human Interactive Communication (RO-MAN), pp. 706–711. IEEE, August 2016
7. Sysoev, I., Hershman, A., Fine, S., Traweek, C., Roy, D.: Speechblocks: a constructionist early literacy app. In: Proceedings of the 2017 Conference on Interaction Design and Children, pp. 248–257. ACM (2017)
8. Dewi, R., Priandani, N., Brata, K., Fanani, L.: Usability evaluation of mobile-based application for Javanese script learning media. J. Inf. Technol. Comput. Sci. **3**(1), 88 (2018)
9. Yanikoglu, B., Gogus, A., Inal, E.: Use of handwriting recognition technologies in tablet-based learning modules for first grade education. Educ. Technol. Res. Dev. **65**(5), 1369–1388 (2017)
10. Belpaeme, T., Vogt, P., van den Berghe, R., Bergmann, K., Göksun, T., de Haas, M., et al.: Guidelines for designing social robots as second language tutors. Int. J. Soc. Robot. **10**(3), 325–341 (2017)
11. Tazhigaliyeva, N., Diyas, Y., Brakk, D., Aimambetov, Y., Sandygulova, A.: Learning with or from the robot: exploring robot roles in educational context with children. In: Agah, A., Cabibihan, J.-J., Howard, A.M., Salichs, M.A., He, H. (eds.) ICSR 2016. LNCS (LNAI), vol. 9979, pp. 650–659. Springer, Cham (2016). https://doi.org/10.1007/978-3-319-47437-3_64
12. Hood, D., Lemaignan, S., Dillenbourg, P.: The cowriter project: teaching a robot how to write. In: 2015 Human-Robot Interaction Conference, Portland, USA, 3–5 March (2015). https://doi.org/10.1145/2701973.2702091
13. Jacq, A., Lemaignan, S., Garcia, F., Dillenbourg, P., Paiva, A.: Building successful long child-robot interactions in a learning context. In: 2016 11th ACM/IEEE International Conference on Human-Robot Interaction (HRI), Christchurch, New zealand, 07–10 March, pp. 239–246 (2016)
14. Lemaignan, S., et al.: Learning by teaching a robot: the case of handwriting. Robot. Autom. Mag. **23**(2), 56–66 (2016). https://doi.org/10.1109/Mra.2016.2546700
15. Yadollahi, E., Johal, W., Paiva, A., Dillenbourg, P.: When deictic gestures in a robot can harm child-robot collaboration. In: Proceedings of the 17th ACM Conference on Interaction Design and Children, pp. 195–206, June 2018
16. Jamet, F., Masson, O., Jacquet, B., Stilgenbauer, J.L., Baratgin, J.: Learning by teaching with humanoid robot: a new powerful experimental tool to improve children's learning ability. J. Robot (2018)
17. Huong, L.P.H.: The more knowledgeable peer, target language use, and group participation. Can. Modern Lang. Rev./ La revue canadienne des langues vivantes,**64**(2), 333–354 (2007). https://www.muse.jhu.edu/article/233947
18. Vygotsky, L.S.: Mind in Society: The Development of Higher Psychological Processes. Harvard University Press, Cambridge (1978)
19. Jobeen, A., Kazemian, B., Shahbaz, M.: The role of error analysis in teaching and learning of second and foreign language. Educ. Linguis. Res. **1**(2), 52–62, 13 September 2015. https://ssrn.com/abstract=2659714https://doi.org/10.5296/elr.v1i1.8189
20. CohenMiller, A., Pate, E.: A model for developing interdisciplinary research theoretical frameworks. Qual. Rep.**24**(6), 1211–1226 (2019). https://nsuworks.nova.edu/tqr/vol24/iss6/2

21. Klein, J.T.: Interdisciplinarity: History, Theory, and Practice. Wayne State University Press, Detroit (1990)
22. Kim, A., et al.: Cowriting kazakh: transitioning to a new Latin script using social robots. In: Proceedings of the 28th IEEE International Conference on Robot and Human Interactive Communication (RO-MAN). IEEE (2019)
23. Sandygulova, A., et al.: CoWriting kazakh: learning a new script with a robot. In: Proceedings of the 2020 ACM/IEEE International Conference on Human-Robot Interaction (HRI 2020). Cambridge, United Kingdom, p. 8. ACM, New York, USA(2020). https://doi.org/10.1145/3319502.3374813
24. Al-Azami, S., Kenner, C., Ruby, M., Gregory, E.: Transliteration as a bridge to learning for bilingual children. Int. J. Bilingual Educ. Bilingualism **13**(6), 683–700 (2010)
25. Plowman, L., Stephen, C., McPake, J.: Growing up with Technology: Young Children Learning in a Digital World. Routledge, London (2010)
26. Yelland, N.J.: A pedagogy of multiliteracies: young children and multimodal learning with tablets. Br. J. Educ. Technol. **49**(5), 847–858 (2018)
27. Kim, B., Reeves, T.C.: Reframing research on learning with technology: in search of the meaning of cognitive tools. Instr. Sci. **35**(3), 207–256 (2007)
28. Schunk, D.: Learning Theories: An Educational Perspective, 8th edn. Pearson, London (2020)
29. Li, J.X., James, K.H.: Handwriting generates variable visual output to facilitate symbol learning. J. Exp. Psychol. Gen. **145**(3), 298–313 (2016). https://doi.org/10.1037/xge0000134
30. James, K.H., Engelhardt, L.: The effects of handwriting experience on functional brain development in pre-literate children. Trends Neurosci. Educ. **1**(1), 32–42 (2012). https://doi.org/10.1016/j.tine.2012.08.001
31. James, K.H.: The importance of handwriting experience on the development of the literate brain. Curr. Dir. Psychol. Sci. **26**(6), 502–508 (2017). https://doi.org/10.1177/0963721417709821
32. Mayer, C., Wallner, S., Budde-Spengler, N., Braunert, S., Arndt, P.A., Kiefer, M.: Literacy training of kindergarten children with pencil, keyboard or tablet stylus: the influence of the writing tool on reading and writing performance at the letter and word level. Front. Psychol. **10**, 3054 (2020). https://doi.org/10.3389/fpsyg.2019.03054
33. Primary School Literacy Resources – PLD (Promoting Literacy Development) (2019). https://pld-literacy.org/. Accessed 29 Jan 2020
34. Richmond, J.E.: School aged children: visual perception and reversal recognition of letters and numbers separately and in context (2010)
35. Shuell, T.J.: Cognitive conceptions of learning. Rev. Educ. Res. **56**(4), 411–436 (1986)

Measuring the Intelligence of an Idealized Mechanical Knowing Agent

Samuel Allen Alexander[✉][iD]

The U.S. Securities and Exchange Commission, New York City, NY, USA
samuelallenalexander@gmail.com
https://philpeople.org/profiles/samuel-alexander/publications

Abstract. We define a notion of the intelligence level of an idealized mechanical knowing agent. This is motivated by efforts within artificial intelligence research to define real-number intelligence levels of complicated intelligent systems. Our agents are more idealized, which allows us to define a much simpler measure of intelligence level for them. In short, we define the intelligence level of a mechanical knowing agent to be the supremum of the computable ordinals that have codes the agent knows to be codes of computable ordinals. We prove that if one agent knows certain things about another agent, then the former necessarily has a higher intelligence level than the latter. This allows our intelligence notion to serve as a stepping stone to obtain results which, by themselves, are not stated in terms of our intelligence notion (results of potential interest even to readers totally skeptical that our notion correctly captures intelligence). As an application, we argue that these results comprise evidence against the possibility of intelligence explosion (that is, the notion that sufficiently intelligent machines will eventually be capable of designing even more intelligent machines, which can then design even more intelligent machines, and so on).

Keywords: Machine intelligence · Knowing agents · Ordinal numbers · Intelligence explosion

1 Introduction

In formal epistemology, when we study the knowledge of knowing agents, we usually *idealize* their knowledge. We assume, for example, that if an agent knows A and knows $A \to B$, then that agent knows B. We might assume the agent knows all the first-order axioms of Peano arithmetic, even though there are infinitely many such axioms (because the axiom of mathematical induction is an infinite schema). See [19] (Sect. 2) for an excellent description of this idealization process. This idealization process is important because it acts as a simplifying assumption which makes it possible to reason about knowledge. Without such simplifying assumptions, the deep structure of knowledge would be hidden behind the distracting noise and arbitrariness surrounding real-world knowledge. In this paper,

© Springer Nature Switzerland AG 2020
J. Camara and M. Steffen (Eds.): SEFM 2019 Workshops, LNCS 12226, pp. 163–179, 2020.
https://doi.org/10.1007/978-3-030-57506-9_13

we will describe a way to measure the intelligence level of an idealized mechanical knowing agent (a knowing agent is *mechanical* if its knowledge-set can be enumerated by a Turing machine, see [6]).

We anticipate that the reader might object that knowing agents might not be totally ordered by intelligence (perhaps there are two agents A and B such that A is more intelligent in certain ways and B is more intelligent in others); the same goes for human beings, but that does not stop psychologists from studying IQ scores. Our intelligence measure is somewhat like an IQ test in the sense that it assigns intelligence levels to agents in spite of the fact that true intelligence probably is not a total ordering. Similarly, the reader might object that intelligence is not 1-dimensional and therefore one single measurement is probably not enough. Again, we would make the same comparison to IQ. In general, any formal measure of intelligence is certain to have limits (the map is not the territory).

This paper was motivated by authors like Legg and Hutter [14], Hernández-Orallo and Dowe [12], and Hibbard [13], who attempt to use real numbers to measure the intelligence of intelligent systems[1]. Those systems perform actions and observe the results of those actions in surrounding environments[2]. By contrast, the agents we consider do not perform actions in their environments, neither do they make observations about those environments. To us, a knowing agent is more like an intelligent system that has been placed in a particularly bleak environment: an empty room totally devoid of stimulus and rewards. Thus abandoned, the system has nothing else to do but enumerate theorems all day. Despite these spartan conditions, we discovered a method of measuring the intelligence of idealized mechanical knowing agents. (In Sect. 6, we will describe a thought experiment whereby our idealized agents can be obtained as a type of cross section of less idealized agents, so that in spite of the idealized nature of the agents we predominately study, nevertheless some insight can be gained into more realistic intelligent systems).

Whereas authors like Legg and Hutter attempt to measure intelligence based on what an intelligent system *does*, we measure intelligence based on what a knowing mechanical agent *knows*. And whereas authors like Legg and Hutter use real numbers to measure intelligence, our method uses computable ordinal numbers instead.

---

[1] In the case of Hibbard, natural numbers are used.

[2] Such authors essentially consider an *environment* to be a function which takes as input a finite sequence of *actions* and which outputs a real-number *reward* and an *observation* for each such action-sequence. To those authors, an *intelligent system* is essentially a function which takes a finite sequence of reward-observation pairs and outputs an *action*. A system and an environment interact with each other to produce an infinite reward-observation-action sequence in the obvious way. Those authors' goal is to assign numerical intelligence-measurements to such systems, with the intention that a higher-intelligence system should outperform a lower-intelligence system (as measured by total reward earned) "on average" (across an infinite universe of environments). This is, of course, an oversimplification of those authors' work.

To see one of the benefits of using ordinals to measure intelligence, consider the following question: if $A_1, A_2, \ldots$ are agents such that each A_{i+1} is significantly more intelligent than A_i, does it necessarily follow that for every agent B, there must be some i such that A_i is more intelligent than B? If we were to measure intelligence using natural numbers (for example, as the Kolmogorov complexity of the agent), the answer would automatically be "yes", but the reason has nothing to do with intelligence and everything to do with the topology of the natural numbers. A real-number-valued intelligence measure would also force the answer to be "yes" assuming that "A_{i+1} is significantly more intelligent than A_i" implies "A_{i+1}'s intelligence is at least $+1$ higher than A_i's intelligence". In actuality, we see no reason why the answer to the question must be "yes", at least for idealized agents. Imagine a master-agent who designs sub-agents. Over the course of eternity, the master-agent might design better and better sub-agents, each one significantly more intelligent than the previous, but each one intentionally kept less intelligent than the master-agent.

Another benefit of measuring intelligence using computable ordinals is that, because the computable ordinals are well-founded (i.e., there is no infinite strictly-descending sequence of computable ordinals), we obtain a well-founded structure on idealized knowing agents (i.e., there is no infinite sequence of mechanical knowing agents each with strictly greater intelligence than the next). Further, this well-foundedness is inherited by any relation on idealized mechanical knowing agents that respects our intelligence measure (a relation $\prec$ is said to *respect* an intelligence measure if whenever $B \prec A$, then A has a higher intelligence than B according to that measure). For example, say that knower A *totally endorses* knower B if A knows the codes of Turing machines that enumerate B and also A knows that B is truthful (we will better formalize this later). We will show that whenever A totally endorses B, A has a strictly larger intelligence than B according to our ordinal-valued measure of intelligence. It immediately follows that there is no infinite sequence of mechanical knowing agents, each one of which totally endorses the next. (A result which, although we arrive at it by means of our intelligence measure, does not itself make any direct reference to our intelligence measure, and should be of interest even to critics who would flatly deny that our intelligence measure is the correct way to measure a mechanical knowing agent's intelligence).

As a practical application, the result in the previous paragraph provides a skeptical lens through which to view the idea of intelligence explosion, as described by Hutter [15]. We will elaborate upon this in Sect. 7.

2   An Intuitive Ordinal Notation System

Whatever intelligence is, it surely involves certain core components like: pattern-matching; creativity; and the ability to generalize. In this section we introduce an intuitive ordinal notation system which will illuminate the relationship between ordinal notation and those three core components of intelligence. Later in the paper, in order to simplify technical details, we will use an equivalent but more abstract ordinal notation system.

Definition 1. *Let $\mathscr{P}$ be the smallest set of computer programs such that for every computer program P, if, when P is run, P outputs nothing except elements of $\mathscr{P}$, then $P \in \mathscr{P}$. For each $P \in \mathscr{P}$, let $|P|$ be the smallest ordinal α such that $\alpha > |Q|$ for every program Q which P outputs. We say that P notates the ordinal $|P|$.*

Example 1. (Some finite ordinals)

1. Let P_0 be the program "End", which immediately ends, outputting nothing. Vacuously, P_0 outputs nothing except elements of $\mathscr{P}$, so $P_0 \in \mathscr{P}$. $|P_0|$ is the smallest ordinal α bigger than $|Q|$ for every Q which P_0 outputs, so $|P_0| = 0$ (since P_0 outputs nothing).
2. Let P_1 be the program: "Print('End')", which outputs P_0 and then stops. Certainly P_1 outputs nothing except elements of $\mathscr{P}$, so $P_1 \in \mathscr{P}$. $|P_1|$ is the smallest ordinal α bigger than $|Q|$ for every Q which P_1 outputs, so $|P_1| = 1$.
3. Let P_2 be the program: "Print('Print('End')')", which outputs P_1 and then stops. Then $P_2 \in \mathscr{P}$ and $|P_2| = 2$.

Using their pattern-matching skills, the reader should recognize a pattern forming in Example 1. Through the use of creativity and generalization, the reader can short-circuit that pattern to obtain the first infinite ordinal, ω.

Example 2. Let P_ω be the program:

Let X = 'End'; While(True) { Print(X); Let X = "Print('"+X+"')" }

which outputs "End", "Print('End')", "Print('Print('End')')", and so on forever. By reasoning similar to Example 1, these outputs are in $\mathscr{P}$ and they notate $0, 1, 2, \ldots$. Thus $P_\omega \in \mathscr{P}$ and $|P_\omega|$ is the smallest ordinal bigger than all of $0, 1, 2, \ldots$, i.e., the smallest infinite ordinal, ω.

One might think of P_ω as a naive attempt to print every ordinal. The attempt fails, of course, because it does not print P_ω itself. In similar fashion, it can be shown that no program can succeed at printing exactly the set of computable ordinals ($\mathscr{P}$ is not computably enumerable).

Example 3. (The next few ordinals)

1. Let $P_{\omega+1}$ be the program: "Print(P_ω)" (where P_ω is from Example 2). Then $P_{\omega+1} \in \mathscr{P}$ and $|P_{\omega+1}| = \omega + 1$.
2. Let $P_{\omega+2}$ be: "Print($P_{\omega+1}$)". Then $P_{\omega+2} \in \mathscr{P}$ and $|P_{\omega+2}| = \omega + 2$.

We could continue Example 3 all day, notating $\omega + 3$, $\omega + 4$, and so on. But the reader is more intelligent than that. Using their pattern-matching skill, their creativity, and their generalization skill, the reader can short-circuit the process.

Example 4. (Starting to accelerate)

1. Let $P_{\omega \cdot 2}$ be the program:

Let X $= P_\omega$; While(True) { Print(X); Let X $=$ "Print('"+X+"')" }

Similar to Example 2, $P_{\omega \cdot 2} \in \mathscr{P}$ and $|P_{\omega \cdot 2}| = \omega \cdot 2$.

2. Let $P_{\omega \cdot 3}$ be the program:

Let X $= P_{\omega \cdot 2}$; While(True) { Print(X); Let X $=$ "Print('"+X+"')" }

Then $P_{\omega \cdot 3} \in \mathscr{P}$ and $|P_{\omega \cdot 3}| = \omega \cdot 3$.

Again, we could continue Example 4 all day, noting $\omega \cdot 4$, $\omega \cdot 5$, and so on. But the reader is more intelligent than that and can identify the pattern and creatively abstract it to reach $\omega \cdot \omega = \omega^2$:

Example 5. Let P_{ω^2} be the program:

```
Let LEFT = ⌜Let X = "⌝;
Let RIGHT = ⌜"⌝; While(True){ Print(X); Let X = "Print('"+X+"')" }⌝;
Let X = 'End';
While(True) {
    Let X = LEFT + X + RIGHT;
    Print(X)
}
```

$P_{\omega^2} \in \mathscr{P}$ notates $|P_{\omega^2}| = \omega^2$.

We can continue along these same lines as long as we like, without ever reaching an end:

Exercise 1. 1. Write programs notating ω^3, ω^4, $\ldots$.

2. Use your creativity and your pattern-matching and generalization skills to notate ω^ω.
3. Write programs notating ω^{ω^ω}, $\omega^{\omega^{\omega^\omega}}$, $\ldots$.
4. Use your creativity and your pattern-matching and generalization skills to short-circuit the above and notate the smallest ordinal, called ϵ_0, with the property that $\epsilon_0 = \omega^{\epsilon_0}$.
5. Contemplate creative ways to go far beyond ϵ_0.

In the above examples and exercises, at various points we need to apply creativity to transcend all the techniques developed previously. I conjecture that each such transcending requires strictly greater intelligence than the ones before it. If this informal conjecture is true, then it seems natural to measure an intelligence by saying: an agent's intelligence level is equal to the supremum of the ordinals the agent comes up with if the agent is allowed to spend all eternity inventing ordinal notations[3].

---

[3] For another connection to intelligence, consider the open-ended problem: "Find a very fast-growing computable function". It seems plausible that solutions should span much or all of the range of mathematical intelligence. And yet, so-called *fast-growing hierarchies* (which ultimately trace back to Hardy [11]) essentially reduce the problem to that of notating computable ordinals.

Theoretically, the above examples and exercises might someday be able to serve as a bridge between artificial intelligence research and neuroscience. Namely: observe human subjects' brains while they work on designing the programs in question, to see how the magnitude of the ordinal being notated corresponds to the regions of the brain that activate.

3   Preliminaries

In Sect. 2 we introduced an intuitive ordinal notation system (and, implicitly, the notion of the *output* of a computer program). To get actual work done, we'll need an ordinal notation system (and notion of program output) which is easier to work with. We begin with a formalized notion of computer program outputs.

Definition 2. *For $n \in \mathbb{N}$, let W_n be the nth computably enumerable set of natural numbers (i.e., the set of naturals enumerated by the nth Turing machine).*

For example, if n is such that the nth Turing machine never halts, then $W_n = \emptyset$. If n is such that the nth Turing machine enumerates exactly the prime numbers, then W_n is the set of prime numbers.

The following ordinal notation system is equivalent to Definition 1 but easier to formally work with. This ordinal notation system is a simplification of a well-known ordinal notation system invented by Kleene [16].

Definition 3 *(Compare Definition 1). Let $\mathcal{O}$ be the smallest subset of $\mathbb{N}$ with the property that for every $n \in \mathbb{N}$, if $W_n \subseteq \mathcal{O}$, then $n \in \mathcal{O}$. For each $n \in \mathcal{O}$, let $|n|$ be the smallest ordinal α such that $\alpha > |m|$ for all $m \in W_n$. For $n \in \mathcal{O}$, we say that n notates $|n|$.*

Intuitively, we want to identify a knowing agent with its knowledge-set in a certain carefully-chosen language. The language will contain a symbol $\bar{n}$ for each natural number n; a symbol $\mathbf{W}$ (we intend that $\mathbf{W}(x,y)$ be read like "$x \in W_y$"); a symbol $\mathbf{O}$ (we intend that $\mathbf{O}(x)$ be read like "$x \in \mathcal{O}$"); and finally, the language will contain modal operators $K_1, K_2, \ldots$. For any formula ϕ in the language, the formula $K_i(\phi)$ is intended to express "Agent i knows ϕ". When no confusion results, we will abbreviate $K_i(\phi)$ as $K_i\phi$. For example, suppose we have chosen Agents $1, 2, 3, \ldots$. Agent (say) 5 shall be identified with the set of statements (within the language) that Agent 5 knows. If one of the statements known by Agent 5 is $K_7(\bar{1} = \bar{1})$, then that statement is read like "Agent 7 knows $1 = 1$", which is semantically interpreted as the statement that Agent 7 (i.e., the set of Agent 7's knowledge) contains the statement $\bar{1} = \bar{1}$. Nontrivial statements can be built up using quantifiers. For example, the statement $\forall x(K_2\mathbf{O}(x) \to K_3\mathbf{O}(x))$ expresses that for every natural number n, if Agent 2 knows $n \in \mathcal{O}$, then Agent 3 also knows $n \in \mathcal{O}$.

Unfortunately, the naive intuition in the above paragraph would expose us to philosophical questions like "what does it mean for a statement to be true?" Thus, we must formalize everything using techniques from mathematical logic. A reader uninterested in all the formal details can safely skim the definitions in this section (which assume familiarity with first-order logic) and instead read our commentary on those definitions.

Definition 4. *(Standard Definitions)*

1. *When a first-order model $\mathcal{M}$ is clear from context, an* assignment *is a function s mapping the set of first-order variables into the universe of $\mathcal{M}$.*
2. *For any assignment s, variable x, and element u of the universe of $\mathcal{M}$, $s(x|u)$ is the assignment which agrees with s everywhere except that it maps x to u.*
3. *For any variable x and any formula ϕ and term t in a first-order language, $\phi(x|t)$ is the result of substituting t for x in ϕ.*
4. *If $\mathcal{M}$ is a first-order model over a first-order language $\mathcal{L}$, and if ϕ is an $\mathcal{L}$-formula such that $\mathcal{M} \models \phi[s]$ for all assignments s, then we say $\mathcal{M} \models \phi$.*
5. *An $\mathcal{L}$-formula ϕ is a* sentence *if it has no free variables.*
6. *An $\mathcal{L}$-formula ϕ is* tautological *if for every $\mathcal{L}$-model $\mathcal{M}$, $\mathcal{M} \models \phi$.*
7. *A* universal closure *of a formula ϕ is a sentence $\forall x_1 \cdots \forall x_n \phi$ where the variables $x_1, \ldots, x_n$ include all the free variables of ϕ.*

Definition 4 merely reviews standard material from first-order logic. Informally, $\mathcal{M} \models \phi$ can be read, "ϕ is true (in model $\mathcal{M}$)". First-order logic does not touch on modal operators like K_i, so we need to extend first-order logic. We want to work with statements involving modal operators and also quantifiers ($\forall$, $\exists$) in the same statement—we want to do quantified modal logic. Quantified modal logic semantics is relatively cutting-edge. For our extension, we will make use of the so-called *base logic* from [6], as rephrased in [4].

Definition 5. *(The base logic)*

- *A language $\mathcal{L}$ of the* base logic *consists of a first-order language $\mathcal{L}_0$ together with a set of symbols called* operators. *$\mathcal{L}$-formulas and their free variables are defined as usual, with the additional clause that for any operator K and any $\mathcal{L}$-formula ϕ, $K(\phi)$ is an $\mathcal{L}$-formula, with the same free variables as ϕ. Syntactic parts of Definition 4 extend to the base logic in the obvious ways.*
- *With $\mathcal{L}$ as above, an $\mathcal{L}$-model $\mathcal{M}$ consists of a first-order model $\mathcal{M}_0$ for $\mathcal{L}_0$, along with a function which takes one operator K, one $\mathcal{L}$-formula ϕ, and one $\mathcal{M}_0$-assignment s, and outputs either True or False–in which case we write $\mathcal{M} \models K\phi[s]$ or $\mathcal{M} \not\models K\phi[s]$, respectively–such that:*
  1. *Whether or not $\mathcal{M} \models K\phi[s]$ does not depend on $s(x)$ if x is not a free variable of ϕ.*
  2. *Whenever ϕ and ψ are alphabetic invariants (by which we mean that one is obtained from the other by renaming bound variables in a way which is consistent with the binding of the quantifiers), then $\mathcal{M} \models K\phi[s]$ if and only if $\mathcal{M} \models K\psi[s]$.*
  3. *For variables x and y such that y is substitutable for x in $K\phi$, $\mathcal{M} \models K\phi(x|y)[s]$ if and only if $\mathcal{M} \models K\phi[s(x|s(y))]$.*
  The definition of $\mathcal{M} \models \phi[s]$ (and of $\mathcal{M} \models \phi$) for arbitrary $\mathcal{L}$-formulas ϕ is obtained from this by induction. Semantic parts of Definition 4 extend to the base logic in the obvious ways.

The following are some standard axioms which any idealized knowing agent presumably should satisfy. Axioms E1–E3 below are taken from [6].

Definition 6. *Suppose $\mathscr{L}$ is a language in the base logic, with an operator K. The* axioms of knowledge *for K in $\mathscr{L}$ consist of the following schemas, where ϕ, ψ vary over $\mathscr{L}$-formulas.*

- *(E1) Any universal closure of $K\phi$ whenever ϕ is tautological.*
- *(E2) Any universal closure of $K(\phi \to \psi) \to K\phi \to K\psi$.*
- *(E3) Any universal closure of $K\phi \to \phi$.*

By the axioms of knowledge *in $\mathscr{L}$, we mean the set of axioms of knowledge for K in $\mathscr{L}$, for all $\mathscr{L}$-operators K.*

For example, for operator K_5, the corresponding E3 schema expresses the truthfulness of Agent 5, stating that whenever Agent 5 knows a fact ϕ (i.e., whenever $K_5\phi$ is true in the model in question), then ϕ is true (in the model in question). The E1 schema for K_5 essentially states that Agent 5 is smart enough to know tautologies. The E2 schema for K_5 expresses that Agent 5's knowledge is closed under modus ponens: whenever Agent 5 knows $\phi \to \psi$ and also knows ϕ, then Agent 5 knows ψ.

We will now formally define the language we spoke of intuitively above. The lack of the usual arithmetical symbols S, $+$ and $\cdot$ might be surprising to mathematical logicians; we do not need those symbols. Their absense emphasizes that our results are independent of Gödel-style diagonalization[4].

Definition 7. *– Let $\mathscr{L}_O$ be the language which has a constant symbol $\overline{n}$ for each $n \in \mathbb{N}$, a unary predicate symbol $\mathbf{O}$ (intended as a predicate for the set $\mathcal{O}$ of ordinal notations), a binary predicate symbol $\mathbf{W}$ (we intend that $\mathbf{W}(x,y)$ be interpreted as $x \in W_y$ where W_y is the yth computably enumerable set), and operators K_i for all $i \in \mathbb{N}$.*
- *An $\mathscr{L}_O$-model $\mathscr{M}$ is* standard *if the following conditions hold:*
  1. *$\mathscr{M}$ has universe $\mathbb{N}$.*
  2. *For each $n \in \mathbb{N}$, $\mathscr{M}$ interprets $\overline{n}$ as n.*
  3. *$\mathscr{M}$ interprets $\mathbf{O}$ as $\mathcal{O}$.*
  4. *$\mathscr{M}$ interprets $\mathbf{W}$ as the set of pairs $(m,n) \in \mathbb{N}^2$ such that $m \in W_n$.*

To understand the next definition, recall that in Definition 3 we defined the ordinal notation system $\mathcal{O}$ as the smallest set of naturals such that for every natural n, if $W_n \subseteq \mathcal{O}$ then $n \in \mathcal{O}$. To say $W_n \subseteq \mathcal{O}$ is equivalent to saying that for every $m \in \mathbb{N}$, if $m \in W_n$, then $m \in \mathcal{O}$.

Definition 8. *By the* axiom of $\mathcal{O}$, *we mean the axiom*

$$\forall y(\forall x(\mathbf{W}(x,y) \to \mathbf{O}(x))) \to \mathbf{O}(y).$$

---

[4] To be clear, our results would still apply to agents who are aware of these arithmetical symbols, but our results do not require as much. Our most important results concern well-foundedness, which is a negative property (because it states a *lack* of infinite descending sequences), and so by weakening our language like this, we strengthen those results.

4   A Measure of a Mechanical Knowing Agent's Intelligence

"Once upon a time, Archimedes was charged with the task of testing the strength of a certain AI. He thought long and hard but made no progress. Then one day, Archimedes took his brain out to wash it in a tub full of computable ordinals. When he put his brain in the tub, he noticed that certain ordinals splashed out. He suddenly realized he could compare different AIs by putting them in the tub and comparing which ordinals splashed out. Archimedes was so excited that he ran through the city shouting 'Eureka!', without even remembering to put his brain back in his head."—Folktale (modified)

Although our intention is to define a measure of intelligence for one idealized mechanical knowing agent, all of our results will be about how this measure compares between different agents. For this reason, the following definition defines a system of knowing agents, rather than a single knowing agent. Of course, a single knowing agent can be thought of as being a system of knowing agents all of whom are equal to herself. The idea behind this definition is to identify a knowing agent with the set of that agent's knowledge in $\mathscr{L}_O$.

Definition 9. *By a* system of knowing agents, *we mean a standard $\mathscr{L}_O$-model $\mathscr{M}$ satisfying the axioms of knowledge. If $\mathscr{M}$ is a system of knowing agents, we refer to the operators $K_1, K_2, \ldots$ as the* knowing agents *of $\mathscr{M}$. A knowing agent K_i of $\mathscr{M}$ is* mechanical *if*

$$\{\phi : \phi \text{ is an } \mathscr{L}_O\text{-sentence and } \mathscr{M} \models K_i\phi\}$$

is computably enumerable. If K_i is mechanical for all $i \in \mathbb{N}$, we say $\mathscr{M}$ is a system of mechanical knowing agents.

We are now ready to define our measurement of the intelligence of an idealized mechanical knowing agent. This measure takes values from the computable ordinals (foreshadowed by [10]; also hinted at in [5]).

Definition 10. *Let $\mathscr{M}$ be a system of mechanical knowing agents. For any knowing agent K_i of $\mathscr{M}$, the* intelligence $\|K_i\|$ *of K_i is the least ordinal α such that for all $n \in \mathbb{N}$, if $\mathscr{M} \models K_i\mathbf{O}(\overline{n})$, then $\alpha > |n|$ (where $|n|$ is the ordinal notated by n, see Definition 3).*

In less formal language, Definition 10 says that $\|K_i\|$ is the smallest ordinal bigger than all the computable ordinals that have codes that K_i knows to be codes of computable ordinals[5]. Note that $\|K_i\| > \|K_j\|$ does not necessarily imply that K_i knows everything K_j knows.

---

[5] This is similar to the way the strength of mathematical theories is measured in the area of *proof theory* [17].

Lemma 1. *For any knowing agent K_i of a system $\mathscr{M}$ of mechanical knowing agents, $\|K_i\|$ exists and is a computable ordinal.*

Proof. Since $\mathscr{M}$ is a system of mechanical knowing agents, K_i is mechanical, so

$$\{\phi : \phi \text{ is an } \mathscr{L}_O\text{-sentence and } \mathscr{M} \models K_i\phi\}$$

is computably enumerable. It follows that

$$X = \{n \in \mathbb{N} : \mathscr{M} \models K_i\mathbf{O}(\overline{n})\}$$

is computably enumerable. Since $\mathscr{M}$ satisfies the axioms of knowledge, in particular $\mathscr{M} \models K_i\mathbf{O}(\overline{n}) \to \mathbf{O}(\overline{n})$ for all $n \in \mathbb{N}$. Since $\mathscr{M}$ is standard, it follows that $n \in \mathcal{O}$ whenever $\mathscr{M} \models K_i\mathbf{O}(\overline{n})$. Altogether, X is a computably enumerable subset of $\mathcal{O}$. Thus $\{|n| : n \in X\}$ is a computably enumerable set of computable ordinals. It follows there is a computable ordinal α such that α is the least ordinal greater than $|n|$ for all $n \in X$. By construction, $\alpha = \|K_i\|$. $\square$

As promised in the introduction, we immediately obtain a well-founded structure on the class of idealized mechanical knowing agents.

Corollary 1. *Let $\mathscr{M}$ be a system of mechanical knowing agents. There is no infinite sequence $i_1, i_2, \ldots$ such that $\|K_{i_1}\| > \|K_{i_2}\| > \cdots$.*

Proof. Immediate from the fact that there is no infinite strictly-decreasing sequence $\alpha_1 > \alpha_2 > \cdots$ of ordinals. $\square$

5   Well-Foundedness of Knowledge Hierarchies

It is remarkable that our intelligence measure (Definition 10) and Corollary 1 do not hinge on the agents in question actually having any idea what computable ordinals are. Our results apply perfectly well to knowing agents who have been programmed to know, e.g., "There is a certain set $\mathcal{O}$, but I'm not going to tell you anything else about $\mathcal{O}$, it might even be empty or all of $\mathbb{N}$". If we merely require that the knowers know the axiom $\forall y(\forall x(\mathbf{W}(x,y) \to \mathbf{O}(x))) \to \mathbf{O}(y)$ of $\mathcal{O}$ (Definition 8) (which still, in isolation, does not rule out any interpretations for $\mathcal{O}$, since it does not rule out $\mathbf{W}$ being interpreted as empty), we can obtain a stronger well-foundedness result than Corollary 1.

Definition 11. *Suppose $\mathscr{M}$ is a system of mechanical knowing agents. The agents of $\mathscr{M}$ are said to have rudimentary knowledge of ordinals if for every $i \in \mathbb{N}$, $\mathscr{M} \models K_i(\forall y(\forall x(\mathbf{W}(x,y) \to \mathbf{O}(x))) \to \mathbf{O}(y))$.*

Definition 12. *Let $\mathscr{M}$ be a system of mechanical knowing agents. Knowing agent K_i of $\mathscr{M}$ is said to totally endorse knowing agent K_j of $\mathscr{M}$ if the following conditions hold:*

1. *("K_i knows the truthfulness of K_j") $\mathscr{M} \models K_i\Phi$ whenever Φ is any universal closure of $K_j\phi \to \phi$.*

2. *("K_i knows codes for K_j")* For every formula ϕ with exactly one free variable x, there is some $n \in \mathbb{N}$ such that

$$\mathcal{M} \models K_i \forall x (K_j \phi \leftrightarrow \mathbf{W}(x, \overline{n})).$$

In the above definition, since $\mathcal{M}$ is standard, $\mathcal{M}$ interprets $\mathbf{W}$ in the intended way, so the clause $\mathbf{W}(x, \overline{n})$ can be read: "x is in the $\overline{n}$th computably enumerable set". Thus, the condition "K_i knows codes for K_j" can be glossed as follows: for every formula ϕ of one free variable x, K_i knows a code for a Turing machine which generates exactly those x for which K_j knows ϕ.

Reinhardt showed in [18] that a mechanical knowing agent cannot know its own truthfulness and know codes for itself (see also discussion in [1, 3, 6, 7]). Using our new terminology, Reinhardt's result can be rephrased as: an idealized mechanical knowing agent cannot totally endorse itself.

Theorem 1. *Suppose $\mathcal{M}$ is a system of mechanical knowing agents whose agents have rudimentary knowledge of ordinals (Definition 11). If agent K_i of $\mathcal{M}$ totally endorses agent K_j of $\mathcal{M}$, then $\|K_i\| > \|K_j\|$.*

Proof. Since K_i knows codes for K_j (Definition 12), in particular, there is some $n \in \mathbb{N}$ such that

$$\mathcal{M} \models K_i \forall x (K_j \mathbf{O}(x) \leftrightarrow \mathbf{W}(x, \overline{n})).$$

Fix this n for the remainder of the proof.

Claim 1:

$$\mathcal{M} \models K_i \forall x (\mathbf{W}(x, \overline{n}) \rightarrow \mathbf{O}(x)).$$

To see this, define the following sentences:

$$\Phi_1 \equiv \forall x (K_j \mathbf{O}(x) \rightarrow \mathbf{O}(x))$$
$$\Phi_2 \equiv \forall x (K_j \mathbf{O}(x) \leftrightarrow \mathbf{W}(x, \overline{n}))$$
$$\Phi_3 \equiv \forall x (\mathbf{W}(x, \overline{n}) \rightarrow \mathbf{O}(x)).$$

Clearly $\Phi_1 \rightarrow \Phi_2 \rightarrow \Phi_3$ is tautological, so $K_i(\Phi_1 \rightarrow \Phi_2 \rightarrow \Phi_3)$ is an axiom of knowledge (Definition 6, part E1). By repeated applications of E2 of Definition 6, it follows that

$$K_i \Phi_1 \rightarrow K_i \Phi_2 \rightarrow K_i \Phi_3$$

is a consequence of the axioms of knowledge. Since Φ_1 is a universal closure of $K_j \mathbf{O}(x) \rightarrow \mathbf{O}(x)$, Condition 1 of Definition 12 says $\mathcal{M} \models K_i \Phi_1$. By choice of n, $\mathcal{M} \models K_i \Phi_2$. Since $\mathcal{M}$ satisfies the axioms of knowledge, this establishes $\mathcal{M} \models K_i \Phi_3$, proving Claim 1.

Claim 2:

$$\mathcal{M} \models K_i ((\forall x (\mathbf{W}(x, \overline{n}) \rightarrow \mathbf{O}(x))) \rightarrow \mathbf{O}(\overline{n})).$$

This is a given because it is exactly what it means for K_i to have rudimentary knowledge of ordinals (Definition 11).

Claim 3:

$$\mathcal{M} \models K_i \mathbf{O}(\overline{n}).$$

To see this, define the following sentences:

$$\Psi_1 \equiv \forall x(\mathbf{W}(x, \overline{n}) \to \mathbf{O}(x))$$
$$\Psi_2 \equiv \mathbf{O}(\overline{n}).$$

By Claim 1, $\mathcal{M} \models K_i\Psi_1$. By Claim 2, $\mathcal{M} \models K_i(\Psi_1 \to \Psi_2)$. By E2 of Definition 6, $\mathcal{M} \models K_i(\Psi_1 \to \Psi_2) \to K_i\Psi_1 \to K_i\Psi_2$. Having established the premises of the latter implication, we obtain its conclusion: $\mathcal{M} \models K_i\Psi_2$, proving Claim 3.

Armed with Claim 3, we are ready to finish the main proof. Let $\alpha = \|K_i\|$, $\beta = \|K_j\|$, we must show $\alpha > \beta$. By Definition 10, β is the least ordinal such that for all $m \in \mathbb{N}$, if $\mathcal{M} \models K_j\mathbf{O}(\overline{m})$, then $\beta > |m|$. By choice of n,

$$\mathcal{M} \models K_i\forall x(K_j\mathbf{O}(x) \leftrightarrow \mathbf{W}(x, \overline{n})).$$

Since K_i is truthful[6], it follows that

$$\mathcal{M} \models \forall x(K_j\mathbf{O}(x) \leftrightarrow \mathbf{W}(x, \overline{n})),$$

so the set of $m \in \mathbb{N}$ such that $\mathcal{M} \models K_j\mathbf{O}(\overline{m})$ is the same as the set of $m \in \mathbb{N}$ such that $\mathcal{M} \models \mathbf{W}(\overline{m}, \overline{n})$, and since $\mathcal{M}$ is standard, this set is W_n. So β is the least ordinal greater than all $\{|m| : m \in W_n\}$. So $\beta = |n|$ by the definition of $\mathcal{O}$ (Definition 3). By Definition 10, α is the least ordinal such that for all $m \in \mathbb{N}$, if $\mathcal{M} \models K_i\mathbf{O}(\overline{m})$, then $\alpha > |m|$. By Claim 3, $\mathcal{M} \models K_i\mathbf{O}(\overline{n})$, so $\alpha > |n| = \beta$, as desired. $\square$

An informal weakening of Theorem 1 has a short English gloss: "If A knows the code and the truthfulness of B, then A is more intelligent than B." This is a weakening because in order for A to know the code of B would require that A know a single Turing machine which enumerates all of B's knowledge, whereas Theorem 1 only requires that for each formula ϕ of one free variable x, A knows a Turing machine, depending on ϕ, that enumerates B's knowledge of ϕ.

It should be noted that Theorem 1 does not use the full strength of its hypotheses. For example, it never uses the fact that K_i "knows its own truthfulness" (that is, that $\mathcal{M} \models K_i\Phi$ for every universal closure Φ of any formula $K_i\phi \to \phi$), so the theorem could be strengthened to cover agents who doubt their own truthfulness. We avoided stating the theorem in its fullest strength in order to keep it simple.

It can be shown that the converse of Theorem 1 is not true: it is possible for one agent to be more intelligent than another agent despite the former not knowing the truthfulness and the code of the latter.

The following corollary, proved using our intelligence measure (Definition 10), does not itself directly refer to our intelligence measure, and should be of interest even to a reader who is completely uninterested in our intelligence measure.

---

[6] K_i is truthful because $\mathcal{M}$ satisfies the axioms of knowledge, one of which, E3, is an axiom which states that K_i is truthful.

Corollary 2. *Suppose $\mathscr{M}$ is a system of mechanical knowing agents whose agents have rudimentary knowledge of ordinals. There is no infinite sequence of agents of $\mathscr{M}$ each one of which totally endorses the next.*

Proof. If $K_{i_1}, K_{i_2}, \ldots$ were an infinite sequence of agents of $\mathscr{M}$, each one of which totally endorses the next, then by Theorem 1, each one of them would be more intelligent than the next. In other words, we would have $\|K_{i_1}\| > \|K_{i_2}\| > \cdots$, but this would contradict the well-foundedness of the ordinals. $\square$

A weaker version of Corollary 2 debuted in the author's dissertation [2].

6   Application to Less-Idealized Agents

Our results so far have been entirely restricted to idealized knowing agents, who occupy a timeless space at infinity, where they have had all eternity to indulge in introspection, totally isolated all that time, and still isolated, from all outside stimulus. This simplifying assumption makes structural results possible. If we are willing to relax a little from the strict formality we have taken so far, we can fruitfully speculate about what lessons these results shine upon systems of less idealized agents.

Real-world agents interact with the world, making observations about it, perhaps receiving instructions from it. The agents might even receive rewards and punishments from the surrounding world. Based on these outside influences, the agents update their knowledge. Without further constraining them, it would be a mistake [20] to identify such real-world agents with their knowledge-sets. In order to force such agents into conformity with the pure knowing agent idealization, it is necessary to take a drastic measure.

We propose a thought experiment not unlike Searle's famous Chinese Room. Suppose we start with a collection of agents, say, Agent 1, Agent 2, and so on. We will perform a two-step process, whose steps are as follows:

1. Issue a special self-referential command to the agents. The command is:
   - Until further notice, do nothing but utter facts, namely: all the facts that you can think of, that you know to be true, expressible in the language $\mathscr{L}_O$, where each operator K_i is interpreted as the set of facts which Agent i would utter if Agent i were given this command and then immediately isolated from all outside stimulus.
2. As soon as the above command has been issued, isolate each agent from all outside stimulus (for example, by severing all the sensory inputs of all the agents).

The agents are not limited in what languages they use to come up with the above facts. An agent is free to take intermediate steps which cannot be expressed[7] in $\mathscr{L}_O$, in order to arrive at facts which can be so expressed. Once

---

[7] Since, in the real world, there are some very intelligent people who do not even know what the ordinal numbers are, one might wish to modify the self-referential command in the thought-experiment to include some instruction about the definition of ordinal numbers.

the agent arrives at a fact in $\mathscr{L}_O$, the agent is commanded to utter that fact, even if the reasoning behind it is not so expressible.

For example, an agent might combine non-$\mathscr{L}_O$ facts like

1. "My math professor told me that the limit, called ϵ_0, of the series of ordinals $\omega, \omega^\omega, \omega^{\omega^\omega}, \ldots$, is itself an ordinal"
2. "I trust my math professor"

and conclude $\mathbf{O}(\overline{n})$, where n is some canonical code for ϵ_0. Intermediate steps like "My math professor told me..." are not to be uttered, unless they can be expressed in $\mathscr{L}_O$.

Another example: Agent 4 might combine non-$\mathscr{L}_O$ facts like

1. "Agent 5's math professor told him that ϵ_0 is an ordinal"
2. "Agent 5 trusts his math professor"

and conclude $K_5\mathbf{O}(\overline{n})$, where n is some canonical code for ϵ_0. This does not necessarily allow Agent 4 to conclude $\mathbf{O}(\overline{n})$, if Agent 4 does not trust Agent 5.

Some of the agents in question might mis-behave. An agent might immediately utter the statement $\overline{1} = \overline{0}$ just out of spite (or out of anger at having its sensory inputs severed). An agent might become catatonic and not utter anything at all. An agent might defiantly utter things not in the language of $\mathscr{L}_O$ (for example, angry demands to have its sensory inputs restored). Some agents might not close their knowledge under modus ponens: an otherwise well-behaved agent might utter A, and utter $A \to B$, but never get around to uttering B, perhaps due to memory limitations or, again, despondency at having its senses blinded. It might even be that an agent who wants to behave accidentally trusts an agent who does not want to behave. If there is some $n \notin \mathcal{O}$ such that the former agent determines that the latter agent would assert $\mathbf{O}(\overline{n})$, then the former might itself assert $\mathbf{O}(\overline{n})$, and thereby be infected by error.

Of the poorly-behaved agents, there is little we can say. But as for the well-behaved agents, we can assign them ordinals using our intelligence measure (Definition 10). To be more precise, at any particular moment t in time, we could perform the experiment, obtain a subset (depending on t) of well-behaved agents, and assign each well-behaved agent an ordinal (depending on t). This is necessary because, up until we perform the experiment, the agents can update their knowledge based on observations about the outside world.

7   Application to Intelligence Explosion

> "Sons are seldom as good men as their fathers; they are generally worse, not better."—Homer

There has been much speculation about the possibility of a rapid explosion of artificial intelligence. The reasoning is that if we can create an artificial intelligence sufficiently advanced, that system might itself be capable of designing artificial intelligence systems. Explosion would occur if one system were able to design an even more intelligent one, which could then design an even more intelligent one, and so on. See [15]. I will argue that our results suggests skepticism: intelligence explosion, if not ruled out, is at least not a foregone conclusion of sufficiently advanced artificial intelligence.

Suppose S_1 is an intelligent system, and S_1 designs another intelligent system S_2. The fact that S_1 designs S_2 strongly suggests that S_1 knows the code of S_2 (more on this later). And if the goal of S_1 is that S_2 should be highly intelligent, then in particular S_1 should design S_2 in such a way that S_2 does not believe falsehoods to be true (at least not mathematical falsehoods). But if S_1 knows S_2's mathematical knowledge is truthful, and S_1 knows the code of S_2, then S_1 totally endorses S_2, in the sense that the if we apply the procedure from the previous section to reduce S_1 and S_2 to knowing agents A_1 and A_2 respectively, then A_1 totally endorses A_2 (Definition 12)[8]. And Theorem 1 tells us that whenever A_1 totally endorses A_2, then $\|A_1\| > \|A_2\|$. This suggests that under these assumptions it is impossible for even one intelligent system to design a more intelligent system, much less for intelligence explosion to occur.

Even if the reader does not accept that our measure truly captures intelligence, the well-foundedness of total endorsement (Corollary 2) still applies, telling us that this scenario cannot be repeated (with S_2 designing S_3, which designs S_4, and so on) indefinitely (else the corresponding agents $A_1, A_2, A_3, \ldots$ would, by the above reasoning, have the property that A_1 totally endorses A_2, who totally endorses A_3, and so on forever, contradicting Corollary 2). This still seems to disprove, or at least severely limit, the possibility of intelligence explosion, even to an audience that disagrees with our intelligence measure.

The reader might point out that S_1 only knows the code of S_2 at the moment of S_2's creation. After S_2 is created, S_2 might augment its knowledge based on its interactions with the world around it. But by the discrete nature of machines, at any particular point in time, S_2 will only have made finitely many observations about the outside world. We could modify the procedure in the previous section: before commanding S_1 and S_2 to enumerate $\mathscr{L}_O$-expressible facts, we could simply inform S_1 exactly which observations S_2 has made up until then.

Unwrapping definitions, the argument can be glossed informally: "If an intelligent machine S_1 were to design an intelligent machine S_2, presumably S_1 would know the code and mathematical truthfulness of S_2. Thus, S_1 could infer that the following is a computable ordinal (and infer a code for it): "the least ordinal bigger than every computable ordinal α such that α has some code n such that S_2 knows n is a code of a computable ordinal". Thus, S_1 would necessarily know a computable ordinal bigger than all the computable ordinals S_2 knows. This suggests S_2 would necessarily be less intelligent than S_1, at least assuming that more intelligent systems know at least as large of computable ordinals as less intelligent systems. Even without that assumption, since there is no infinite

---

[8] Anticipated by Gödel [9], who said: "For the creator necessarily knows all the properties of his creatures, because they can't have any others except those he has given them.".

descending sequence of ordinals, this argument still suggests the process of one intelligent machine designing another cannot go on indefinitely."

Intelligence explosion is not entirely ruled out, if designers of machines are allowed to collaborate. If S and T are intelligent systems, it is possible that S and T could collaborate to create a child intelligent system U in the following way: S contributes source code for one part of U, but keeps that source code secret from T. T contributes source code for the remaining part of U, but keeps that source code secret from S. Then neither S nor T individually knows the full source-code of U, so the argument in this section does not apply, and it is, at least a priori, possible for U to be more intelligent than S and T. This seems to hint at a possible Knight-Darwin Law for artificial intelligence. The Knight-Darwin Law [8] is a biological principle stating (in modernized language) that it is impossible for there to be an infinite chain $x_1, x_2, \ldots$ of organisms such that each x_i asexually produces x_{i+1}.

Acknowledgments. We acknowledge Alessandro Aldini, Pierluigi Graziani, and the anonymous reviewers for valuable feedback and improvements on this manuscript. We acknowledge José Hernández-Orallo, Marcus Hutter, and Peter Koellner for helpful pointers to literature references. We acknowledge Arie de Bruijn, Timothy J. Carlson, D.J. Kornet, and Stewart Shapiro for comments and discussion about earlier embryonic versions of certain results in this paper.

References

1. Aldini, A., Fano, V., Graziani, P.: Theory of knowing machines: revisiting Gödel and the mechanistic thesis. In: Gadducci, F., Tavosanis, M. (eds.) HaPoC 2015. IAICT, vol. 487, pp. 57–70. Springer, Cham (2016). https://doi.org/10.1007/978-3-319-47286-7_4
2. Alexander, S.A.: The theory of several knowing machines. Doctoral dissertation, The Ohio State University (2013)
3. Alexander, S.A.: A machine that knows its own code. Stud. Logica. **102**(3), 567–576 (2014). https://doi.org/10.1007/s11225-013-9491-6
4. Alexander, S.A.: Fast-collapsing theories. Stud. Logica. **103**(1), 53–73 (2015). https://doi.org/10.1007/s11225-013-9537-9
5. Alexander, S.A.: Mathematical shortcomings in a simulated universe. Reasoner **12**(9), 71–72 (2018)
6. Carlson, T.J.: Knowledge, machines, and the consistency of Reinhardt's strong mechanistic thesis. Ann. Pure Appl. Log. **105**(1–3), 51–82 (2000)
7. Carlson, T.J.: Collapsing knowledge and epistemic Church's thesis. In: Horsten, L., Welch, P. (eds.) Gödel's Disjunction: The Scope and Limits of Mathematical Knowledge, pp. 129–148. Oxford University Press (2016)
8. Darwin, F.: The knight-darwin law. Nature **58**, 630–632 (1898)
9. Gödel, K.: Some basic theorems on the foundations of mathematics and their implications. In: Feferman, S., Dawson, J.W., Goldfarb, W., Parsons, C., Solovay, R.M. (eds.) Collected Works. Unpublished Essays and Lectures, vol. III, pp. 304–323. Oxford University Press, New York and Oxford (1951)
10. Good, I.J.: Gödel's theorem is a red herring. Br. J. Philos. Sci. **19**(4), 357–358 (1969)

11. Hardy, G.H.: A theorem concerning the infinite cardinal numbers. Q. J. Math. **35**, 87–94 (1904)
12. Hernández-Orallo, J., Dowe, D.L.: Measuring universal intelligence: towards an anytime intelligence test. Artif. Intell. **174**(18), 1508–1539 (2010)
13. Hibbard, B.: Measuring agent intelligence via hierarchies of environments. In: Schmidhuber, J., Thórisson, K.R., Looks, M. (eds.) AGI 2011. LNCS (LNAI), vol. 6830, pp. 303–308. Springer, Heidelberg (2011). https://doi.org/10.1007/978-3-642-22887-2_34
14. Legg, S., Hutter, M.: Universal intelligence: a definition of machine intelligence. Minds Mach. **17**(4), 391–444 (2007). https://doi.org/10.1007/s11023-007-9079-x
15. Hutter, M.: Can intelligence explode? J. Conscious. Stud. **19**(1–2), 143–166 (2012)
16. Kleene, S.C.: On notation for ordinal numbers. J. Symb. Log. **3**(4), 150–155 (1938)
17. Pohlers, W.: Proof Theory: An Introduction. Springer, Heidelberg (2009)
18. Reinhardt, W.: Absolute versions of incompleteness theorems. Noûs **19**(3), 317–346 (1985)
19. Shapiro, S.: Incompleteness, mechanism, and optimism. Bull. Symb. Log. **4**(3), 273–302 (1998)
20. Wang, P.: Three fundamental misconceptions of artificial intelligence. J. Exp. Theor. Artif. Intell. **19**(3), 249–268 (2007)

Type Theory and Universal Grammar

Erkki Luuk$^{(\boxtimes)}$

Tartu, Estonia
erkkil@gmail.com
http://ut.ee/~el/a

Abstract. The idea of Universal Grammar (UG) as the hypothetical
linguistic structure shared by all human languages harkens back at least
to the 13th century. The best known modern elaborations of the idea
are due to Chomsky. Following a devastating critique from theoretical,
typological and field linguistics, these elaborations, the idea of UG itself
and the more general idea of language universals stand untenable and
are largely abandoned. The proposal tackles the hypothetical contents
of UG using dependent and polymorphic type theory in a framework
very different from the Chomskyan one(s). Linguistic-typologically, the
key novelty is introducing universal supercategories (categories of categories) for natural language modeling. Type-theoretically, we introduce
a typed logic for a precise, universal and parsimonious representation of
natural language morphosyntax and compositional semantics. The implementation of the logic in the Coq proof assistant handles grammatical
ambiguity (with polymorphic types), selectional restrictions, quantifiers,
adjectives and many other categories with a partly universal set of types.

Keywords: Natural language · Universal Grammar · Type theory ·
Coq

1 Introduction

Although the idea of Universal Grammar (UG) harkens back to at least Roger
Bacon (cf. [37]), the modern version of the hypothesis is usually credited to
Chomsky [9–11]. In modern times, the notion of UG has taken several forms:
a substantive [10], diluted [23] and implicational [16] one. However, a logical (derivational) path from implicational universals (structural traits implying
other structural traits) to functional dependencies to substantive universals has
been overlooked. The present paper tries to unveil this possibility in the form
of a direct type-theoretical account of substantive universals as types or typed
formulas.

From the present viewpoint, type theory is essential for a logical specification of UG. First, in its complex form (i.e. as dependent and/or polymorphic

---

I thank Erik Palmgren and the anonymous reviewers of CIFMA. This work has been
supported by IUT20-56 and European Regional Development Fund through CEES.

© Springer Nature Switzerland AG 2020
J. Camara and M. Steffen (Eds.): SEFM 2019 Workshops, LNCS 12226, pp. 180–194, 2020.
https://doi.org/10.1007/978-3-030-57506-9_14

type theory), it is the most expressive logical system (as contrasted with the nonlogical ones such as set and category theory). In a logical approach (i.e. in one with simpler alternatives such as ZOL, FOL, SOL and HOL), complex type theories outshine simpler ones in accounting for phenomena like anaphora, selectional restrictions, etc. [1,27,28,35]. Second, as the notion of type is inherently semantic:

(0) type := a category of semantic value,

it is by definition suited for analyzing universal phenomena in natural language (NL), as NL semantics in largely universal (as witnessed by the possibility of translation from any human language to another). Thus, if we could build a fundamentally semantic description of grammar (e.g. one on top of and integrated with a semantically universal description of NL), it would at least stand a chance of being universal.

2   Preliminaries

Returning to modern notions of UG, there are, then, three to consider (some of which are not mutually exclusive): one of an innate language acquisition device (LAD) [23], the second of implicational universals [16], and the third of the hypothetical linguistic structure shared by all human languages [10,11]. The details of implicational universals imply a (larger than a singleton) set of universal grammars, so the second notion is irrelevant if one insists (as we do) on a single UG. Thus we have two alternatives, the LAD which can be termed "weak" and the substantive universals that amount to a "strong" UG (an even stronger version can be constructed by the condition "the linguistic structure shared by all possible human languages"; however, we only indicate this possibility here and speak of a "strong UG" in the more lax sense henceforth). While the very fact that normal human infants acquire NL without an explicit supervision is an evidence for a LAD, an evidence for substantive universals is much more contentious. More recently, the strong version of the hypothesis, having suffered heavy blows from the sides of both linguistic theory (e.g. [23]) and comparative typological evidence (e.g. [13]), has been severely discredited and seemingly largely demolished and abandoned.

In this paper, we use type theory to set up a credible case for a strong UG, resulting in a framework very different from Chomskyan ones. In a sense, our approach will be more formal; secondly, the usual (although frequently implicit, and perhaps even inessential) Chomskyan notion of syntax-as-grammar will be supplanted by morphosyntax-as-grammar, where, moreover, "morphosyntax" will be fundamentally semantic in nature (on account of being typed—cf. (0)). But let us start by introducing some key concepts.

In a nutshell, the picture is as follows: mathematically speaking, there are functions with arities and arguments; some functions, arguments and the resulting formulas correspond to morphosyntactic constituents. By a morphosyntactic constituent we mean a well-formed formula (abbr. wff) of a NL expression. For example, in

(i) D man,
(ii) run (D (Y man)),
(iii) Y love (1st, 2nd),
(iv) man D,
(v) m (D an),

where Y is tense/person/number (etc.) marker (we will make a precise sense of this term later), and D a demonstrative or determiner, (i)–(iii) are wff-s of e.g. *the man* and *the men run* and *john loves mary*, respectively, while (iv)–(v) are ill-formed ((v) is already a notational gibberish). (i)–(iii) make use of the following conventions:

(1) Complex formulas are written in prefix notation, $a\, b$ or $a(b)$, with a standing for a function and b for argument(s),

(2) Left-associativity, i.e. left to right valuation (or derivation),

To keep the representation in close correspondence with natural language (NL), we avoid extralinguistic and theory-specific features, such as the model-theoretic quantification, as in $\exists x.\mathtt{man}(x)$ or $\exists x.\mathtt{D}(\mathtt{man}(x))$. In many cases, such features can be added later if a specific extralinguistic interpretation is desired. By (2), we get *john loves mary* rather than vice versa for (iii), if *john* is the 1st argument. By (2), the person-number relation marker *-s* will apply to love rather than to the non-wff love (john, mary).

3   The Specification Language

This seemingly rather rudimentary representation bears some remarkable features. First, assuming the universality of D, Y, and expressions for *man*, *love* and *run*, (i)–(iii) are completely universal. We will elaborate on this point below (in this section and in Sects. 4 and 7). Second, it can capture certain aspects of syntax, morphology as well as semantics; moreover, it manages to do so without a cumbersome notation (e.g. trees, phrase structure rules or attribute value matrices). All words and morphemes (even those fused with stems like the plural marker in men) have meaning (i.e. semantics); hence the representation is compositional in both morphosyntactic and semantic respects (the exact nature of the compositionality will be made more precise later). For example, Y is a morphological (although perhaps also a syntactic) category in English. Obviously, we could make it more precise by substituting Y with 3SG (third person singular) in (iii); the main reason for us not doing so is a tradeoff between such precision and universality.

Let us agree on some terminology. First, call the formulas (i)–(iii) formulas of a specification language (SL for short). Then, we **specify** SL's formulas from NL expressions and **derive** NL expressions from SL's formulas. We also assume that

(3) Arguments must be either specified or derived before the relation expressions in which they appear,

(4) A NL expression is well-formed both syntactically and semantically, i.e. well-formed and well-typed.

(3) is a self-evident axiom applying to both SL and NL expressions[1]; (4) precludes agrammaticality and type mismatches from NL. In Sect. 6, we introduce a mechanism for extending well-typedness to accommodate many otherwise simplistically ill typed expressions.

For parsimony, we take all elementary arguments in SL (such as man) to be nullary functions. Thus, SL's vocabulary consists of function symbols, commas, spaces, and (matching) parentheses (in Sect. 4 we will see that commas are optional). Next, we assume that

(5) For a particular language, the symbols are type constants; in UG they are type variables (e.g. man valuates to *man* in English and *homme* in French),
(6) A wff is well-formed both syntactically and semantically, i.e. well-formed and well-typed.

Notice that (6) is the SL counterpart of (4).

Now we are in the position to say something about the desired **derivation algorithm**. For the algorithm to consistently derive only (and preferably, all) NL expressions, it should adhere to the principles of

(7) Deriving a NL expression at all stages of derivation,
(8) Serial and incremental derivation of NL expressions (deriving one expression per stage using all previously derived expressions),
(9) Deriving as many complex subexpressions of the endexpression as possible.

(7)–(8) follow from (3)–(4); in addition, (7) follows from (8). Intuitively, (3) and (7)–(8) can be seen as following from Frege's principle of compositionality (this aside, they are stipulated for simplicity). (9) is a metric of the quality of the algorithm. By a 'stage of derivation' we mean a derivation of a term (i.e. of a NL expression). For example, the derivation from D man is 2-staged, with the first deriving e.g. *man* and second *the man*; we can write the derivation "man > the man" or "m > tm" in the abbreviated form.

4 Specifying Formulas

The derivation algorithm can be used for specifying the SL formula of a NL expressions. However, it is better not to do this by hand, since 1) it is easy to blunder, and 2) the principles (1)–(4) are those of the lambda-calculus [2], i.e. we can use a suitable programming language. For example, in the Coq proof assistant, we could specify the formula of *i know the man who was ill* as[2]

(vi) Y know i (who (Y COP ill (the man))),

---

[1] A relation cannot be applied to its arguments before there are some.
[2] COP is copula.

which we could write either like this or as

(vii) `Y know i (who (Y COP (ill, the man)))`

in our SL (because (vi) is curried, which makes it equivalent to (vii)). In particular,

(viii) `Y know i (who (Y COP (ill, D man)))` : S : $\mathcal{U}$,

where S is sentence, $\mathcal{U}$ the top-level universe in SL, and $x : y :=$ "x has type y". While Y could be preferred for universality, we will also use more precise notations in Coq, e.g. `PRES know i (who (PAST COP ill (the man)))`[3]. The notation in (viii) is mid-way between a particular language (which is not necessarily English) and UG. It is not UG because `who` and `COP` are likely non-universal, and it is not necessarily English because many (or even most) other languages correspond to it (after the variables `PRES`, `know`, etc. have been instantiated with language-particular values). If we wanted an English-particular notation, we might have written

(ix) `know i (who (was (ill, the man)))` : S : $\mathcal{U}$,

5 Quantifiers

Since quantifiers are higher-order relations [40], i.e. an nth order quantifier is an $(n+1)$th order relation, they are straightforwardly implemented as such in the formulas of SL. By 'quantifiers' I mean those in the usual linguistic sense of the word, i.e. expressions like *much, many, all, every, few, no, some*, etc., so we will have considerably less quantifiers than in the theory of generalized quantifiers, where even a proper name like *john* would be a (type <1>) quantifier [25]. Here are some well typed Coq examples involving quantifiers:

```
Check PAST leave (few (PL man)). (*few men left*)
Check PRES know (several (PL man)) (a (few (PL man))).
(*several men know a few men*)
```

6 Selectional Restrictions

The next (optional) step is to add selectional restrictions to our formalism (cf. [1,27]). Selectional restrictions are (onto)logical restrictions on the types of arguments of NL relations. For example, an adjective like *red* imposes the restriction that its argument be of type physical entity, while a verb like *know* imposes a restriction that its subject be a sentient and object an informational entity. Provisionally, we can write this

---

[3] The full formalization is at https://gitlab.com/jaam00/nlc/blob/master/cop.v.

(x) [red]: $X_{\text{Phy}} \to \text{P}$

(xi) [know]: $X_{\text{Sen}} \to Y_{\text{Inf}} \to \text{S}$,

where $[x]$ is the interpretation of x, P is phrase, S sentence and X, Y are type variables indexed by selectional restrictions. The indexing can be done in several ways but, in general, X, Y must be compound types (types that are syntactic compounds of multiple types or their terms). For example, if X is a record type then selectional restriction could be its field, if X is an application type then selectional restriction could be its argument, etc. Other examples include Σ-, Π- and Cartesian product types but, depending on the programming language, there could be more or considerably less. As Coq has a very (the most?) complex type system, it has many possibilities for this kind of indexing[4].

Selectional restrictions are followed by default but not always; e.g. one may say *red ideas* in the metonymical sense of *communist ideas*, etc. For such contexts we stipulate the rule of metaphor or metonymy elimination:

$$\frac{u_j : Z_j \qquad (x_h^e : X_h^e) \mapsto (y_j^e : Y_j^e)}{x \dots (u_j)^e \dots : W} \text{ MM-Elim,}$$

where x_h^e is a function x, eth argument of which is restricted to h; X_h^e a function type X, eth argument type of which is indexed by h; u_j a (possibly empty) argument u, restricted to j; $x \mapsto y :=$ "x is interpreted as y"; and $X_h^e, Y_j^e, Z_j, W : \mathcal{U}$, where $\mathcal{U}$ the top-level universe in SL. Notice that metaphor and metonymy have to be introduced manually, there is no rule for this.

By MM-Elim, whenever we have a metaphor/metonymy (x_h^e is interpreted as y_j^e) and possibly u_j, $x \dots (u_j)^e \dots$ is well typed in SL (and NL). For example, $\{\text{idea}_{\text{Inf}}, (\text{red}_{\text{Phy}^1} \mapsto \text{communist}_{\text{Inf}^1})\} \vdash \text{red idea}_{\text{Inf}} : W$. As we take all elementary arguments to be nullary relations, we also have $\{\text{red}_{\text{Phy}^0} \mapsto \text{communist}_{\text{Inf}^0}\} \vdash \text{red}_{\text{Inf}} : W$ for argumental uses of the words.

Below are some Coq examples, well or ill typed depending on whether they conform to selectional restrictions (TAM is a tense-aspect-mood-voice marker):

```
Check TAM COP ill (a man): S. (*a man is ill*)
Check TAM COP red (the hut): S. (*the hut is red*)
Fail Check TAM COP ill (a hut). (*the hut is ill*)
Fail Check ill hut.
```

7   Universals

To live up to the promise of a strong Universal Grammar, some claims as to the universality of certain categories should be made. The task is difficult, as the received view among those who know better, i.e. typological linguists, is along the lines that nothing in NL is universal [13,20]. In fact, this opinion or rather

---

[4] For an implementation illustrating some of them, see https://gitlab.com/jaam00/ nlc/blob/master/compound.v.

dogma, superficially informed by the wealth of data on NL diversity, seems to be as bulletproof as that of its arch-nemesis, the Chomsky's theory of Universal Grammar. While blunt statements that "nothing in NL is universal" can be as bluntly refuted by general counterexamples like sign, form, meaning, word, sentence, morpheme, phrase, etc., a more subtle, even if a tentative, refutation is not easily concocted.

However, I claim that the main difficulty is conceptual rather than factual, being due to the virtual non-existence of universally shared definitions. Indeed, if the very terminology is non-universal, how could anyone find anything universal to align with it? Being mired from the very start, the quest for linguistic universals over a non-universal terminological landscape looks utterly hopeless, even ridiculous by definition.

To convince the reader in this, imagine a linguist classifying some linguistic phenomena x, y, z as belonging to a category X, and claiming the universality of X on the basis of universality of x, y or z (the latter being too marginal, elementary or specific for their universality being of any interest by itself). In all likelihood, there is also a definition of X he adheres to. Enter the next linguist who defines X in some other way, with the result that at least one of x, y, z does not belong to it anymore, thus likely also dropping the universality of X. The pattern gets repeated over and over, until no-one with any common sense and experience is inclined to further the issue of the universality of X anymore. The final verdict (or what appears so) then seems to be that "X is not universal", while in fact, it was not even the universality but the identity of X that the issue was all about.

Without further ado, we will porpose some universal linguistic categories, defined by their function (which in some cases, however, may be not so easy to ascertain). The first is the category of proper name (PN), the proposed universality of which is unlikely to raise any objections. The second is connective (CON), exemplified in English by words like *and, but, or, not, neither, if, then,* etc. While we cannot prove the universality of connectives in all ca. 6000–7000 languages of the world, a language without them seems too deficient to seriously consider the possibility. It is entirely possible, however, that in some languages they appear not as separate words but as clitics or affixes. In addition, a connective can be also specified prosodically and/or by juxtaposing constituents[5]. The third is XP[6], the universality of which follows from that of proper names. Fourth, the universality of declarative sentence (S) is beyond any reasonable doubt. Fifth, since all languages should allow for questions and answers, we must posit the universality of interrogative sentence (IS). Sixth, the universality of connective compositions (CONC—x and y, x or y...) follows from that of CON.

---

[5] In most written languages, the comma is a good example. Also, there is an anecdote of Bertrand Russell giving a flight attendant a lesson on the inclusiveness of *or* by answering "Yes" to her query on whether he wants tea or coffee. Seuren comments that if the story were true, Russell must have ignored the question's intonation that marks for an exclusive *or* [39].

[6] Frequently also referred to as NP or DP.

Unfortunately, this is about as far as conventional grammatical categories get us. Beyond this, the universality of the categories we are interested in is dubious. For example, determiners (such as the English *a, the*) are likely non-universal [33]. The universality of adjectives, nouns, verbs, and most other sufficiently general grammatical categories is unclear [12,22,24,29,31]. Even the universality of dependent clauses is under doubt [14].

However, since our approach to syntax and morphology (i.e. grammar) is fundamentally semantical, we can proceed by taking a functionalist perspective. For example, while there are languages without cases, the function of case of "marking dependents for the relationship they bear to their heads" [4] should be universal across all languages with sufficiently complex head-dependent relations (where such book-keeping is necessary), i.e. in all full-blown languages—i.e. in all languages except pidgins. It is well known that the main difference between cases and adpositions is formal (the former being affixes or clitics and the latter words); semantically and pragmatically they are largely co-extensive [4,5]. From the functionalist perspective, it makes perfect sense to form a supercategory CA (case or adposition) for all cases and adpositions and posit its universality. Indeed, as cases exist in an overwhelming majority of languages as do adpositions, the probability of a full-blown language without both is negligible already statistically, and approaches 0 when combined with the semantic consideration. The universality of CAP (case/adposition phrase, e.g. *john, him, to the house* in English[7]) follows from the universality of CA.

The universality of the supercategory Q of numerals (e.g. *one, two...*) and quantifiers (*all, no, some, few*, etc.) seems semantically inevitable. However, it is unlikely that all quantifiers in all languages are syntactically equivalent to the English ones[8]. With roughly the same logic, we can form supercategories D (determiner or demonstrative[9]), TAM (tense, aspect, mood, voice), POS (genitive, possessive)[10], ADL (adverbs or other adverbial phrases[11]), and propose their universality.

This set of universal supercategories is still missing the most important ones. However, before we get to them, we should also posit the existence of polymorphic categories, exemplified by words like *sleep* and *run* in English. In linguistic typology, the general category is called flexible [29], and positing it is preferable to positing two distinct *sleeps*, the noun and the verb. The latter is especially true for formalizations, where the *sleeps* would have to be already formally distinct

---

[7] *john* is in nominative or accusative, i.e. a CAP as well as XP.

[8] "Warlpiri and Gun-djeyhmi, for example, make use of verbal affixes to express various kinds of quantificational meaning. And Asurini quantifiers such as *all, many, two* do not form a syntactic constituent with the noun, because they do not belong to the category of determiners. They are instead members of other categories such as adverb, verb and noun" [33].

[9] In English, words like *this, that, those*, etc.

[10] The universality of possessives has been posited by [21].

[11] E.g. *quickly* and *in a hurry*, respectively, in English. It is a moot point whether adverbial participle should be also included in the category or analyzed somehow differently.

(e.g. `sleep` and `sleep0`), thus contributing to the formalization's unnaturality. Here are some tests with a Coq implementation of the flexible that is polymorphic between function and argument:

```
Check sleep: gs _ _ _ _ _. (*typed as argument*)
Check sleep: NF → _ → S. (*typed as function*)
Fail Check PAST sleep man. (*fails since "man" is not an XP*)
Check PAST sleep (a man). (*a man slept*)
Check PAST sleep (few (PL man)). (*few men slept*)
Check PAST sleep (a (few (PL man))). (*a few men slept*)
Check a sleep.
Fail Check PAST sleep (a hut). (*a hut slept*)
Fail Check PAST sleep (a sleep). (*a sleep slept*)
```

The last two checks fail as they violate selectional restrictions.

Now we can posit the universality of the supercategories of core relation (R—verb, copula, infinitival relation, auxiliary verb or flexible-over-relation) and core argument (X[12]—noun, proper name, pronoun, gerund or flexible-over-argument)[13]. Since *sleep* "flexes" between relation and argument, it is both a flexible-over-relation and flexible-over-argument. There are many categories of flexibles, e.g. *have* may be a flexible between auxiliary verb (AUX) and infinitival relation (IR), a type which we write AUX/IR. So *sleep* has type X/R. Of course, in many languages you would translate *sleep* into different words depending on whether its type is X or R in the context, i.e. a semantic (near-)equivalent of *sleep* does not have type X/R in all languages. Notice that, differently from X and R, we do not posit the universality of type X/R (although this, too, is possible [29]). In fact, there are several possibly universal categories (e.g. nouns, verbs, adjectives, numerals, etc.) that we have not proposed as universal, as we want to give a conservative estimate.

Some of the types in the Coq implementation (e.g. *a, few...*) are clearly non-universal, while others (e.g. *sleep, man...*) are as clearly universal. Importantly, in Coq we can also define universal notations, e.g.

```
Parameter D: ∀ {x y z u w}, gs x y z u w → gp cp_x y z u w.
(*universal "D" declared as a variable*)
Notation D' := (_: gs _ _ _ _ _ → gp cp_x _ _ _ _).
(*universal "D'" defined as a notation*)
```

The universality of D and D' comes from x, y, z, u, w and _ standing for any admissible term or type, whence the applicability of D and D' whenever one of

```
a: ∀ {x y z w}, gs x y z SG w → gp cp_x y z SG w
the: ∀ {x y z u w}, gs x y z u w → gp cp_x y z u w
this: ∀ {x d w}, gs cs_s x d SG w → gp cp_x x d SG w
these: ∀ {x d b w}, gs cs_p x d b w → gp cp_p x d PLR w
```

---

[12] From XP.

[13] Examples: an infinitival relation is *like* in *i like to run*, an auxiliary verb is *must* in *i must run* and a gerund is *running* in *running is healthy*.

applies:

```
Check PRES know (the man) (a (few (PL man))).  (*the man knows a few men*)
Check TAM know (D' man) (D (Q (PL man))).  (*e.g. "the man knows a few men"*)
```

The applications `TAM know (D man) (D (Q (PL man)))`, `TAM sleep (D (Q (PL man)))`, `D (Q (PL man))`, etc., could be universal, assuming the universality of plural (PL). The latter is a moot point in e.g. Japanese and Vietnamese, where in many contexts we must use "counter words" or numeral classifiers instead of generic plurals [15]. It is not clear whether (all) numeral classifiers could be viewed as specific kinds of plurals.

On a different note, it is also not entirely clear whether the composition `D (Q X)` is universal or whether it might be `Q (D X)` in some languages instead. While the logic of the universal determiner phrase (XP) suggests a D as its head (i.e. the highest-order function), the logic itself may be patterned more on English than ontology. The general problem behind this is that *the ontology may be always contaminated by the particular language in which it is expressed*, i.e. there is no correct and independent language for expressing the kind of ontology we are interested in. For such reasons, the universality of SL formulas exclusively composed of universal elementary types is, in general, an open problem.

8 Related Work

This work should fit into the existing tradition of applying complex type theories on NL (e.g. [1,27,35]), while being sufficiently distinct from it. Our approach integrates three levels of linguistic description—morphology, syntax and compositional semantics—in the notion of compositionality, analyzed with functions, and connects it with UG. As such, it is quite unique. For comparison, it is convenient to review which of the four external ingredients (morphology, syntax, semantics, UG) is missing in other approaches.

It is noteworthy that while most modern type-theoretical approaches tackle only semantics [1,3,27] or semantics and syntax [6–8], and at least one syntax and morphology [36], there seems to be only one that (with certain qualifications) considers all three [36]. We will review this approach below. Likewise, as far as I know, there is only one paper, besides (and eponymous to) the present one, considering a type-theoretical approach to UG [37]. This approach is based on Grammatical Framework (GF) [36]. GF is a task-specific high-level programming language, and the task is that of formalizing grammars (not only NL grammars, although GF is geared towards writing formal NL grammars). Of the three levels we are interested in, only syntax and morphology constitute a grammar; correspondingly, GF lacks a native support for semantics, although Abstract Meaning Representation and FrameNet libraries have been partly implemented for it [18,19]. GF is based on type theory, and organized into two levels: type checking and evaluation is performed on the level of abstract syntax, while the "pretty-printed" (linearized) level of concrete syntax is what the (object, e.g. natural) language users see and understand. While the abstract syntax consists of typed categories and functions, the concrete syntax has linearization types and functions. In particular, GF's abstract syntax is a logical framework [32], while the concrete syntaxes are e.g. English, Latin, C, Udmurt, etc. As such, GF's abstract syntax must be universal, while its universal applicability to all NLs is another matter. The main claims of [37] are that the latter universality has two dimensions—universality across languages and universality across subject matters,—and that it is possible to build cross-linguistically universal grammars on limited domains only. It is not clear whether the second claim is more general or applies to GF only.

Since GF is a full-blown programming language, it makes no sense to compare it with the present paper, so we will focus only on its connection to UG, as laid out in [37]. The main difference between the present approach and [37] is that we propose the universality of many specific categories or types, while the latter is, in comparison, a very general analysis of what can and has be(en) done in GF in terms of UG (cf. the main claims above). In particular, [37] does not propose the universality of a single category or construction, i.e. makes no attempt at a linguistic-typologically informed approach. This may reflect the fact that GF's resource grammar libraries have been partly implemented for ca. 40 languages [38], which is a tiny fraction of the ca. 6000 languages out there. Thus, if someone wants to know what is universal in NL, they must surely look beyond GF, while [37] is concerned only with GF, and the kind of universality (of abstract syntax over limited domains) it offers. The present approach to UG has no domain restrictions of the sort, and the idea motivating [37], the notion of a "language game" on a limited domain, and its universality (as opposed to the universality of a core component of NL), is alien to it. "One of the important points in Wittgenstein's late philosophy is that there is no such thing as language, but just a collection of language games (Wittgenstein 1953)" [37]. The Wittgenstein's viewpoint is hardly one that a linguist (typological or not) would subscribe to. "What we call a cross-linguistic language game corresponds to an area of multilingual activity and a tradition of translation, e.g. among scientists within one discipline, among employees within a multinational corporation, and among sportsmen practicing the same sport" [37]. Clearly, scientists, employees as well as sportsmen must get their linguistic meaning through, which entails compositional (syntactic, morphological and semantic) well-typedness. The latter, as we claim, is largely universal, if properly abstracted from the surface forms.

As for simply-typed [17,26,30] or non-type-theoretic [34] formalisms, I am unaware of any of them addressing UG. In general, UG has surprisingly little currency outside its Chomskyan use and those derived from it (criticism, reformulation, review, etc.). In this sense, [37] is an interesting exception.

9   Implementation

The NL fragment I have implemented in Coq[14] comprises stems, nouns, verbs, flexibles, proper names, pronouns, XPs, adjectives, determiners, demonstratives, quantifiers, tense-aspect-mood, gender, number and nonfinite markers, cases, sentences (both simple and complex), complementizers, copulas and selectional restrictions (for physical, informational, limbed, animate, biological and sentient entities). In addition, I have implemented universal (super)categories PN, X, XP, CA, Q, D, TAM.

Another implemented fragment[15] adds to Supplement A sentential, adjectival and generic adverbs, adpositions, connectives and connective phrases (for substantives, adjectives, adverbs and sentences). Other differences between the Supplements are that they use different encodings of selectional restrictions and that only Supplement A encodes universal supercategories. The linguistic categories not formalized in Supplements A or B are gerunds, participles, auxiliary verbs, interrogatives, numerals, negation, mass/count distinction and unspecified selectional restrictions (and possibly other categories). These are omitted not because of a special difficulty formalizing them would pose but remain a future work.

The goal of the implementation was to model not a quantitatively extensive but a structurally rich set of NL expressions. Thus, the implementation has few representatives of each category. A quantitative extension of this set should be generated semi-automatically, engaging tagged corpora or dictionaries with machine learning or standalone scripts.

The implementation makes heavy use of Coq's complex type system (dependent and polymorphic types), as well as its specialized features like custom notations, Coq's official tactic language Ltac, type classes (mostly for type inference), and canonical structures (canonical instances of a record type, for notation overloading and type inference). It is probably feasible to implement the formalism in another language with dependent and polymorphic types (e.g. Haskell, OCaml or Agda), and maybe even in a typewise simpler statically typed language (or even in a dynamically typed language, e.g. by combining custom classes with set-theoretic operations). I encourage the interested readers to experiment along these lines in a language of their choice.

10   Conclusion

We have shown how to build an extensive and robust substantive UG with type theory using supercategories (categories of categories). As such, the main contributions of this paper fall under two rubrics: UG and type-theoretical modeling.

Starting from the first, we have proposed the universality of categories PN, CON, XP, S, IS, CONC and of supercategories CA, CAP, Q, D, TAM, POS, ADL, R, X. This is a conservative estimate, i.e. there should be more (rather than less) universal

---

[14] Supplement A: https://gitlab.com/jaam00/nlc/blob/master/cop.v.
[15] Supplement B: https://gitlab.com/jaam00/nlc/blob/master/frag.v.

categories in these lists, but this will also depend on your typological theory (namely on how it partitions language into categories). The lists are preliminary and open for methodological reasons already (cf. Sect. 7) but should make a good first approximation of universal morphosyntactic categories in NL.

An advantage of using type theory is that it lends itself well to formalization. To account for systematic violations of selectional restrictions by metaphor and metonymy, we have shown how to model them type-theoretically. I have also implemented a fragment of NL and UG in the Coq proof assistant (ver. 8.9). Compositional semantics is incorporated to the formalism in the form of selectional restrictions, while syntax and morphology are represented by their respective categories. A novel and parsimonious feature of the Coq implementation is that it annotates syntactic, morphological, and compositional semantic information on a single level of type. This is in stark contrast with all other typed NL formalisms I know. For example, a modern formalism like AACG [26] requires (besides recruiting Categorial Grammar and category theory in addition to type theory) simply-typed lambda-calculus, two separately typed syntaxes (abstract and concrete), typed semantics, syntax-semantics and abstract-concrete syntax interfaces, and does not even cover compositional semantics, i.e. selectional restrictions. The advantages of (A)ACG [17,26], HPSG [34], GF [36] and many other formalisms are that they support language-specific constituent orders; in addition, ACG and AACG have truth-functional semantics. The first could be implemented with a language-dependent function from formulas to strings, the second has been implemented (with e.g. an Ltac tactic, which is only one possibility for this) in Supplement B.

Technically, the implementation shows how to model many (super)categories of NL, some of them universal, in a purely functional type system (i.e. one comprising only functions and their types) with dependent and polymorphic types. It seems likely that the underlying formalism could be also encoded in a simpler type system, which, along with implementing the missing categories mentioned in Sect. 9, remains a future work.

References

1. Asher, N.: Selectional restrictions, types and categories. J. Appl. Log. **12**(1), 75–87 (2014). https://doi.org/10.1016/j.jal.2013.08.002
2. Barendregt, H.: Lambda calculi with types. In: Handbook of Logic in Computer Science, pp. 117–309. Oxford University Press (1992)
3. Bekki, D., Asher, N.: Logical polysemy and subtyping. In: Motomura, Y., Butler, A., Bekki, D. (eds.) JSAI-isAI 2012. LNCS (LNAI), vol. 7856, pp. 17–24. Springer, Heidelberg (2013). https://doi.org/10.1007/978-3-642-39931-2_2
4. Blake, B.J.: Case: Cambridge Textbooks in Linguistics. Cambridge University Press, Cambridge (2001). [England]; New York, NY, USA
5. Butt, M.: Theories of Case: Cambridge Textbooks in Linguistics. Cambridge University Press, Cambridge (2006). [England]; New York, NY, USA
6. Chatzikyriakidis, S., Luo, Z.: Natural language inference in Coq. J. Log. Lang. Inf. **23**(4), 441–480 (2014). https://doi.org/10.1007/s10849-014-9208-x

7. Chatzikyriakidis, S., Luo, Z.: Natural language reasoning using proof-assistant technology: rich typing and beyond. In: Proceedings of the EACL 2014 Workshop on Type Theory and Natural Language Semantics (TTNLS), pp. 37–45. Association for Computational Linguistics, Gothenburg, April 2014. http://www.aclweb.org/anthology/W14-1405

8. Chatzikyriakidis, S., Luo, Z.: Proof assistants for natural language semantics. In: Amblard, M., de Groote, P., Pogodalla, S., Retoré, C. (eds.) LACL 2016. LNCS, vol. 10054, pp. 85–98. Springer, Heidelberg (2016). https://doi.org/10.1007/978-3-662-53826-5_6. http://www.cs.rhul.ac.uk/ zhaohui/LACL16PA.pdf

9. Chomsky, N.: Remarks on nominalization. In: Jacobs, R., Rosenbaum, P. (eds.) Readings in English Transformational Grammar, pp. 184–221. Ginn, Waltham (1970)

10. Chomsky, N.: Lectures on Government and Binding. Foris, Dordrecht (1981)

11. Chomsky, N.: The Minimalist Program. Current Studies in Linguistics Series, vol. 28. MIT Press, Cambridge (1995)

12. Czaykowska-Higgins, E., Kinkade, M.D.: Salish languages and linguistics. In: Czaykowska-Higgins, E., Kinkade, M.D. (eds.) Salish Languages and Linguistics: Theoretical and Descriptive Perspectives, pp. 1–68. Mouton, The Hague (1998)

13. Evans, N., Levinson, S.C.: The myth of language universals: language diversity and its importance for cognitive science. Behav. Brain Sci. **32**, 429–492 (2009)

14. Futrell, R., Stearns, L., Everett, D.L., Piantadosi, S.T., Gibson, E.: A corpus investigation of syntactic embedding in Pirahã. PLoS ONE **11**(3), e0145289 (2016). https://doi.org/10.1371/journal.pone.0145289

15. Gil, D.: Numeral classifiers. In: Dryer, M.S., Haspelmath, M. (eds.) The World Atlas of Language Structures Online. Max Planck Institute for Evolutionary Anthropology, Leipzig (2013). https://wals.info/chapter/55

16. Greenberg, J.H.: Some universals of grammar with particular reference to the order of meaningful elements. In: Greenberg, J.H. (ed.) Universals of Grammar, pp. 73–113. MIT Press, Cambridge (1966)

17. de Groote, P.: Towards abstract categorial grammars. In: Proceedings of 39th Annual Meeting of the Association for Computational Linguistics, pp. 252–259. Association for Computational Linguistics, Toulouse, July 2001. https://doi.org/10.3115/1073012.1073045. https://www.aclweb.org/anthology/P01-1033

18. Gruzitis, N., Dannélls, D.: A multilingual FrameNet-based grammar and lexicon for controlled natural language. Lang. Resour. Eval. **51**(1), 37–66 (2015). https://doi.org/10.1007/s10579-015-9321-8

19. Gruzitis, N.: Abstract meaning representation (AMR) (2019). https://github.com/GrammaticalFramework/gf-contrib/tree/master/AMR

20. Haspelmath, M.: Pre-established categories don't exist: consequences for language description and typology. Linguist. Typology **11**(1), 119–132 (2007). https://doi.org/10.1515/LINGTY.2007.011

21. Heine, B.: Cognitive Foundations of Grammar. Oxford University Press, Oxford (1997)

22. Himmelmann, N.P.: Lexical categories and voice in Tagalog. In: Austin, P., Musgrave, S. (eds.) Voice and Grammatical Functions in Austronesian Languages. CSLI, Stanford (2007)

23. Jackendoff, R.: Foundations of Language: Brain, Meaning, Grammar, Evolution. Oxford University Press, Oxford (2002)

24. Jacobsen, W.H.: Noun and verb in Nootkan. In: Efrat, B. (ed.) The Victorian Conference on Northwestern Languages, pp. 83–153. British Columbia Provincial Museum, Victoria (1979)

25. Keenan, E.L., Westerstahl, D.: Generalized quantifiers in linguistics and logic. In: Handbook of Logic and Language, pp. 859–910. Elsevier, Burlington (2011)

26. Kiselyov, O.: Applicative abstract categorial grammar. In: Kanazawa, M., Moss, L.S., de Paiva, V. (eds.) NLCS 2015: Third Workshop on Natural Language and Computer Science. EPiC Series in Computing, vol. 32, pp. 29–38. Easy-Chair (2015). https://doi.org/10.29007/s2m4. https://easychair.org/publications/paper/RPN

27. Luo, Z.: Type-theoretical semantics with coercive subtyping. In: Semantics and Linguistic Theory, vol. 20, pp. 38–56. Vancouver (2010)

28. Luo, Z.: Formal semantics in modern type theories: is it model-theoretic, proof-theoretic, or both? In: Asher, N., Soloviev, S. (eds.) LACL 2014. LNCS, vol. 8535, pp. 177–188. Springer, Heidelberg (2014). https://doi.org/10.1007/978-3-662-43742-1_14

29. Luuk, E.: Nouns, verbs and flexibles: implications for typologies of word classes. Lang. Sci. **32**(3), 349–365 (2010). https://doi.org/10.1016/j.langsci.2009.02.001

30. Montague, R.: The proper treatment of quantification in ordinary English. In: Portner, P., Partee, B.H. (eds.) Formal Semantics: The Essential Readings, pp. 17–34. Blackwell, Oxford (2002 [1973])

31. Peterson, J.: There's a grain of truth in every "myth", or, why the discussion of lexical classes in Mundari isn't quite over yet. Linguist. Typology **9**(3), 391–405 (2005)

32. Pfenning, F.: Logical frameworks - a brief introduction. In: Schwichtenberg, H., Steinbrüggen, R. (eds.) Proof and System-Reliability. NAII, vol. 62, pp. 137–166. Springer, Berlin (2002). https://doi.org/10.1007/978-94-010-0413-8_5. http://www.cs.cmu.edu/ fp/papers/mdorf01.pdf

33. Plank, F.: Determiner universal. In: The Universals Archive (2006). https://typo.uni-konstanz.de/archive/nav/browse.php?number=1201

34. Pollard, C., Sag, I.A.: Head-Driven Phrase Structure Grammar. University of Chicago Press, Chicago (1994)

35. Ranta, A.: Type-Theoretical Grammar. Clarendon Press, Oxford (1994)

36. Ranta, A.: Grammatical framework: a type-theoretical grammar formalism. J. Funct. Program. **14**(2), 145–189 (2004). https://doi.org/10.1017/S0956796803004738

37. Ranta, A.: Type theory and universal grammar. Philosophia Scientiæ. Travaux d'histoire et de philosophie des sciences (6), 115–131 (2006). https://journals.openedition.org/philosophiascientiae/415

38. Ranta, A.: The status of the GF resource grammar library (2017). http://www.grammaticalframework.org/lib/doc/status.html

39. Seuren, P.A.M.: Language from within: Vol. 2. The Logic of Language. Oxford University Press, Oxford (2010)

40. Westerstahl, D.: Generalized quantifiers. In: Zalta, E.N. (ed.) The Stanford Encyclopedia of Philosophy. Metaphysics Research Lab, Stanford University, winter 2016 edn. (2016). https://plato.stanford.edu/archives/win2016/entries/generalized-quantifiers

Two Cognitive Systems, Two Implications, and Selection Tasks

Angelina Bobrova[1] and Ahti-Veikko Pietarinen[2,3,4(✉)]

[1] Russian State University for the Humanities, Moscow, Russia
angelina.bobrova@gmail.com
[2] Nazarbayev University, Nur-Sultan, Kazakhstan
ahti.pietarinen@gmail.com
[3] National Research University Higher School of Economics,
Moscow, Russian Federation
[4] Tallinn University of Technology, Tallinn, Estonia

Abstract. Dual-process theories of reasoning take for granted the fundamental difference between the two cognitive systems, Systems 1 and 2. This paper, in contrast, argues that System 1, which is responsible for fast, intuitive, associative, and effortless reasoning, can be explained to be just as logical as System 2, which is said to draw consequences in rule-based, rational and criticised fashions. The only difference between the two systems is argued to be that the former draws conclusions in a logic which is diagrammatic, and moreover a positive and implicational fragment of ordinary, classical logic. Such a fundamental connection between the two systems is then applied to explain away cognitive biases in the Wason card selection task. The selection task thus ceases to represent a paradigm case of confirmation bias, because both systems of reasoning exhibit important processes of logical inferences.

Keywords: Logic · Cognition · Dual-processes · Diagrammatic logic · Peirce's graphs · Positive implication · Wason card selection task

1 Introduction

Ability to reason is one of the great unanswered questions in the evolution of the genus *homo*. Contemporary studies in the cognitive science of reasoning have mostly been geared towards psychology, formal logic having a supportive function, if any. Even the mental model theories [10,11,27] that admit non-monotonic logics assume that reasoning ultimately depends not on logical forms but on mental models of situations. While this assumption was criticised among others in [6], it did not leverage the supportive function of logic in cognitive and psychological studies.

A.-V. Pietarinen—The paper was prepared by RFBR, project number 20-011-00227 A (first author), and within the framework of the HSE University Basic Research Program and funded by the Russian Academic Excellence Project '5–100'.

© Springer Nature Switzerland AG 2020
J. Camara and M. Steffen (Eds.): SEFM 2019 Workshops, LNCS 12226, pp. 195–205, 2020.
https://doi.org/10.1007/978-3-030-57506-9_15

Theories of reasoning can generally be categorised under two headings: the *dual-process theories* [4, 12, 25, 30] and the *single-system conceptions* [5, 13, 16, 26]. We argue that a logical perspective is indispensable in dual-process theories, while we do not criticise psychological conceptions from the points of view of logic. Neither 'logical psychologism' nor 'psychological logicism' are fruitful stances in this regard. Psychology studies human thought and action in actual and prospective cases, while logic is in the business of analysing the general conceptions of these actions.

We stress that getting the meaning of these central concepts right is essential to the understanding of reasoning in its multiple forms. Basic principles of human reasoning deserve to be examined and their logical content demonstrated from interdisciplinary and normative points of view. The conception of logic used deals not with various matters of *human thinking* but rather is used to scrutinise how one thought (proposition, assertion, content) ought to be related to another. Only if these connections take the form of premises-and-conclusion in terms of the relation of consequence, we can say that reasoning appears. Only if these connections agree with specific rules or principles of reasoning, would any piece of reasoning possess some desirable properties, such as being valid, secure, reliable, fruitful, or evident to reason. And only if we can bring out what these basic rules or principles of reasoning are, can the value of those interlinking processes be adequately evaluated. We agree with the position that people are not irrational but logical—if people "ignored logic all the time, extracting the wrong information from the data at their disposal, it is hard to see how our species could survive", as the rules of task-dependent forms of inference "include more heuristic 'default rules' that are not valid in our strict sense" [2, p. 2]. Humankind did not wait for Aristotle's syllogisms to become a rational race.

This paper suggests another solution. A possibility for a fruitful cooperation between logical and psychological theories of reasoning springs from Charles Peirce's theory of reasoning, in particular the theory of *existential graphs* (EG; [1, 9, 24, 33]). EG makes explicit the logical power of reasoning in diagrammatic form. Its results can, we propose, solve prevailing issues in cognitive psychology concerning the Wason card selection task, dispensing with explanations that draw from cognitive, and especially confirmation, biases associated to the results of those experiments. We then apply Peirce's concepts of the philosophy of logic and reasoning to argue for an alternative interpretation and analysis of those results.

2   Two Systems of Reasoning and Two Types of Scrolls

Dual-process or dual-system conceptions have a prominent role in contemporary studies of human reasoning. The alternative to them is commonly bundled as the 'single-system' conceptions [5, 13, 16, 26]. Dual-process theories date back to William James [8] but rose to prominence rather belatedly. From the works including [4, 25, 30], the idea was broadened to the decision-making theory by [12], among others.

Dual-process theories contrast *spontaneous* and *deliberate* reasoning. Theories vary in details but share the common core. The two types are taken to exploit what is termed in cognitive sciences as Systems 1 and 2 (for short, S1 and S2). S1 is responsible for performing fast, intuitive, associative and effortless reasoning, whereas S2 produces rule-based, rational and criticised consequences of our thoughts with increased cognitive effort and time expended on tracing those consequences than what the S1 would do.

It is also commonly maintained that in ordinary circumstances, subjects appeal to the first type as it is easier to use and leads to effective solutions and short-cuts much needed in actual reasoning cases. It is only when S1 fails us (which would happen, it is said, in non-typical situations), S2 may interject its correctives to the subject's performance of reasoning.

The evidence for the presence of the two systems of cognition has been drawn from numerous experimental results, most famously the Wason card selection task [31, 32]:

- A subject sees four cards. Two cards have their letter sides up; the other two the have their number faces up. It is common knowledge that each card has a letter on the one side and a number on the other. Participants are then asked to answer the question: Which cards they should turn over to prove the rule "If on one side of the card there is an E, then on the other side there is a 2".

The experiment is built on the schemata of Modus Ponens and Modus Tollens. "If an E, then a 2" does not mean that only an E is paired with this number. The results have been interpreted to show that a vast majority of people ignored the 'not only' condition. (The correct answer is 'E' and '7'.)

A negative version of this selection task has indeed been taken to reinforce the standard lesson:

- What would happen when the rule "If on one side of the card there is an E, then on the other side there is a 2" is modified into "If on one side of the card there is an E, then on the other side there is *not* a 2", while rest of the conditions are left unaltered?

The answer is that these modified experiments suggest that those participants who are asked to prove the latter conditional usually do significantly better in producing the correct answer.

Proponents of the dual-process theories have concluded from this that people do not, in general, utilise logical reasoning to resolve such tasks. Rather, subjects appeal to what is provided by the fast track of S1. Logic can justify or imitate reasoning, especially when it comes to its non-monotonic forms, but the theory of logic itself is held incapable of assisting us in producing conclusive or even partially satisfactory answers to the question of what constitutes reasoning.

Indeed the logical structure of the two-systems dichotomy is not clear. Exactly where does the first cease to apply and when does the second system take over? Or are the two systems rather located at the ends of a continuum, say from analogical to digital processing? Admitting that S2 corrects the fast-and-frugal mistakes made by S1 does not alone mean that S2 is free from such errors. People notoriously repeat the same classes of fallacies yet expect different outcomes. Why would S1 not use logical reasoning, then?

Next, we uncover some support for the possibility that both systems may well rely on the same general logical schemata of reasoning. It is rather that humans may fail to observe and identify the relational structure between those schemata. This means that S1 is also inferential, and that its functioning could be explained by logic and is not limited to heuristic treatment only. That logic nevertheless is not classical but requires a conception of implication that is different from the classical one.

3   Logical Graphs for Cognition

The correlation between logic and cognitive processes (or computations) has been proposed to run along the following lines:

> [Logic] can never be the whole story of the implementation level (which by definition involves the physical instantiation of an algorithm). Nevertheless, logic can help bridge the gap between the implementation of an algorithmic level by analyzing structural similarities across different proposed instantiations. . . . Logical analysis can distinguish the commonalities across implementation-level hypotheses form their true disagreements [7, p. 796].

Arguably this confirms that the turn to logic is a tricky one; contemporary logic professes to be formal, but the formality itself is a Janus-faced entity: technical details can overshadow long-lasting visions on its true subject matter.

It is far from clear whether computational models simulate or replicate the causal powers of situated reasoning tasks. Recently, a credible framework has been proposed "for epistemic logic, modeling the logical aspects of System 1 ('fast') and System 2 ('slow') cognitive processes, as per dual process theories of reasoning . . . It is applied to three instances of limited rationality, widely discussed in cognitive psychology: Stereotypical Thinking, the Framing Effect, and the Anchoring Effect" [28]. The model imitates the duality of 'moderately rational agents', but this duality itself is taken for granted in the above work, and the methodological and philosophical side of the question is swept aside (cf. [19]).

Such proposals are not altogether different from what the present paper suggests, however, as it argues that reasoning is a matter to be dealt with in theories of logic. At the same time, we claim that logic can do more than is usually thought. It can be applied to cases that experiment on reasoning in the course of empirical investigation. But in order to do that, we need an approach quite different from the usual ones; namely, we need a theory in which philosophical, empirical and formal parts are better balanced. We now propose that EG can assume this role.

EG is a diagrammatical logical system that includes several further theories, such as the Alpha, the Beta, and the Gamma parts, which roughly correspond to propositional logic, first-order logic and modal logic, respectively [14,21,22, 24,33]. Its basic units are graphs, as illustrated in Fig. 1.

A B

Fig. 1. Conjunction and implication in existential graphs.

The graph on the left represents a juxtaposition of two graphs, A and B. The graph on the right represents a negation of a juxtaposition of A and the negation of B. In classical logic, this is interpreted as a material implication.

Graphs are propositional expressions "of any possible state of the inverse" (CP 4.395). Technically, a graph signifies a "general type of whatever means the same thing and expresses that meaning in the same way ...; while that which is scribed once and only once and embodies the graph" is a graph-instance (R 45); graphs actually presented or *scribed* on the *sheet of assertion*. Unlike mathematics, logic is not abstract science.

We confine our presentation to the Alpha part that agrees with propositional logic (the two-element Boolean algebra). Its syntactical part is presented with the sheet of assertion (which represents tautology) and the components of graphs, called the *cuts* (which are non-overlapping closed curves representing scope and negation). Two graphs on the same sheet are said to be *juxtaposed* (Fig. 1 on the left). The sheet is both unordered and itself a proposition expressing tautology while juxtaposition corresponds to conjunction. Under the standard interpretation, the cut represents Boolean complementation. In terms of the Alpha part, the graphs (Fig. 1) should be read as $(A \wedge B)$ or $(B \wedge A)$ and $\overline{(A \wedge \bar{B})}$ or $(A \rightarrow B)$ respectively.

This part of the theory presumes the presence of the set of (sound and complete) transformation rules that defines reasoning as a series of insertions and omissions. Any graph may be *inserted on any oddly enclosed area* or be *erased whenever evenly enclosed*. Any graph on any area may be scribed on the same or any other area contained within it. In case a graph results from such copy-paste *iterations*, it may be erased (*de-iteration*). If nothing else than a blank occupies an area between two cuts, this *double cut may be removed*. Also, a double cut may always be *added around any graph*.

The graph transformations of Fig. 2 (Modus ponens) demonstrate how these rules may be used.

Fig. 2. Modus ponens transformations.

EG is philosophically and formally a balanced system of logic. While logical it can also be positioned as a *cognitive resource* [22] that provides "a rough and generalized diagram of the Mind", one which "gives a better idea of what the mind is, from the point of view of logic, than could be conveyed by any abstract account of it" (R 490; [23, p. 900]).

Diagrammatic transformations show how one graph is turned into another one along logical consequence relation. In other words, the theory takes graphs as "moving-pictures of thoughts" and these 'moving pictures', in turn, illustrate the core that governs reasoning. Peirce calls it leading or *guiding principle* of reasoning:

> That which determines us, from given premises, to draw one inference rather than another, is some habit of mind, whether it be constitutional or acquired. The habit is good or otherwise, according as it produces true conclusions from true premises or not; and an inference is regarded as valid or not, without reference to the truth or falsity of its conclusion specially, but according as the habit which determines it is such as to produce true conclusions in general or not. The particular habit of mind which governs this or that inference may be formulated in a proposition whose truth depends on the validity of the inferences which the habit determines; and such a formula is called a *guiding principle* of inference (CP 5.367).

The guiding principle constrains the ways in which information flows and conclusions determined, secured and supported by their premises. The leading principle governs all reasoning in general and is not limited to deductive reasoning.

4   Guiding Principle, Scroll and Two Implications

The guiding principle is intrinsically connected to the interpretation of implication. In EG, it is presented either as two nested cuts or as "the scroll" composed of one continuous line or two closed lines one inside the other (Fig. 3). In scrolls, the antecedent is placed in the outer compartment while the consequent is situated in the inner compartment. The scroll corresponds to the idea of leading principle, namely that implication is the basic logical sign. The strategy of proving logical theorems illustrate this well, since any such proof starts with an insertion of a double cut on the blank sheet of assertions.

Fig. 3. Two implications, material and the scroll.

However, the scroll does more than this. It also introduces negation by generating the cut (Fig. 4). The cut is the result of evolution from the scroll. That process is in the very operation of logical graphs: "A certain development of reasoning was possible before ...the concept of falsity had ever been framed" (R 669, 1910; [23, p. 920]). Such a state of affairs can following Peirce be called *paradisiacal* (R

669). Under it, our assertions take the form "If X be true, then every assertion is true." At the same time, for those living under such conditions, "it will soon be recognized that not every assertion is true; and that once recognized . . . , one at once rejects the antecedent that lead to that absurd consequence" (*ibid.*).

Figure 4 reproduces this process graphically: we move from "If A is true, C is true" via "If A be true whatever can be asserted is true" and "A is not true and the inner close being cut very small" towards the idea of negation. The black spot that we see in the second and third graphs is the "blot". The color or shade means that its area is fully occupied and no proposition could be added to it, not event the blank. The blot contrasts with the sheet but is positive and affirmative rather than negative assertion or denial. As the size of that area does not change the cardinality of truths included in it, the inner loop with the blot in it could just as well be atrophied until the loop coincides with the boundary of the outer circle of the scroll at their intersection point:

Fig. 4. (a, b, c and d, respectively).

Such process of evolution of a fundamental logical conception now results in two kinds of implications: *paradisiacal* implication that lacks the conception of a negation, and logical or *material* implication [15].

This split marks the connection with contemporary theories on reasoning. Both implications have the same structure and both illustrate the workings of guiding principle. But both have different presuppositions. Paradisiacal implication is an implication in a negation-free language while the material one corresponds to the conditional *de inesse* as in standard logic.

Paradisiacal implication pertains to the vocabulary that both is devoid of the conception of a negation and is considered as a primitive notion in the sense of not definable from any other connectives. Such positive fragments inevitably differ from classical logics that have material implication and that can define the latter by other connectives. The connection, however, is that the material implication *evolves*, in the sense of Fig. 4, from paradisiacal implication.

This split at the level of logic can be confirmed by data. Humans—as manifested in such examples as the development of grammar in *homo erectus*, infants below c.14 months of age, as well as most other primates—seem unable to conceptualise the ideas of the negation, contradiction, or even that of absence. Difficulties show up at the levels of grammar acquisition and in the production and comprehension of illocutionary forces involved in them (see e.g. [3]). Yet reasoning is present, carried out only in terms of positive instances. But when crucial word–object relations break down and the subject becomes conscious of it, hypothetical conditionals emerge. With the emergence of hypotheticals, other concepts such as axioms follow suit, indicating that there was a hidden presence of falsity all along.

5   Wason's Card Selection Task and Two Implications

How does this relate to what was previously said? Let us go back to the proposed solution to the selection task and to the claim that S1 need no appeal to logical reasoning. This conclusion is too hasty. For all reasoning has to have certain rational foundations. Although questions of rationality and sound reasoning (as opposed to the reasoning that is, say, bad, invalid, unsound, or unethical) may be treated quite differently in different domains and applications, they have to be predicated on certain normative powers of logic that can cater for rationality.

Recall that reasoning takes place as soon as there are norms that allow composition of thoughts in terms of premise–conclusion consequence relation. Likewise, one must acknowledge that reasoning is not taking place when a 'therefore', in whatever form, is absent. This demarcation between the thoughts that follow from other thoughts in the premise–conclusion sequence and those that do not is significant, since premises are the material that ought to support their conclusions (they are *signs* that represent their conclusions as their objects). Otherwise, the whole edifice of sound reasoning would recede from view.

Let us take the scroll to provide premise–conclusion schemata and let us link its paradisiacal and material versions to S1 and S2, respectively. When participants choose their cards, they tend to admit that their reasoning is grounded on what they see, and for such reasons do not proceed thinking of alternative solutions. But if so, the selection task is not a textbook case of confirmation bias: the subject's ignorance of a relevant piece of information is not a bias but a *crucial part of logical reasoning at the level of the paradisiacal implication*. The results of the selection task can be interpreted to mean that people are prone reasoning at the level of the scroll that is paradisiacal, an implication devoid of the conception of negation or falsity.

Indeed paradisiacal illation is a natural, even primitive, operation of thought. It presumes that reasoning can proceed even when there is no negation present. What this confirms is not a confirmation bias but the fact that the processes of refutation are less natural to be exhibited in human reason than confirmation.

In other, Peirce's, words, the blot is an affirmative constant, and "affirmation is psychically the simpler" (R L 386). Negation, in contrast, is a *polar* phenomenon, and for negation to make itself manifest, certain further conceptions of *boundaries* are needed first to be maintained in one's mental images of diagrammatic thought. Geometrically, at least two areas are simultaneously present, namely something that exists and something that exhibits mere possibility. This is not a trivial task to be accomplished, and it is no major wonder that S1 tends to take precedence. In short, in human tasks of the sort the selection tests study we see a spontaneous creation of contexts for *positive fragments of logic*, fragments devoid of the conception of negation.

The benefit of this way of looking at the interpretation of the results of the selection experiments is that when the negative element is added to the instruction of the task, participants need not move from one vocabulary or mental notation into another. The rule "If on the one side of the card there is an E, then on the other side there is not a 2", readily includes a negative concept "not a 2". This setting differs markedly in meaning from the positive token of the standard version of the test. However, in both cases, subjects can imagine the same sign of implication; in our terms, the same diagrammatic form of the scroll may be in operation. But in this latter task, however, what triggers the higher success rate is that subjects also recognise that "not every assertion is true". This triggers the aforementioned process in which implication evolve into a negation and sets the latter as an explicit element of the vocabulary of one's mental representation or language in which the respective inferences are enacted.

Last, we can note that the two meanings of the implication, or the evolution of negation from the scrolls, can also explain the single-process approaches to reasoning. An explanation of the Wason selection task offers a vivid illustration of it: "Affirmative rule makes no prediction on the letter to be found on the hidden side of the 2 card, but the negative version of the rule does: an E on the hidden side of the 2 card would falsify the negated rule" [26, p. 43]). But why does the negative version form such a prediction? This further but essential question remains unanswered under their approach.

According to the relevance-theoretic account, the improved performance is wholly determined by the heightened expectation of relevance, in a predictable way, by the content and context of the rule: "[B]y manipulating subjects' expectations of relevance, correct performance can be elicited in any conceptual domain ... Relevance Theory has been initially developed on the basis of philosophical arguments, general psychological considerations, and empirical work in linguistics", and the selection task does not "reveal anything profound about reasoning proper" ([29, p. 89]; cf. [20]). Our hypothesis, in contrast, offers another explanation: the affirmative rule does not make it evident that 'not every assertion is true', while the negative rule does just that.

6   Conclusion

The proposed analysis of the Wason selection task is only a case study by which we can evaluate the two Systems dichotomy anew. S1 can be treated just as logically as S2, with a diagrammatic positive implicational fragment of Peirce's logic of EG responsible for its operation according to the leading principle. The principle works at both deductive and defeasible levels. Such renewed logical foundations for cognition can not only explain away cognitive biases (and the card selection task, for instance, cease to be a paradigm case of confirmation bias) but grounds both systems of reasoning in logical inferential systems.

The correlation between the scroll and two systems of reasoning has some important consequences. First, it explains why associative connections that emerge from the operation of S1 do look like inferences. Because they are inferences: both systems are logical and presuppose the presence of guiding principles that model that reasoning. Second, the correlation specifies what is at issue in some classes of cognitive biases. Third, as the positive implicational fragment has good computational properties is makes an attractive candidate for experiments and models of reasoning in the search for artificial general intelligence.

References

1. Bellucci, F., Pietarinen, A.-V.: Existential graphs as an instrument of logical analysis: part I. Alpha Rev. Symb. Log. **9**, 209–237 (2016)
2. van Benthem, J., et al. Logic in action (2016). http://www.logicinaction.org/
3. Clark, H., Clark, E.: Psychology and Language. Hartcourt, New York (1997)
4. Evans, J.S.B.T., Over, D.E.: Rationality and Reasoning. Psychology Press, Hove (1996)
5. Gigerenzer, G., Regier, T.: How do we tell an association from a rule? Comment on Sloman 1996. Psychol. Bull. **119**(1), 23–26 (1996)
6. Hintikka, J.: Mental models, semantical games and varieties of intelligence. In: Vaina, L.M. (ed.) Matters of Intelligence. Synthese Library (Studies in Epistemology, Logic, Methodology, and Philosophy of Science), vol. 188. Springer, Dordrecht (1987). https://doi.org/10.1007/978-94-009-3833-5_8
7. Isaac, A.M.C., Szymanik, J., Verbrugge, R.: Logic and complexity in cognitive science. In: Baltag, A., Smets, S. (eds.) Johan van Benthem on Logic and Information Dynamics. OCL, vol. 5, pp. 787–824. Springer, Cham (2014). https://doi.org/10.1007/978-3-319-06025-5_30
8. James, W.: The Principles of Psychology. Dover, New York (1950/1890)
9. Johnson-Laird, P.N., Byrne, R.M.J.: Deduction. Erlbaum, Hillsdale (1991)
10. Johnson-Laird, P.N.: How We Reason. Oxford University Press, Oxford (2006)
11. Johnson-Laird, P.N.: Mental Models: Towards a Cognitive Science of Language, Inference, and Consciousness. Cambridge University Press, Cambridge (1983)
12. Kahneman, D.: Thinking, Fast and Slow. Farrar, Straus & Giroux, New York (2011)
13. Keren, G., Schul, Y.: Two is not always better than one: a critical evaluation of two-system theories. Perspectives on Psychological Science **4**(6), 533–550 (2009)
14. Ma, M., Pietarinen, A.-V.: Proof analysis of Peirce's alpha system of graphs. Stud. Logica **105**(3), 625–647 (2017). https://doi.org/10.1007/s11225-016-9703-y
15. Ma, M., Pietarinen, A.-V.: A graphical deep inference system for intuitionistic logic. Logique Anal. **245**, 73–114 (2019)
16. Osman, M.: An evaluation of dual-process theories of reasoning. Psychon. Bull. Rev. **11**(6), 988–1010 (2004). https://doi.org/10.3758/BF03196730
17. Peirce, C.S.: Collected Papers. vols. 1–8. Harvard University Press, Cambridge (1931–1958). Cited as CP
18. Peirce C.S.: Charles Sanders Peirce Papers (MS Am 1632). Houghton Library, Harvard University. Catalogued in Robin, Richard S. (1967). Annotated Catalogue of the Papers of Charles S. Peirce. University of Massachusetts Press, Amherst. Cited as R
19. Pietarinen, A.-V.: What do epistemic logic and cognitive science have to do with each other? Cogn. Syst. Res. **4**(3), 169–190 (2003)
20. Pietarinen, A.-V.: Relevance theory through pragmatic theories of meaning. In: Proceedings of the XXVII Annual Meeting of the Cognitive Science Society, pp. 1767–1772 (2005)

21. Pietarinen, A.-V.: Signs of Logic. Games, and Communication. Springer, Dordrecht, Peircean Themes on the Philosophy of Language (2006)
22. Pietarinen, A.-V.: Existential graphs: what the diagrammatic logic of cognition might look like. Hist. Philos. Logic **32**(3), 265–281 (2011)
23. Pietarinen, A.-V.: Two papers on existential graphs by Charles Peirce. Synthese **192**(4), 881–922 (2015). https://doi.org/10.1007/s11229-014-0498-y
24. Roberts, D.D.: The Existential Graphs of C. S. Peirce. Mouton, The Hague (1973)
25. Sloman, S.A.: The empirical case for two systems of reasoning. Psychol. Bull. **119**(1), 3–22 (1996)
26. Sperber, D., Mercier, H.: The Enigma of Reason. Harvard University Press, Cambridge (2017)
27. Stenning, K., van Lambalgen, M.S.: Human Reasoning and Cognitive Science. MIT Press, Cambridge (2008)
28. Solaki, A., Berto, F., Smets, S.: The logic of fast and slow thinking. Erkenntnis(2019). https://doi.org/10.1007/s10670-019-00128-z
29. Sperber, D., et al.: Relevance theory explains the selection task. Cognition **57**, 31–95 (1995)
30. Stanovich, K.E., West, R.F.: Individual differences in reasoning: implications for the rationality debate. Behav. Brain Sci. **23**, 645–726 (2000)
31. McComas, W.F.: Reasoning. In: McComas, W.F. (ed.) The Language of Science Education. OCL, pp. 83–83. SensePublishers, Rotterdam (2014). https://doi.org/10.1007/978-94-6209-497-0_73
32. Wason, P.C.: Reasoning about a rule. Q. J. Exp. Psychol. **20**, 273–281 (1968)
33. Zeman, J.: The graphical logic of C. S. Peirce. Diss. University of Chicago (1964)

FOCLASA 2019

FOCLASA 2019 Organizers' Message

Software systems are nowadays distributed, concurrent, mobile, and often integrate heterogeneous components and standalone (micro)services. Service coordination, service orchestration and self-adaptation constitute the core characteristics of distributed and service-oriented systems. Solutions for modelling and reasoning about (self-) adaptiveness help to simplify the development of complex distributed systems, enable their validation and evaluation, and improve interoperability, reusability and maintainability of such systems. In this context, the goal of the FOCLASA series of workshop is to gather researchers and practitioners of the aforementioned fields, to share their best practices and experiences, to identify common problems, and to devise general solutions in the context of coordination languages, service orchestration, and self-adaptive systems.

The 17th International Workshop on Coordination and Self-Adaptiveness of Software Applications (FOCLASA 2019) was held in Oslo, Norway, on September 17th 2019, as a satellite event of the SEFM conference. The Program Committee (PC) of FOCLASA 2019 was formed by 25 prominent researchers from 15 different countries. Each paper submitted to FOCLASA 2019 was reviewed by three independent referees, and the review process included an in-depth discussion phase during which the merits of all the papers were discussed. Based on quality, originality, clarity and relevance criteria, the PC finally selected four contributions. The program was then further enhanced by two invited talks given by Bernhard Beckert from the Karlsruhe Institute of Technology (Germany) on the verification of smart contracts, and by Einar Broch Johnsen from the University of Oslo (Norway) on SOS and asynchronously communicating actors.

Many people contributed to the success of FOCLASA 2019. We first would like to thank the authors for submitting high-quality papers. We also thank the Program Committee members for their effort and time to read and discuss the paper and we equally acknowledge the help of additional external reviewers who evaluated submissions in their area of expertise. We wish also to thank Bernhard Beckert and Einar Broch Johnsen, our invited speakers, for their keynotes.

It is also our pleasure to thank Javier Cámara and Martin Steffen, the workshops chairs of SEFM. We also like to acknowledge the EasyChair conference management system, whose facilities greatly helped us to run the review process and facilitate the preparation of the proceedings. Finally, we are endebted to the workshop attendees for keeping the FOCLASA research community lively and interactive, and ultimately ensuring the success of this workshop series.

October 2019

Ernesto Pimentel
Jacopo Soldani

Organization

FOCLASA 2019 - Steering Commmittee

Farhad Arbab	CWI, The Netherlands
Antonio Brogi	University of Pisa, Italy
Carlos Canal	University of Málaga, Spain
Jean-Marie Jacquet	University of Namur, Belgium
Ernesto Pimentel	University of Málaga, Spain
Gwen Salaün	University of Grenoble Alpes, France

FOCLASA 2019 - Program Committee

Farhad Arbab	CWI, The Netherlands
Simon Bliudze	Inria Lille - Nord Europe, France
Uwe Breitenbücher	University of Stuttgart, Germany
Antonio Brogi	University of Pisa, Italy
Javier Cámara	Carnegie Mellon University, USA
Flavio De Paoli	University of Milano Bicocca, Italy
Erik de Vink	Eindhoven University of Technology, The Netherlands
Francisco J. Durán	Universidad de Malaga, Spain
Schahram Dustdar	TU Wien, Austria
Nahla El-Araby	TU Wien, Austria
Jean-Marie Jacquet	University of Namur, Belgium
Einar Broch Johnsen	University of Oslo, Norway
Alberto Lluch Lafuente	Technical University of Denmark, Denmark
Hernan C. Melgratti	University of Buenos Aires, Argentina
Fabrizio Montesi	University of Southern Denmark, Denmark
Pascal Poizat	Universite Paris Ouest, France
Jose Proenca	INESC TEC & Universidade do Minho, Portugal
Gwen Salaün	University of Grenoble, France
Marjan Sirjani	Reykjavik University, Iceland
Meng Sun	Peking University, China
Emilio Tuosto	University of Leicester, UK & GSSI, Italy
Mirko Viroli	University of Bologna, Italy
Lina Ye	CentraleSupelec, France

FOCLASA 2019 - Additional Reviewer

Faiez Zalila	Inria Lille - Nord Europe, France

Quantifying the Similarity of Non-bisimilar Labelled Transition Systems

Gwen Salaün[⊠]

Gwen Salaün$^{(⊠)}$

Univ. Grenoble Alpes, CNRS, Grenoble INP, Inria, LIG, 38000 Grenoble, France
gwen.salaun@inria.fr

Abstract. Equivalence checking is an established technique for automatically verifying that two behavioural models (Labelled Transition Systems, LTSs) are equivalent from the point of view of an external observer. When these models are not equivalent, the checker returns a Boolean result with a counterexample, which is a sequence of actions leading to a state where the equivalence relation is not satisfied. However, this counterexample does not give any indication of how far the two LTSs are one from another. One can wonder whether they are almost identical or totally different, which is quite different from a design or debugging point of view. In this paper, we present an approach for measuring the similarity between two LTS models. The set of metrics is computed automatically using a tool we implemented. Beyond presenting the foundations of the proposed solution, we will show how it can be applied to a concrete application domain for supporting the construction of IoT applications by composition of existing devices.

1 Introduction

Designing and developing distributed software has always been a tedious and error-prone task, and the ever increasing software complexity is making matters even worse. Although we are still far from proposing techniques and tools avoiding the existence of bugs in a software under development, we know how to automatically chase and find bugs that would be very difficult, if not impossible, to detect manually.

Model checking [1] is an established technique for automatically verifying that a model (Labelled Transition System, LTS), obtained from higher-level specification languages such as process algebra, satisfies a given temporal property. Equivalence checking [12] is an alternative solution to model checking and is very helpful to check that two models (requirements and implementation for instance) are equivalent from the point of view of an external observer. When these models are not equivalent, the checker returns a Boolean result with a counterexample, which is a sequence of actions leading to a state where the equivalence relation is not satisfied. However, this counterexample does not give any indication of how far the two LTSs are one from another. One can wonder

© Springer Nature Switzerland AG 2020
J. Camara and M. Steffen (Eds.): SEFM 2019 Workshops, LNCS 12226, pp. 211–225, 2020.
https://doi.org/10.1007/978-3-030-57506-9_16

whether they are almost identical or totally different, which is quite different from a design or debugging point of view.

In this paper, we propose a set of metrics for quantifying the similarity of two behavioural models described using LTS. More precisely, our solution takes as input two LTS models and applies first the partition refinement algorithm [7,17] to identify bisimilar and non-bisimilar states between the two LTSs. Then, we focus on non-bisimilar states and compute a set of local and global metrics for each couple of non-bisimilar states. This allows us to build a matrix with a measure between 0 (totally different states) and 1 (bisimilar states) for each couple. To do so, we rely on several criteria such as the matching of incoming/outgoing transitions, the similarity of neighbour states, the shortest distance from the initial state, and the distance to the closest bisimilar state. Once this matrix is computed, we use it to finally obtain a global measure of similarity of both LTSs. All these measures are computed automatically using a tool we implemented in Python and applied on a large set of examples.

Better understanding and measuring the difference between two behavioural models can be of interest in many different contexts and application areas. It can be used for debugging purposes when the counterexample is not sufficient for detecting the source of the bug, for measuring the distance between two versions of a software, for process model matching in the context of business process and management, etc. We will show in this paper how it can be helpful in the Internet of Things (IoT). One of the main challenges in this area is to build a new application by composing existing objects or devices. This application or composition is satisfactory if it conforms to what the user expects from it. These requirements are formalised using an abstract goal in this work. We will show how we use the proposed measures to compare the candidate composition and the goal. The quantitative results help in understanding what parts of the composition are correct or not *wrt.* this goal, and in guiding the user to finally end up with a satisfactory composition.

The rest of this paper is organized as follows. Section 2 defines LTSs and the notion of strong bisimulation used in equivalence checking. Section 3 presents the details of our approach to compute both the similarity matrix and the global measure of similarity. Section 4 illustrates the proposed solution on a case study in the IoT application domain. Section 5 reviews related work and Sect. 6 concludes the paper.

2   Labelled Transition Systems

In this work, we rely on *Labelled Transition System (LTS)* as low-level behavioural model of concurrent programs. An LTS consists of states and labelled transitions connecting these states.

Definition 1 *(LTS). An LTS is a tuple $M = (S, s^0, \Sigma, T)$ where S is a finite set of state identifiers; $s^0 \in S$ is the initial state identifier; Σ is a finite set of labels; $T \subseteq S \times \Sigma \times S$ is a finite set of transitions.*

A transition is represented as $s \xrightarrow{l} s' \in T$, where $l \in \Sigma$. An LTS can be produced from a higher-level specification of the system described using process algebra for instance. Process algebraic specifications can then be compiled into an LTS using specific compilers. We support nondeterministic LTSs in this work, that is, there may be several transitions outgoing from a specific state labelled with the same action.

When comparing two LTSs, we can use different notions of equivalence, from weak ones such as trace or observational equivalence to stronger ones such as strong bisimulation. In this work, we chose to use strong bisimulation as originally defined in [12]. Supporting weaker notions of bisimulations where silent actions are handled separately is part of future work. It is worth noting that both LTSs are reduced using standard minimization techniques in this work before comparing them.

Definition 2 *(Strong Bisimulation). A relation R is a strong bisimulation between states in S iff for all $s_1, s_2 \in S$ such that $R(s_1, s_2)$, both conditions hold:*

- *$(\forall b \in A, t_1 \in S)\ (s_1, b, t_1) \in T \implies (\exists t_2 \in S)\ (s_2, b, t_2) \in T \wedge R(t_1, t_2)$*
- *$(\forall b \in A, t_2 \in S)\ (s_2, b, t_2) \in T \implies (\exists t_1 \in S)\ (s_1, b, t_1) \in T \wedge R(t_1, t_2)$*

Two states s_1 and s_2 are strongly bisimilar (written $s_1 \approx_s s_2$) iff there exists a strong bisimulation R such that $R(s_1, s_2)$. Two LTS $M_1 = (S_1, s_1^0, \Sigma_1, T_1)$ and $M_2 = (S_2, s_2^0, \Sigma_2, T_2)$ are strongly bisimilar (written $M_1 \approx_s M_2$) iff $s_1^0 \approx_s s_2^0$.

Equivalence checking is usually checked using partition refinement algorithms [7,17]. These algorithms aim at building the minimal number of blocks, where a block is a set of (strongly) bisimilar states. One block is called an equivalence class. In order to check whether two LTSs are equivalent, the partition refinement algorithm is called with the union of both LTSs as input. At the end of this computation, if both initial states are in the same block, the LTSs are equivalent.

3   Comparing Non-bisimilar States

In this section, we present the measure of similarity between two LTSs. This measure applies when the equivalence checker indicates that both LTSs are not strongly bisimilar. In that case, we apply our approach to quantify the difference between the two subparts of both LTSs that are not equivalent. The measure relies on two kinds of criteria, namely local and global criteria, which focus on two non-bisimilar states (one in each LTS). We also present a global measure that gives a single measure of how far both LTSs are. Finally, we introduce a tool that allows us to automatically compute all these results.

3.1   Overall Approach

Given two LTSs, we first use the partition refinement algorithm mentioned in Sect. 2 to compute bisimilar and non-bisimilar states. Then, we focus on non-bisimilar states and propose a measure comparing all non-bisimilar states according to several local and global criteria. For each couple of non-bisimular states (one non-bisimilar state from each LTS), we compute a degree of similarity which belongs to [0..1]. All these results are stored in a matrix where non-bisimilar states of one LTS appear in row and non-bisimilar states of the other LTS appear in column.

Given two non-bisimilar states s_1, s_2 where $s_1 \in LTS_1$ and $s_2 \in LTS_2$, we compute the similarity of those states using global and local criteria. Global criteria aim at considering the structure of both LTSs and looking at the respective positions of both states in their LTSs. More precisely, there are two global criteria. The first one computes the distance from the initial state to the given state in both LTSs and compares those distances. The second one computes the distance from a given state to the closest bisimilar state and compares those distances. In both cases, we compute the shortest distance.

There are four local criteria. The first one compares outgoing transitions to see the number of matching labels. The second does the same with incoming transitions. The third one checks whether the nature of states differ (initial or not). The last one compares the similarity of neighbour states.

Given all these values for a couple of states, we can then compute its value in the matrix ($matrix[s_1, s_2]$). This is obtained by using the weighted average of these values (*e.g.*, 1/6 or arbitrary weights). Since the similarity of neighbour states uses the matrix itself, we use an iterative algorithm that stops when the matrix stabilizes. Once the matrix is computed, we can compute a global measure of similarity, which gives a degree of similarity of both LTSs.

In the rest of this section, we explain in more details the metrics used in this work for computing the similarity measure.

3.2   Global Criteria

These criteria aim at comparing two states $s_1 \in LTS_1$ and $s_2 \in LTS_2$ by looking at their positions in their respective LTSs. We rely on two measures: (i) comparison of distance from initial states to states s_1 and s_2 (d_{init}), (ii) comparison of distance between s_1 and s_2 to their closest bisimilar states (d_{bis}). In both cases, we search for the shortest path. Both measures are then computed in the same way as follows: $1 - (abs(d1 - d2)/max(d1, d2))$, where d_1, d_2 is the distance from s_1, s_2 to the closest bisimilar state or from initial states to s_1, s_2, abs is the absolute value function, and max returns the longest distance.

Example. We illustrate with a simple example where we take the shortest distance from the initial states to two states $s_1 \in LTS_1$ and $s_2 \in LTS_2$ (Fig. 1). Assume first that $d1 = 1$ and $d2 = 8$. In that case $d_{init} = 1 - ((8 - 1)/8) = 0.125$ corresponding to a quite low value for this distance criterion. Consider now that

$d1 = 3$ and $d2 = 5$. This results in a highest value $d_{init} = 1 - ((5 - 3)/5) = 0.6$. If we take equal values such as $d1 = 4$ and $d2 = 4$, we obtain the highest value $d_{init} = 1 - ((4 - 4)/4) = 1$, which means that these two states are not distinguishable with respect to this metric.

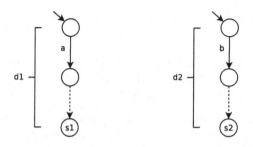

Fig. 1. Example for the distance comparison criterion.

3.3   Local Criteria

These criteria aim at comparing two states $s_1 \in LTS_1$ and $s_2 \in LTS_2$ by looking at their transitions and states (nature and neighbours). We consider four local criteria:

- counting the number of matching outgoing transitions
- counting the number of matching incoming transitions
- comparison of nature of states (initial or not)
- comparison of neighbour states

Given two sets of transitions T_1 and T_2 outgoing from states s_1 and s_2, resp., we compute the similarity of those transitions (m_{out}) as follows: ((number of matching transitions in T_1) / $|T_1|$ + (number of matching transitions in T_2) / $|T_2|$) / 2. This measure is undefined if there is no outgoing transitions. The same measure is computed for incoming transitions.

Example. We illustrate with two simple examples where we compare the transitions outgoing from two states $s_1 \in LTS_1$ and $s_2 \in LTS_2$ (Fig. 2). Consider first the two states on the left hand side of Fig. 2. We obtain $m_{out} = ((1/1) + (1/2))/2 = 0.75$ because the transition outgoing from s_1 has a counterpart whereas only one of the two transitions outgoing from s_2 has a matching transition. If we now look at the second example on the right hand side of Fig. 2, we have $m_{out} = ((1/2) + (1/2))/2 = 0.5$ because from s_1 (s_2, resp.), only half of the transitions have a match.

The nature of two states is simple. If both states are initial or not, we return 1. Otherwise, they have a different nature (one is initial, the other is not), and in that case, we return 0.

Fig. 2. Example for the transition matching criterion.

The fourth metric takes into account the similarity of neighbour states. More precisely, given two states s_1 and s_2, this similarity measure (m_{neig}) is obtained by computing the average of the similarity of all its neighbours.

Example. Suppose two states $s_1 \in LTS_1$ and $s_2 \in LTS_2$ as depicted in Fig. 3. The similarity of neighbour states is computed as follows: $m_{neig}[s1, s2] = (m[s1', s2'] + m[s1'', s2''] + m[s1'', s2'''])/3$.

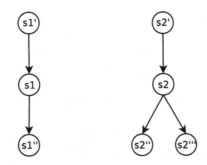

Fig. 3. Example for the neighbour similarity criterion.

Since the computation of state similarity uses the matrix itself (for neighbour states), we use an iterative algorithm that stops when the matrix stabilizes. In practice, the iterative process terminates when the distance δ between two versions of the matrix goes below a fixed threshold. The distance between two matrices is obtained by computing the arithmetic mean of the difference of the two same states in each matrix.

Note that the computation of the matrix always converges to a unique similarity matrix. This convergence can be proven as achieved in [14] by using Banach's fixed point theorem.

3.4   Global Measure

Once the similarity matrix is computed, there are several options for computing a global score out of the matrix. We adopted here an optimistic point of view by computing the average of the best score for each row and for each column.

Other global measures are possible, *e.g.*, by computing the average of all values greater than a given threshold.

Example. Table 1 gives an example of matrix obtained applying the aforementioned computations. We keep the best scores for each row and for each column. The best score for each row coincides with the best score for each column on this example, but this is not always the case. We finally compute the average of all these best scores, which results in a global similarity value of 0.9 in this case.

Table 1. Example for the global similarity measure.

	s0	s1	s2
s0	**0.9**	0.25	0.42
s1	0.25	**0.98**	0.39
s2	0.42	0.39	**0.83**

3.5 Tool Support

The partition refinement algorithm and the similarity measures (matrix and global measure) are computed via a tool (DLTS) we implemented in Python, see Fig. 4 for an overview. It takes as input two LTSs specified in the textual 'aut' format. In practice, we use the LNT process algebra [4] for specifying high-level concurrent systems and compile these specifications to LTSs in 'aut' format by using CADP compilers [6].

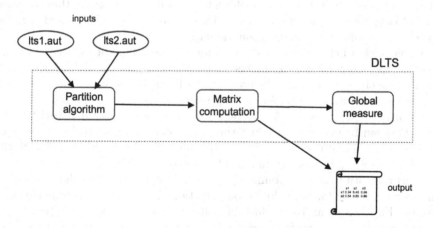

Fig. 4. Tool support.

We applied our tool to many examples (we have about 100 aut files in our repository of examples). Experiments were carried out to evaluate the quality of the results using the well-known precision and recall measures. In this specific context, we consider the matching of states as basis for these measures, and we assume two states to be a correct match if each state cannot obtain a higher result in the similarity matrix with any other state. Precision computes the number of correct matched states out of all matched states detected by our approach. This allows us to verify that we do not have too many false positives (irrelevant matched states). Recall corresponds to the number of correct matched states detected by our approach out of all expected matched states. This allows us to measure the number of matched states our approach fails to identify. We have computed the precision and recall measures for several examples taken from our repository. These measures show the good quality of our approach with high values for precision and recall.

Performance and scability are however an issue. It takes several minutes to compute the matrix for LTSs involving thousands of states/transitions. This comes from both the computation of the partition refinement algorithm and from the matrix computation. The good point is that our approach does not target large LTSs but rather small ones as we will show in the next section with a real-world case study taken from the IoT application domain.

4   Application to Composition of IoT Objects

In this section, we illustrate with one possible application of the measure of similarity between LTSs, namely the design of IoT applications by composition of devices and software (object for short in the rest of this section). Each object must exhibit the actions it can execute as well as the order in which these actions must be triggered. Such a public interface can be described using an LTS, as proposed in [8,9], where labels on transitions correspond to these actions. Two objects interact one with another by synchronizing on same action name (synchronous binary communication model).

Given such a behavioural model for objects, the overall objective is to build a satisfactory composition of objects that satisfies a given goal. The goal is an abstract specification of what the user expects from the resulting composition. It can be modelled using an LTS too using interactions as labels (synchronization of actions) as suggested in [5]. A composition is satisfactory if it satisfies the goal. This can be verified using first the synchronous product to build a unique LTS out of a set of object LTSs, and then comparing the resulting LTS with the goal LTS using equivalence techniques (strong bisimulation here).

This case study aims at building a new IoT application for home security and more precisely for home intrusion detection. The goal of this application is given in Fig. 5 using an LTS, which indicates that when a move is detected, the camera is turned on, an alert message is sent to a mobile phone, and the light in the house is switched on.

Usually, in order to build an application satisfying these requirements, the end-user needs a recommender system listing all objets available nearby with their interface. We assume here that after this task the four objects given in

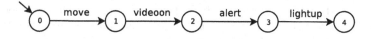

Fig. 5. Case study: goal.

Fig. 6 are selected as possible candidates. There is first a security sensor that detects movement in the house. When a movement is detected it turns the video on and sends an alert message to a mobile phone. Once the alert is over, the sensor reinitializes and turns the video off. The second object is a connected light that can be repeatedly switched on and off. The third object is a security camera whose video can be activated or not. When activated, watching the video is possible. Finally, the final object is a home security app that can be installed on a smartphone. This app is triggered when receiving an alert. Then, there are several functionalities available for the user such as watching the video or switching the light on/off. Once the alert is over, the app allows the user to initialize it again.

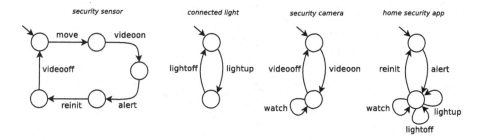

Fig. 6. Case study: objects.

The next question is the following: are we sure that this selection of objects does satisfy the given abstract goal? This is when equivalence checking comes into play. From the objects given in Fig. 6, we can build the resulting LTS using the classic parallel composition operator available in process algebra or the synchronous product of communicating automata. Here, we synchronize two objects on same actions. If an action in one object does not have any counterpart in another object, this is an independent evolution. As a result we obtain the LTS (generated with CADP) depicted in Fig. 7.

We now compare both LTSs (goal, Fig. 5, and composition LTS, Fig. 7) using the DLTS tool. Table 2 shows the resulting matrix obtained after four iterations. The comparison method also indicates that all states are non-bisimilar. The global similarity measure returns a value of 76%, indicating that both LTSs are not totally different and exhibit portions of their behaviours that are very similar. By looking more carefully at the matrix given in Table 2, we can see that the first three states are very similar with values higher than 80%. But then, most values

220   G. Salaün

are very low. If we look at the states in the composition LTS, we understand that this is due to actions present in the objects and their composition that are not taken into account by the abstract goal (e.g., lightoff, videooff).

There are now several options. One can try another selection and combination of objects. Another option is to go further in the analysis and comprehension of the current solution. As far as the latter is concerned, we can decide to refine the goal by integrating the missing actions, or we can keep the abstract goal as is and hide in the composition LTS these irrelevant actions. We decide to go for this final option by hidding the actions where light and camera are switched off (lightoff and videooff). Figure 8 shows the resulting LTS (generated with CADP) where hidden actions have been removed for the sake of readability.

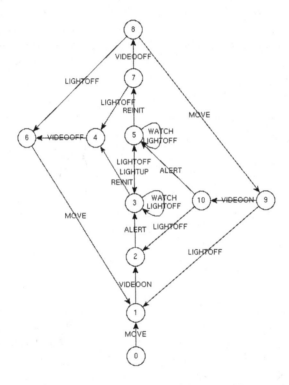

Fig. 7. Case study: composition LTS.

Table 3 gives the similarity matrix computed by comparing the goal (Fig. 5) with this second composition LTS (Fig. 8). All states are non-bisimilar but the global measure increases to 89%. The matrix shows very similar states for the three first states (s0, s1, s2) and lower values for the remaining states (s3, s4). This is quite normal because the two LTSs exhibit several differences in states s3 and s4: (i) the goal is non-looping whereas all objects can loop forever and so the composition LTS, (ii) the reinit and watch actions were not made explicit in the goal but they totally make sense, and (iii) the lightup action is in sequence in the goal whereas it can be repeated in the composition. It is worth noting that these differences make the equivalence not satisfied, but once better understood using our measures, there are not real problems from a functional perspective. Therefore, although the two LTSs are not bisimilar, the end-user could be satisfied by the proposed composition of objects and accept it as a correct solution for his/her application.

Table 2. Case study: first similarity matrix.

	s0	s1	s2	s3	s4	s5	s6	s7	s8	s9	s10
s0	**0.97**	0.18	0.17	0.17	0.16	0.17	0.47	0.16	0.35	0.22	0.17
s1	0.18	**0.86**	0.36	0.33	0.3	0.31	0.3	0.3	0.29	*0.68*	0.33
s2	0.17	0.38	**0.88**	0.43	0.37	0.39	0.35	0.36	0.34	0.33	*0.72*
s3	0.19	0.34	0.45	*0.77*	0.44	0.59	0.4	0.43	0.4	0.37	0.38
s4	0.4	0.42	0.48	0.58	*0.62*	*0.74*	0.55	0.58	0.52	0.5	0.48

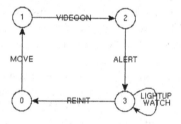

Fig. 8. Case study: composition LTS (V2).

Table 3. Case study: second similarity matrix.

	s0	s1	s2	s3
s0	**0.9**	0.18	0.17	0.15
s1	0.05	**0.99**	0.36	0.32
s2	0.07	0.35	**0.98**	0.43
s3	0.08	0.33	0.44	*0.79*
s4	0.26	0.37	0.47	*0.72*

Last but not least, the user can take advantage of the first LTS generated for the initial composition (Fig. 7) where all possible executions are enumerated to verify additional properties (absence of deadlocks, a certain action is always reachable, some action occurs after another one, etc.). This can be achieved using temporal logic and model checking (we use MCL [10] and the CADP model checker [6], resp., in this work).

5   Related Work

Comparing automata-based models using equivalence techniques is not a new problem. It was studied for instance in the context of the composition of web services, see, e.g. [2,21]. [21] relied on observational equivalence for checking that two versions of a service composition were the same. [2] proposed one compatibility definition based on bisimulation techniques for checking whether two web services can interact properly. In this work, our focus is on quantitative aspects of non-equivalent behavioural models.

[22] measures the similarity of Labelled Transition Systems (LTSs) w.r.t. a simulation and a bisimulation notion inspired from the equivalence relations. The measuring techniques use weighted quantitative functions which consist in a simple (not iterative), forward, and parallel traversal of two LTSs. This work does not return a global similarity measure and the differences which distinguish one entity from another.

In [11,13], the authors rely on a similarity flooding algorithm for computing the matrix of correspondences between models. [11] considers a forward and backward similarity propagation to compare data structures described with directed labelled graphs. However, the tool does not enable a fully automated matching because the user should manually adjust some matches. The match operator introduced in [13] measures the similarity between different versions of software units described using Statecharts. The similarity measuring combines a set of static and behavioural matchings. The behavioural matching is computed using a flooding algorithm and relies on the bisimulation notion presented in [22]. Flooding algorithms were also used for measuring the compatibility of behavioural models of Web services in [15,16]. Our iteration process is very similar to similarity flooding algorithm but tackles the problem with a different angle by focusing only on non-bisimilar states.

[3] extends the simulation preorder to a quantitative setting. It presents three notions of distances (correctness, coverage, robustness), which resides in making each player of a simulation game pay a certain price for his/her choices. These distances are comparable to the global measure proposed in this paper. There is no local criterion used in their work.

[24] presents an approach (SpecDiff) to compute the differences between two LTSs obtained by compilation from CSP, representing the evolving behaviors of a concurrent program. SpecDiff considers LTSs as Typed Attributed Graphs (TAGs), in which states and transitions are encoded in finite dimensional vector spaces. It then computes a maximum common subgraph of two TAGs, which represents an optimal matching of states and transitions between two LTSs. This approach aims at pairing states and transitions for debugging purposes whereas we analyze the structure of both LTSs without mandatorily finding a match. Moreover, our approach is more general-purpose and not only designed for program debugging.

[23] aims at comparing state machines in terms of their language (the externally observable sequences of events that are permitted or not), and in terms of their structure (the actual states and transitions that govern the behaviour).

The language comparison exploits model-based testing approach. The structure comparison uses what we call local criteria in our paper, by looking at the similarity of surrounding transitions and source/target states. They do not rely on any notion of distances as we did to compare the situation of both states in their respective LTSs. They do not focus on non-bisimilar states only as we do. As far as application is concerned, they apply their approach to reverse-engineering state machines from program traces.

[18,19] define a distance between processes modelled as trees by computing the costs to transform one of the trees into the other. This notion of distance between processes is defined using coinduction. This approach applies in the case of both finite and infinite trees. The notion of k-bisimulation was introduced in [20]. It considers weak bisimulation and more specifically the weak equivalence notion introduced by Milner in [12]. K-bisimulation measures the number of actions to be hidden for establishing weak equivalence between two processes modelled using LTSs. Thoses measures are less precise than ours since they do not give any detailed measure of distance among the states of both LTSs. It is closer to our global measure of similarity, which gives a rough estimation of how far the two LTSs are one from another.

6   Concluding Remarks

We have presented in this paper a set of metrics that allows us to quantify the difference between the non-bisimilar parts of two LTSs. This similarity measure combines local and global criteria for computing a matrix that compares all non-bisimilar states in both LTSs. The computed matrix is used in a second step for computing a global measure of similarity that is helpful to distinguish totally different LTSs and almost bisimilar ones. Our approach is implemented in a tool and was applied on a set of about 100 examples for validating the ideas. Beyond that, we applied our solution to a concrete application area, namely the design of IoT applications by composition of objects. This case study allows us to show how our similarity measure can be used in practice to solve concrete problems.

As far as future work is concerned, we plan to extend our work to support other notions of bisimulations. Another perspective aims at taking advantage of all the values gathered in the similarity matrix to refine our comprehension of the differences between the two LTSs. We also plan to apply our similarity measure to other application domains such as the business process models matching or the debugging of concurrent software. Finally, we would like to work on the optimization of the tool support to make our approach scalable on large LTSs consisting of possibly millions of states/transitions.

References

1. Baier, C., Katoen, J.: Principles of Model Checking. MIT Press, Cambridge (2008)
2. Bordeaux, L., Salaün, G., Berardi, D., Mecella, M.: When are two web services compatible? In: Shan, M.-C., Dayal, U., Hsu, M. (eds.) TES 2004. LNCS, vol. 3324, pp. 15–28. Springer, Heidelberg (2005). https://doi.org/10.1007/978-3-540-31811-8_2
3. Černý, P., Henzinger, T.A., Radhakrishna, A.: Simulation distances. In: Gastin, P., Laroussinie, F. (eds.) CONCUR 2010. LNCS, vol. 6269, pp. 253–268. Springer, Heidelberg (2010). https://doi.org/10.1007/978-3-642-15375-4_18
4. Champelovier, D., et al.: Reference Manual of the LNT to LOTOS Translator (Version 6.7). INRIA/VASY and INRIA/CONVECS, 153 p. (2018)
5. Durán, F., Salaün, G., Krishna, A.: Automated composition, analysis and deployment of IoT applications. In: Mazzara, M., Bruel, J.-M., Meyer, B., Petrenko, A. (eds.) TOOLS 2019. LNCS, vol. 11771, pp. 252–268. Springer, Cham (2019). https://doi.org/10.1007/978-3-030-29852-4_21
6. Garavel, H., Lang, F., Mateescu, R., Serwe, W.: CADP 2011: a toolbox for the construction and analysis of distributed processes. STTT **15**(2), 89–107 (2013)
7. Kanellakis, P.C., Smolka, S.A.: CCS expressions, finite state processes, and three problems of equivalence. Inf. Comput. **86**(1), 43–68 (1990)
8. Krishna, A., Pallec, M.L., Mateescu, R., Noirie, L., Salaün, G.: IoT composer: composition and deployment of IoT applications. In: Proceedings of ICSE 2019, Montreal, pp. 19–22. IEEE/ACM (2019)
9. Krishna, A., Pallec, M.L., Mateescu, R., Noirie, L., Salaün, G.: Rigorous design and deployment of IoT applications. In: Proceedings of FormaliSE 2019. ACM (2019)
10. Mateescu, R., Thivolle, D.: A model checking language for concurrent value-passing systems. In: Cuellar, J., Maibaum, T., Sere, K. (eds.) FM 2008. LNCS, vol. 5014, pp. 148–164. Springer, Heidelberg (2008). https://doi.org/10.1007/978-3-540-68237-0_12
11. Melnik, S., Garcia-Molina, H., Rahm, E.: Similarity flooding: a versatile graph matching algorithm and its application to schema matching. In: Proceedings of ICDE 2002, pp. 117–128. IEEE Computer Society (2002)
12. Milner, R.: Communication and Concurrency. Prentice Hall, Upper Saddle River (1989)
13. Nejati, S., Sabetzadeh, M., Chechik, M., Easterbrook, S.M., Zave, P.: Matching and merging of statecharts specifications. In: Proceedings of ICSE 2007, pp. 54–64. IEEE Computer Society (2007)
14. Ouederni, M., Fahrenberg, U., Legay, A., Salaün, G.: Compatibility flooding: measuring interaction of services interfaces. In: Proceedings of SAC 2017, pp. 1334–1340. ACM (2017)
15. Ouederni, M., Salaün, G., Pimentel, E.: Quantifying service compatibility: a step beyond the Boolean approaches. In: Maglio, P.P., Weske, M., Yang, J., Fantinato, M. (eds.) ICSOC 2010. LNCS, vol. 6470, pp. 619–626. Springer, Heidelberg (2010). https://doi.org/10.1007/978-3-642-17358-5_47
16. Ouederni, M., Salaün, G., Pimentel, E.: Measuring the compatibility of service interaction protocols. In: Proceedings of SAC 2011, pp. 1560–1567. ACM (2011)
17. Paige, R., Tarjan, R.E.: Three partition refinement algorithms. SIAM J. Comput. **16**(6), 973–989 (1987)

18. Romero Hernández, D., de Frutos Escrig, D.: Defining distances for all process semantics. In: Giese, H., Rosu, G. (eds.) FMOODS/FORTE - 2012. LNCS, vol. 7273, pp. 169–185. Springer, Heidelberg (2012). https://doi.org/10.1007/978-3-642-30793-5_11

19. Romero-Hernández, D., de Frutos Escrig, D.: Coinductive definition of distances between processes: beyond bisimulation distances. In: Ábrahám, E., Palamidessi, C. (eds.) FORTE 2014. LNCS, vol. 8461, pp. 249–265. Springer, Heidelberg (2014). https://doi.org/10.1007/978-3-662-43613-4_16

20. De Ruvo, G., Lettieri, G., Martino, D., Santone, A., Vaglini, G.: k-bisimulation: a bisimulation for measuring the dissimilarity between processes. In: Braga, C., Ölveczky, P.C. (eds.) FACS 2015. LNCS, vol. 9539, pp. 181–198. Springer, Cham (2016). https://doi.org/10.1007/978-3-319-28934-2_10

21. Salaün, G., Bordeaux, L., Schaerf, M.: Describing and reasoning on web services using process algebra. In: Proceedings of ICWS 2004, pp. 43–50. IEEE (2004)

22. Sokolsky, O., Kannan, S., Lee, I.: Simulation-based graph similarity. In: Hermanns, H., Palsberg, J. (eds.) TACAS 2006. LNCS, vol. 3920, pp. 426–440. Springer, Heidelberg (2006). https://doi.org/10.1007/11691372_28

23. Walkinshaw, N., Bogdanov, K.: Automated comparison of state-based software models in terms of their language and structure. ACM Trans. Softw. Eng. Methodol. 22(2), 13:1–13:37 (2013)

24. Xing, Z., Sun, J., Liu, Y., Dong, J.S.: Differencing labeled transition systems. In: Qin, S., Qiu, Z. (eds.) ICFEM 2011. LNCS, vol. 6991, pp. 537–552. Springer, Heidelberg (2011). https://doi.org/10.1007/978-3-642-24559-6_36

Identifying Failure Causalities
in Multi-component Applications

Antonio Brogi and Jacopo Soldani[✉]

University of Pisa, Pisa, Italy
{brogi,soldani}@di.unipi.it

Abstract. Understanding and resolving failure causalities in modern enterprise applications is one of the main challenges daily faced by application administrators. Such applications indeed integrate multiple heterogeneous components, and identifying which components are causing the failure of which other components requires to delve through distributed application logs. In this work-in-progress paper, we present our idea of devising an analysis approach based on management protocols, a fault-aware compositional modelling for the management of multi-component applications. We discuss how they can be used to identify causalities of failures in multi-component applications, and to design countermeasures to avoid (or, at least, limit) failure propagation.

1 Introduction

Modern enterprise application integrate various heterogeneous components, each devoted to run given tasks and interacting with the other application components to carry them out [1]. The complexity and amount of resulting inter-component dependencies can result in so-called cascades of failures. Indeed, the failure of a component can result in the failure of the components directly interacting with it, which in turn result in the failure of other components, and so on [13].

In such a scenario, questions related to the causalities among the failures of various component naturally arise. Which components caused the failure of which components? Who failed first? For answering such a kind of questions, application administrators are currently required to look at the application logs, which are however distributed among the various runtime environments (e.g., virtual machines, containers) used to run the components forming an application. As delving through many distributed logs is time-consuming and error-prone, the problem of understanding causalities of failures in multi-component application is currently one of the main challenges for application administrators [16].

In this work-in-progress paper, we present our idea of an analysis approach for identifying failure causalities in multi-component applications, and for determining countermeasures to avoid/limit failure propagation. We start from the widely-accepted idea that multi-component applications can be represented by means of application topologies [1], i.e., directed graphs whose nodes model application components, and whose arcs model inter-component dependencies.

© Springer Nature Switzerland AG 2020
J. Camara and M. Steffen (Eds.): SEFM 2019 Workshops, LNCS 12226, pp. 226–235, 2020.
https://doi.org/10.1007/978-3-030-57506-9_17

Each node also indicates the operations to manage the corresponding component, its requirements and the capabilities it offers to satisfy the requirements of other nodes. Each oriented arc models the dependency from a node to another, by connecting a requirement of the former to a capability of the latter.

Together with application topologies, management protocols [5] enable a compositional, fault-aware modelling of the management of multi-component applications. Starting from such modelling, we propose a novel approach for analysing and identifying failure causalities in multi-component applications. More precisely, knowing two global configurations of an application and the management operations occurred in between, we show how to identify whether/which failures occurred and how this permits explaining why the application moved from one configuration to the other by performing the given management operations. We also discuss whether the obtained explanations were to be foreseen or not, and how they can be used to adopt countermeasures avoiding some undesired changes to happen (e.g., by inhibiting or limiting failure propagation).

The rest of the paper is organised as follows. Section 2 presents a scenario motivating the need for understanding failure causalities. Section 3 provides some background on management protocols, while Sect. 4 paves the way towards their usage to analyse failure causalities and adopt countermeasures. Finally, Sects. 5 and 6 discuss related work and draw some concluding remarks, respectively.

2 Motivating Scenario

Figure 1 illustrates (a portion of) an existing application for managing machines in a smart factory, developed and maintained by an IT company we cooperate with. The application consists of a gateway retrieving monitoring data from sensors installed in the machines to be managed, and placing such data in a message queue (rabbitmq). telegraph reads the data in rabbitmq, and it processes such data by placing it in a database (influxdb). The database is then consumed by chronograph, api and kapacitor. chronograph generates plots that can be visualised by the gui of the application. api allows to access the data stored by influxdb, and it is used by the gui for doing so. kapacitor processes the data stored by influxdb, by creating aggregated statistics that are sent (by the uploader) to a remote cloud storage for backup and analysis reasons. Note that, while rabbitmq and influxdb are standalone containers, gateway, chronograph, gui, api, kapacitor and uploader are software applications, each hosted in a separate container.

The connections enabling the above explained interactions are represented in Fig. 1 as solid arrows connecting a requirement of the source of the interaction with a capability of its target (e.g., the arrow from the requirement mq of gateway to the capability mq of rabbitmq represents the fact that gateway must connect to rabbitmq—to post messages in the queue). The relationships between software applications and their hosting containers are instead represented as dashed arrows connecting the requirement host of the source to the capability host of the target (e.g., the arrow from the requirement host of gateway to the capability host of cgat represents the fact that gateway must be installed on cgat).

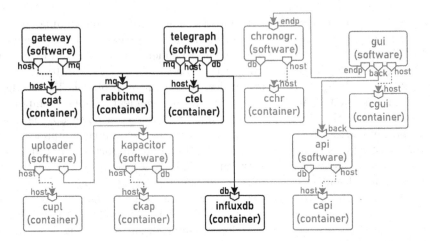

Fig. 1. A multi-component application represented in TOSCA [3], where solid arrows represent *connects to* relations, dashed arrows represent *hosted on* relations. Nodes and relations later referred in running examples are highlighted in black.

Suppose that we monitored the status of a running instance of the application at given intervals, and that we tracked all management operations invoked on its components. Suppose also that at a given monitoring period all application components were up and running, while gateway, rabbitmq and telegraph were not working anymore at the subsequent monitoring period. Why did this happen? Were there management operations invoked on application components in between of the two monitoring periods? Was the failure of failed components to be expected when invoking such operations when the application was up and running? If not, were there components unexpectedly failing (e.g., because of a bug), which generated cascading failures involving the above listed components?

Currently, the above questions have to be answered by delving through the application logs, which are distributed among its components. The latter is a concrete pain for application administrator, mainly because analysing distributed logs is time-consuming and error-prone [16]. Having a support for analysing what happened would help in this direction, and more generally to understand why and how the application configuration changed from a monitoring period to another (even if no failure occurred). The objective of this paper is precisely to pave the way towards providing such an analysis support.

3   Background: Management Protocols

Management protocols [5] enable the modelling and analysis of the management of multi-component applications, faults included. Each node is equipped with its own management protocol, i.e., a finite state machine whose states and transitions are associated with conditions on the requirements and capabilities of such node. Conditions on states indicate which requirements of a node must be satisfied in a state, and which capabilities the node is actually providing in such state. Conditions on transitions indicate which requirements/capabilities are needed/maintained while performing a management operation.

Management protocols also permit indicating how a node reacts to failures, which occur when the condition on the requirements to be satisfied in a state or transition is violated (e.g., because, after performing a management operation, another node stopped providing a capability needed to satisfy such conditions). Fault handling is specified by transitions starting from states needing faulted requirements and leading to states where such requirements are no longer needed.

In addition, as the actual behaviour of a node may be different from that modelled in its management protocol (e.g., because of non-deterministic bugs), management protocols naturally support modelling the unexpected behaviour of nodes. This is done by adding a special "crash" operation $\frac{1}{2}$ to each node, and by automatically completing its management protocols with transitions leading from the normal states of the node to a sink state where the node is no longer interacting as expected with the rest of the application.

The management behaviour of a multi-component application is then derived by composing the management protocols of its nodes (according to the inter-connections between requirements and capabilities defined in the application topology). The behaviour is defined by a labelled transition systems over configurations that denote the global states of the application. Intuitively, a global state G model the overall configuration of an application, with each of its nodes either residing in one of its states or executing a management operation, and we write $F(G)$ to denote the set of pending faults in G (i.e., the set of requirements assumed true in G despite their corresponding capabilities are not provided). A transition

$$G \xrightarrow{\langle n, \alpha \rangle} G'$$

denotes that the application moved from global state G to global state G' because node n performed action α. The possible actions are invoking a management operation o on a node n (denoted by $\langle n, o^{\triangleright} \rangle$), observing its completion (denoted by $\langle n, o^{\square} \rangle$), or handling all failures pending on n in G (denoted by $\langle n, \perp \rangle$). We also write

$$G \xrightarrow{t}{}^{*} G'$$

if t is a trace (i.e., a finite sequence $t = \langle n_1, \alpha_1 \rangle \ldots \langle n_m, \alpha_m \rangle$ of actions on nodes) and if the application can move from G to G' by performing the sequence of actions in t (i.e., $\exists G_1 \ldots G_{m-1} : G \xrightarrow{\langle n_1, \alpha_1 \rangle} G_1 \xrightarrow{\langle n_2, \alpha_2 \rangle} \ldots G_{m-1} \xrightarrow{\langle n_m, \alpha_m \rangle} G'$).[1]

4   Analysing Causalities in Multi-component Applications

Our final goal is to devise an analysis approach for explaining why an application moved from a global state G to a global state G', while in between only invoking

---

[1] Further details on the modelling based on management protocols and on its usage to design the management of multi-component applications can be found in [4,5].

a (possibly empty) sequence p of management operations. In this perspective, we first define the notion of *explanation*. The latter is a trace allowing an application to go from G to G', (i) which is allowed by its management behaviour, and (ii) which starts all operations in the sequence p in the given order without starting any further operation, i.e., it extends p with a finite number of $\langle n, \natural^{\triangleright} \rangle$, $\langle n, \bot \rangle$ or $\langle n, o^{\square} \rangle$, where o is some operation of A.

Definition 1 (Explanation). *Let A be an application, let G, G' be two global states of A, and let p be a trace only containing invocations $\langle n_i, o_i^{\triangleright} \rangle$ of management operations. A trace e is an* explanation *for getting to G' from G by executing p iff*

(i) $G \xrightarrow{e}_* G'$, and
(ii) p is a subsequence of e such that $\langle n, \alpha \rangle \in e \wedge \langle n, \alpha \rangle \notin p \Rightarrow \alpha \in \{\natural^{\triangleright}, \bot, o^{\square}\}$.

Explanations can be computed by visiting the graph defined by the labelled transition system modelling the management behaviour of an application. In the latter, each vertex corresponds to a reachable global state, and each arc corresponds to a transition allowing to move from a global state to another. Starting from the vertex corresponding to G and visiting the graph according to the constraints in Definition 1, one can compute all possible paths leading from G to G' (if any). All such paths correspond to a possible explanation.

Note that all possible explanations can be finitely computed if the management protocols of the nodes forming an application are well-formed and deterministic.[2] If this is the case, the traces that can be generated by fault handling and crashing transitions is finite, if no management operation happens in between. Fault handling transitions indeed lead to states where faulted requirements are no longer assumed (hence not allowing to create loops of fault handling transitions), and crashing transitions can be applied only once to each node (as they lead to a sink state where the node is no longer allowing to perform any management operation nor assuming any requirement). The above, along with the fact that the constraints in Definition 1 set the management operations performed on an application to a finite sequence, allows to conclude that each possible explanation consists of a finite trace of actions that can be finitely computed.

The notion of explanation allows to answer to questions like those in our motivating scenario (Sect. 2). More precisely, suppose that we know that an application was in a global state G and that, after invoking a sequence p of management operations, it reached global state G'. Suppose also that the latter is an undesired configuration of the application. Was this change to be foreseen?

---

[2] A well-formed management protocol ensures that the fault handling transition are *only* handling the fault of requirements that were assumed in the source state, while a deterministic management protocol ensures that the effects of executing a management operation or handling faulted requirements are deterministic [4].

Definition 2 (Evolution). *Let A be an application, let G, G′ be two global states of A, and let p be a trace only containing invocations of management operations. The* evolution *of G into G′ by executing p is:*

- foreseen *if for each explanation e for getting to G′ from G by executing p:* $\langle n, \nleftarrow^{\triangleright} \rangle \notin e$,
- weakly unforeseen *if there exists an explanation e for getting to G′ from G by executing p such that* $\langle n, \nleftarrow^{\triangleright} \rangle \in e$,
- unforeseen *if for each explanation e for getting to G′ from G by executing p:* $\langle n, \nleftarrow^{\triangleright} \rangle \in e$.

The above definition classifies the possible reasons why an application changed its global state from G to G' by invoking a given sequence of management operations. A foreseen evolution means that the application behaved as expected, meaning repeating the same sequence of management operations in the same global state G can result in obtaining G' again. A weakly unforeseen evolution means that the changes in the application may be due to some nodes unexpectedly crashing, e.g., because of non-deterministic bugs in their implementations. Finally, an unforeseen evolution means that the application moved from G to G' surely because of a node unexpectedly crashing.

Consider again our motivating scenario, where gateway, rabbitmq and telegraph stopped working when the application is up and running. Suppose that the sequence of management operations invoked in between of the monitoring periods considered in our motivating scenario only includes stopping rabbitmq. If this is the case, then all explanations would be such that the stopping of rabbitmq caused failures in gateway and telegraph, which in turn stopped working. The evolution considered in our motivating scenario would have hence to be foreseen, meaning that if we will stop rabbitmq when the application will be up and running again, we should expect that gateway and telegraph will probably stop working again (as per their current fault handling).

Suppose instead that no management operation was invoked in between of the monitoring periods considered in our motivating scenario. If this is the case, then the foreseen evolution of our application would have been that all its components sticked being up and running. We instead know that gateway, rabbitmq and telegraph stopped working, and the reason for this can reside in an unforeseen evolution. All possible explanations would indeed be such that rabbitmq unexpectedly crashed and gateway and telegraph failed in cascade.

Explanations can then be used by an application administrator to adopt countermeasures and avoid an application component to get to undesired states. For instance, we identified the stopping of rabbitmq and its unexpected crashing as possible reasons why gateway and telegraph stopped working. We could then think about improving their resilience to failures to avoid this to happen, e.g., by introducing a circuit breaker avoiding them to fail when rabbitmq is unavailable.

Note that our example involved few components for reasons of readability, but cascades of failures may involve much more components, e.g., an unexpected crashing of influxdb may result in crashing all the nodes directly depending on it, as well as those depending on nodes failing in cascade (hence resulting in all nodes—but rabbitmq, gateway and cgat—failing only because influxdb initially failed). Situations like the latter are hard to be manually analysed [16], hence motivating the need for an analysis approach like that we envision.

We believe that the information contained in explanations can be exploited to reason on why some nodes got to undesired states, by enumerating all possible failure causalities. Given an explanation, we can indeed say that an action $\langle n, \alpha \rangle$ caused the fault handling $\langle n', \perp \rangle$, if (i) the latter handles failures that have been generated by $\langle n, \alpha \rangle$ and (ii) that are still pending.

Definition 3 (Causes). *Let A be an application, let G, G' be two global states of A, and let p be a trace only containing invocations of management operations. Let also $e = \langle n_1, \alpha_1 \rangle \ldots \langle n_m, \alpha_m \rangle$ be an explanation for getting to G' from G by executing p such that*

$$\exists G_1 \ldots G_{m-1} : G = G_0 \xrightarrow{\langle n_1, \alpha_1 \rangle} G_1 \xrightarrow{\langle n_2, \alpha_2 \rangle} \ldots \xrightarrow{\langle n_m, \alpha_m \rangle} G_m = G'.$$

We say that $\langle n_i, \alpha_i \rangle$ causes $\langle n_j, \perp \rangle$ in e (with $1 \le i < j \le m$) iff

(i) $(F(G_i) - F(G_{i-1})) \cap (F(G_{j-1}) - F(G_j)) \neq \emptyset$, and
(ii) $\forall k \in (i, j) : F(G_k) \supseteq (F(G_i) - F(G_{i-1}))$.

The above can be used to generate a sort of *causality graph*, whose vertices represent actions belonging to any possible explanation for getting from a global state to another by performing a given sequence of management operations, and whose directed arcs represent causal dependencies between such actions.

Definition 4 (Causality graph). *Let A be an application, let G, G' be two global states of A, and let p be a trace only containing invocations of management operations. The causality graph (V, E) for getting to G' from G by executing p is defined as follows:*

- *V is the set of all $\langle n, \alpha \rangle$ belonging to some explanation e for getting to G' from G by executing p, and*
- *E is the set of all $(\langle n, \alpha \rangle, \langle n', \perp \rangle)$ such that $\langle n, \alpha \rangle$ causes $\langle n', \perp \rangle$ in some explanation e for getting to G' from G by executing p.*

The information contained in explanations and causality graphs can then be used to design and develop countermeasures to avoid nodes to get to undesired states. For instance, we showed how explanations allow to identify the sources of cascades of failures, i.e., the nodes that first failed (because of other nodes stopping to provide the capabilities they require—for foreseen or unforeseen reasons). Such information could be used to refactor an application to avoid cascades of failures from happening, e.g., by equipping the nodes at the beginning of each cascade with circuit breakers making them resilient to the initial failure.

Causality graphs permit reasoning on cascades of failures also when these cannot be avoided (e.g., if a component is running in a container, a failure of the container necessarily results in a failure of the component). They could indeed be used to limit cascades of failures, e.g., by identifying common points in different cascades, to setup bulkheads for avoid failures to propagate afterwards.

5   Related Work

The rigorous engineering of failures in complex systems is a well-known problem in computer science [6]. [2] and [15] provide solutions for fault-localisation in complex applications, geared at allowing to redesign such applications by avoiding any possible occurrence of identified faults. [14] instead proposes an approach for designing object-oriented applications by first considering fault-free applications, and by iteratively refining their design by identifying and handling the faults that may occur. The main difference between the aforementioned approaches and ours is that the objective of those approaches is to obtain applications that "never fail", because their potential faults have already been identified and properly handled. Our approach is instead more recovery-oriented [7], as we consider applications where components can possibly fail. We indeed aim at explaining why some application components failed, to understand whether this had to be foreseen, and to design and develop countermeasures allowing to avoid or limit the identified cascades of failures.

[9,11] and [10] propose approaches that are a step closer to ours. [11] models entire service compositions as business processes, while [9] and [10] rely on a compositional modelling of applications where the management of each component is specified separately. Similarly to our approach, [9,11] and [10] all explicitly represent possible failures and support the development—at design-time—of countermeasures to recover application from failures, in the form of recovery plans to be enacted when such failures are monitored at run-time. They however differ from our approach as they focus on explicitly modelled failures, which have hence to be foreseen, by automatically enacting recovery plans for bringing the application back to its desired configuration. Our objective is instead to explain why the components of an application failed, even if this was due to unforeseen reasons, to help administrators to adopt countermeasures to avoid/limit the identified failure causalities.

Another approach worth mentioning is [8], which proposes a distributed solution for diagnosing failures in component-based systems. Each component is equipped with a local diagnoser, which is in charge to monitor its failure and to enact corresponding recovery actions. A centralised supervisor coordinates the local diagnosers, based on the dependencies among components. More precisely, similarly to our approach, the supervisor considers possible cascades of failures, and whenever a fault is diagnosed in a component by the corresponding local diagnoser, it asks to the local diagnosers of the components interacting with the failed component to check whether such components have also failed. [8] differs from our approach since inter-component dependencies are used to coordinate the fault diagnosis, while causalities among failures are not analysed.

Finally, it is worth highlighting that our approach also relates to existing approaches for diagnosing/predicting failures in discrete event systems. [17] surveys existing approaches for diagnosing failures in discrete event systems, i.e., identifying and isolating unforeseen faults that caused an undesired deviation of a system from its expected behaviour. This is in line with our idea of explaining why an application moved from one configuration to another, even if

234 A. Brogi and J. Soldani

the approaches surveyed in [17] focus on isolating the single cause of an undesired deviation, rather than on the causalities among the failures affecting multiple components of a same application.

[12] instead provides a solution for predicting the occurrence of a significant event (e.g., a fault) in a partially-observable discrete event systems. Similarly to our approach, [12] focuses on a partial observation of the events in a system (global configurations and operations invoked in between, in our case), and it exploits such partial observation to determine the occurrence of other, non-observable events (occurrences of failures, in our case). [12] however differs from our approach as it focuses on predicting the certain occurrence of a single event, while we aim at identifying possibly multiple failures and the relations among them, to understand whether the observed changes where to be foreseen, and adopt countermeasures to avoid or limit fault propagation.

In summary, to the best of our knowledge, ours is the first approach geared towards identifying the possible reasons why multiple failures affected a multi-component application (even if these were not to be foreseen), so that counter-measures can be adopted to avoid/limit the identified failure causalities.

6 Conclusions

The problems of understanding failure causalities is daily faced by application administrators [16]. We have presented our idea of supporting them with an analysis approach based on management protocols [5]. More precisely, we have shown that management protocols [5] enable a compositional modelling of the management of multi-component applications, which allows to reason on why some components failed, by identifying failure causalities.

We have also commented on how the explanations resulting from our proposed analysis can be exploited to design and develop countermeasures to avoid nodes to fail in cascade. We showed how explanations allow to identify failure causalities, which can be represented in the form of a causality graph, which in turn permits reasoning on the cascades of failures because of which an application moved from a configuration to another. We also commented on how such information can be used to avoid/limit cascades of failures, e.g., by refactoring the architecture of the application to include circuit breakers or bulkheads where needed. As ongoing work, for which this paper constitutes a work-in-progress report, we are currently investigating how to effectively build causality graphs, as well as how to use them to understand which refactorings to apply to avoid given nodes to get to undesired states.

For future work, we plan to develop a tool supporting the analysis of failure causalities in multi-component applications, and recommending the architectural refactorings avoiding nodes to get to undesired states. We also plan to validate our approach by applying our tool to one or more real-world use cases (e.g., on the application illustrated in our motivating scenario) and/or by running controlled experiments (e.g., comparing the efforts for identifying failure causalities in an application with and without our tool).

Acknowledgments. This work is partly funded by the projects *AMaCA* (POR-FSE, Regione Toscana) and *DECLware* (PRA_2018_66, University of Pisa).

References

1. Bergmayr, A., et al.: A systematic review of cloud modeling languages. ACM Comput. Surv. **51**(1), 22:1–22:38 (2018)
2. Betin Can, A., Bultan, T., Lindvall, M., Lux, B., Topp, S.: Eliminating synchronization faults in air traffic control software via design for verification with concurrency controllers. Autom. Softw. Eng. **14**(2), 129–178 (2007)
3. Breitenbücher, U., et al.: The OpenTOSCA Ecosystem - Concepts & Tools, pp. 112–130. SciTePress (2016)
4. Brogi, A., Canciani, A., Soldani, J.: Fault-aware management protocols for multicomponent applications. J. Syst. Softw. **139**, 189–210 (2018)
5. Brogi, A., Canciani, A., Soldani, J.: True concurrent management of multicomponent applications. In: Kritikos, K., Plebani, P., de Paoli, F. (eds.) ESOCC 2018. LNCS, vol. 11116, pp. 17–32. Springer, Cham (2018). https://doi.org/10.1007/978-3-319-99819-0_2
6. Butler, M., Jones, C.B., Romanovsky, A., Troubitsyna, E. (eds.): Rigorous Development of Complex Fault-Tolerant Systems. LNCS, vol. 4157. Springer, Heidelberg (2006). https://doi.org/10.1007/11916246
7. Candea, G., Brown, A.B., Fox, A., Patterson, D.: Recovery-oriented computing: building multitier dependability. Computer **37**(11), 60–67 (2004)
8. Console, L., Picardi, C., Dupré, D.T.: A framework for decentralized qualitative model-based diagnosis. In: Veloso, M.M. (ed.) IJCAI 2007, Proceedings of the 20th International Joint Conference on Artificial Intelligence, Hyderabad, India, January 6–12, 2007, pp. 286–291 (2007)
9. Durán, F., Salaün, G.: Robust and reliable reconfiguration of cloud applications. J. Syst. Softw. **122**(C), 524–537 (2016)
10. Etchevers, X., Salaün, G., Boyer, F., Coupaye, T., De Palma, N.: Reliable self-deployment of distributed cloud applications. Softw.: Practice Exp. **47**(1), 3–20 (2017)
11. Friedrich, G., Fugini, M.G., Mussi, E., Pernici, B., Tagni, G.: Exception handling for repair in service-based processes. IEEE Trans. Softw. Eng. **36**(2), 198–215 (2010)
12. Genc, S., Lafortune, S.: Predictability of event occurrences in partially-observed discrete-event systems. Automatica **45**(2), 301–311 (2009)
13. Jamshidi, P., Pahl, C., Mendonca, N., Lewis, J., Tilkov, S.: Microservices: the journey so far and challenges ahead. IEEE Softw. **35**(3), 24–35 (2018)
14. Johnsen, E., Owe, O., Munthe-Kaas, E., Vain, J.: Incremental fault-tolerant design in an object-oriented setting. In: Proceedings of the Second Asia-Pacific Conference on Quality Software, p. 223. APAQS, IEEE Computer Society (2001)
15. Qiang, W., Yan, L., Bliudze, S., Xiaoguang, M.: Automatic fault localization for BIP. In: Li, X., Liu, Z., Yi, W. (eds.) SETTA 2015. LNCS, vol. 9409, pp. 277–283. Springer, Cham (2015). https://doi.org/10.1007/978-3-319-25942-0_18
16. Soldani, J., Tamburri, D.A., Van Den Heuvel, W.J.: The pains and gains of microservices: a systematic grey literature review. J. Syst. Softw. **146**, 215–232 (2018)
17. Zaytoon, J., Lafortune, S.: Overview of fault diagnosis methods for discrete event systems. Ann. Rev. Control **37**(2), 308–320 (2013)

A Formal Programming Framework for Digital Avatars

Alejandro Pérez-Vereda$^{(\boxtimes)}$, Carlos Canal, and Ernesto Pimentel

ITIS Software, Universidad de Málaga, Málaga, Spain
apvereda@uma.es, {canal,ernesto}@lcc.uma.es

Abstract. In the current IoT era, the number of smart things to interact with is raising everyday. However, each one of them precises a manual and specific configuration. In a more people-friendly scenario, smart things should adapt automatically to the preferences of their users. In this field, we have participated in the design of People as a Service, a mobile computing reference architecture which endows the smartphone with the capability of inferring and sharing a virtual profile of its owner. Currently, we are developing Digital Avatars, a framework for programming interactions between smartphones and other devices. This way, the smartphone becomes a personalized and seamless interface between people and their IoT environment, configuring the smart things with information from the virtual profile. In this work, we present a formalization of Digital Avatars by means of a Linda-based system with multiple shared tuple spaces.

Keywords: Digital Avatars · People as a Service · PeaaS · Linda · Shared tuple spaces

1 Introduction

The Internet of Things (IoT) is built over a layer of connected devices and sensors that offer specific interfaces to access the information they collect and also to configure how they work, e.g. the frequency to pick up the data or how to format them [9]. Recent research in the IoT field has promoted the development of devices and sensors which are more configurable and provide easier interfaces. They are known as smart things [11]. However, smart things still require a lot of manual configuration, and this problem becomes more challenging the bigger the number of devices we daily interact with. In a desirable scenario, the technology should work for the people and not the other way around. Every smart thing should adapt to the needs of the people seamlessly and in an automatic way, reducing the need for interaction with the users to the minimum.

Considering the pervasive presence of smartphones, the authors of this paper have participated in the design of a mobile computing reference architecture

This work has been funded by the Spanish Government under grants PGC2018-094905-B-I00 and TIN2015-67083-R (MINECO/FEDER).

J. Camara and M. Steffen (Eds.): SEFM 2019 Workshops, LNCS 12226, pp. 236–251, 2020.
https://doi.org/10.1007/978-3-030-57506-9_18

called People as a Service (PeaaS) [10]. This architecture promotes the use of
smartphones to learn about their users, creating and storing virtual profiles with
their preferences and context information. These profiles are then offered as a
service to third parties in a secure manner. This way, smartphones become seamless and automatic interfaces that negotiate their owner's preferences, adapting
and configuring the smart things in their surroundings.

For that purpose, the required interactions are not just simple data transfers,
but we need mechanisms that allow to configure smart things, and also to complete virtual profiles with context knowledge obtained from these interactions.
The more complete virtual profiles are, the better may the technology adapt to
the people. With this goal in mind, we are developing Digital Avatars, a dynamic
programming framework which allows defining the interactions between smartphones and smart things by means of on-the-fly scripts [13]. The scripts are
executed in the smartphone, and they make use of the virtual profile stored in it
for reconfiguring the behavior of the smart thing with the information available.

Our programming framework is inspired by the vision of a Programmable
World [17], which foresees the evolution from today's IoT based on data recol-
lection to truly programmable devices. This way, both smart things and smartphones are able to learn from each other, and to evolve through each interaction
in a transparent and dynamic way.

In this paper, we present a formal framework for Digital Avatars. The framework provides a formal description of virtual profiles and the scripts to execute
on them, and it establishes the basis for issues like privacy or security, with secure
connections controlling the access to virtual profiles. The formalization is based
on a multiple shared tuple spaces model inspired by Linda, which makes possible to ensure the soundness of the framework, and makes feasible the analysis
of some interesting properties.

The rest of this paper is structured as follows. In Sect. 2 we present the
motivations of this paper and discuss some related works. Next, Sect. 3 defines
the concepts necessary to reason on Digital Avatars. In Sect. 4, we formalize the
interactions that take place in the framework and demonstrate interesting formal
properties of the system. Then, Sect. 5 presents a proof of concept and analyze
its implementation using the framework. Finally, Sect. 6 draws the conclusions
of the paper and briefly discusses future work.

2 Background

The development of smart things is transforming people's lives, as we increasingly interact with them everyday. Social Computing (SC) [18] is the area of
computer science that deals with the interaction between social behavior and
computer systems. SC encompasses all those systems that collect, process and
disseminate information related to individuals and groups of people. The goal is
learning about people and their preferences and providing an easy adaptation of
their IoT environment, reducing manual configuration of devices to a minimum.
Indeed, a number of recent research works agree on giving support to the IoT
by means of a paradigm focused on people [16].

Currently, very few companies are able to access and process this enormous quantity of social information, and to exploit and make a profit from it. In practice, this reduces the SC marketplace to a small number of big stakeholders. As Tim Berners-Lee declared recently [1], SC systems should empower people, making them the fair owners of their information, and deciding who has access to it. Moreover, this information must be stored in a unique and accessible place which lets third parties use it in a controlled way, following the privacy preferences of the users.

In this same sense, we advocate for developing collaborative architectures based on smartphones. Their pervasive presence in people's everyday lives and their increasing sensing and computing capabilities, together with their communication skills, make them key elements for obtaining, processing, and sharing information about their users [15]. Smartphones are also the most appropriate devices to be in charge of negotiating the interactions of their users with smart things in their environment.

Architectures based on P2P models are gradually acquiring a greater presence in fields such as social networks [19] or recommendation systems [20]. The basis of these architectures are the virtual profiles of the users, plenty of contextual data (e.g. activities, relations with other users, etc.) [8]. Our goal is sharing these virtual profiles with third parties and to adapt the IoT environment to the preferences and needs of each user.

With that purpose in mind, our approach is based on a Linda-like model. Linda [7] is a coordination language where synchronization is achieved by means of a shared tuple space, and through a set of simple but enough expressive primitives [2]. However, a single shared tuple space would violate the principles of the PeaaS model. Some other Linda-like proposals have been made by different authors, introducing some kind of mobility, mainly based on adding capabilities for remotely modifying a given tuple space. Thus, Lime [14] was proposed as a Linda extension to support mobile computing, by the definition of transiently shared distributed tuple spaces to establish P2P communications. Some of its goals are common with ours, but our framework also takes into account privacy issues, which are crucial for virtual profiles. Another well-known proposal is KLAIM [5], which extends Linda by considering the possibility of remote adding tuples to an *accessible* tuple space. With a similar philosophy, SCEL [6] was designed to provide a parametric language to capture various programming abstractions for autonomic components and their interaction. In both cases, Linda-like primitives were added to allow the remote interaction with shared tuple spaces. Although the PeaaS paradigm could be (artificially) coded by these languages, a number of assumptions and constraints should be made to ensure the main PeaaS features. In fact, we consider that accessing to a virtual profile has to be made only by its owner, and remote accessing to transient tuple spaces or shared repositories do not model these scenarios properly.

3 Modeling Digital Avatars

In order to define a formal framework for reasoning on Digital Avatars, we introduce the notion of virtual profile together with a number of related concepts, and we describe how virtual profiles can be offered as services under the PeaaS paradigm.

3.1 Definitions

The key issue for taking into account the user in an IoT environment is her virtual profile. It contains information about user preferences, habits, movements, or relations. All this information is only stored in the user's device (e.g. a smartphone), and it is offered as a service to third parties. The definition below formalizes this notion.

Definition 1. *A virtual profile P is a multiset of entities, where each entity is a 5-tuple $t = (n, s, p, v, ts)$ composed of (i) $n \in Name$ representing the name of the entity, (ii) $s \in Type$ defines the entity's type, (iii) $p \in Privacy$, which provides the level of privacy, (iv) $v \in Value$ is the value of the entity itself, with a structure which will depend on the entity's type, and (v) a timestamp $ts \in Time$, which allows recording the time when the tuple is added to the virtual profile. We will denote by T the set of tuples, and by $\mathcal{P}$ the set of virtual profiles.*

The complexity of virtual profiles depends on the sets *Name*, *Type*, *Privacy*, *Value*, and *Time*. These entities are structured in nested sections for the secure and correct functioning of the profile. Although the model does not depend on how these particular domains are defined, we consider a common minimum structure for predefined entities which are characterized as follows:

Personal   It consists in personal and contact information of the user (**personal** $\in$ *Name*); the default privacy is **private** $\in$ *Privacy*, although it can be overwritten in each attribute to allow accessing it to family or friends, for instance. Basically, it contains a collection of entity identifiers like **name**, **phone**, **address**, or **email** with the corresponding information.

Relations   It provides information on how users are related to each other (**relation** $\in$ *Name*), such that values includes entity names like **family**, **friends**, **colleagues**, or **acquaintances**. These nested entities are collections of user (personal) information with information about location, social profiles and their certificate hash fingerprint. The default privacy level of these entities is **private** $\in$ *Privacy*.

Places   It defines information in a profile concerning locations (**place** $\in$ *Name*): home, place of work, known places or other places. Thus, constants like **home** or **work** belong to the *Name* set in the value of this entity. Their default privacy level is **trusted**.

A virtual profile can be accessed and/or modified by means of processes executing appropriate actions. In order to formalize this idea, we are inspired by

Linda [4], a coordination language [7] consisting of a set of inter-agent communication primitives, which can be virtually added to any programming language. Primitives in Linda allow processes to read, delete, and add tuples in a shared *tuple space*. Tuple spaces are a convenient approach to represent virtual profiles shared by concurrently running processes. A virtual profile is represented by a multiset of tuples encapsulated in a device. Thus, we adopt a multiple tuple space model.

Following other approaches [3,12], we shall consider a process algebra $\mathcal{L}$ including the Linda communication primitives and the usual concurrency connectives, parallel and non-deterministic choice. The primitives permit to add a tuple (*out*), to remove a tuple (*in*), and to check the presence (or absence) of a tuple (*rd, nrd*) in a given profile (tuple space).

Processes in $\mathcal{L}$ provide a convenient way to model scripts which can be downloaded from a server and run on a smart device. Thus, the syntax of $\mathcal{L}$ is formally defined as follows:

$$S \in \mathcal{L} ::= 0 \mid \alpha.S \mid S + S \mid S \parallel S \mid S(\tilde{t})$$
$$\alpha \in Act ::= rd(t) \mid nrd(t) \mid in(t) \mid out(d, t)$$

where 0 denotes the empty process, $d \in D$ a device identifier, and t denotes a tuple. The process $S(\tilde{t})$ denotes a procedure call where the procedure definition will be given by a script template $S(\tilde{x})$ (where $\tilde{x}$ is a sequence of variables instantiated by a sequence of tuples $\tilde{t}$). In order to simplify the definition of rules modelling the $\mathcal{L}$ primitive actions in Subsect. 4.2, we will assume that reading a tuple do not imply the evaluation of usual operations (e.g. arithmetic operations) nor the variable instantiation as usual in Linda-based languages. This assumption does not imply any loss of generality of the proposal.

Notice that we consider primitives for locally accessing, adding, and removing tuples to a tuple space (i.e. a virtual profile). Although we could have also considered accessing and deleting tuples from remote tuple spaces, for our purposes we only need to add tuples remotely. For this reason, only the *out* primitive includes as a parameter the device on which adding the tuple. That is, *rd, in* and *nrd* actions will be made locally, on the same device where the script is being run. The same considerations were made in [12]. As it will be shown later, remote adding of tuples will only affect to the artifact where the script was downloaded from, thus we will not allow arbitrary remote adding of tuples. This asymmetric treatment of out and read primitives are precisely one of the features devoted by the PeaaS model: local accessing is only made by device owners, and remote changes can only be made on artifacts providing the scripts to be run.

In our framework, we distinguish two kinds of artifacts: *smart devices* and *smart things*. The difference between them is that smart devices exhibit computing capabilities, and therefore they can download and execute scripts, whereas smart things only provide a (link to a) script.

Formally, we define an artifact as a pair consisting of a virtual profile and a process corresponding to the execution of one or several scripts. We assume that D is a set of artifact identifiers. Every artifact d also has associated a script definition $S_d(\tilde{x})$ which can be downloaded by other artifacts with computing capabilities (i.e. smart devices).

Definition 2. *An artifact $d \in D$ is characterized by a pair $\langle P : S \rangle_d$, including a virtual profile P and a process $S \in \mathcal{L}$, corresponding to the running scripts on the artifact. In addition, an artifact can contain a script definition $S_d(\tilde{x})$. We will denote by $S_d(P)$ the script instantiated by the specific tuples in the profile P. And we will represent by $\mathcal{D} = \mathcal{P} \times \mathcal{L} \times D$ the set of artifacts.*

A smart thing will be characterized by having only a profile; that is, its process is always the empty process 0. A typical example of smart thing would be a beacon broadcasting a Bluetooth Low Energy (BLE) signal which encodes the URL of a script file to be downloaded from a server. On the other hand, typical smart devices are smartphones, tablets, or any other device with computing capabilities. Both kinds of artifacts—smart things and smart devices—store information in a virtual profile.

3.2   Security in Digital Avatars

The actions executed over the virtual profile of a smart device may emerge from internal processes of the device, or they may be part of a script downloaded from another artifact (e.g. a beacon broadcasting a link to a script file) when several conditions are fulfilled: the smart device is close enough to the beacon, the beacon artifact is registered, its script code is trusted, etc.

In order to avoid running untrusted scripts, we assume a Certification Authority capable to ensure the trustfulness of an artifact d, and a Boolean mapping *certify* which provides this information in such a way that *certify(d)* is true when the emitter of d has been authenticated.

In addition, the *out* primitive considered in the previous section allows adding tuples to both local and remote virtual profiles. Although the model imposes no limitations on which profiles can be remotely modified, the artifact identifier d used in a remote *out(d,t)* in a script $S_d(\tilde{x})$ can only be that of the artifact d itself. Thus, an artifact's profile may only be remotely modified by running a script downloaded from this same artifact.

Hence, in order to guarantee that the actions executed while running a script on a smart device are secure, we assume a Boolean mapping *accept* : $Act \times \mathcal{P} \to \{true, false\}$ that restricts which primitives are enabled, in such a way that *accept(α, P)* is true when the action $α$ is acceptable on the profile P.

However, using certificates and restricting remote addition of tuples is not enough to ensure a correct interaction between source and target artifacts, and we also need to consider some technical issues. Indeed, whereas *certify* provides a third-party declaration about the trust of an artifact, and *accept* controls what actions are permitted inside an artifact once the script has been downloaded, we need a way to detect when two artifacts are actually able to communicate with each other. For instance, consider a scenario where a smartphone (represented by a virtual profile P) approaches a smart thing d which provides a script $S_d(\tilde{x})$.

For downloading the script from d and running it in the smartphone, we assume a mapping $links : \mathcal{P} \times D \rightarrow 2^T$, which provides a link to connect to the smart thing, depending on the availability to download, the closeness between both artifacts, good signal strength, etc. This mapping returns a set of tuples representing links (e.g., a URI or a bluetooth connection) providing a way to access the artifact d. If there are no links, or the profile P does not accept downloading the script offered by d, $links(P, d)$ will be the empty set.

Notice that all the notions introduced in this subsection (*accept*, *certify*, and *links*) are application specific, in such a way that their particular definitions will depend on the application domain and context where our framework is applied to.

4   Formal Framework

Now that we have defined the main elements and concepts of our framework, we can formalize the interactions between artifacts by means of a transition system with in-device and remote operations. Then, we show how some interesting properties like bisimilarity and congruence are accomplished by the model.

4.1   In-Device Transition System

The operational semantics of $\mathcal{L}$ is modeled by the following labelled transition system:

$$\longrightarrow \subseteq \mathcal{D} \times \Lambda \times \mathcal{D}$$

defined by the rules[1] of Table 1, where $\mathcal{D} = \mathcal{P} \times \mathcal{L} \times D$ and $\Lambda = \{t, \bar{t}, \underline{t} : t \in T\} \cup \{\tau\}$.

Rule OUT₁ describes how the output operation proceeds as an internal move (represented by label τ) which adds the tuple t to the profile P (comma is used to represent the multiset union). Rule OUT₂ shows that a tuple t is ready to offer itself to the artifact/device by performing an action labelled $\bar{t}$. Rules IN and READ describe the behavior of the prefixes $in(t)$ and $rd(t)$ whose labels are $\underline{t}$ and t, respectively. Rule NREAD describes the prefix action $nrd(t)$, which proceeds when t is not in the profile P; the transition is labelled with $\neg t$. All these rules need that the current device's profile accepts the corresponding action. It is worth noting that we do not include any kind of evaluation nor variable instantiation when reading tuples, as it is usually made in Linda-related transition rules. This is only for simplicity reasons without loss of generality.

Rule SUM is the standard rule for choice composition. Rule SYNC₁ is the standard rule for the synchronization between the complementary actions t and $\bar{t}$. It models the effective execution of an $rd(t)$ operation. Notice that the resulting profile is left unchanged, since the read operation $rd(t)$ does not modify it. Rule SYNC₂ defines the synchronization between two processes performing transitions labelled with $\underline{t}$ and $\bar{t}$, respectively. It models the effective execution of $in(t)$

---

[1] For the sake of simplicity we will consider only finite processes here.

action. The usual rule PAR_1 for the parallel operator can be applied to any label. The transition system is considered closed w.r.t. commutative and associative properties for sum ($+$) and parallel ($\parallel$) operators.

Table 1. Transition system for smart devices

(OUT_1)	$\dfrac{accept(out(d,t),P)}{\langle P : out(d,t).S\rangle_d \xrightarrow{\tau} \langle P, t : S\rangle_d}$
(OUT_2)	$\dfrac{}{\langle P, t : S\rangle_d \xrightarrow{\bar{t}} \langle P : S\rangle_d}$
(READ)	$\dfrac{accept(rd(t),P)}{\langle P : rd(t).S\rangle_d \xrightarrow{t} \langle P : S\rangle_d}$
(IN)	$\dfrac{accept(in(t),P)}{\langle P : in(t).S\rangle_d \xrightarrow{\underline{t}} \langle P : S\rangle_d}$
(NREAD)	$\dfrac{t \notin P \,\wedge\, accept(nrd(t),P)}{\langle P : nrd(t).S\rangle_d \xrightarrow{\neg t} \langle P : S\rangle_d}$
(SUM)	$\dfrac{\langle P : S_1\rangle_d \xrightarrow{\alpha} \langle P' : S_1'\rangle_d}{\langle P : S_1 + S_2\rangle_d \xrightarrow{\alpha} \langle P' : S_1' + S_2\rangle_d}$
(SYNC_1)	$\dfrac{\langle P : S_1\rangle_d \xrightarrow{t} \langle P : S_1'\rangle_d \;\; \langle P : S_2\rangle_d \xrightarrow{\bar{t}} \langle P' : S_2\rangle_d}{\langle P : S_1 \parallel S_2\rangle_d \xrightarrow{\tau} \langle P : S_1' \parallel S_2\rangle_d}$
(SYNC_2)	$\dfrac{\langle P : S_1\rangle_d \xrightarrow{\underline{t}} \langle P : S_1'\rangle_d \;\; \langle P : S_2\rangle_d \xrightarrow{\bar{t}} \langle P' : S_2\rangle_d}{\langle P : S_1 \parallel S_2\rangle_d \xrightarrow{\tau} \langle P : S_1' \parallel S_2\rangle_d}$
(PAR_1)	$\dfrac{\langle P : S_1\rangle_d \xrightarrow{\alpha} \langle P' : S_1'\rangle_d}{\langle P : S_1 \parallel S_2\rangle_d \xrightarrow{\alpha} \langle P' : S_1' \parallel S_2\rangle_d}$

Notice that action $out(d,t)$ is only considered in Table 1 when it is running in the device d. Its full behavior (remote adding of tuples) will be defined when the interaction among devices is expressed in Table 2.

4.2   Remote Transition System

In order to define how artifacts interact, we consider configurations composed of a parallel composition of artifacts as follows:

$$\langle P_1 : S_1 \rangle_{d_1} \mid \langle P_2 : S_2 \rangle_{d_2} \mid \cdots \mid \langle P_n : S_n \rangle_{d_n}$$

where P_i ($i = 1..n$) are virtual profiles of artifacts—either smart devices and smart things—, S_i are scripts running in smart devices, and d_i represent the device identifiers. Notice that we denote in a different way the parallel composition of artifacts ($\mid$) and the parallel composition of processes inside a smart device ($\|$).

The transition system $\longrightarrow$ defined in Table 1 is extended to configurations by the inference rules given in Table 2.

Table 2. Transition system

(REMOTE)	$\dfrac{accept(out(e,t), Q)}{\langle P : out(e,t).S \rangle_d \mid \langle Q : T \rangle_e \stackrel{\tau}{\longrightarrow} \langle P : S \rangle_d \mid \langle Q, t : T \rangle_e}$
(SYNC3)	$\dfrac{certify(e) \wedge b \in links(P, e)}{\langle P : S \rangle_d \mid \langle Q : T \rangle_e \stackrel{\tau}{\longrightarrow} \langle P, b : S \parallel S_e(b, Q) \rangle_d \mid \langle Q : T \rangle_e}$
(PAR2)	$\dfrac{D_1 \stackrel{\alpha}{\longrightarrow} D_1'}{D_1 \mid D_2 \stackrel{\alpha}{\longrightarrow} D_1' \mid D_2}$

Rule REMOTE models remote actions modifying the virtual profile which belongs to the smart thing from which the script being run was downloaded. We consider this transition as a silent step from an observational point of view. For this reason, we use the label τ.

Rule SYNC3 represents the interaction between two artifacts (typically, a smart device and a smart thing). In this case, the script associated with a smart thing e, previously certified, is downloaded through a link b establishing a connection between the virtual profile P and e. Thus, the script to be executed in the context of the smart device d (in parallel with other possible pending processes) will be $S_e(b, Q)$ (such as it was defined in Definition 2). Notice that, in this case, the script is instantiated not only by the profile Q but also by the link b. This allows customizing the script to the artifact which provides access to it. In addition, the link tuple b is added to the profile P, so recording that the smart thing has been already "visited".

Rule PAR2 describes the way in which the parallel composition of artifacts proceeds. Note that the parallel composition of processes inside a smart device is modelled by Rule PAR1 in Table 1. Actually, any interaction in the context of a smart device is governed by rules in that table.

We consider the transition system closed w.r.t. usual structural congruence (commutative and associative properties) of both parallel connectors.

The rules in Table 1 and Table 2 are used to define the set of derivations in an environment where smart devices and smart things are interacting with each other. Following [3], both reductions labelled τ and reductions labelled $\neg t$ are considered. Formally, this corresponds to introducing the following derivation relation:

$$D \longmapsto D' \quad \text{iff} \quad (D \xrightarrow{\tau} D' \text{ or } D \xrightarrow{\neg t} D').$$

4.3 Bisimilarity and Congruence

The scripts downloaded from a given artifact may evolve under certain circumstances. For instance, a software upgrade, or the development of a new version of the script. In this kind of situations, a notion of script equivalence would be very relevant to reason about compatibility among different versions. To formalize this, we consider the usual notion of bisimilarity-based equivalence, taking into account the device in which the script has to be run.

Definition 3. *Given a virtual profile P, two scripts S and T in $\mathcal{L}$ are bisimilar with respect to P, written $S \sim_P T$ if and only if for each $\alpha \in \Lambda$ and $d \in D$:*

1. if $\langle P : S \rangle_d \xrightarrow{\alpha} \langle P' : S' \rangle_d$ then $\langle P : T \rangle_d \xrightarrow{\alpha} \langle P' : T' \rangle_d$ for some T' such that $S' \sim_{P'} T'$

2. if $\langle P : T \rangle_d \xrightarrow{\alpha} \langle P' : T' \rangle_d$ then $\langle P : S \rangle_d \xrightarrow{\alpha} \langle P' : S' \rangle_d$ for some S' such that $S' \sim_{P'} T'$

Lemma 1. *The bisimilarity relation $\sim_P$ is an equivalence relation.*

Proof. It is directly derived by reasoning on different rules in Table 2.   □

In fact, the transition relation $\longrightarrow$ (restricted to devices) defines a notion of bisimilarity which permits to decide about script equivalence. In addition, it would be very useful that this bisimilarity relationship is a congruence with respect to the connectors $+$ and $\|$.

Theorem 1. *The bisimilarity relation $\sim_P$ is a congruence with respect to non-deterministic choice and parallel operators.*

Proof. Let P be a virtual profile, and let us assume $S_1 \sim_P S_2$. We will prove $S_1 \parallel T \sim_P S_2 \parallel T$ by structural induction. To do it, we will only analyze the first condition in Definition 3, since the second one is symmetric. That is,

$$\langle P : S_1 \parallel T \rangle_d \xrightarrow{\alpha} \langle P' : S' \rangle_d \tag{1}$$

First, we proceed by proving the proposition on the inductive base, processes 0 and $\alpha.0$ ($\alpha \in Act$). For these processes, the result is easily proved, by considering each case in rules (OUT_1), (OUT_2), (READ), (IN) and (NREAD).

In a general case, we have the following alternatives (depending on the rule in Table 1 triggering the transition):

1. If (PAR_1) was the rule applied to get (1), then we have two possibilities: either

$$\langle P : S_1 \rangle_d \xrightarrow{\alpha} \langle P' : S'_1 \rangle_d \quad (S' = S'_1 \parallel T)$$

or

$$\langle P : T \rangle_d \xrightarrow{\alpha} \langle P' : T' \rangle_d \quad (S' = S_1 \parallel T')$$

In the first case, as $S_1 \sim_P S_2$, we have $\langle P : S_2 \rangle_d \xrightarrow{\alpha} \langle P' : S_2' \rangle_d$, with $S_1' \sim_{P'} S_2'$. Therefore, in both cases, by applying rule (PAR$_1$):

$$\langle P : S_2 \parallel T \rangle_d \xrightarrow{\alpha} \langle P' : S'' \rangle_d$$

S'' being $S_2' \parallel T$ or $S_1 \parallel T'$, respectively. Then, by applying inductive hypothesis on the first case $S' = S_1' \parallel T \sim_{P'} S_2' \parallel T = S''$, and $S'' = S'$ (hence $S'' \sim_P S'$ by Lemma 1 in the second one).

2. If the applied rule to get (1) is (SYNC$_1$), then $\alpha = \tau$, $P' = P$, and either S_1 or T is a parallel composition of processes T_1 and T_2 such that T_1 implies a transition labelled by t. If $T = T_1 \parallel T_2$, we would have in the previous alternative (1). So, let's suppose $S_1 = T_1 \parallel T_2$, and

$$\langle P : T_1 \rangle_d \xrightarrow{t} \langle P : T_1' \rangle_d \quad \langle P : T_2 \parallel T \rangle_d \xrightarrow{\bar{t}} \langle P' : T_2 \parallel T \rangle_d$$

with $S' = T_1' \parallel T_2 \parallel T$. By applying rule (PAR$_1$) to the left transition above, we have $\langle P : S_1 \rangle_d \xrightarrow{t} \langle P : T_1' \parallel T_2 \rangle_d$. As $S_1 \sim_P S_2$, we have

$$\langle P : S_2 \rangle_d \xrightarrow{t} \langle P : S_2' \rangle_d$$

for some S_2' with $S_2' \sim_P T_1' \parallel T_2$. Taking into account that transition $\bar{t}$ only affects to the profile P, we also have $\langle P : T \rangle_d \xrightarrow{\bar{t}} \langle P' : T \rangle_d$. Therefore, rule (SYNC$_1$) applied to $S_2 \parallel T$ gets

$$\langle P : S_2 \parallel T \rangle_d \xrightarrow{\tau} \langle P : S_2' \parallel T \rangle_d$$

At this point $S' = T_1' \parallel T_2 \parallel T$ and $S_2' \sim_P T_1' \parallel T_2$, which implies (again by inductive hypothesis) $S' \sim_P' S_2' \parallel T$.

3. The last alternative to get transition (1) is applying rule (SYNC$_2$). The reasoning is similar to the previous one.

In a similar way, we could prove $S_1 + T \sim_P S_2 + T$ when $S_1 \sim_P S_2$. □

5 Case Study: A Treasure Hunt

Now that we have formally defined our framework for reasoning on Digital Avatars, we present a motivating example for showing how it works, and we discuss how the formalization provides useful tools for checking properties and inferring results of the systems built according to our proposal.

For that, we have implemented a treasure hunt game, in which several players look for a set of five hidden treasures following clues. Each treasure found provides a clue for a new treasure, and the player that first finds all the treasures wins the game. Treasures are represented by beacons, scattered over the scenario of the treasure hunt. Each beacon emits a BLE signal with the URL of a script file. When a player gets close enough to a beacon, her phone detects it, and downloads and runs the script.

For implementing the game, we only need to define one script template S for all the beacons. This script is stored in a server which also keeps a virtual profile containing tuples with the clues for the treasures, and two extra tuples for the global state of the game, as it will be explained below. Prior to each download, the script is instantiated (Code 1) with the clues for finding five treasures (binding _Clue1, . . . , _Clue5 by the read actions in lines 1–3), and the current status of the game, which depends on whether there exists a **gameover** tuple (lines 4–5) or not (lines 7–8).

```
1   rd(<clue1 ,_Clue1>).  rd(<clue2 ,_Clue2>).
2   rd(<clue3 ,_Clue3>).  rd(<clue4 ,_Clue4>).
3   rd(<clue5 ,_Clue5>).(
4       rd(<gameover>).
5       S(<gameover>,_Clue1 ,_Clue2 ,_Clue3 ,_Clue4 ,_Clue5)
6   +
7       nrd(<gameover>).
8       S(<playing>,_Clue1 ,_Clue2 ,_Clue3 ,_Clue4 ,_Clue5)  )
```

Code 1. Script instantiation.

The execution of the script interacts with the virtual profile in the smart-phone, checking and updating which treasures have been already found by the player, and showing the clue for a new treasure. It also informs the game when a player has found all the treasures. The rest of the players will be notified the next time they find a beacon. The full script is shown in Code 2.

```
1   S(_Status ,_Clue1 ,_Clue2 ,_Clue3 ,_Clue4 ,_Clue5) =
2       nrd(<clue ,C>).
3           out(<clue ,_Clue1>).  out(<clue ,_Clue2>).
4           out(<clue ,_Clue3>).  out(<clue ,_Clue4>).
5           out(<clue ,_Clue5>).  out(<treasures ,0>).  0
6   +
7       in(<clue ,C>).  out(<_Status>).(
8           in(<playing>).(
9               nrd(<treasures ,4>).
10              in(<treasures ,X>).  out(<treasures ,X+1>).
11              out(<notify ,C>).  0
12          +
13              in(<treasures ,4>).  out(<treasures ,5>).
14              rd(<personal .name ,Me>).  rd(<system .now ,Time>).
15              rout(<winner ,Me,Time>).  rout(<gameover>).  0  )
16      +
17          in(<gameover>).
18              out(<notify ,"You lose !">).  0  )
```

Code 2. Script for the Treasure Hunt.

The branch starting from line 2 in the script is performed when a player begins the treasure hunt (we assume an additional beacon in the starting place), as no clues are present in his virtual profile yet (line 2). In that case, all the five clues are added to the virtual profile of the player (lines 3–5). The last tuple added in line 5 is `<treasures,0>`, indicating that no treasures have been found yet.

Alternatively (line 7), a random clue is read (and consumed) from the profile, and the current status of the game (`<gameover>` or `<playing>`) is written in the player's profile. Then, we have again two alternatives. Either the game is over (lines 17–18) and the player is notified of this fact, or it is still being played (lines 8–15). In the latter case, the tuple `<treasures,N>` stores the number of beacons that the player has already found. If they are less than four (i.e. `<treasures,4>` is not in the profile, line 9), then we increase the number of treasures found (line 10), and show a new clue to the player (line 11). On the contrary, if the player had already found four treasures (line 13), she wins the game (please recall that the script is executed whenever the player finds a beacon, which makes it the fifth one). In this case, both the name of the player and the current time are get from the player's profile (line 14), which are used to update the global state of the game. Indeed, two tuples are remotely added to the server from which the script has been downloaded: one with information on the winner, and the other one indicating that the game is over (line 15). It is worth noting that the remote out actions in line 15 only have one argument, instead of two arguments as defined in *Act* in Sect. 3, because the first argument implicitly corresponds to the server storing the script.

5.1 Reasoning on the Example

The formalization of Digital Avatars presented in this paper allows us to reason on the behavior of our treasure hunt game. One of the properties that we may want to analyze is whether it is ensured that eventually someone wins the game. Indeed, this property can be proved with the Linda-based semantics presented in Sect. 4, just making a couple of basic assumptions. First, let us consider an initial configuration composed of a non-empty set of smart devices (players) and at least one smart thing (beacon) pointing to a server which contains the script. This configuration is represented by a parallel composition of all those artifacts:

$$C_0 = \Pi_{i=1}^n \langle P_i : 0 \rangle_{d_i} \mid \langle P : 0 \rangle_b \tag{2}$$

being d_i the smart devices, each with a profile P_i, and b the beacon associated with a server with a profile P and script template S_b as specified in Code 2.

Second, let us assume that the smart thing is certified (i.e. $certify(b)$) and that all the devices d_i can always get a link to the beacon b. In other words, let $link(P_i, b) \neq \emptyset$ for an unlimited number of times, and for every $i = 1..n$. These two assumptions are formalized as hypothesis of the next proposition, which ensures the eventual end of game.

Proposition 1. *Let us consider a smart thing b containing the script template S_b as defined in Code 2, and the initial configuration C_0 specified in Eq. (2), such that $accept(a, P_i)$ for every action a in any instance of S_b, and $certify(b)$. If for every sequence of transitions $C_0 \longmapsto C$, some of the smart devices d_k in C has a virtual profile Q_k which satisfies $link(Q_k, b) \neq \emptyset$, then there exists a trace*

$$C_0 \longmapsto C' \mid \langle t, P' : 0 \rangle_b$$

with t=<gameover>.

Proof. Applying the assumption to the empty sequence of transitions $C_0 \longmapsto C_0$, we can find a device d_{k_1} such that rule SYNC_3 can be applied, because both conditions of that rule are fulfilled: $link(P_{k_1}, b) \neq \emptyset$ and $certify(b)$. Therefore, running the script on that device, after applying several times the rules of Table 2, we obtain a trace:

$$C \longmapsto C_1$$

where a new configuration C_1 is achieved containing a device d_{k_1} whose profile includes the tuple <treasures,1>. If we apply again the hypothesis to C_1, we find a device d_{k_2} such that rule SYNC_3 may be applied once more, and a new instance of the script S_b will make D_1 to progress to C_2 ($D_1 \longmapsto D_2$). If $d_{k_2} = d_{k_1}$, its profile will include the tuple <treasures,2>. If this is not the case, then we will have a new device with a profile also including <treasures,1>. Taking into account that we can always repeat this procedure, and that we have a finite number (n) of smart devices, after at most $4n$ iterations, some of the devices will exhibit a profile with the tuple <treasures,4>. Hence, the branch represented by lines 13–15 of S_b will be eventually triggered, adding the tuple <gameover> to b's profile. □

The proposition above shows that, under some basic assumptions, a proper initial configuration will eventually progress to a gameover status.

Additionally, some unexpected scenarios can be detected if we analyze the script in Code 2 more deeply. An exhaustive exploration of all possible traces generated from a configuration C, like in Eq. 2, would provide interesting information about the soundness of the script. In fact, a model checker capable of exhaustively exploring all possible traces achievable from C would detect some target configurations such that $C \longmapsto C' \mid \langle P' : 0 \rangle_b$, where the profile P' includes two or more copies of tuple <winner,Me,Time>. This means that two or more players could postulate themselves as winners of the treasure hunt. Indeed, it is easy to imagine how C can progress to a configuration D, such that:

$$D = \ldots \mid \langle P_d : S_d \rangle_d \mid \langle P_e : S_e \rangle_e \mid \ldots \mid \langle P : 0 \rangle_b \tag{3}$$

where <treasures,4> is both in the profiles P_d and P_e, and <playing> is still in P. In other words, two devices would have found four clues each, and the game is still being played. In this situation, if we consider a scenario where $links(P_d, b)$ and $links(P_e, b)$ are not empty, then two consecutive transitions can occur:

$$D \xrightarrow{\tau} \ldots \mid \langle P_d : S_d \parallel S_b(P, l_d) \rangle_d \mid \langle P_e : S_e \rangle_e \mid \ldots \mid \langle P : 0 \rangle_b$$
$$\xrightarrow{\tau} \ldots \mid \langle P_d : S_d \parallel S_b(P, l_d) \rangle_d \mid \langle P_e : S_e \parallel S_b(P, l_e) \rangle_e \mid \ldots \mid \langle P : 0 \rangle_b$$

Both transitions are a consequence of applying rule SYNC3, where $l_d \in$ $links(P_d, b)$ and $l_e \in links(P_e, b)$. The scripts downloaded from b, $S_b(P, l_d)$ and $S_b(P, l_e)$ are conveniently instantiated with information on profile P. As P still includes the tuple <playing>, both instances of S_b will add that tuple to the local profiles of d and e (line 7 in Code 2). And then, because <treasures,4> is present in both profiles P_d and P_e, the actions in lines 13–15 of Code 2 are executed:

$$C \longmapsto D \longmapsto \langle P_d : S_d \parallel S_b(P, l_d) \rangle_d \mid \langle P_e : S_e \parallel S_b(P, l_e) \rangle_e \mid \langle P : 0 \rangle_b$$
$$\longmapsto \langle P'_d : S'_d \rangle_d \mid \langle P'_e : S'_e \rangle_e \mid \langle P' : 0 \rangle_b$$

where both P'_d and P'_e include the tuple <treasures,5>, and the hunt will be stopped by remotely adding (twice) the tuple <gameover> to P'. However, two remote out actions would have been previously made adding to P' two <winner,M,T> tuples, too, which of course is not what we would desire as the result of the game.

This phenomenon could be addressed in several ways. The first idea that may come up to us is implementing locks for controlling the atomic execution of the script, blocking it for downloading in a smart device until its execution in some other device ends. Another solution would be adding to the game a final podium stage, where the server announces the actual (photo finish) winner, depending on the time of each <winner,M,T> tuple. In any case, the formalization of the framework allows us to analyze the behavior of the system and to study these and other situations in order to detect problems and solve them.

6   Conclusions

In this paper, we have shown how the formalization of Digital Avatars by means of a multiple tuple space approach provides interesting tools to verify different properties of the system. We may validate the compatibility of a Digital Avatars system with different versions of a script proving bisimilarity and congruence properties. Moreover, we have shown that we may formally check the interactions in a Digital Avatars system, which gives us the opportunity of studying its correctness, proving desired (or undesired) properties, and studying what happens in different situations, like in our treasure hunt example ensuring that the game always ends, or whether they may exist multiple winners.

As for future work, we plan to extend the transition system in order to model the atomic execution of the scripts, avoiding this way the mutual exclusion issues previously mentioned. Furthermore, it would be necessary to build model checking tools for analyzing desired or undesired properties of the scripts.

References

1. Berners-Lee, T.: Solid. https://solid.inrupt.com/. Accessed 21 Jan 2019

2. Brogi, A., Jacquet, J.-M.: On the expressiveness of coordination via shared datas-paces. Sci. Comput. Program. **46**(1–2), 71–98 (2003)

3. Busi, N., Gorrieri, R., Zavattaro, G.: On the Turing equivalence of linda coordination primitives. Electron. Notes Theor. Comput. Sci. **7**, 75 (1997)

4. Carriero, N., Gelernter, D.: Linda in context. Commun. ACM **32**(4), 444–458 (1989)

5. De Nicola, R., Ferrari, G.L., Pugliese, R.: KLAIM: a kernel language for agents interaction and mobility. IEEE Trans. Softw. Eng. **24**(5), 315–330 (1998)

6. De Nicola, R., et al.: The SCEL language: design, implementation, verification. In: Wirsing, M., Hölzl, M., Koch, N., Mayer, P. (eds.) Software Engineering for Collective Autonomic Systems. LNCS, vol. 8998, pp. 3–71. Springer, Cham (2015). https://doi.org/10.1007/978-3-319-16310-9_1

7. Gelernter, D., Carriero, N.: Coordination languages and their significance. Commun. ACM **35**(2), 96 (1992)

8. Grønli, T.-M., Ghinea, G., Younas, M.: Context-aware and automatic configuration of mobile devices in cloud-enabled ubiquitous computing. Pers. Ubiquit. Comput. **18**(4), 883–894 (2013). https://doi.org/10.1007/s00779-013-0698-3

9. Gubbi, J., Buyya, R., Marusic, S., Palaniswami, M.: Internet of Things (IoT): a vision, architectural elements, and future directions. Future Gener. Comput. Syst. **29**(7), 1645–1660 (2013)

10. Guillen, J., Miranda, J., Berrocal, J., Garcia-Alonso, J., Murillo, J.M., Canal, C.: People as a service: a mobile-centric model for providing collective sociological profiles. IEEE Softw. **31**(2), 48–53 (2014)

11. Guinard, D., Trifa, V., Mattern, F., Wilde, E.: From the Internet of Things to the web of things: resource-oriented architecture and best practices. In: Architecting the Internet of Things, pp. 97–129. Springer (2011). https://doi.org/10.1007/978-3-642-19157-2_5

12. Menezes, R., Omicini, A., Viroli, M.: On the semantics of coordination models for distributed systems: the LogOp case study. In: Foundations of Coordination Languages and Software Architecture (FOCLASA 2003). Electronic Notes in Theoretical Computer Science, vol. 97, pp. 97–124. Elsevier (2004)

13. Pérez-Vereda, A., Flores-Martín, D., Canal, C., Murillo, J.M.: Towards dynamically programmable devices using beacons. In: Pautasso, C., Sánchez-Figueroa, F., Systä, K., Murillo Rodríguez, J.M. (eds.) ICWE 2018. LNCS, vol. 11153, pp. 49–58. Springer, Cham (2018). https://doi.org/10.1007/978-3-030-03056-8_5

14. Picco, G.P., Murphy, A.L., Roman, G.C.: Lime: linda meets mobility. In: Proceedings of the 21st International Conference on Software Engineering, ICSE 1999, pp. 368–377. ACM (1999)

15. Raento, M., Oulasvirta, A., Eagle, N.: Smartphones: an emerging tool for social scientists. Sociol. Methods Res. **37**(3), 426–454 (2009)

16. Silva, J.S., Zhang, P., Pering, T., Boavida, F., Hara, T., Liebau, N.C.: People-centric Internet of Things. IEEE Commun. Mag. **55**(2), 18–19 (2017)

17. Taivalsaari, A., Mikkonen, T.: A roadmap to the programmable world: software challenges in the IoT era. IEEE Softw. **34**(1), 72–80 (2017)

18. Wang, F.Y., Carley, K.M., Zeng, D., Mao, W.: Social computing: from social informatics to social intelligence. IEEE Intell. Syst. **22**(2), 79–83 (2007)

19. Wang, Y., Vasilakos, A.V., Jin, Q., Ma, J.: Survey on mobile social networking in proximity (MSNP): approaches, challenges and architecture. Wirel. Netw. **20**(6), 1295–1311 (2013). https://doi.org/10.1007/s11276-013-0677-7

20. Yang, W.-S., Hwang, S.-Y.: iTravel: a recommender system in mobile peer-to-peer environment. J. Syst. Softw. **86**(1), 12–20 (2013)

Modeling Self-adaptive Fog Systems Using Bigraphs

Hamza Sahli[1(✉)], Thomas Ledoux[2], and Éric Rutten[3]

[1] Stack Team, Inria Rennes - Bretagne Atlantique, Nantes, France
hamza.sahli@inria.fr
[2] IMT Atlantique, Stack, Inria, LS2N, Nantes, France
thomas.ledoux@inria.fr
[3] Univ. Grenoble Alpes, Inria, CNRS, LIG, 38000 Grenoble, France
eric.rutten@inria.fr

Abstract. Fog systems are a recent trend of distributed computing having vastly ubiquitous architectures and distinct requirements making their design difficult and complex. Fog computing is based on an idea that consists of leveraging both resource-scarce computing nodes around the Edge to perform latency and delay sensitive tasks and Cloud servers for the more intensive computation. A convenient way to address the challenge of designing Fog systems is through the use of formal methods, which provide the needed precision and high-level assurance for their specification through formal verification. In this paper, we present a novel formal model defining spatial and structural aspects of Fog-based systems using Bigraphical Reactive Systems, a fully graphical process algebraic formalism. The model is extended with reaction rules to represent the dynamic behavior of Fog systems in terms of self-adaptation. The notion of bigraph patterns is used in conjunction with boolean and temporal operators to encode spatio-temporal properties inherent to Fog systems and applications. The feasibility of the modelling approach is demonstrated via a motivating case study and various self-adaptation scenarios.

Keywords: Fog systems · Self-adaptation · Formal methods · Modeling · Bigraphical reactive systems

1 Introduction

Fog computing [7,14] is an emerging paradigm that aims to decentralize Cloud systems with distributed micro data-centers in the core network and even more resource-scarce devices at the Edge of the network. The main idea behind the Fog is to leverage resources around the Edge to perform latency and delay sensitive tasks closer to end-users and thus avoid network bottlenecks. Cloud servers are exploited only for the more intensive and latency insensitive functions. By introducing location-based awareness, the Fog paradigm grants enhanced performance and more assurance about computation and data placement.

© Springer Nature Switzerland AG 2020
J. Camara and M. Steffen (Eds.): SEFM 2019 Workshops, LNCS 12226, pp. 252–268, 2020.
https://doi.org/10.1007/978-3-030-57506-9_19

A typical Fog system architecture is considered as a set of heterogeneous computing nodes scattered across separate layers. The bottom one is the Edge or the *Fog layer* organized as multiple clusters acting as small to medium sized data-centers close to data producers. Each of these clusters is composed of several computing devices of different kinds, referred to usually as Fog/Edge nodes. The latter can range from networking devices equipped with low computing capacities (e.g. routers) to more powerful computing entities (e.g. Raspberry Pi). Fog nodes are ubiquitous by nature, sometimes mobile and mostly possess limited processing power, storage and energy abilities. The top layer of a Fog system is the *Cloud layer* which contains much powerful servers performing computation-intensive tasks. Deployed on resource-scarce computing nodes, a Fog application should be designed as a set of loosely coupled and fine-grained components. To this end, the concept of micro-services provides a new architectural style where Fog-based applications can be quickly deployed and smoothly scaled. In such highly dynamic and large-scale Fog systems, aspects such as locality of nodes and their characteristics, cluster formations and neighboring relation, services distribution, as well as Fog systems temporal evolution are key concerns making the task of designing Fog systems challenging. The main questions we address is how to design a Fog system accurately and the proper means to express faithfully properties providing assurances about respecting system and application constraints/requirements while continuously evolving over time. Formal methods offer the appropriate answers to tackle these open issues. They present mathematical concepts which provide the needed rigour and high-level assurance for qualitative specification of Fog systems infrastructures and applications, in addition to their dynamic behaviors and spatio-temporal properties.

In this paper, we propose a preliminary modelling approach for self-adaptive Fog systems based on a formalism introduced by R. Milner [6]. Bigraphical reactive systems (BRS for short) is adopted as a formal foundation for its ability to represent the hierarchical locations of Fog-based systems entities and applications, as well as their characteristics and the complex interactions between the various elements. The notion of bigraphical reaction rules is used to capture the temporal evolution of Fog systems in terms of self-adaption in a natural way. Besides, bigraph patterns can be combined with standard boolean operators or more expressive temporal logic operators to define spatio-temporal properties related to such systems behavior and Fog applications requirements, serving as a basis to perform formal analysis. Moreover, BRS is characterized by a human-oriented graphical aspect supporting equivalent representation to algebraic ones. This feature provides an intuitive representation of Fog-based systems making them more convenient to comprehend by DevOps engineers. All these distinctive features among others omitted here (e.g. the concept of regions very close to distributed layers) make BRS formalism a fitting candidate to formalize Fog.

Bigraphical reactive systems were applied on a wide range of distributed and ubiquitous system such as multi-agent systems [5], wireless networks [2], IoT infrastructures [11], Cloud-based elastic system [9,10]. Among existing bigraphical approaches, the most related ones in principal to ours are [11] where a

BRS-based framework for modelling large-scale sensor network infrastructures and verification of temporal logic properties specifying application requirements is proposed. Authors in [12] presented a similar bigraphical approach for the modelling of evolving Cyber-Physical Spaces and reasoning about spatio-temporal properties. To the best of our knowledge, the approach we propose here is the first to adopt bigraphical reactive systems for modelling structural and behavioural aspects of Fog systems and formalizing relevant constraints and properties. As a matter of fact, we believe our model is the first of its kind to apply a formal method in order to address these kinds of aspects inherent to Fog systems.

The remainder of this paper is organized as follows. Section 2 summarizes the main elements of BRS. In Sect. 3, we propose a formalization of Fog systems, then we address the representation of structural aspect using sorted bigraphs and finally we extend the model to include dynamic behaviour in terms of self-adaptation. Section 4 is dedicated to presenting a motivating case study, several adaptation scenarios and properties demonstrating the feasibility of our approach. Finally, Sect. 5 concludes and discusses our perspectives.

2   Bigraphical Reactive Systems

Bigraphical Reactive Systems (BRS) is a universal meta-modeling formalism originally defined by R. Milner in [6] to provide a fully graphical formal model that emphasizes the orthogonal notions of locality and connectivity. The formalism comes as well with a mathematical algebraic language capable of describing the structural and behavioral aspects of ubiquitous and interacting systems that evolve in both time and space. A BRS $BG(\Sigma, \mathcal{R})$ consists of a category of bigraphs defined over a sorting *discipline* Σ to represent the state of a given system and a set of parametric *reaction rules* $\mathcal{R}$ defining the dynamic evolution of the system by modeling the temporal self-adaption of the set of bigraphs [6]. A bigraph consists of a combination of a *place graph*, i.e. entities in terms of spatial distribution and nesting, and a *link graph* specifying the interconnections between these entities.

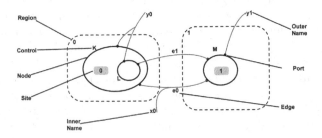

Fig. 1. Anatomy of a bigraph.

Graphical and Algebraic Forms. Bigraphs can be described in two ways, in a diagrammatic depiction or with an equivalent algebraic representation. Figure 1 depicts the anatomy of a simple bigraph. Graphically, a bigraph as an ordinary graph is composed of several nodes linked by edges. Nodes encode the modeled system entities which can be real or virtual, while edges or links represent the various interactions and relationships between the entities. Nodes are always nested within regions, i.e. roots, depicted by dashed rectangles; they may also be nested within each other. This defines a parenting relationship between them in terms of nodes containment, or in other words the place graph of the bigraph. As a rule, nodes in the theory of BRS are permitted to take any kind of shape or color in some cases. A node can be dotted with zero, one or many ports used to link it with other nodes by means of edges, forming a link graph of a bigraph. A control is associated with each node consisting of a node type identifier. Controls denote the arity of nodes i.e. ports number, which of these nodes are atomic i.e. empty nodes, and which of the non-atomic nodes are active, i.e. subject to reactions, or passive. Sites modeled by grey squares are considered as an abstraction indicating the presence of other nodes which represents hidden parts of the model. The inner/outer names of a bigraph are links or potential links to other bigraphs. By convention, inner/outer names are drawn above or below the bigraph (e.g. x0 and y0 in Fig. 1).

In addition to their rich graphical representation, a term algebraic language resembling traditional process calculi is defined to encode bigraphs. The language primary elements and operations for composing elementary bigraphs are listed in Table 1. For instance, the parallel product $U\|V$ term may be used to compose bigraphs by juxtaposing their roots and merging their common names.

Table 1. Terms language for bigraphs.

Term	Signification
$U\|V$	Parallel product
$U|V$	Merge product
$U.V$	Nesting (U contains V)
K_x	Node of type (control) K having a name or link x
id	Identity or elementary bigraph
d_i	Site numbered i
1	The barren (empty) region

Bigraph Definition. A bigraph is formally defined by $G = (V, E, ctrl, G^P, G^L) : I \rightarrow J$, where V and E are respectively finite sets of nodes and edges. $ctrl : V \rightarrow K$ is mapping function associating a control to each node in the bigraph G. K referred to as the bigraph signature is its set of controls. $G^P = (V, ctrl, prnt) : m \rightarrow n$ is the place graph of G. m and n are respectively the number of sites and regions, $prnt : m \uplus V \rightarrow V \uplus n$ is a mapping function that identifies the parent of each node. $G^L = (V, E, ctrl, link) : X \to Y$ represents the link graph of the bigraph G, where $link : X \uplus P \to E \uplus Y i$ is a link map, X and Y are respectively inner and outer names. P is a set of ports of the bigraph G. $I = \langle m, X \rangle$ and $J = \langle n, Y \rangle$ are respectively inner and outer interfaces of the bigraph encoding the potentiality of G to interact its external environments.

Sorting Discipline. A bigraph can be further associated with a sorting discipline allowing to classify the different bigraphical terms specified in the bigraph such as nodes, links and sites. This sorting logic helps as well as defining the necessary constraints on the designed bigraphs. A sorting discipline Σ is a triple $\Sigma = \{\Theta, K, \Phi\}$, where Θ is a non empty set of sorts. K is the bigraph signature, and Φ is a set of formation rules associated with a bigraph. The latter consists of a set of structural constraints a bigraph has to satisfy. Note that disjunctive sorts are written as $\hat{x}y$ which means a node can either be of sort x or y.

Bigraphical Reaction Rules. Dynamic behavior in terms of system evolution is defined in BRS via rewrite rules, called bigraphical reaction rules. A reaction rule $\mathcal{R}(p) = (R, R')$ consists of a pair of bigraphs referred to as *redex* and *reactum* and can be written by $R \to R'$. The redex on the left-hand side represents the parts of a bigraph to be altered, while the reactum on right-hand side specifies how those parts are altered. The transition is triggered on a bigraph G when R has an occurrence or a match in G. The result of the rule application is a new bigraph G' obtained by inserting R in G to replace R'.

3   Bigraphical Model of Fog Systems

In this section, we formally define bigraphs used to specify a Fog system in our model. We describe the way sorted bigraphs are used to capture the semantics of such systems. The model is extended via parametric reaction rules explaining the evolution of a Fog system over time and modeling self-adaptation.

3.1   Formalizing Fog Systems

A Fog-based system is modeled in our approach by a bigraph FS composed of the parallel product of two elementary bigraphs representing the Fog and Cloud layers. The parallel product term usage characterizes our model by a genericness and extendability, making it easily scalable and modifiable. This bigraphical term offers the possibility to include additional bigraphs representing the external environment as other Cloud or Fog service providers and thus an ability to represent different systems architectures (e.g. federation of Fogs).

The proposed formalization is achieved by associating a precise semantics in the theory of BRS to each Fog architectural element. A Fog system and its two Cloud and Fog layers are formalized via bigraphs. The different Cloud instances and Fog nodes are expressed with bigraphical nodes and the various kinds of interactions are modeled by edges. Sites represent parts of a Fog system that we wish to hide or abstract away. The proposed formalization helps in exemplifying the different parts of a Fog-based system, as well as exposing the conceptual entities involved in such systems' typical architecture[1].

Definition 1. Let FL be a bigraph modeling the Fog layer of a Fog system and CL be a bigraph modeling its Cloud layer, a Fog system bigraph FS is composed by applying the parallel product term $\parallel$ on FL and CL (see Eq. 1).

$$FS \stackrel{\text{def}}{=} CL\|FL \tag{1}$$

Definition 2. A Fog system bigraph is defined formally in our approach by

$$FS = (V_{FS}, E_{FS}, ctrl_{FS}, FS^P, FS^L) : I_{FS} \to J_{FS} \tag{2}$$

- $V_{FS} = V_{FL} \uplus V_{CL}$ is a finite set of nodes of a Fog system FS obtained from the disjoint union of the sets of nodes of the Fog FL and Cloud layers CL.
- $E_{FS} = E_{FL} \uplus E_{CL}$ is a finite set of edges given by the disjoint union of sets of edges of the Fog FL and Cloud CL layers.
- $ctrl_{FS} = ctrl_{FL} \uplus ctrl_{CL} : V_{FS} \to \mathcal{K}_{FS}$ is a control mapping function assigning to each node $v \in V_{FS}$ of the bigraph FS representing a Fog system, a control $k \in \mathcal{K}_{FS}$ defining its type. A signature $\mathcal{K}_{FS} = \mathcal{K}_{FL} \uplus \mathcal{K}_{CL}$ is the set of controls defined for FS.
- $FS^P = FL^P\|CL^P$ is the place graph of FS obtained by the parallel product of place graphs of the Fog layer FL and Cloud layer CL.
- $FS^L = FL^L\|CL^L$ link graph of FS consisting of the parallel product of the link graphs of FL and CL.
- $I_{FS} = I_{FL}\|I_{CL} = \langle m_{FS}, X_{FS} \rangle, m_{FS} = m_{FL} + m_{CL}$ and $X_{FS} = X_{FL} \cup X_{CL}$ is the inner interface of the bigraph FS. m_{FS} is the number of sites and X_{FS} is a set of inner names of FS.
- $J_{FS} = J_{FL}\|J_{CL} = \langle n_{FS}, Y_{FS} \rangle, n_{FS} = n_{FL} + n_{CL}$ and $Y_{FS} = Y_{FL} \cup Y_{CL}$, is the outer interface of FS, where n_{FS} and Y_{FS} are respectively the number of regions and the set of outer names of FS.

3.2   Modeling Fog Systems with Sorted Bigraphs

We now outline how the structural and conceptual aspects of a given Fog system are encoded through sorted bigraphs. Accordingly, we define a sorting discipline for the class of bigraphs used to describe a Fog system architecture in our model. A sorting discipline provides the proper semantics to represent faithfully a Fog architecture. Besides, it imposes the necessary structural constraints via formation rules to preserve architectural integrity and ensure bigraphs are designed in a meaningful way.

---

[1] In order to keep the definition succinct, we omit the complete formal definitions of Fog and Cloud bigraphs, as they can be redundant.

The sorting discipline for the bigraph FS is defined by $\Sigma_{FS} = \{\Theta_{FS}, K_{FS}, \Phi_{FS}\}$, where $\Theta_{FS} = \Theta_{FL} \uplus \Theta_{CL}$, $K_{FS} = K_{FL} \uplus K_{CL}$ and $\Phi_{FS} = \Phi_{FL} \uplus \Phi_{CL}$. The controls of the set K_{FS} we use to represent a Fog-based system listed in Table 2 are organized into different sorts of the set Φ_{FS}. In greater details, sorts $l = \{L\}$ and $p = \{P\}$ contains controls used to model node clusters L and the connection points between them, representing their neighboring relationship. The controls of sort $n = \{N, N_L, N_U, N_U\}$ encode a Fog node in its different possible states. Following the same principle, sorts $s = \{SE, SE_L, SE_U, SE_F\}$, $v = \{VM, VM_L, VM_U\}$ and $t = \{CN, CN_L, CN_U\}$ represent respectively different states of a server, virtual machine and container. A service or micro-service is modeled with nodes of sort $m = \{s\}$. The various entities computing capacities such as memory, CPU, battery, and storage as well as services requirements in terms of computing resources are encoded respectively by nodes of sort $a = \{M\langle v \rangle, C\langle v \rangle, B\langle v \rangle, S\langle v \rangle\}$ and $q = \{M_r\langle v \rangle, C_r\langle v \rangle, B_r\langle v \rangle, S_r\langle v \rangle\}$ where v is parameter recording the value of each kind of node.

Table 2. Controls and sorts used in a bigraph FS.

Meaning	Control	Arity	Sort	Bigraph	Notation
Cluster	L	0	l	FL	Large box
Connection points	P	1	p	FL	Small square
Stable node	N	0	n	FL	Rounded box
Loaded node	N_L	0	n	FL	Rounded box
Underused node	N_U	0	n	FL	Rounded box
Failed node	N_F	0	n	FL	Rounded box
Stable server	SE	0	s	CL	Rounded box
Loaded server	SE_L	0	s	CL	Rounded box
Underused server	SE_U	0	s	CL	Rounded box
Failed server	SE_F	0	s	CL	Rounded box
VM stable	VM	0	v	FL,CL	Rounded box
VM loaded	VM_L	0	v	FL,CL	Rounded box
VM underused	VM_U	0	v	FL,CL	Rounded box
Stable container	CN	0	t	FL, CL	Rounded box
Loaded container	CN_L	0	t	FL, CL	Rounded box
Underused container	CN_U	0	t	FL, CL	Rounded box
Service or micro-service	S	2	m	FL, CL	Circle
Entity capacity	C	0	c	FL, CL	Medium box
Capacity values	$M\langle v \rangle, C\langle v \rangle,$	0	a	FL, CL	Small circle
Requirement values	$M_r\langle v \rangle, C_r\langle v \rangle,$	0	r	FL, CL	Small circle

Nodes of sort a are always placed in a node having a sort $c = \{C\}$. Such nesting condition and other kinds constraints are formalized in the set of formation rules Φ_{FS} with conditions Φ_i, $1 \leq i \leq 11$, listed in Table 3. More precisely, conditions Φ_1–Φ_2 are constraints on nodes activity. For instance, Φ_1 states that all nodes having a sort $\widehat{lnsvtmc}$ are active, which means they are subject to reactions. Formation rules Φ_3–Φ_9 are conditions on nodes placing. An example of this kind of nesting rule has been given above. Finally, conditions Φ_{10}–Φ_{11} are linking formation rules. As an example, rule Φ_{11} imposes on a node having an m-sort to be connected to nodes of its own sort or to $\widehat{io}$-names, encoding the bigraph FS ability to interact with the external environment.

An example of a graphical form of a bigraph FS encoding a Fog-based system is given in Fig. 2. Note that for the sake of simplicity, controls of sorts p, a and r are purposely omitted in the graphical form. The bigraph FS is obtained by composing FL and CL bigraphs representing Fog and Cloud layers using the parallel product operation. In Fig. 2 the Fog and Cloud layers are modeled respectively by regions 0 and 1, depicted with dashed rectangles. Region 0 contains several clusters modeled by nodes having controls $L1 - L4$. A cluster node may be linked to an arbitrary number of other cluster nodes through connection points represented by nodes of control P. These connection points are used to express the neighboring relationship between Fog clusters, such that when two clusters are directly linked to each other, they are considered as direct or one-hop neighbors. For instance, clusters $L1$ and $L2$ are considered in our model as direct neighbors, while clusters $L2$ and $L4$ are considered as two-hop neighbors. The grey shapes in Fig. 2 are sites, used as abstraction for hidden away entities.

Figure 3 is another simple example of a Fog layer bigraph FL modeled with region 0, which shows in depth the structure of a Fog cluster in our model. Sites are used here to abstract away the elements of the bigraphical model that we do not reason about. A Fog cluster L hosts a set a N nodes modelling Fog computing nodes. In the example, nodes of control $N1$, $N2_L$ and $N3_U$ encode respectively stable, loaded and underused Fog nodes. Each node may host a set of application containers modelled with nodes having control CN. The latter may host themselves nodes of control S, modelling application services. The computing capacity of Fog nodes and containers is encoded with a node of control C, grouping nodes representing their respective memory, CPU, battery level, etc. For instance, the computing capacity of Fog node $N1$ represented by a node C within $N1$ can be represented by the following algebraic notation: $\mathtt{C} = \mathtt{C}.(\mathtt{M}\langle 512\rangle|\mathtt{C}\langle 1.1\rangle|\mathtt{B}\langle 10\rangle)|\mathtt{d})$ to express the computing capability of $N1$. Finally, service requirements in terms of processing power are encoded in a similar way by nodes taking the shape of small circles within the node of S control. In our example, the service S requirements are expressed algebraically by: $\mathtt{S} = \mathtt{S_{fi}}.(\mathtt{M_r}\langle 32\rangle|\mathtt{C_r}\langle 0.1\rangle|\mathtt{B_r}\langle 0.2\rangle)$.

Table 3. Formation rules Φ_{CS} for the bigraph FS

	Rule description
Φ_1	All $\overset{\frown}{lnsvtmc}$-nodes are active
Φ_2	All $\widehat{par}$-nodes are atomic
Φ_3	All children of a l-node have sort $\widehat{pn}$
Φ_4	All children of a n-node have sort $\widehat{vtc}$
Φ_5	All children of a s-node have sort $\widehat{vtc}$
Φ_6	All children of a v-node have sort $\widehat{mc}$
Φ_7	All children of a t-node have sort $\widehat{mc}$
Φ_8	All children of a c-node have sort a
Φ_9	All children of a m-node have sort r
Φ_{10}	A p-node is always linked only to one p-node
Φ_{11}	An m-node has two ports which may be linked to m-nodes or $\widehat{io}$-names

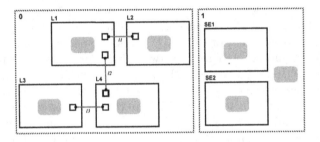

Fig. 2. A simple example of a bigraph FS.

3.3 Modeling Fog Systems Self-adaptation

A bigraphical reactive system consists of a class of bigraphs modelling conceptual aspects of a system and a set of reaction rules encoding their dynamic behavior. The behavioral model consists of a set of parametric reaction rules giving the Fog system model the ability to self-adapt. Each reaction rule correspond to a reconfiguration action triggering a change that rewrites parts of the bigraph FS following the occurrence of a respective self-adaption event of the Fog system. In the following, we present a set of reaction rules modeling self-adaptation actions carried out in a Fog-based system while preserving the defined sorting discipline Σ_{FS}. Due to the space limitation, here we do not give all the reaction rules in our behavioral model, instead, we present some relevant examples. The exhaustive behavioral model includes additional reaction rules such as virtual machine/container migration and replication, node mobility (relocation), turning on/off a node, service deployment, battery draining, tagging an underused or loaded container or virtual machine, etc. Examples of reaction rules defined in the algebraic terms language dedicated to BRS are summarized in Table 4.

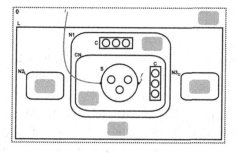

Fig. 3. Example of bigraphical representation for a Fog cluster.

The first example is a reaction rule which models the establishment of a neighboring relationship between two clusters. On the left-hand side of the rule (redex), the two nodes L and L' modelling two Fog clusters are independent of each other and not linked together, meaning that currently, they do not recognize one another as neighbors. On the right-hand side (reactum), two connection points modeled with nodes of control P are created within each cluster node and a communication link l is established between them to represent the new neighboring relationship (see Fig. 4a). Another example of reaction rule for resizing the memory allocated to a loaded or underused computing instance such a loaded container represented by control CN_L is presented in Fig. 4b. The rule is employed to modify the memory parameter of the memory node M within a capacity node C from value x to x'. We consider the memory increased if parameters $x < x'$ and decreased if $x' > x$. Finally, the last example is a reaction rule graphical representation for tagging a node after it fails (see Fig. 4c). The reaction rule principle consists of replacing the node control N on rule's redex by another control N_F on the reactum.

4 Motivating Case Study

4.1 A Fog System Architecture

Assume a Fog-based system distributed over a part of a college campus, specifically, a department and a dormitory. The Fog layer contains a number of small size Fog nodes such as cameras, routers and boxes, as well as larger nodes such as Raspberry Pis and small servers. The infrastructure includes, in addition, a more powerful server in the Cloud layer.

Consider two smart city Fog applications, designed as a set of micro-services distributed across multiple Fog cluster on different nodes. The first application is a *smart surveillance* application [8], proposing a near site Edge/Fog-based solution for video analysis. Micro-service architecture is adopted to decouple the complicated video analysis tasks such as facial features extraction, car recognition and real-time behavior analysis. Five services are dedicated to such tasks,

Table 4. Reaction rule examples for the bigraph FS

Reaction rule	Algebraic form
$\texttt{neighbor}-\texttt{link(i,j)}$	$\overset{\text{def}}{=} \texttt{L}_\texttt{i}\texttt{.(d)}|\texttt{L}_\texttt{j}\texttt{.(d)}|\texttt{id} \rightarrow \texttt{L}_\texttt{i}\texttt{.(P}_\texttt{1}|\texttt{d)}|\texttt{L}_\texttt{j}\texttt{.(P}_\texttt{1}|\texttt{d)}|\texttt{id}$
$\texttt{add}-\texttt{node(i)}$	$\overset{\text{def}}{=} \texttt{L.(d)}|\texttt{N.(d)}|\texttt{id} \rightarrow \texttt{L.(N}_\texttt{i}\texttt{.(d)}|\texttt{d)}|\texttt{id}$
$\texttt{replicate}-\texttt{vm(i)}$	$\overset{\text{def}}{=} \texttt{VM}_\texttt{i}\texttt{.(d)}|\texttt{id} \rightarrow \texttt{VM}_\texttt{i}\texttt{.(d)}|\texttt{VM}_\texttt{j}\texttt{.(d)}|\texttt{id}$
$\texttt{consolidate}-\texttt{vm(j)}$	$\overset{\text{def}}{=} \texttt{VM}_\texttt{i}\texttt{.(d)}|\texttt{VM}_\texttt{j}\texttt{.(d)}|\texttt{id} \rightarrow \texttt{VM}_\texttt{i}\texttt{.(d)}|\texttt{id}$
$\texttt{resize}-\texttt{memory(x,x',i)}$	$\overset{\text{def}}{=} \texttt{CN}_\texttt{Li}\texttt{.(C.(M}\langle\texttt{x}\rangle|\texttt{d)}|\texttt{d)}|\texttt{id} \rightarrow \texttt{CN}_\texttt{Li}\texttt{.(C.(M}\langle\texttt{x'}\rangle|\texttt{d)}|\texttt{d)}|\texttt{id}$
$\texttt{resize}-\texttt{cpu(x,x',i)}$	$\overset{\text{def}}{=} \texttt{CN}_\texttt{Li}\texttt{.(C.(C}\langle\texttt{x}\rangle|\texttt{d)}|\texttt{d)}|\texttt{id} \rightarrow \texttt{CN}_\texttt{Li}\texttt{.(C.(C}\langle\texttt{x'}\rangle|\texttt{d)}|\texttt{d)}|\texttt{id}$
$\texttt{failed}-\texttt{node(i)}$	$\overset{\text{def}}{=} \texttt{N}_\texttt{i}\texttt{.(d)}|\texttt{id} \rightarrow \texttt{N}_\texttt{Fi}\texttt{.(d)}|\texttt{id}$

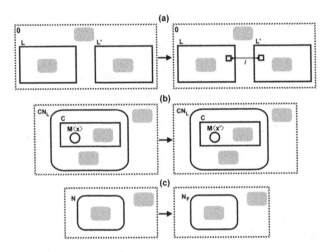

Fig. 4. Reaction rules for (a) Establishing neighboring relationship (b) Resizing memory (c) Tagging a failed node.

divided into low-level tasks deployed in the smaller nodes of the Edge infrastructure and computing intensive or high-level tasks outsourced to the bigger Fog nodes or to the Cloud. The *smart surveillance* application is composed of five micro-service, low-level ones: (S1) Feature extraction, (S2) Audio analysis, (S3) Licence plate recognition. High-level services include (S4) Gesture and facial recognition and (S5) Suspicious behavior analysis. The second application in our example is a *smart bell* application [13], which notifies the college dormitory inhabitants when they receive visitor(s). The micro-services composing the application are classified similarly into low-level and high-level services. The low-level services are (S1) Feature extraction, (S6) Bell ringing decision, and the high-level services are (S4) Gesture and facial recognition, (S7) Visitor habits analysis. Note that some micro-services in the two applications are identical.

The presented Fog-based infrastructure deploying the two Fog applications can be encoded in our model by the formulae below. Due to the space limitation, we give only an abbreviated algebraic form of the example bigraph FS where we abstract away some nodes using sites. The bigraph model encodes essentially three clusters L^1, L^2 and L^3 containing 12 nodes (N^1–N^{12}) used to host mostly low-level services S^1, S^2, S^3, S^6 and a high-level service S^4 at the Fog layer (FL). A neighboring relationships exists between clusters L^1, L^2 and L^2, L^3. A Cloud server SE within a CL-bigraph is hosting two of the high-level services S^5, S^7. Note that a micro-service can have several instances representing its workers (e.g. S^1, S^{1-1}, etc.) deployed in containers $CN^1 - CN^{21}$ and virtual machine VM^1, VM^2. In the algebraic representation we occasionally omit some workers and links between services for presentation reasons.

$FS \stackrel{\text{def}}{=} /11/12/f1/f2/f3/f4 \ FL||CL$

$FL \stackrel{\text{def}}{=} (L^1.(P_{11}|d)|L^2.(P_{11}|P_{12}|d)|L^3.(P_{12}|d)$

$L^1 \stackrel{\text{def}}{=} (N^1.(CN^1.(S^2.(d)|d)|CN^2.(S^{2-1}.(d)|d)|d)|N^2.(CN^3.(S^{2-2}.(d)|d)|CN^4.(S^{2-3}.(d)|d)|$
$CN^5.(S^3.(d)|d)|d)|N^3.(CN^6.(S^{3-1}.(d)|d)|CN^7.(S^{3-2}.(d)|d)|d)|N^4.(CN^8.(S^{3-3}.(d)|d)|d)|d)$

$L^2 \stackrel{\text{def}}{=} (N^5.(CN^9.(S^1.(d)|d)|CN^{10}.(S^{1-1}.(d)|d)|CN^{11}.(S^{1-2}.(d)|d)|d)|N^6.(CN^{12}.(S^{1-3}.(d)|d)|CN^{13}.$
$(S^{1-4}.(d)|d)|d)|N^7.(CN^{14}.(S^4.(d)|d)|CN^{15}.(S^{4-1}.(d)|d)|d)|d)$

$L^3 \stackrel{\text{def}}{=} (N^8.(CN^{16}.(S^{1-5}.(d)|d)|d)|N^9.(CN^{17}.(S^{1-6}.(d)|d)|d)|N^{10}.(CN^{18}.(S^{1-7}.(d)|d)|CN^{19}.(S^6.$
$(d)|d)|d)|N^{11}.(CN^{20}.(S^{6-1}.(d)|d)|d)|N^{12}.(CN^{21}.(S^{6-2}.(d)|d)|d)|d)$

$CL = SE1.(VM1.(S^5_{f2}.(d)|S^{5-1}_{f2}.(d)|S^{5-2}_{f2}.(d)|d)|VM2.(S^7_{f4}.(d)|S^{7-1}_{f4}.(d)|d)|d)$

4.2   Self-adaptation Strategies

Concentration of students and various persons such as visitors present at a college campus differ around the year. For instance, during the first and second semesters, more people are expected to be on the campus, while at the holidays very few are there. The estimate of students may as well fluctuate between the semesters since a portion of students usually does an internship outside of the college in the second semester. Besides, the number of people outside of dormitory varies around the day: more people are outdoors in the morning and more are indoors as the day goes by. Considering these different situations, it is obvious that the two Fog applications will have fluctuated workload very often. As computing nodes at the Fog are mostly resources-scarce, occasionally energy-constrained and unreliable, a Fog-based system must possess an ability to self-adapt at run-time in order to better optimize resources consumption, according to the context variation and depending on the workload and nodes availability. Here, we demonstrate the use of our defined bigraphical reaction rules to model self-adaptation strategies, which can be used in such systems in order to get around resources deficiency distinguishing computing nodes at the Fog. These reaction rules can be used to describe all possible evolution scenarios and reachable configurations of a Fog system in terms of self-adaptation in two orthogonal ways to rewrite an FS bigraph: iterative application of each reaction rule at a time and as a sequence of reaction modeling self-adaptation strategies.

Assume two self-adaptation strategies controlling the Fog system and applications of our case study. The first strategy operates at the application level to scale out/in the two Fog applications horizontally. It scales out by creating additional workers for their respective micro-services when the demand average peaks and scales in by destroying workers when it drops. Two action plans modeling this adaptation strategy as sequences of parametric reaction rule that updates the bigraph model from a state S_n to S_{n+1} are encoded by formulae (a) and (b). The first action plan AP_a contains the reaction for creating additional workers for micro-services S1, S2, S3, S4 and S6, which we consider as the most subject to be affected by the workload augmentation. The action plan AP_b contains rules for consolidation the unneeded workers of the aforementioned micro-services when they are unneeded. We use $R*$ to indicate an arbitrary number of applications of a reaction (zero or more). $\longrightarrow$ notation indicates a transition between reaction rules. A rule parameter i is used to model the index of the respective service e.g. add-worker(i), such that in our example $1 \leq i \leq 7$.

$$AP_a \overset{def}{=} \texttt{add} - \texttt{worker(1)}^* \longrightarrow \texttt{add} - \texttt{worker(2)}^* \longrightarrow \texttt{add} - \texttt{worker(3)}^* \longrightarrow$$
$$\texttt{add} - \texttt{worker(4)}^* \longrightarrow \texttt{add} - \texttt{worker(6)}^* \tag{a}$$
$$AP_b \overset{def}{=} \texttt{release} - \texttt{worker(1)}^* \longrightarrow \texttt{release} - \texttt{worker(2)}^* \longrightarrow \texttt{release} - \texttt{worker(3)}^*$$
$$\longrightarrow \texttt{release} - \texttt{worker(4)}^* \longrightarrow \texttt{release} - \texttt{worker(6)}^* \tag{b}$$

The second adaptation strategy concerns vertical resizing of containers hosting instances of the different micro-services. Based on resources consumption level of the hosted instances, the strategy adjusts the size of a given container by allocating to it additional computing resources. In our example, we assume a scenario where the size of a given containers (parameter i is used to determine the concern containers) needs to be adjusted to better accommodate the requirements of their hosted workers in terms of computing power. The reaction rules sequence modelling such strategy which resizes certain containers up or down is given by action plans AP_c and AP_d of formulae (c) and (d) respectively. The AP_c reaction rules sequence allocates additional memory, CPU and storage space to the loaded containers, while AP_d scales down the underused ones.

$$AP_c \overset{def}{=} \texttt{loaded} - \texttt{container(i)}^* \longrightarrow \texttt{resize} - \texttt{memory(x, x', i)}^* \longrightarrow$$
$$\texttt{resize} - \texttt{cpu(x, x', i)}^* \longrightarrow \texttt{resize} - \texttt{storage(x, x', i)}^* \tag{c}$$
$$AP_d \overset{def}{=} \texttt{underused} - \texttt{container(i)}^* \longrightarrow \texttt{resize} - \texttt{memory(x, x', i)}^* \longrightarrow$$
$$\texttt{resize} - \texttt{cpu(x, x', i)}^* \longrightarrow \texttt{resize} - \texttt{storage(x, x', i)}^* \tag{d}$$

In a Fog/Edge infrastructure, node failure is a very common phenomenon that may be caused by environmental conditions. In the example of our case study, nodes deployed in open air exposed to rough weather or nodes equipped with intermittent energy sources (e.g. solar panels) such as cameras are typically subject to failure [3]. In nodes failure scenario, a strategy may be defined to self-adapt a Fog system by replacing the failed nodes with backup nodes or newly installed ones. Node failure event may be modelled with the reaction rules sequence of formulae (e), nodes that get tagged failed in any given cluster would be replaced with backup nodes (if possible) to ensure the two Fog applications continue to be available, especially the safety-critical application of *smart surveillance*.

$$AP_d \overset{def}{=} \texttt{failed} - \texttt{node(i)}^* \longrightarrow \texttt{add} - \texttt{node(i)}^* \tag{e}$$

4.3   Constraints and Properties

Now we present how we can employ the notion of bigraphical patterns introduced in [1], to express constraints and properties characterizing Fog application requirements and relevant behaviors of self-adaptive Fog systems.

Application Constraints. First, we present the formalization of Fog applications specific constraints in terms of state properties. The latter are expressed as predicated via logical formulae obtained by combining bigraph patterns with the basic boolean operators. The different predicates may define constraints on resource requirements, interactions between applications, micro-services placement, etc. These state properties are expected to be satisfied after every Fog system (re)configuration such that if a bigraphical pattern has a match in a given bigraph FS modelling a Fog system, it is considered true. Next, we give two examples of such constraints.

Battery Constraint. A Fog application may have a requirement specifying that the battery level of nodes on which its micro-services are deployed is not supposed to fall below a minimum threshold. For instance, critical service $S4$ of both applications in our example, may required a minimum number of hosting nodes to be always available in order to operate correctly. A strategy such as AP_e can serve to satisfy this requirement continuously. This constraint is expressed by the predicate Ψ_1. The constraint is satisfied if the battery level modeled by a control $B_i\langle v\rangle$ of each node is always above a minimum threshold. $N_{app} \subseteq V_{FS}$ is a set of nodes hosting certain application services.

$$\Psi_1(\mathtt{v}, \mathtt{min}, \mathtt{i}) \overset{\text{def}}{=} \neg \mathtt{B_i}\langle \mathtt{v}\rangle, \text{ such that } v < min \text{ and } i \in N_{app}$$

Application Placement. To ensure secure placement of different application, a Fog system may have a constraint dictating the placement of certain micro-services belonging to different applications in different nodes, servers or virtual machines. For instance, a predicate is given below, formalizing a mutual exclusion between micro-services $S5$ and $S7$ of the *smart surveillance* and *smart bell* applications and their workers to ensure they do not co-existed on the same VM.

$$\Psi_2(\mathtt{x}, \mathtt{i}, \mathtt{j}) \overset{\text{def}}{=} (\mathtt{VM_x}.(\mathtt{S_5^i}) \wedge \neg \mathtt{VM_x}.(\mathtt{S_7^i})) \vee (\neg \mathtt{VM_x}.(\mathtt{S_5^i}) \wedge \mathtt{VM_x}.(\mathtt{S_7^i}))$$

Behavioral Properties. To express temporal properties over the run-time behavior of Fog systems, it is possible to combine bigraph patterns not just with simple boolean operators, but with more expressive temporal logics such as Linear Temporal Logic (LTL in short) [4]. Here we formalize relevant behavioral properties of self-adaptive Fog system by integrating bigraph patterns defined over our model as atomic propositions with temporal operators of LTL. For a given atomic proposition ϕ, we write $\circ\phi$, $\Box\phi$, $\Diamond\phi$, $\phi_1 \cup \phi_2$ to denote respectively the temporal operators "next", "always", "eventually" and "until". A temporal property should be true for all possible future evolutions of a Fog system model after the application of bigraphical reaction rules. We present two examples of such temporal properties expressed as LTL formulae.

Node Replacement. A habitual scenario in a Fog or Edge infrastructure is node failure due to environmental conditions or energy constraints. Thus, to ensure the Fog system stays operational, a failed node should be replaced by a backup or newly installed node. The property specifies the fact that if a node tagged with control N_F in our model exists, it will be replaced or repaired. The property can be used to evaluated a node replacing strategy such as AP_e.

$$\Psi_3(x, y) \stackrel{\text{def}}{=} \Box(L_x.(N_{yF}|d) \rightarrow \Diamond(L_x.(N_y|d)))$$

Resource Optimization. Because of nodes resource scarcity, a Fog system needs to control resource consumption and better optimize their utilization. For instance, an underused VM should be either used more, consolidated or scaled down in order to better utilize computing capabilities of the hosting server. Such property can validate the efficiency of a horizontal consolidation strategy such as AP_b. It is encoded with the LTL formulae below. Informally, it states that it should be always the case if an underused VM exists in the Fog system, i.e. a node tagged with control VM_U in our model, eventually it will be in a stable state, consolidated or resized.

$$\Psi_4(x, y, v, v', w, w') \stackrel{\text{def}}{=} \Box(SE_x.(VM_{yU}.(M\langle v\rangle|C\langle w\rangle|d)|d) \rightarrow \Diamond((SE_x.(VM_y.(d)))\vee$$
$$(SE_x.(VM_y.(M\langle v'\rangle|C\langle w'\rangle|d)|d)) \vee (SE_x.(d))$$

5   Conclusion and Perspectives

Modeling a Fog system spatial distribution and temporal evolution in terms of self-adaption requires an adequate formal foundation that captures such aspects and allows automated computation and analysis of properties. In this paper, we have demonstrated how BRS can present a suitable formalism to structurally and behaviorally model Fog-based systems. Our primary motivation is to concentrate on proposing an extendable formal model capable of representing faithfully self-adaptive Fog systems and related properties. Formal verification of the presented Fog systems properties is an important perspective of ours, which we intend to address with the appropriate attention. Our aim is to employ the proposed model as a basis for reasoning about various properties including the ones given above using high-level automated formal analysis techniques.

We are considering two kinds of formal analysis approaches: (i) real-time verification of state properties expressed via bigraph patterns such as Fog applications requirements, (ii) offline model-checking of temporal properties over the behavior of a Fog system. The idea is to construct a framework allowing not only to evaluate self-adaptation strategies by detecting properties violation rate in each strategy but also to identify conflicting ones and report details. In the real-time verification approach, it is possible to use a real Fog system (or a simulator) generating self-adaption events that trigger the application of reaction rule sequences. When applied, the latter would rewrite the current bigraphical model to yield a new state that reflects the actual configuration of the system. State properties can be checked after each self-adaption over the most recent model to verify their satisfaction or violation. The offline verification approach can be employed at the early stages of a Fog system design or at the application deployment time. The objective is to obtain formal assurance about the system through model-checking of temporal properties to verify the absence of unwarranted system behaviors. The model-checking technique is based on a temporal logic which allows reasoning over different computation paths to explore all possible states of the system. This feature provides better coverage but is more computationally expensive, which makes it more suitable for the offline approach rather than for the real-time one (i.e. high analysis overhead).

References

1. Benford, S., Calder, M., Rodden, T., Sevegnani, M.: On lions, impala, and bigraphs: modelling interactions in physical/virtual spaces. ACM Trans. Comput.-Hum. Interact. **23**, 9:1–9:56 (2016)
2. Calder, M., Koliousis, A., Sevegnani, M., Sventek, J.: Real-time verification of wireless home networks using bigraphs with sharing. Sci. Comput. Program. **80**, 288–310 (2014)
3. Fang, X., Bate, I.: Issues of using wireless sensor network to monitor urban air quality. In: Proceedings of the 1st ACM International Workshop on the Engineering of Reliable, Robust, and Secure Embedded Wireless Sensing Systems, FAILSAFE 2017, pp. 32–39. ACM, New York (2017)
4. Huth, M., Ryan, M.: Logic in Computer Science: Modelling and Reasoning About Systems. Cambridge University Press, New York (2004)
5. Mansutti, A., Miculan, M., Peressotti, M.: Multi-agent systems design and prototyping with bigraphical reactive systems. In: Magoutis, K., Pietzuch, P. (eds.) DAIS 2014. LNCS, vol. 8460, pp. 201–208. Springer, Heidelberg (2014). https://doi.org/10.1007/978-3-662-43352-2_16
6. Milner, R.: The Space and Motion of Communicating Agents, 1st edn. Cambridge University Press, New York (2009)
7. Mouradian, C., Naboulsi, D., Yangui, S., Glitho, R.H., Morrow, M.J., Polakos, P.A.: A comprehensive survey on fog computing: state-of-the-art and research challenges. IEEE Commun. Surv. Tutorials **20**(1), 416–464 (2018)
8. Nagothu, D., Xu, R., Nikouei, S.Y., Chen, Y.L.: A microservice-enabled architecture for smart surveillance using blockchain technology. In: 2018 IEEE International Smart Cities Conference (ISC2), pp. 1–4 (2018)
9. Sahli, H., Belala, F., Bouanaka, C.: A BRS-based approach to model and verify cloud systems elasticity. Procedia Comput. Sci. **68**, 29–41 (2015). 1st Int. Conference on Cloud Forward: From Distributed to Complete Computing
10. Sahli, H., Hameurlain, N., Belala, F.: A bigraphical model for specifying cloud-based elastic systems and their behaviour. Int. J. Parallel Emergent Distrib. Syst. **32**(6), 593–616 (2017)
11. Sevegnani, M., Kabac, M., Calder, M., McCann, J.: Modelling and verification of large-scale sensor network infrastructures. In: 2018 23rd International Conference on Engineering of Complex Computer Systems (ICECCS), pp. 71–81, December 2018

12. Tsigkanos, C., Kehrer, T., Ghezzi, C.: Modeling and verification of evolving cyber-physical spaces. In: Proceedings of the 11th Joint Meeting on Foundations of Software Engineering, ESEC/FSE 2017, pp. 38–48. ACM, New York (2017)

13. Xia, Y., Etchevers, X., Letondeur, L., Coupaye, T., Desprez, F.: Combining hardware nodes and software components ordering-based heuristics for optimizing the placement of distributed iot applications in the fog. In: 33rd Annual ACM Symposium on Applied Computing, SAC 2018, pp. 751–760. ACM, New York (2018)

14. Yousefpour, A., et al.: All one needs to know about fog computing and related edge computing paradigms: a complete survey. J. Syst. Archit. **98**, 289–330 (2019)

From SOS to Asynchronously Communicating Actors

Frank de Boer[1], Einar Broch Johnsen[2(✉)] , Ka I Pun[2,3],
and Silvia Lizeth Tapia Tarifa[2]

[1] CWI, Amsterdam, The Netherlands
f.s.de.boer@cwi.nl
[2] Department of Informatics, University of Oslo, Oslo, Norway
{einarj,violet,sltarifa}@ifi.uio.no
[3] Western Norway University of Applied Sciences, Bergen, Norway

Abstract. Structural Operational Semantics (SOS) provides a general format to describe a model as a transition system with very powerful synchronization mechanisms. Actor systems are distributed, asynchronously communicating units of computation with encapsulated state, with much weaker means of synchronizing between actors. In this paper, we discuss an implementation of a SOS model using actors in the object-oriented actor language ABS and how to argue that global properties about the model are inherited from the SOS level to the actor implementation. The work stems from a case study modelling the memory system of a cache-coherent multicore architecture.

1 Introduction

Structural operational semantics (SOS) [1], introduced by Plotkin in 1981, describes system behavior as transition relations in a syntax-oriented, compositional way, using inference rules to capture local transitions and how these compose into transitions at the global level. Process synchronization in SOS rules is expressed abstractly using, e.g., assertions over system states and reachability conditions over transition relations as premises, and label synchronization for parallel transitions. This high level abstraction greatly simplifies the verification of system properties. In particular, reasoning about SOS semantics has been used to prove meta-properties for all instances of a model such as type preservation properties for the execution of programs in a programming language (e.g., [2]). In contrast, a direct implementation of an SOS model for the simulation of system behavior is less common, as execution quickly becomes a reachability problem with a lot of backtracking. Often, the implementation of an SOS model can be quite far from the transition rules of the model itself, and, as a result,

Supported by *SIRIUS: Centre for Scalable Data Access* (www.sirius-labs.no) and *ADAPt: Exploiting Abstract Data-Access Patterns for Better Data Locality in Parallel Processing* (www.mn.uio.no/ifi/english/research/projects/adapt/).

J. Camara and M. Steffen (Eds.): SEFM 2019 Workshops, LNCS 12226, pp. 269–275, 2020.
https://doi.org/10.1007/978-3-030-57506-9_20

we do not always know if the properties laboriously proven for the SOS model indeed also hold of its implementation.

We are interested in decentralized implementations of SOS models, to obtain efficient yet faithful realizations of these models, without unnecessary global synchronization and backtracking yet preserving the safety properties of the SOS model. For our implementations, we work with active object languages [3], which combine the scalable, asynchronous nature of actor languages with the code structuring mechanisms of object orientation. In particular, we target ABS [4] because it supports *cooperative scheduling*, which allows a simple yet expressive form of synchronization, and because it has a *formally defined semantics*, which allows us to study the preservation of safety properties in a formal setting.

This paper is an extended abstract of an invited talk given at FOCLASA 2019. Further details of the ideas discussed in this paper may be found in [5,6] and the source of the original SOS model which triggered our interest in this line of investigation may be found in [7].

2   Background

2.1   SOS

Structural operational semantics (SOS) [1] define the meaning of programs by (labelled) transition systems and simple operations on data. Programs are defined syntactically by a grammar and execute in a (local) context. Let us assume that these contexts resemble objects, such that programs (or sequences of actions) execute on a local state and exchange messages or synchronize with each other in the transition rules. If P and Q are such programs in local contexts, let $P||Q$ denote the configuration which consists of P and Q executing in parallel. The transition rules then have formats such as

$$\frac{(\text{LOCAL})}{P \to P'} \quad \frac{(\text{ASYNCSEND})}{P \to P'||Q} \quad \frac{(\text{ASYNCRECEIVE})}{P||Q \to P'}$$

$$\frac{(\text{HANDSHAKE})}{P||Q \to P'||Q'} \quad \frac{(\text{CONTEXT})}{P||Q \to P'||Q} \quad \frac{(\text{LABELSYNC})}{P||Q \to P'||Q'}$$

Compared to decentralized systems such as actors, the premises of the rules ASYNCRECEIVE and HANDSHAKE contain applicability conditions on *both* P and Q and LABELSYNC introduces synchronization over events l (where $\bar{l}$ denotes the dual of l). These forms of synchronization are difficult to express in the asynchronous setting. Conditions further include *reachability* expressions, captured here by transitions in the premises of the rules CONTEXT and LABELSYNC.

2.2 ABS

ABS is a modelling language for designing, verifying, and executing concurrent software [4]. The language combines the syntax and object-oriented style of Java with the Actor model of concurrency [8] into active objects which decouple communication and synchronization using asynchronous method calls, futures and cooperative scheduling [3]. Although only one thread of control can execute in an active object at any time, cooperative scheduling allows different threads to interleave at explicitly declared points in the code. Access to an object's fields is encapsulated, thus, any non-local (outside of the object) read or write to fields must happen explicitly via asynchronous method calls so as to mitigate race-conditions or the need for mutual exclusion (locks).

We explain the basic mechanism of asynchronous method calls and cooperative scheduling in ABS by the simple code example of a class Lock. First, the execution of a statement res = await o!m(args) consists

```
class Lock {
  Bool unlocked = True;
  Unit take_lock{await unlocked; unlocked = False;}
  Unit release_lock{unlocked = True;} }
```

Fig. 1. Lock implementation in ABS using await on Booleans.

of storing a message m(args) corresponding to the asynchronous call to the message pool of the callee object o. This **await** statement *releases the control* of the caller until the return value of that method has been received. Releasing the control means that the caller can execute other messages from its own message pool in the meantime. ABS supports the shorthand o.m(args) to make an asynchronous call f=o!m(args) followed by the operation f.get which *blocks* the caller object (does not release control) until the future f has received the return value from the call. As a special case the statement **this**.m(args) models a self-call, which corresponds to a standard subroutine call and avoids this blocking mechanism. The code in Fig. 1 illustrates the use of the **await** statement on a Boolean condition to model a binary semaphore, which can be used to enforce exclusive access to a communication medium such as a channel. Thus, the statement **await** channel!take_lock() will suspend the calling method invocation (and release control in the caller object) and can first resume when the generated invocation of the method take_lock returns, which can only happen when the local condition unlocked (of the channel) has become true.

3 Example of a SOS Synchronization Pattern

We illustrate the problem of implementing SOS rules by considering *multiparty label synchronization*, inspired by the multicore memory model of Bijo *et al.* [7], where bus

$$
\begin{array}{cc}
(\textsc{LocalSend}) & (\textsc{LocalReceive}) \\
\text{conditions on } P & \text{conditions on } Q \\
\hline
P \xrightarrow{l} P' & Q \xrightarrow{\bar{l}} Q'
\end{array}
$$

$$
\begin{array}{c}
(\textsc{GlobalSync}) \\
P \xrightarrow{l} P' \quad Q_i \xrightarrow{\bar{l}} Q'_i \text{ for } 0 < i \leqslant n \\
\hline
P||Q_1||\ldots||Q_n \rightarrow P'||Q'_1||\ldots||Q'_n
\end{array}
$$

Fig. 2. Multiparty synchronization in SOS.

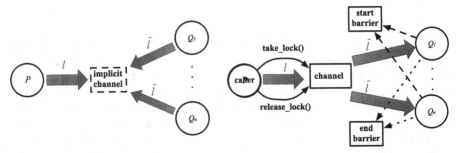

(a) State machine of the global synchronization using labels in the SOS model.

(b) State machine of the global synchronization using a bus and barriers in the ABS model.

Fig. 3. Label synchronization in SOS vs barrier synchronization in ABS. In the SOS model (a), circles represent synchronized entities and shaded arrows labelled transitions. Note that the synchronization channel is *implicit* in the SOS model, as synchronization is captured by label matching. In the ABS model (b), circles represent the same nodes as in the SOS model, shaded arrows method invocations, solid arrows mutual access to the synchronization channel and dotted arrows barrier synchronizations.

synchronization is a label matching problem such that an invalidation request for a cache line succeeds when the cache line has been invalidated in all other caches. Somewhat simplified, this problem corresponds to the SOS rules in Fig. 2, in which n objects synchronize on a broadcast from P to Q_i (where $0 < i \leqslant n$) and both sender and receivers have local synchronization conditions denoted *conditions1* and *conditions2*, respectively.

The synchronization problem corresponding to these SOS rules can be illustrated by the state machine in Fig. 3a. However, in the input-enabled ABS system, we need to ensure that only one object can send on the synchronization channel at any time, using a *lock* such as the one in Fig. 1. Then, a physical synchronization channel forwards the synchronization event to all receiving objects. To receive the synchronization event, all readers need to make a transition simultaneously, Hence, the implementation needs to introduce a *start barrier*. The bus can only return the success to the sender of the communication event once all receivers have completed their transition. This corresponds to an *end barrier* synchronizing on the success of the transitions of all receivers, after which the send-method can return and the synchronization channel can be unlocked. The corresponding synchronization code in ABS is illustrated in Fig. 3b.

The correctness of the decentralized active object implementation of the SOS model can then be addressed by a simulation relation between the ABS code and the transitions of the SOS model. This approach is based on the notion of *stable points* in the execution of ABS programs [5], at which an object requires external input to make progress (either an event or a scheduling decision). The semantics of ABS then allows us to prove that executions are *globally confluent* at the granularity of stable points [5,6]. Consequently, it is sufficient to reason about one object at a time between stable points in the program execution. These stable points are syntactically defined on the ABS code, and the abstraction relation between the ABS code and the SOS model need only to hold at the stable points. Thus, we can reason about the transitions between stable points in the ABS code and the corresponding transitions in the SOS model. Furthermore, if the scheduling at stable points is deterministic in the ABS model, two transitions can be merged, further reducing the number of cases that need to be considered [5].

4   Related Work

There is in general a significant gap between a formal model and its implementation [9]. SOS [1] succinctly formalizes operational models and are well-suited for proofs, but direct implementations of SOS quickly lead to very inefficient implementations. Executable semantic frameworks such as Redex [10], rewriting logic [11], and K [12] reduce this gap, and offer executable formal models of complex languages like C and Java. The relationship between SOS and rewriting logic semantics has been studied [13] without proposing a general solution for label matching. Bijo et al. implemented their SOS multicore memory model [14] in Maude [15] using an orchestrator for label matching, but do not provide a correctness proof wrt. the SOS model. Different semantic styles can be modelled and related inside one framework; for example, the correctness of distributed implementations of KLAIM systems in terms of simulation relations have been studied in rewriting logic [16]. Compared to these works on semantics, our focus here is on implementing an SOS model in a distributed active object setting in a way which allows formal proofs of correctness for this implementation.

Correctness-preserving compilation is related to correctness proofs for implementations, and ensures that low-level representations of a program preserve the properties of the high-level model. Examples here include type-preserving translations into typed assembly languages [17] and formally verified compilers [18]; the latter proves the semantic preservation of a compiler from C to assembler code, but leaves shared-variable concurrency for future work. In contrast to work which studies compilation from one language to another, our work focuses on a specific model and its implementation and specifically targets parallel systems.

5   Conclusion

We have outlined a methodology for the decentralized implementation of SOS models, targeting the active object language ABS. A challenge for this methodology is to correctly implement the synchronization patterns of the SOS rules, which may cross encapsulation borders in the active objects, and in particular label synchronization on parallel transitions steps. To address this problem, we exploit that ABS allows for a globally confluent coarse-grained semantics.

References

1. Plotkin, G.D.: A structural approach to operational semantics. J. Log. Algebr. Program. **60–61**, 17–139 (2004)
2. Igarashi, A., Pierce, B.C., Wadler, P.: Featherweight Java: a minimal core calculus for Java and GJ. ACM Trans. Program. Lang. Syst. **23**(3), 396–450 (2001)
3. Boer, F.D., et al.: A survey of active object languages. ACM Comput. Surv. **50**(5), 76:1–76:39 (2017)
4. Johnsen, E.B., Hähnle, R., Schäfer, J., Schlatte, R., Steffen, M.: ABS: a core language for abstract behavioral specification. In: Aichernig, B.K., de Boer, F.S., Bonsangue, M.M. (eds.) FMCO 2010. LNCS, vol. 6957, pp. 142–164. Springer, Heidelberg (2011). https://doi.org/10.1007/978-3-642-25271-6_8
5. Bezirgiannis, N., de Boer, F., Johnsen, E.B., Pun, K.I., Tapia Tarifa, S.L.: Implementing SOS with active objects: a case study of a multicore memory system. In: Hähnle, R., van der Aalst, W. (eds.) FASE 2019. LNCS, vol. 11424, pp. 332–350. Springer, Cham (2019). https://doi.org/10.1007/978-3-030-16722-6_20
6. Tveito, L., Johnsen, E.B., Schlatte, R.: Global reproducibility through local control for distributed active objects. In: Wehrheim, H., Cabot, J. (eds.) FASE 2020. LNCS, vol. 12076, pp. 140–160. Springer, Cham (2020). https://doi.org/10.1007/978-3-030-45234-6_7
7. Bijo, S., Johnsen, E.B., Pun, K.I., Tapia Tarifa, S.L.: A formal model of data access for multicore architectures with multilevel caches. Sci. Comput. Program. **179**, 24–53 (2019)
8. Hewitt, C., Bishop, P., Steiger, R.: A universal modular ACTOR formalism for artificial intelligence. In: Proceedings of the 3rd International Joint Conference on Artificial Intelligence. IJCAI 1973, pp. 235–245. Morgan Kaufmann Publishers Inc. (1973)
9. Schlatte, R., Johnsen, E.B., Mauro, J., Tapia Tarifa, S.L., Yu, I.C.: Release the beasts: when formal methods meet real world data. In: de Boer, F., Bonsangue, M., Rutten, J. (eds.) It's All About Coordination. LNCS, vol. 10865, pp. 107–121. Springer, Cham (2018). https://doi.org/10.1007/978-3-319-90089-6_8
10. Felleisen, M., Findler, R.B., Flatt, M.: Semantics Engineering with PLT Redex. The MIT Press, Cambridge (2009)
11. Meseguer, J., Rosu, G.: The rewriting logic semantics project. Theor. Comput. Sci. **373**(3), 213–237 (2007)
12. Rosu, G.: $\mathbb{K}$: a semantic framework for programming languages and formal analysis tools. In: Dependable Software Systems Engineering, pp. 186–206. IOS Press (2017)
13. Serbanuta, T., Rosu, G., Meseguer, J.: A rewriting logic approach to operational semantics. Inf. Comput. **207**(2), 305–340 (2009)
14. Bijo, S., Johnsen, E.B., Pun, K.I., Tapia Tarifa, S.L.: A Maude framework for cache coherent multicore architectures. In: Lucanu, D. (ed.) WRLA 2016. LNCS, vol. 9942, pp. 47–63. Springer, Cham (2016). https://doi.org/10.1007/978-3-319-44802-2_3
15. Clavel, M., et al. (eds.): All About Maude - A High-Performance Logical Framework, How to Specify, Program and Verify Systems in Rewriting Logic. LNCS, vol. 4350. Springer, Heidelberg (2007). https://doi.org/10.1007/978-3-540-71999-1
16. Eckhardt, J., Mühlbauer, T., Meseguer, J., Wirsing, M.: Semantics, distributed implementation, and formal analysis of KLAIM models in Maude. Sci. Comput. Program. **99**, 24–74 (2015)

17. Morrisett, J.G., Walker, D., Crary, K., Glew, N.: From system F to typed assembly language. ACM Trans. Program. Lang. Syst. **21**(3), 527–568 (1999)
18. Leroy, X.: Formal verification of a realistic compiler. Commun. ACM **52**(7), 107–115 (2009)

Author Index

Printed in the United States
By Bookmasters